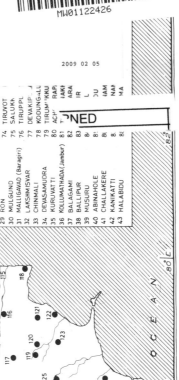

13 ALAMPUR
14 ADONI
15 VELPAMADUGU
16 PRODDATUR
17 PADDUKARA
18 ANIMALA
19 HEMAVATI
20 LEPAKSHI
21 BASINIKONDA
22 TIRUCHCHANOOR
23 NARAYANAVANAM
24 YALAMARI

MAHARASHTRA
25 KOLHAPUR

KARNATAKA
26 MANIKYAVALLI
27 HULI or PULI
28 ABLUR
29 RON
30 MULGUND
31 MALLIGAVAD (Baragiri)
32 LAKSHMISVAR
33 CHINMALI
34 DEVASAMUDRA
35 KURUVATTI
36 KOLLUMATHADA (Jambur)
37 BALAGAMI
38 BALLIPUR
39 MUSURU
40 ABINAHOLE
41 CHALLAKERE
42 KANIKATTI
43 HALABIDU

59 VEPP
60 KANCI
61 VAYAL
62 VEPPA
63 MANI
64 KULAT
65 PILLAI
66 ARPAK
67 PERUN
68 SENBA
69 MAHAB
70 KUNNA
71 TIRUKK
72 TIRUKK
73 UTTIRAM
74 TIRUVOT
75 SALUKK
76 TIRUPPL
77 DEVAKIP
78 KODUNG-LL
79 TIRUM'KKU
80 ACH
81 RAP

Detail, figured coverlet, Kalamkari, Deccan, Golconda, AD 1630–40. (Collection: National Museum, New Delhi).
Courtesy *An Age of Splendour - Islamic Art in India* (Marg Publications)

Textiles and Weavers
in
South India

Textiles and Weavers
in
South India

Second Edition

VIJAYA RAMASWAMY

OXFORD
UNIVERSITY PRESS

OXFORD

UNIVERSITY PRESS

YMCA Library Building, Jai Singh Road, New Delhi 110001

Oxford University Press is a department of the University of Oxford. It
furthers the University's objective of excellence in research, scholarship, and
education by publishing worldwide in

Oxford New York
Auckland Cape Town Dar es Salaam Hong Kong Karachi
Kuala Lumpur Madrid Melbourne Mexico City Nairobi
New Delhi Shanghai Taipei Toronto

With offices in
Argentina Austria Brazil Chile Czech Republic France Greece
Guatemala Hungary Italy Japan Poland Portugal Singapore
South Korea Switzerland Thailand Turkey Ukraine Vietnam

Oxford is a registered trade mark of Oxford University Press
in the UK and in certain other countries

Published in India
by Oxford University Press, New Delhi

© Oxford University Press 1985

ISBN-13: 978-0-19-567633-4
ISBN-10: 0-19-567633-5

Typeset by Taj Services Ltd, Noida
Printed in India at De-Unique, New Delhi 110 018
Published by Oxford University Press
YMCA Library Building, Jai Singh Road, New Delhi 110 001

To my Gurus
Sringeri Jagadguru Sri Abhinava Vidyateerta Svamigal
Sringeri Jagadguru Sri Bharati Theertha Svamigal
and
Amma, Krish, and Ram

Contents

Appendices and Glossaries

Tables

Maps

Figures

Plates

Frontispiece—Detail, figured coverlet, Kalamkari, Deccan, Golconda,
AD 1630–40

(*between pp. 116 and 117*)

Bijapur wall-hanging dated around 1640—a medley of Christian,
Islamic and Hindu figures

Vishnu and Lakshmi at the centrepiece with scenes from the
Bhagavatam in surrounding panels

Preface to the Second Edition

Bridging the Gap

The first edition of *Textiles and Weavers in Medieval South India* was published in 1985, more than twenty years ago. At the time of its publication the book was considered a pioneering study. Based on more than a decade of fieldwork among weavers especially the Sengunthar (also known as Kaikkolar), Saliya, and the Devanga community, the study sought to integrate diverse methodologies to provide multiple perspectives on the socio-economic world of the weaving communities. The book attempted a holistic picture of the ways of the medieval weavers, concerning itself as much with the oral traditions of weavers, their origin myths, and status and role in medieval South Indian society as with textile centres, production technology, cloth dyeing and printing, and trade and taxation. The utilization of local records, weaver folk traditions which were entirely in the Tamil, Kannada, and Telugu languages and regional chronicles enabled me to provide a 'view from below' of textile production and trade in Peninsular India. This was in contra-distinction to the many extremely competent studies written primarily in English with the exception of the monograph by Sergio Aiolfi[1] which mainly utilized European sources. These books are too many and fairly well known to the specialist academicians to be cited here at length. Suffice it to say that studies like K.N. Chaudhuri's *The Trading World of Asia and the English East India Company 1600–1760* (Cambridge, 1978), Tapan Raychaudhuri's *Jan Company on the Coromandel Coast 1605–1690* (Hague, 1962), and the many writings of Chinnappa Arasaratnam, especially *Merchants, Companies and Commerce on the Coromandel Coast 1650–1740* (New Delhi, 1986), made invaluable contribution to the study of textile history but touched only peripherally, if at all, on the lives of the weavers. The comparatively unnoticed monograph by Aiolfi however filled some essential gaps in the textile history and therefore deserves special mention. It focuses on the linkages between the English textile printing industry and the production of bleached cotton cloth in India. His period of study involved the process of transition within the Indian weaving industry when the British manufacturing lobby successfully prevented the entry of finished goods from India while buying bleached cloth from the Coromandel weavers, to finish the cloth in England. Aiolfi's work therefore looked closely at the training given to South Indian weavers and bleachers in the Company workshops and also studied the incipient formation of wage labour in the textile industry.

D.B. Mitra in his *Cotton Weavers of Bengal* (Calcutta, 1978) and Hameeda Hossain in *Company Weavers of Bengal* (Delhi, 1988) also provided a view from below of the world of the pre-colonial weaver communities. I would like to draw particular attention to Mattison Mines in *The Warrior Merchants: Textiles, Trade and Territory in South India* (Cambridge, 1984). Mines had not utilized any of the sources available in the South Indian languages but nevertheless produced an extremely convincing monograph on the Kaikkola community of weavers in relation to commerce and the colonial state. Joseph J. Brennig[2] provided interesting insights into the life and times of the weavers and comprador merchants working for the Dutch East India Company but unfortunately Brennig never published his thesis. Among the studies deeply rooted in indigenous sources including literary texts is K. Bhagavati's *Tamizhar Adaigal* written in Tamil (Chennai, 1980) although I was not aware of this interesting work when I submitted my thesis in 1980.

In the 1970s when as a fledgling researcher at Jawaharlal Nehru University I began working on the handloom industry of South India following a methodology best described as anthropological history, through intense fieldwork in villages of weavers, living with weaver families, I was regarded as a maverick historian. Since then this style of researching outside the 'Archives' has earned a degree of broad acceptance. Today many researchers doing what came to be broadly described as 'Subaltern Studies', have moved out of archives and closed spaces to pursue their research.

At the same time Non Resident Indian (NRI) scholars based in foreign universities are coming up with very interesting works, combining the knowledge of local sources with sophisticated western theories and methodologies. One such book in recent times is Prasannan Parthasarathy's *The Transition to a Colonial Economy: Weavers, Merchants and Kings in South India 1720–1800* (Cambridge, 2001). Parthasarathy has argued that 'poverty in South Asia did not originate with deindustrialization, as an earlier stream of writings argued, but with the profound political reordering which accompanied British rule.'[3] The work then further studies the relatively prosperous condition of weavers before the onslaught of British rule and their continuous impoverishment thereafter. I would say that my own study *The Textiles and Weavers in Medieval South India* which closed with the British ban on Indian calico in 1720, provided the foreground for Parthasarathy's study which took forward the story of the insidious penetration of the British regime into the production organization through multiple controls including the system of advances and the creation of *careedar*s or master-weavers/middlemen who served the interests of the imperial administration.

Some of the studies in the last two decades have also looked at weavers' cooperatives, another area of textile history which has been largely neglected by researchers. In this context Yvonne J. Arterburn's *The Loom of Interdependence: Silkweaving Cooperatives in Kanchipuram* (New Delhi, 1982) stands out as an exceptional contribution to textile history. The Cooperative Credit Society Act of 1904 legitimized the formation of cooperatives and in 1905 the first weavers' cooperative society was started in Kanchipuram. Arterburn's work looks primarily at the rootedness of certain weaving communities like the Kaikkolar and the Saliyar, the vicissitudes of the cooperative movement as a result of economic and political pressures, and the organizational changes in the Kanchipuram weaving cooperatives. It is a pity that this extremely perspicacious work has not yet received the kind of attention it deserves among textile historians. Another interesting work which may not even have drawn the attention of scholars is S. Shanmugasundaram's *Weavers' Cooperatives: A Study of their Utilization in Coimbatore District* (Coimbatore, 1987) because the publisher, Rainbow Publications, do not have any visibility outside their immediate region. Although very traditional in its approach, the study does look at the strengths and weaknesses of the cooperative sector in Coimbatore, regarded a leading textile centre even today and the site of South Indian Textile Research Association (SITRA).

I would like to conclude this bird's-eye view of the historiography of textile history around the time my book was first published in 1985 and subsequent to its publication by drawing attention to the Harvard University series, some of which have looked at the South Indian textile industry. One such title in the series called Harvard Studies is their monograph number 17 titled *The Challenge of Reform: How Tamil Nadu's Textile and Apparel Industry is Facing the Pressures of Liberalization* (Chennai, 2001). The study points out how handlooms in Tamil Nadu (and by the same logic in other traditional handloom centres), have become buyer-driven and market-driven rather than craft-driven, resulting in loss of cultural identity for weavers and loss of ethnic authenticity for discriminating consumers who are different from the global buyers. This point was made effectively by Nalli Kuppusami Chettiar who belongs to the two thousand year old Saliya community of weavers in a lengthy interview with the author.[4] In the context of the New Textile Policy brought out by the Tamil Nadu Government in 2001, I had raised some of these issues in my article 'Silencing the Singing Looms' published in *Hindu Business Line*, Monday, 29 January, 2001.

This second edition of makes no claims about substantial revision of the original text. The new section, 'Afterword . Rewind Forwards' attempts to take the story of the South Indian handloom industry into the colonial period and beyond. This brief introductory survey tries to situate this volume within the growing literature on Indian textile history. I do believe that the book will continue to hold its own because of the fact that it cuts across disciplines (making it in a sense trans-disciplinary) and uses multiple sources and diverse methodologies—interviews with weavers, loom songs, archival records, literary evidence, and hardcore epigraphical data—in order to understand the world of the weavers in early South Indian history.

Vijaya Ramaswamy

NOTES

1. Sergio Aiolfi, *Calicos und Gedrucktes Zeug: Die Entwicklung der Englischen Textilveredelung und der Tuchhandel der East India Company, 1650–1750*, (Stuttgart 1987).
2. Joseph J. Brennig, 'The Textile Trade of Seventeenth Century Northern Coromandel', unpublished PhD Thesis, University Microfilms, Ann Arbor, Michigan, 1983.
3. Prasannan Parthasarathy, *The Transition to a Colonial Economy: Weavers, Merchants, and Kings in South India 1720–1800*, Cambridge, 2001, p. 5.
4. Vijaya Ramaswamy, 'Nalli: A Soft Corner Silks', *Hindu Business Line*, 20 March 2000.

Preface to the First Edition

'It is the grave pit, not the loom pit' (*tarikuzhi alla chavu kuzhi*) quoted a weaver when I asked him about present-day conditions in the handloom industry. As an enthusiastic recruit to the field of research I was in Gugai in Salem, trying to get the feel of my subject. The stark reality which confronted me was totally unexpected. I found the weavers in their pits poor and emaciated. The master weaver told me that for a whole day's work they were paid 4 to 5 rupees and they managed to weave only 3 to 4 yards a day. In many of the places I visited the looms used were completely primitive and could well have belonged to the fifteenth century: this was specially true of coarse carpet weaving in Salem district.

The Indian handloom industry in the twentieth century has been hit not by the competition of Lancaster or Manchester but by the country's own powerlooms. After the great *khadi* movement, interest in handlooms has declined and in the post-independence period Indian mill textiles have displaced handlooms at home and abroad. The insidious penetration of powerlooms has been such that block-printed mill imitations are available even of such inimitable textiles as the *kalamkaris* of the Andhra region and the Madurai tie-and-dye sarees called *chungdis*. The recommendations of the Kanungo Textile Enquiry Committee of 1952 reiterated support to powerlooms, and excise duties were exempt on domestic units of not more than four powerlooms, a clause the mill owners exploited to get the maximum benefit.

In addition to powerloom competition the handloom weavers find that they are compelled to be dependent on the market for yarn, and even for dyes, since vegetable dyes have rapidly gone out of fashion and chemical dyes provide a wider range of colours. Indebtedness is, as it has been since the seventeenth century, the single major problem of weavers. They are indebted to the master weavers, the village moneylenders or merchants, and these continue to get the major share of profits from the sale of handlooms.

It is essential, if the handloom industry is to be protected, that weavers be financed adequately and given the necessary yarn and dyes on fair terms. Long before independence many handloom weavers organized themselves into co-operative societies. Madras, with the highest number of handlooms and producing many export varieties, was the first state to build up a co-operative organization among handloom weavers, even before the Second World War. During the War years weavers' co-operative societies were utilized for producing varieties like gauze, bandage cloth and mosquito nets for soldiers.

However, these societies have been only partially successful in solving the difficulties of handloom weavers. They have been ineffective in combating private merchants and middlemen and the master weavers. In fact the Santanam Committee appointed by the Government of Tamil Nadu in 1972 reported that only 30 per cent of handlooms in Tamil Nadu were under co-operatives and the bulk of the remaining 70 per cent were working for private producers. Even now many weavers prefer to work for master weavers because the weaver is able to get advances and other assistance in times of need, as at the time of marriages and funerals.

Remedies have been tried and are still being tried to solve the manifold problems of weavers. Efforts are being made to bring more and more weavers into the co-operatives. The Santanam Committee proposed that excise duty on powerlooms should be brought on a par with the duty on handloom cloth and loans at concessional rates of interest should be granted to handloom co-operatives. Certain export sectors should be reserved for handlooms and, besides England, other European countries and the United States, possible markets for handlooms in Latin America and Africa must also be explored. Although in recent times export incentives have been extended to handloom fabrics also, these are benefiting the middlemen—the exporters but not the weavers. As things stand today kalamkari painters and specialist handloom weavers are rapidly losing ground and the fact that their products are once again becoming fashion-wear in India and the west has not led to any fundamental improvement in their condition. If the handloom weaver has continued to survive it is perhaps because, as Alfred Chatterton the British civil servant said at the turn of the century, he has learnt to live on less and less.

The prosperity of weavers reached its zenith under the Vijayanagar empire when they were vested with significant social and ritual privileges in recognition of their economic importance, a period when they even participated in the administration at various levels. However, their steady decline began with the cotton revolution in England in the eighteenth century. A touching reminder of their past glory is to be found in a lullaby of the Saliya weavers:

velli midi palagai vengalathal nadavum
alli midi midikka adainjavanar vun maman.

The song tries to convey the idea of past prosperity among the weavers by saying that the Saliya forefather of the child (in the song) wove on a loom that had a silver plank and rope made of an expensive bronze alloy.

This is a sketch of the current situation and it remains for administrators and social reformers to help solve the problems of handloom weavers. But present conditions in the weaving community can be better understood if the causes and nature of its changing fortunes are studied over a period of time. A study of various aspects of the handloom industry in the past does throw light on recent problems. For instance the hold of the master weaver and the merchant-middleman today can be appreciated only if it is realized that their dominant role in textile production organization goes back to the late Vijayanagar period. What is therefore attempted in this work is a historical retrospect, a case history of South Indian textiles and weavers.

This study of the vicissitudes of the handloom industry and the weaving communities stretches spasmodically over seven hundred years, the idea being that when a theme in history is best studied in terms of epochs or phases, to strait-lace it in pure chronology would be poor methodology. My effort has also been to adopt as comprehensive an approach as possible and my study is as vitally concerned with the status and role of weavers in medieval society as with economic aspects such as loom technology, production organization and domestic and foreign trade in textiles.

Vijaya Ramaswamy

Acknowledgements

I wish to acknowledge my debt to the History Department of Jawaharlal Nehru University for all its help in the course of my research. I would specially like to thank Dr R. Champakalakshmi, Professor S. Bhattacharya and Dr Satish Saberwal for going through the initial drafts of some of these chapters. Professor R.P. Jain of the Centre for German Studies, Jawaharlal Nehru University, was kind enough to translate some important German and Sanskrit texts for me. I am grateful to Professor Dharma Kumar of the Delhi School of Economics, Dr K.N. Chaudhuri of the School of Oriental and African Studies, London, and Mr Joseph Brennig for going through the script and making useful suggestions. My special thanks are also due to C.N. Subramaniam of the Centre for Historical Studies, Jawaharlal Nehru University, for the lengthy discussions he has had with me on various aspects of South Indian history.

For their great help and co-operation in the collection and translation of weaver community literature, I wish to thank the Devanga Co-operative Weavers' Association of Gugai (Salem District), the Saurashtra Sabha of Madurai and Salem, and the Sengunta Sabha at Madras. I would like to express my gratitude to Thiru Muthukumaraswami of the Maraimalai Adigal Library, Kavignar N. Kandaswami of Rasipuram and Dr Busnagi Rajannan for their great personal help. I am grateful to Yuchido Norihiko for putting me in touch with the literature on the Pattunulkaran caste and to Mr T.J. Ayyan of the Saurashtrian Community for his information on Pattunulkaran folklore.

Thanks are also due to the Victoria and Albert Museum and the India Office, London; the National Museum, Delhi (specially to Mrs Krishna Lal); Dr M.L. Nigam of the Salar Jung Museum, Hyderabad; Mr Karl Kandalavala and Dr Harbans Mukhia for allowing me to reproduce prints in their collections.

Finally, my sincere thanks to Oxford University Press for the efficiency with which this book has been brought out.

Abbreviations

A.P.G.E.S.	*Andhra Pradesh Government Epigraphical Series*
A.R.E.	*Annual Report of (South Indian) Epigraphy*
Dispatches	*Dispatches from England*
E.C.	*Epigraphica Carnatica*
E.I.	*Epigraphica Indica*
E.P.W.	*Economic and Political Weekly*
E.F.I.	William Foster, *The English Factories in India*
Hak.Soc.	Hakluyt Society
H.E.H.	*Corpus of Inscriptions in the Nizam's Dominions (Hyderbad Archaeology series)*
I.S.P.P.	*Indian Studies Past and Present*
J.I.H.	*Journal of Indian History*
J.I.T.H.	*Journal of Indian Textile History*
Letters	*Letters from Fort St. George*
M.A.R.	*Mysore Archaeological Report*
Mac.Mss.	Mackenzie Manuscripts
N.D.I.	*Nellore District Inscriptions*
P.I.H.R.C.	*Proceedings of the Indian Historical Records Commission*
S.I.I.	*South Indian Inscriptions*
S.I.T.I.	*South Indian Temple Inscriptions*
T.T.I.	*Tirumalai–Tirupati Devasthanam Inscriptions*

Author's Note

In the pronounciation of names and words in South Indian Languages, an effort has been made to keep as close as possible to the modern English usage because a very strict transliteration of native words may have posed problems to the general reader. However, where it was found unavoidable, the usual system of Romanization has been followed, for example the use of *c*, which is always pronounced as the palatal *ch*. The use of double *o* or double *e* has been avoided where long or double consonants occur. For instance, in Ottakkuttar *u* is used rather than a double *o*. The letters *r* and *rr* are trilled and *rr* is pronounced *tra*. A guide to the pronounciation of all the important native names and terms is provided in Glossary 2 and the Index, where diacritical marks have been used.

When an inscription is mentioned in the text for the first time, the place name is followed by the name of the district where it is located to enable identification. However, in all subsequent references to the same place the district is not mentioned. It is easy to look this up in the table provided in Chapter 1, which lists the *taluk* as well as the district.

Clarification has also to be made regarding the usage of terms such as 'Kaikkola', 'Saliya', and Devanga'. Three kinds of usages will be found. For example, 'Kaikkolar' refers to weavers in the collective, but 'Kaikkolan' is singular. Wherever there is a general reference to this community, 'Kaikkola' is used. Thus: the 'Kaikkola' weavers, the 'Kaikkolan' Kannan Arasu and the 'Kaikkolar' of Kamakshiamman temple.

Textiles and Weavers Down the Ages

The history of South Indian textiles goes back to prehistoric times. Evidence of what appear to have been spindles was found in archaeological sites like Paiyampalli in the North Arcot district of Tamil Nadu.[1] These were usually made of arecanut beads or were circular potsherds pierced with a hole. Surprisingly, even evidence of cloth has survived in a few archaeological sites like Adichchanallur and the Nilgiri hills.[2]

Cotton textiles of very superior quality were being produced and exported from centres like Kanchipuram, Madurai and Tanjavur. The evidence for this is to be found in many of the Sangam classics (first century BC to sixth century AD) like *Silappadikaram*[3] and *Manimekalai*.[4] *Silappadikaram* refers to the weaving of cotton and silk cloth and its export from the port of Pumpuhar, otherwise called Kaveripumpattinam. It describes the separate streets for weavers which were called *karugar vidi* or *aruvai vidi*.[5] Madurai also boasted equally prosperous and skilled weavers; even Kautilya in his *Arthashastra* refers to the fine textiles of Madurai.[6] In Sangam texts one finds descriptions of 'beautiful cloth so fine that the eye cannot follow the course of the yarn', and cloth bearing such delicate designs as to make it look like 'the slough of a snake'.[7] Some are described as soft as fresh blossoms and others as light as smoke.[8] Fine woven cloth is said to be as delicate and transparent as the vapours of milk. Garments were woven with borders or with embroidery on them.[9] Silk cloth is referred to as *pattadai*.

The spinning and weaving of cotton cloth was very much a part of everyday life in ancient India. The loom is used as a poetic image in several ancient texts. The *Atharvana Veda* says that day and night spread light and darkness over the earth as the weavers throw a shuttle on the loom.[10] The Hindu god Vishnu is called *tantuvardan* or 'weaver' because he is said to have woven the rays of the sun into a garment for himself. The words *tantu* (warp) and *ottu* (woof) are to be found in the *Rig Veda*.[11]

Specific references to textile technology in ancient South India are also to be found in other literary texts. In *Agananuru*[12] as well as *Narrinai*,[13] both Sangam texts, the carder's bow is used as a poetic simile—the fluffy clouds in the sky after the rains are said to resemble cotton well beaten by the carder's bow. Such evidence shows that the bow for carding was introduced in South India between the second and sixth centuries, not in the medieval period as has hitherto been believed.[14] There are several references to the spinning of yarn, and from the texts it is clear that this was mainly the occupation of widows.[15] The earliest type of loom in operation seems to have been the vertical loom. A verse from the *Atharvana Veda* says, 'A man weaves it, ties it up; a man hath borne it upon the firmament. These pegs propped up the sky; the chants, they made shuttles for weaving. . . . ' (*sic.* The rhythmic sound made by the shuttle as it lifts the woof or vertical threads and passes through the weaving shed is referred to in the last line.)[16] The evidence points to a primitive vertical loom.

The Sangam texts are also replete with references to Indian dyes. Indigo was a commonly used vegetable dye and cloth dyed with indigo is referred to as *nilikachchai* in *Purananaru*.[17] Huge brick dyeing vats pertaining to the first and second centuries have been unearthed from Arikamedu[18] in Pondicherry and Uraiyur[19] in Tiruchirapalli, both known to be important weaving centres from the accounts of *Periplus*.

From sculptures, paintings and ancient literary accounts it appears that in antiquity it was the lower strata of people—common soldiers, menials, elephant mahouts, palace attendants, singers and dancers—who wore stitched garments such as blouses, trousers and waistcoats. Such garments are not described as the apparel of upper classes or royalty. Nor are they depicted on images of gods and goddesses. *Silappadikaram* describes the king's bodyguards as wearing shirts and turbans on their heads. Tailors are referred to as *tunnakkarar*.[20] The references to *tunnar* and *tunnavinajnar* also come from *Manimekalai*.[21]

The evidence of ancient texts points not only to the production and technology of textiles but also to the trade in cloth. The indigenous textile merchants were called *aruvai vanigar*. *Silappadikaram* describes the *aruvai vanigar vidi* or the street of cloth merchants where quantities of cloth woven of cotton thread, hair or silk were sold.[22] Interestingly, it describes the existence of wholesale shops as

well as streets of petty shops, the latter perhaps being the place
where weavers spread out their goods and sold them. Cloth
merchants are also referred to as *aruvai vanigar* in a Brahmi
inscription from Alaganmalai pertaining to the second century.[23] An
important poet of the Sangam age was known by the name of
Aruvai Vanigar Elavettanar,[24] indicating that he must have been a
cloth merchant of considerable prominence.

While the cotton industry in India was flourishing, in Europe
cotton was still virtually unknown. Herodotus (fifth century BC)
thought that cotton was a kind of animal hair like sheep's hair.[25] At
the beginning of the Christian era Indian textiles figured prominent-
ly in the trade with Rome. The Roman historian Arrian testifies to
the export of dyed cloth from Masulia, i.e. Masulipatnam.[26] It is
said that Indian cloth and the Chinese silk re-exported from India
were purchased for their weight in gold.[27] This was probably the
reason for Pliny's oft-quoted lament that India was draining away
the wealth of Rome.[28] *Periplus of the Erythrean Sea* refers to
Dhanayakataka (Dharanikotta on the Krishna river, near Amaravati) as an important centre of the textile industry and trade.[29] It also
says that 'argaritic' muslins were exported to Egypt and Rome.[30]
Argaru was the Roman name for Uraiyur in Trichnopoly district,
the capital of the Sangam Cholas. *Periplus* also refers to Poduca,[31] i.e.
Pondicherry, whose historical importance as a textile centre is
evident from the Arikkamedu excavations. The quality of Indian
dyeing, too, was proverbial in the ancient world, and in St. Jerome's
fourth century Latin translation of the Bible Job says that wisdom is
more enduring than the dyed colours of India. The extent of Rome's
trade with South India can be gauged by the fact that more than
1007 coins of the Emperor Tiberius have been unearthed in South
India alone. Indian textiles even passed into Roman vocabulary, as
is seen by the use as early as 200 BC of an Indian word for cotton,
carbasina, derived from the Sanskrit *karpasa*.

This brief account sums up the condition of South Indian textiles
and weavers in the ancient period. The focus of the present study is,
however, the period stretching from the tenth to the seventeenth
centuries.

The handloom industry of South India generally prospered
during the medieval period except when there were famines or
periods of political instability, such as the interlude between the fall
of the later Chola empire and the establishment of the Vijayanagar

empire. The heyday of the weaving industry was the Vijayanagar period in the fifteenth to sixteenth centuries, when the kings provided an added impetus to textile production by giving facilities and privileges to weavers and traders of cloth. With economic prosperity there was marked upward social mobility among weavers, resulting in their securing ritual and other privileges from the state and society. This was also the age of the heterodox Bhakti movements in the South, initially Virasaivism and later Tengalai Sri-Vaishnavism, in which weavers participated in large numbers. Upward economic mobility caused a flux in society and social status was sought to be determined through violent clashes between and within the left-hand (*idangai*) and right-hand (*valangai*) castes. The nerve centres of society were the temples.

With the establishment of rival European companies in the seventeenth century, the lives of weavers no longer revolved around the temple but around European factories and Black Towns. The quarrels of the left-hand and right-hand castes invariably involved the question of who was to secure the company's contract for cloth. While merchants turned middlemen, weavers gradually began to work on the basis of company advances; soon a situation was reached when poor weavers 'could not even put the cloth on the loom without an advance', as the Agent of Fort St. George, Langhorne, commented in 1675. Their creativity and skill were also being destroyed since the companies' injunction was to make them work 'to the perfection of the pattern'. With this the age of economic and social power, of the acquisition of land and privileges, of donations to temples and effective corporate functioning, was definitely over for Indian weavers in the South. With the turn of the eighteenth century their plight worsened. The cotton revolution in England rendered redundant the products of Indian handlooms and, instead of Indian cloth being exported abroad, the Indian market was flooded by Manchester and Lancashire goods. The words attributed to Lord Bentinck—'The bones of the cotton weavers are bleaching the plains of India'—are dramatic but apt as a description of the fate of handloom weavers.

The rise and decline of Coromandel textiles thus constitutes a fascinating but tragic study. In the present work the vicissitudes of the weaving communities have been examined in the light of the changing fortunes of the cotton textile industry in medieval India. The study covers a long period to enable analysis of the dynamics of social change and the correlation between economic power and social mobility over a span of time. I have endeavoured to demonstrate that the social status of a professional caste group was determined not by its ritual or theoretical status in the *varna* system, but by the extent of economic power which it enjoyed in that particular society.

The sources used in this study vary in nature and content since the canvas is spread over seven hundred years. For the later Chola and Vijayanagar periods inscriptions and literary texts, and to some extent traveller's accounts, are the main sources of information. For the seventeenth century inscriptions are few and far between and literary accounts of this period seldom deal with concrete realities or show an awareness of existing political and commercial tensions. Thus one is dependent mainly on company records, which suffer from one grave drawback. All the available records are those maintained by the East India Company establishments, and even private accounts are of individuals such as Streynsham Master, Schorrer or Hodges who were attached to Dutch, English and French concerns. Thus where political relationships arising out of trade contacts or commercial disputes with middlemen are referred to, the account is entirely one-sided. This is a handicap the researcher can only be conscious of, since it cannot be remedied. It is again the non-availability of sizeable indigenous source material that leads to a major gap in the data concerning the textile trade. While a clear picture of international trade emerges from company records, no parallel data is forthcoming either for a knowledge of domestic trade in textiles or for the extent of participation of indigenous merchants in foreign textile trade, although a broad outline of their activities has been drawn on the basis of inscriptions.

It is necessary to draw special attention to one other type of source used extensively—oral tradition. Various categories of oral tradition, such as religious songs, ritual folk dance and music, caste names and titles, and even proverbs and riddles, have been used as corroborative evidence. There is an acute paucity of information on the social structure of medieval times, and inscriptions, however accurate, are brief, sometimes to the point of being cryptic. Thus oral traditions have been used in conjunction with inscriptions and literary texts. Although their chronology is dubious and their facts interspersed with myths and fancies, these folk traditions are invaluable as substantive and corroborative evidence when used to bolster up other sources.

CHAPTER I

The Weavers, Textile Production and Trade

(Tenth to Fourteenth Centuries)

In 1957 a detailed survey of the textile centres of Tamil Nadu was made. This showed that the largest concentration of textiles was in Coimbatore, where more than forty per cent of the total workers in the cotton industry were agglomerated. This was followed by Madurai, Madras, Tirunelveli, Tiruchirapalli, Salem and Tanjavur districts.[1] A comparison of this recent survey of textile centres in Tamil Nadu with the geographical distribution of weaving centres in medieval South India shows that the traditional centres of weaving have more or less continued down the centuries from early medieval times. Despite the tremendous mechanization that has taken place in the textile industry, the primary criteria for determining the location of the industry, apart from the establishment of rail links, have essentially remained the same. As this survey reveals, the criteria continued to be the availability of raw material, skilled labour and transport and marketing facilities. In the medieval period the location of the weaving industry was dependent on the same factors, while proximity to ports replaced the modern preoccupation with rail transport.

The textile centres in medieval South India, by and large, had three factors in common—a similar type of soil, availability of dyes and proximity to ports. The centres were usually rich in black soil or the ferruginous loam soil best suited to cotton cultivation. According to the 1957 economic report, cotton cultivation was predominant in the black soil regions of Coimbatore, Madurai, Ramanathapuram and Tirunelveli districts. In North Coromandel the places surrounding Masulipatnam such as Chirala, Guntur, Ellur and others are known for their cotton production. In Bijapur, Dharwar and Belgaum districts cotton is the main crop on the basis of acreage. Many of these regions were also the areas of weavers' concentration in the medieval period. Coupled with the availability of cotton was

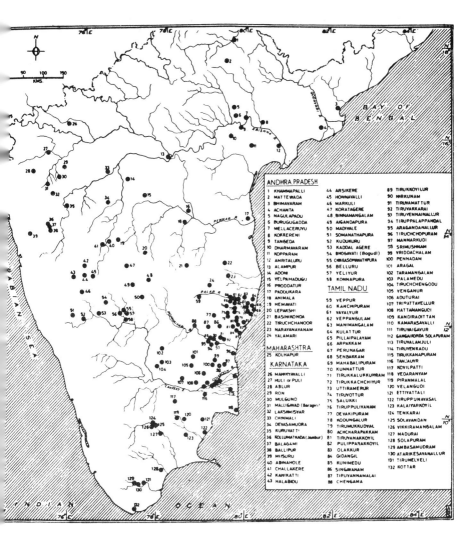

Map 1. Weaving Centres in Medieval South India AD 1000–1500 (based on inscriptional evidence)

S. No.	District	Weaving Centre	Taluq	Inscriptional Reference
		Andhra Pradesh		
1	Karimnagar	Kammapalli	Manthera	*A.P.G.E.S.*, vol. VIII, no. 34
2	Warangal	Mattewada	Warangal	*H.A.S.*, vol. 13, no. 10, 13 and 14
3	E. Godavari	Bhimavaram	Kakinada	*S.I.I.*, vol. V, no. 85
4	W. Godavari	Achanta	Narasapuram	*S.I.I.*, vol. X, no. 239
5	Nalgonda	Nagulapadu	Suryapet	*H.A.S.*, vol. 13, no. 30
6	Nalgonda	Burugugadda	Huzurnagar	*H.A.S.*, vol. 13, no. 18
7	Nalgonda	Mellaceruvu	Huzurnagar	*H.A.S.*, vol. 13, no. 52
8	Krishna	Kokkerini	Nandigama	*S.I.I.*, vol. X, no. 507
9	Guntur	Tangeda	Palnad	*A.R.E.*, 387 of 1926
10	Guntur	Dharmavaram	Ongole	V. Rangacharya, *Inscriptions of Madras Presidency*, no. 362
11	Guntur	Kopparam	Narasapeta	*S.I.I.*, vol. X, no. 533
12	Guntur	Amritaluru	Tenali	*S.I.I.*, vol. XVI, no. 334
13	Mahboobnagar	Alampur	Gadwal	*H.A.S.*, vol. 13, no. 55
14	Adoni	Adoni	Adoni	*A.R.E.*, 1 of 1915–16, Appendix D.
15	Anantapur	Velpamadugu	Gooty	*S.I.I.*, vol. IX, pt. 2, no. 516
16	Cuddappah	Proddatur	Proddatur	*A.R.E.*, 333 of 1935–6
17	Nellore	Paddukara	Kovur	*S.I.I.*, vol. XII, pt. I, no. 5; *A.R.E, C.P.* 1 of 1933.
18	Cuddappah	Animala	Kamalapuram	*A.R.E.*, 200 of 1937–8
19	Anantapur	Hemavati	Madakasira	*A.R.E.*, 15 and 16 of 1917–18
20	Anantapur	Lepakshi	Hindapur	*A.R.E.*, C.P. 18 of 1917–18
21	Chittoor	Basinikonda	Madanapalli	*A.R.E.*, 342 of 1912–13
22	Chittoor	Tirchchanoor	Tirupati	*T.T.*, vol. I, no. 34
23	Chittoor	Narayanava-nam	Puttur	*S.I.I.*, vol. XVI, no. 315
24	Chittoor	Yalamari	Chittoor	*A.R.E.*, 68 of 1959–60.
		Maharashtra		
25	Kolhapur State	Kolhapur		*E.C.*, vol. XIX, no. 4

S. No.	District	Weaving Centre	Taluq	Inscriptional Reference
			Karnataka	
26	Bijapur	Manikyavalli	Bugewadi	*E.C.*, vol. V, no. 3A
27	Belgaum	Huli or Puli	Parasagad	*E.I.*, XVIII, no. 22.E
28	Chittaldroog	Abbur	Kod	*A.R.E.*, 58 of 1951–2
29	Dharwar	Ron	Ron	*E.I.*, vol. XIII, no. 16
30	Dharwar	Mulgund	Gadag	*S.I.I.*, vol. XI, pt. 1, no. 97
31	Dharwar	Malligavad (Baragiri)	Hubli	*E.C.*, vol. V, no. 102
32	Dharwar	Lakshmisvar	Shiratti	*S.I.I.*, vol. XX, no. 11
33	Raichur	Chinmali	Sidhdhanur	*A.P.G.E.S.*, vol. IX, no. 15
34	Chittaldroog	Devasamudra	Molakalamuru	*E.C.*, vol. XI, Mk. 1
35	Bellary	Kuruvatti	Haddagalli	*S.I.I.*, vol. IX, no. 165
36	Shimoga	Kollumathada (Jambur)	Shikarpur	*E.C.*, vol. VII, Sk. 145
37	Shimoga	Balgami	Shikarpur	*E.C.*, vol. VII, Sk. 95
38	Shimoga	Ballipur	Shikarpur	*E.C.*, vol. VII, Sk. 95
39	Shimoga	Musuru	Shikarpur	*E.C.*, vol. VIII, Nr. 33
40	Chittaldroog	Abinahole	Hiriyur	*E.C.*, vol. XI, Hr. 37
41	Chittaldroog	Challakere	Hiriyur	*E.C.*, Hr. no. 87
42	Hasan	Kanikatti	Arsikere	*E.C.*, vol. V, Ak. 40
43	Hasan	Halabidu	Belur	*E.C.* V(ii) Bl. Supplement, no. 236
44	Hasan	Arsikere	Arsikere	*M.A.R.* 1930, no. i Ak. 110
45	Tumkur	Honnavalli	Tiptur	*E.C.* vol. XII, Tp. 130
46	Hasan	Markuli	Hasan	*E.C.*, vol. V, Hn. 119
47	Tumkur	Koratagere	Koratagere	*E.C.*, vol. XII, Ml. 31
48	Bangalore	Binnamanga-lam	Devanahalli (Nilamangalam)	*E.C.*, vol. IX, Nl. no. 3
49	Bangalore	Aigandapura	Nilamangalam	*E.C.*, vol. IX, Nl. no. 38
50	Bangalore	Madivale	Bangalore	*E.C.*, vol. IX, Bn. 66
51	Mysore	Somanatha-pura	Tirumakudlu-Narsipur	*E.C.*, vol. III, Tn. no. 97
52	Mysore	Kudukuru	Hunasur	*E.C.*, vol. IV, Hs. 97

S. No.	District	Weaving Centres	Taluq	Inscriptional Reference
53	Mysore	Kaddalagere	Serinagapatam	*E.C.*, vol. III, Sr. 104
54	Mandya	Bhogavati (Bhogudi)	Nagamangala	*M.A.R.*, 1940, no. 29
55	Bangalore	Chikkasoma-nathapura	Chennapatna	*M.A.R.*, 1942, no. 26
56	Mandya	Belluru	Madur (Nagamangala)	*E.C.*, vol. IV, Ng. no.38
57	Bangalore	Yeliyur	Chennapatna	*E.C.*, vol. IX, Cp.66
58	Mandya	Konnapura	Malavalli	*M.A.R.*, 1945 no. 17

Tamil Nadu

S. No.	District	Weaving Centres	Taluq	Inscriptional Reference
59	North Arcot	Veppur	Gudiyattam	*S.I.I.*, vol. IV, no. 343
60	Chingleput	Kanchipuram	Kanchipuram	*S.I.I.*, vol. II, pt. III no. 73
61	Chingleput	Vayalur	Kanchipuram	*A.R.E.*, 364 of 1908
62	Chingleput	Veppangulam	Kanchipuram	*S.I.I.*, vol. VIII, no. 4
63	Chingleput	Manimangalam	Saidapet	*S.I.I.*, vol. VI, no. 255
64	Chingleput	Kulattur	Chingleput	*A.R.E.*, 16 of 1935
65	Chingleput	Pillaipalayam	Kanchipuram	*A.R.E.*, 88 of 1921-2
66	Chingleput	Arpakkam	Kanchipuram	*S.I.I.*, vol. VI, no. 456
67	Chingleput	Perunagar	Chingleput	*A.R.E.*, 370 of 1923
68	Chingleput	Senpakkam	Chingleput	*A.R.E.*, 113 of 1933-4
69	Chingleput	Mahabali-puram	Kanchipuram	*A.R.E.*, 303 of 1961-2
70	Chingleput	Kunnattur	Chingleput	*A.R.E.*, 221 of 1929-30
71	Chingleput	Tirukkaluk-kunram	Chingleput	*A.R.E.*, 170 of 1933
72	Chingleput	Tirukkach-chiyur	Chingleput	*A.R.E*, 300 of 1909
73	Chingleput	Uttiramerur	Kanchipuram	*A.R.E.*, 195 of 1922-3
74	North Arcot	Tiruvottur	Cheyyar	*S.I.I.*, vol. VII of 109
75	North Arcot	Salukki	Wandiwash	*A.R.E.*, 471 of 1920-1
76	Chingleput	Tiruppuliva-nam	Kanchipuram	*A.R.E.*, 201 of 1923
77	North Arcot	Devakipuram	Arni	*A.R.E.*, 364 of 1912
78	North Arcot	Kodungalur	Wandiwash	*A.R.E.*, 143 of 1923-4
79	Chingleput	Tirumakkudal	Madurantakam	*A.R.E.*, 182 of 1916 .

S. No.	District	Weaving Centre	Taluq	Inscriptional Reference
80	Chingleput	Achcharapakkam	Madurantakam	S.I.I., vol. VII, no. 448
81	Chingleput	Tiruvanakkoyil	Madurantakam	A.R.E, 286 of 1910
82	Chingleput	Puliparakkoyil	Madurantakam	A.R.E., 293 of 1910
83	South Arcot	Olakkur	Dindivanam	A.R.E., 354 of 1907
84	South Arcot	Gidanigil	Dindivanam	S.I.I., vol. VII, no. 936
85	South Arcot	Kunimedu	Dindivanam	S.I.I., vol. XVII of 264
86	South Arcot	Singavaram	Gingee	S.I.I., vol. XVII, no. 248
87	North Arcot	Tiruvananamalai	Tiruvananamalai	S.I.I., VIII, no. 7
88	North Arcot	Chengam	Tiruvananamalai	S.I.I., vol. VII, no. 117
89	South Arcot	Tirukkoyilur	Tirukkoyilur	S.I.I., vol. VII, no. 936
90	South Arcot	Nerkunram	Tirukkoyilur	A.R.E., 218 of 1934–5
91	South Arcot	Tiruvamattur	Viluppuram	A.R.E., 10 of 1922–3
92	South Arcot	Tiruvakkarai	Viluppuram	S.I.I., vol. XVII, no. 221
93	South Arcot	Tiruvennainallur	Tirukkoyilur	S.I.I., vol. VII, no. 379
94	South Arcot	Tiruppalappandal	Cuddalore	S.I.I., vol. XVII, no. 180
95	South Arcot	Argandanallur	Dindivanam	S.I.I., vol. II, no. 1018
96	South Arcot	Tiruchchopuram	Cuddalore	S.I.I., vol. XVII, no. 130
97	South Arcot	Mannarkudi	Vilupuram	S.I.I., vol. VI, no. 70
98	South Arcot	Srimushnam	Chidambaram	A.R.E., 252 of 1916–17
99	South Arcot	Vriddachalam	Vriddachalam	A.R.E., 68 of 1918–19
100	South Arcot	Pennadam	Vriddachalam	A.R.E, 263 of 1928–9
101	Salem	Aragal	Attur	A.R.E., 409 of 1913
102	Salem	Taramangalam	Omalur	S.I.I., vol. VII, no. 22
103	Salem	Palamedu	Tiruchchengodu	A.R.E., 346 of 1959–60
104	Salem	Tiruchchengodu	Tiruchchengodu	A.R.E., 140 of 1915–16
105	Trichinopoly	Venganur	Perambalur	A.R.E., 2 of 1913–14
106	Trichinopoly	Aduturai	Perambalur	A.R.E., 30 of 1913–14

S. No.	District	Weaving Centre	Taluq	Inscriptional Reference
107	Trichinopoly	Tripattavellur	Musiri	*A.R.E.*, 311 of 1968–9
108	Trichinopoly	Nattamangudi	Lalgudi	*A.R.E.*, 152 of 1928–9
109	Trichinopoly	Kandiradittam	Udayarpalayam	*A.R.E.*, 203 of 1928–9
110	Trichinopoly	Kamarasavalli	Udaiyarpalayam	*A.R.E.*, 88 of 1914–15
111	Tanjavur	Tiruvaigavur	Papanasam	*A.R.E.*, 59 of 1914–15
112	Trichinopoly	Gangaikonda Cholapuram	Udaiyarpalayam	*S.I.I.*, vol. IV, no. 524
113	Tanjavur	Tiruvalanjuli	Kumbakonam	*S.I.I.*, vol. VIII, no. 22
114	Tanjavur	Tiruvenkadu	Srikali	*S.I.I.*, vol. V, no. 176
115	Tanjavur	Tirukkanapuram	Nannilam	*A.R.E.*, 508 of 1922–3
116	Tanjavur	Tanjavur	Tanjavur	*S.I.I.*, vol. II, no. 66
117	Trichnopoly	Kovilpatti	Kulittalai	*A.R.E.*, 286 of 1964–65
118	Tanjavur	Vedaranyam	Tirutturaipundi	*S.I.I.*, vol. XVII, no. 452
119	Ramnad	Piranmalai	Tirupattur	*S.I.I.*, vol. VII, no. 442
120	Ramnad	Velangudi	Tirupattur	*A.R.E.*, 507 of 1958–9
121	Tanjavur	Ettiyattali	Aratangi	*A.R.E.*, 132 of 1915–16
122	Tanjavur	Tiruppunavasal	Arantangi	*S.I.I.*, vol. VIII, no. 21
123	Ramnad	Kalaiyarkoyil	Sivagangai	*S.I.I.*, vol. VII, no. 177
124	Madurai	Tenkarai	Nilakkottai	*S.I.I.*, vol. V, no. 301
125	Madurai	Cholavandan	Nilakkottai	*S.I.I.*, vol. V, no. 301
126	Madurai	Vikkiramangalam	Nilakkottai	*S.I.I.*, vol. V, no. 303
127	Madurai	Madurai	Madurai	*S.I.I.*, vol. IV, no. 371
128	Tirunelveli	Cholapuram	Kovilpatti	*S.I.I.*, vol. XVI, no. 221
129	Tirunelveli	Ambasamudram	Ambasamudram	*A.R.E.*, 310 of 1916–17
130	Tirunelveli	Harikesavanallur	Ambasamudram	*A.R.E.*, 454 of 1916–17
131	Tirunelveli	Tirunelveli	Tirunelveli	*A.R.E.*, 48 of 1945–6
132	Travancore State	Kottar	Nagarcoil	*S.I.I.*, vol. III. pt. II, no. 73

the easy accessibility of vegetable dyes and mordants. The references in inscriptions to these plants are numerous.[2] The proximity to ports was another leading factor in the growth of textile centres because land transport was expensive and slow, consisting mostly of pack bullocks and carts, while transport by sea was easier, cheaper and swifter.

The Weaving Communities

The weaving communities were concentrated in textile centres which were invariably linked to ports, as shown in the map. Certain weaving communities were traditionally associated with certain geographical regions, although it is not easy to make a precise demarcation of the spread of these communities over regions. This is on account of the mobility displayed by some of the weaver castes. The Devanga weavers originally hailed either from the Andhra or Karnataka region. Inscriptions relating to them have been found in both these regions[3] and the language spoken by them is either Telugu or Kanarese. But at some stage the Devangas seem to have moved into the Tamil country, and more specifically the Kongu region, in large numbers. It is possible that these migrations took place during the period of expansion under the Vijayanagar empire. The reasons for the migrations were the enormous opportunities offered by the new Telugu ruling class and the desire for economic advancement. The reference to the Devanga weavers in the Tamil country comes from Chingleput, Tanjavur and South Arcot districts,[4] besides Salem and Coimbatore where they were numerous.

An important weaver community of medieval times was the Sale or the Saliga community, classified as the Padma Sale and the Pattu Sale. This was probably the same community as the Saliya of the Tamil country for the root of both names is the Sanskrit *shalika*, meaning 'weaver'.[5] In the Dharwar and Belgaum districts they are referred to as Salige[6] and are termed Salevaru in the Andhra regions of Guntur, Krishna and Nalgonda districts.[7] The Tirumalai – Tirupati inscriptions also refer to them as Saliya.[8] The references to the Saliya in the Tamil country are of course numerous. A further proof of the close links between the Sale and the Saliya is the worship of the common deity called Salisvara. In course of time they must have acquired different cultural habits, and for that matter today, even within Tamil Nadu, the Saliyar of Tanjavur do not intermarry with the Saliyar of Tirunelveli.[9] The Jeda or Jedara caste of weavers was concentrated mainly in the Karnataka region. The reference to the Jedara caste of weavers is to be found as early as the twelfth century,[10] and in fact Jedara Dasimayya, the famous Sudra saint, belonged to this period.[11] The Senigar formed another weaving community of the Andhra-Karnataka region in the medieval period.[12]

The leading weaver communities of the Tamil country were the Saliyar and the Kaikkolar. During the Chola period, i.e. roughly from the tenth to the fourteenth centuries, it was the Saliyar who formed the major weaving community. In fact they were called the Choliya-Saliyar.[13] References to them are found in Chingleput, South Arcot and Tirunelveli[14] where they are to be found in considerable numbers, and also in Coimbatore, North Arcot and Tanjavur.[15]

However, the other major weaving community of Tamil Nadu, the Kaikkolar, seem to have functioned in the Chola period primarily as soldiers and members of the special troop of the king. The Chola inscriptions refer to the Kaikkola-*perumpadai* and the Kaikkola-*senapati*.[16] They are more often referred to as the Terinja-Kaikkolar (Terinja means trusted and they were so called because they formed the king's bodyguard.) Thus there were Samarakesari Terinja Kaikkolar, Vikramasinga Terinja Kaikkolar and Virasola Terinja Kaikkolar[17] (all referring to Parantaka I, 907–55), Arulmolideva Terinja Kaikkolar and Rajaraja Terinja Kaikkolar[18] (both referring to Rajaraja I, 985–1016). It is significant that the most frequent reference to the Terinja Kaikkolar comes from Tanjavur, the seat of Chola power. There is no inscription which directly relates the Kaikkolar with the weaving profession till the beginning of the thirteenth century. The earliest mention of loom tax on the Kaikkolar comes from the period of Sundara Pandya in the thirteenth century.[19] The Kaikkolar also find mention in connection with the loom tax in the period of Rajanarayana Sambuvaraya in the fourteenth century.[20] Even the literary evidence relating to the period confirms that the Kaikkolar functioned predominantly as soldiers in the Chola period. The twelfth century poet Ottakuttar's *Itti Elupatu* is a panegyric on the bravery and prowess of arms of Kaikkola warriors. The evidence that the Kaikkolar served in the Chola army is further strengthened by a late

literary work of the community, *Vira Narayana Vijayam*.[21]
However, it is probable that even during the Chola period the
Kaikkolar combined weaving with soldiering. Weaving must have
been their occupation during peacetime, except for those Kaikkolar
employed permanently as bodyguards of the king. Thus, while most
of the references from Tanjavur district (the seat of Chola power)
during this period relate to the Terinja Kaikkolar, the majority of
inscriptions from all other districts refer merely to the Kaikkolar and
not to the Kaikkolar soldiers. Hence in these regions the Kaikkolar
must have continued to pursue their traditional occupation of
weaving. It must be noted that in the inscriptions the caste name
and the professional name were considered synonymous. If the
inscription mentioned 'Banajiga' or 'Chetti' it could be assumed
automatically that the reference was to a merchant, and if it
mentioned 'Saliya' or 'Kaikkola' it would be quite natural to assume
that the reference was to a weaver. While technically the term
tantuvaya stood for weaver, in practice no inscription refers to a
Saliya *tantuvaya* or a Kaikkola *tantuvaya*. Thus one can assume that in
those places where the nomenclatures Terinja or Senapati have not
been used, the reference is to a weaver. The assumption that the
Kaikkolar pursued weaving side by side with soldiering is strongly
substantiated by the eighth century lexicon *Adi Diwakaram* written
by the Jaina saint Diwakaram Munivar which says, 'Senguntar,[22]
Padaiyar [soldiers], senai talaivar [army commanders], Karugar [a
term for weavers occurring as early as the *Silappadikaram*][23]
Kaikkolar'.[24]

With the disbanding of the army of Rajaraja III and the
foundation of the Vijayanagar empire, the Kaikkolar became
full-fledged weavers and emerged as the predominant weaving
community in Tamil Nadu, displacing the Saliyar. Though concentrated in large numbers in the Tamil country, the Kaikkolar are to
be found in Mysore and Bangalore[25] where they are referred to as
Kaikkolaru, and also in Chittoor in Andhra.[26] It is significant that
these instances pertain to the Vijayanagar period, when weaver
migrations took place.

The association between soldiering and weaving seems to have
been common in many weaver communities. The Kaikkolar, for
instance, claim to have been the soldiers of Virabahu, the divine
lieutenant of the Hindu deity Kartikeya.[27] The Togata weavers of
the Andhra region styled themselves Ekangaviras and fought for the

Mahamandalesvara of Parugallu.[28] The Devanga, like the Kaikkolar, claim divine origin as the soldiers of their patron deity
Chaudambike.[29] Similarly the leader of the Sale or Salapu was
called *senapati*.[30] One reason for the continuous evidence of such
an association could be the existence of caste-based armies under the
Cholas.[31]

The weavers were usually settled in the *tirumadaivilagam*[32] of the
temple, i.e. the temple square, also called the temple town.[33] In the
Rajarajesvara temple of Tanjavur, the Saliyatteru or the Saliya
street is referred to as being within the temple square (*ullalai*) in
contrast to the streets of some other professionals which were outside
(*purambadi*).[34] In every town weavers had their own separate
quarters. During the period of Uttama Chola (tenth century), the
Pattusales were settled in the four quarters of Kanchipuram (called
Kachchipedu in the inscription) known as Karuvulanpatti, Karisa-
hanappatti, Atimanappatti and Eruvalichcheri.[35] The reference to
the street of the weavers (Kaikkolatteru) to the north of the
tirumadaivilagam of Tiruvalanturaiudaiya Nayinar temple in
Tiruchirapalli comes from Parakrama Chola-Pandya's reign, dated
1077.[36]

Textile Varieties

The weavers produced various types of cloth for the requirement of
the temple, the royal household and the common people. One of the
main articles of weaving was the *pudavai*. The *pudavai* (sari) was (and
still is) the dress of the women. The *Jivaka Chintamani* says that
women wore sarees with folds and drapes at the end.[37] The *pudavai*
was probably not very different from what it is today, of a length
between five to six yards. The main articles of clothing woven for the
common man were *vetti* and *uttiriyam*, the *vetti* worn from the waist
downwards being roughly one and a half yards in length and the
uttiriyam worn to cover the upper body. Headgear was worn by the
king and nobles but not perhaps by the common people. During the
period of Kulottunga Chola (1070–1122) reference is made to the
surrupudavai, niravadi pudavai, pavadai pudavai (a three-yard piece), and
men's apparel such as *uddi* and *uttiriyam*.[38] The weaving of ordinary
cotton sarees (*parutti pudavai*) is referred to in an inscription from
Nilamangalam in Bangalore.[39] Reference to *vetti* and *pudavai* is also
made in the reign of Rajaraja III in 1243.[40]

Evidence for the wearing of rich clothes and the use of headgear by the nobility is available from Karahalli Hobli in 1290.[41] The epigraph says that the Mahamandalesvara Someya Nayaka put on his gold coloured silk cloth (*pumpattigal kattida nulpattu*) and wound the turban around his head (*darasira pattigalam*). That the nobles wore costly shawls is clear from the evidence from Challakere which reveals that the Mahamandelesvara presented the king with a *hodake*,[42] a thin fine shawl.

Along with weaving, the allied craft of tailoring also occupied an important place. Evidence of stitched garments, especially the blouse or waistcoat (*kanchuk*) and trousers is to be found in ancient Indian sculpture.[43] References to tailors are to be found in Sangam literature. As stated earlier, the *Pugarkandam* of the *Silappadikaram* refers to *tunnakarar*, and in the *Manimekalai* they are referred to as *tunnar* and *tunnavinagnar*.[44] As in the Sangam period, it is not the upper class but the lower strata of society which is shown wearing stitched garments. Depictions of attendants wearing frock coats with full sleeves pertaining to the tenth century have been found in the Brahadisvaram temple at Tanjavur.[45]

Professional tailors were attached to the Tanjavur temple in the period of Rajaraja I (tenth century).[46] An order of Rajaraja Chola assigning a share in the produce of certain lands to a number of artisans and professionals refers to tailors called *tayyan* (the root *tayyal* means 'stitch') and *peruntunnan* (*tunnan* refers to one who cuts up the cloth) who were assigned one share of temple paddy each, and to a jewel stitcher (*ratna tayyan*) called Achchan Karundittai who was given one-and-a-half shares. He apparently belonged to a special category. A detailed *prasasti* (panegyric) dated 1139 on the tailors' corporation is available from Halabidu in Belur.[47] It refers to the corporation of tailors (*gottali* or *kottali*) of five cities and says that of these the tailors of Dwarasamudra were producers of decorative dresses (*vastrakandita-sringara chitrobhavarum*), skilled in the art of embellishing with many pieces of cloth (*aneka vastrakandita sringara vidya pravinaragi*), and that they also stitched decorative blouses. A great corporation (*mahasabha*) of tailors and 'tailors of god' (*Jagati kottali* and *Jeda kottali*) is referred to during the reign of Hoysala Ballaladeva in 1209 from Kanikatti Hobli.[48]

In cottons, muslins and chintz were mainly woven. Muslin was called sella. The Masulipatnam region was famous for its muslin. Chintz was known as vichitra. The *Manosollasa*[49] of Someshwar, which belongs to the twelfth century, refers to the excellent textiles of Poddalapura, Chirapalli, Negapatna and Cholapatna, and also to the cloth of Tondaimandalam.[50] It describes the production of cotton (*karpas*) as well as silk (*pattusutram*). Chintz vichitra is referred to, and cloth varieties and patterns are enumerated in detail. It describes sarees variegated by lines in different colours and with five colours in the *pallav*, circular patterns with lines and squares, and sarees with dots.[51] The text also refers to the tie-and-dye as *tantu banda*.[52] The *Jivaka Chintamani* of the tenth century refers to both silk and cotton cloth starched with rice-water (*kanji*) and perfumed with fragrant smoke.[53] The work also refers to *pum pattu, pachchilai pattu, konkala pattu* and *ven pattu*.[54] A reference to the different types of silk in the period of Vikrama Chola (twelfth century) comes from Coimbatore.[55] The inscription refers to *pachchai pattu, puliyur pattu* and *pattavala pattu* (patola).[56] The record bestows on the Idaiyar (shepherd) community the right to wear these varieties of silks as a special privilege, along with other privileges such as covering their houses with plaster. *Pumpattigal kattida nulpattu*, which can be translated as 'flowered silk cloth', was woven at Karahalli Hobli in 1290.[57] From Gulbarga district there is reference to a gift of 960 silk garments to the temple deity.[58] The reference to *pachchai pattu* and *dasuri pattu* comes from Warangal district at the beginning of the fourteenth century, in 1317.[59] *Dasuri pattu* is now called tassore silk.[60] Though the term *pachchai pattu* occurs repeatedly in these inscriptions, its quality is not clear. The reference to tassore silk and its processing also comes from the *Mitakshara*[61] of Vijnanesvara, pertaining to the twelfth century.

Cloth Dyeing and Printing

Cloth was dyed with vegetable dyes. A twelfth-century record from Shimoga district refers to the use of *kusumba* or red safflower as a principal dye.[62] The Hoysala king Vishnuvardana (twelfth century) is said to have imposed duty on safflower in Belur district.[63] *Kusumba* gave a pleasing red colour that was bright and lasting. The references to *nili* (indigo) and *manjishta* (madder, the red dye) come from Warangal from the period of Kakatiya Ganapatideva, in connection with joint donations by foreign and native merchants from a levy on their items of trade.[64] The *Mitakshara* refers to the processing of different types of textiles in some detail. Silks like *tassore* and *amsupattu* were purified by the use of water, alkaline earth and cow's urine,[65] which acted as caustic agents. It says that this process was repeated again and again after the cloth was dried. *Srifruit* or *bel* and *arishta* or *rita* were also used as caustic agents.[66] Another important caustic agent was *myrobalan* or *kadukkai*.[67] With regard to cotton and linen, the *Mitakshara* instructs that they should be processed in a solution of white mustard, water and cow's urine, apparently because of their astringent quality. Describing the process the text says, 'After being dried for some time in the sun, the clothes dyed with flower colour must be sprinkled by hand [with the solution], again sprinkled with water and then used in the performance.'[68] The final reference is to the painting or printing of the cloth after the processing. The term 'flower colour' probably refers to *kusumba* (red dye) and also *haridra* (turmeric) which cannot bear washing but must be sprinkled by hand in contrast to *manjishta* (madder) which can be washed. *The Manasollasa* also makes references to the variety of dyes in use. It says that in tie-and-dye weaving, pleasing colours were used. Reference is made to *manjishta*, *laksha* (lac) used as a mordant, *kusumba*, *haridra* and *nili*.[69] It also refers to *abhayarasa* as yielding black dye and *nisha* (deep blue or black). Cloth dyed the colour of peacock blue is also mentioned.[70]

Dyeing had gradually emerged as an independent profession and reference to a tax on dyers is to be found in several inscriptions. A tax on dyers, *kaibanna nulu karbuna*, is alluded to in a record from Grama Hobli in Hassan district, dated 1173.[71] A similar tax on dyers called Sivapputoyar in the Tamil country is mentioned from Tiruvorriyur in the year 1223.[72] Another instance of the same tax comes from Virupakshapuram Hobli in 1288.[73]

Cloth printing is an important aspect of textile production but its origin is extremely difficult to determine. Irfan Habib who has done a great deal of work on this aspect is unable to trace it back earlier than the seventeenth century.[74] However it seems probable that block printing existed in India even in the twelfth century. To begin with there is the term used for printed calico, i.e. chintz, *chit* or *chint* (the Tamil word is *chiti*). Habib cites the *Bahar-i-Ajam* to affirm that it was the Hindi *chint* which passed into Persian vocabulary. What is very interesting is that the words for chintz, *chit* or *chiti*, are corruptions of the Sanskrit word *vichitra*.[75] Now one might conclude that *vichitra* refers to painted rather than printed calico,[76] except for the reference in the *Manasollasa*[77] which states that the cloth was dyed and then printed with the instrument. To quote the relevant line: '*Prakshale adhikarangani ranjitani cha yantrakaihi.*' If the term *yantraka* used here pertains to the wooden block, then the process of block printing can be pushed back to the twelfth century. The evidence is, however, inconclusive since the precise meaning of the term *yantraka* here is ambiguous. The word can mean 'an instrument' or it can mean 'tied' or 'bound', which would point to an entirely different process. But the former interpretation does seem more tenable.

Textile Technology

Some stray references to the existing textile technology are to be found in the contemporary literature and epigraphical records. In medieval literature the loom is a part of innumerable poetic similies and metaphors. A tenth century verse of the saint Manikkavasagar compares flights of fancy to the rapid movements of a shuttle on the loom.[78] A description of the processes involved in preparing the yarn for weaving comes from the Jaina author Malayagiri (twelfth century) in the *Sripindanajukti*.[79] It says that batting ('by a woman') means making loose the cotton (*ruta*) by means of the bow (*pinjana*). It also says that the cotton was ginned in the gin (*lotinyam lotayanti*). The description of *Pinjana* as batting instrument, a bow for loosening the fibres, is confirmed by the Sanskrit dictionary *Abidana Chintamani*[80] of Hemchandra, also pertaining to the twelfth century. The evidence of the continued use of the spindle for spinning yarn in the thirteenth century comes from the Jaina saint and poet, Bhavanandi Munivar. In his *Nannul*,[81] a work on grammar, he compares poetic composition to the process of spinning—'With words as cotton, ideas as the thread and my imagination as the spindle [*kadir*], I shall spin my yarn.'[82] It appears that the spinning wheel with the crank handle was introduced in India only in the fourteenth century by the Turks.

The vertical loom seems to have been the most primitive type in existence in India.[83] Evidence of the operation of the vertical loom in the medieval period comes from the reign of Vira Ballaladeva in a record dated 1184 from the brahmin village (*agraharam*) of Jambur in Shimoga district.[84] The inscription refers to 'looms which are tied to the roof with a rope.' The folk songs of the weaving communities (which are ancient but cannot be dated) seem to indicate that

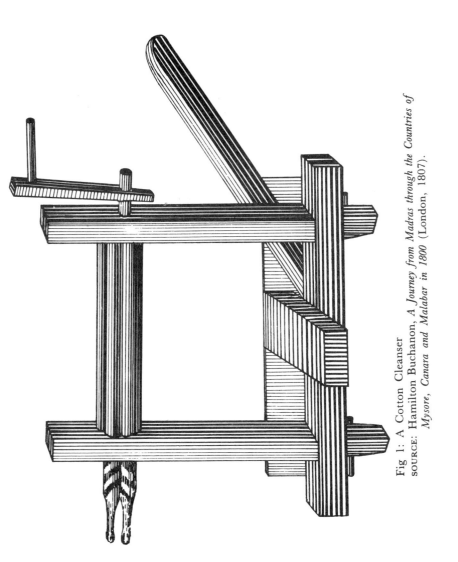

Fig 1: A Cotton Cleanser
SOURCE: Hamilton Buchanon, *A Journey from Madras through the Countries of Mysore, Canara and Malabar in 1800* (London, 1807).

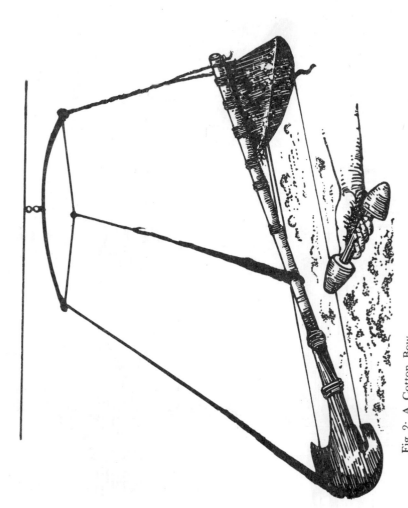

Fig 2: A Cotton Bow
SOURCE: Elijah Hoole, *A Mission to the South of India* (London, 1829).

Fig 3: A Spinning Wheel
SOURCE: Elijah Hoole, *A Mission to the South of India* (London, 1829)

horizontal looms were also in use. A folk song sung by the Nainar or Kuttar (minstrels) belonging to the Kaikkola community refers to the process of weaving with different deities representing different parts of the loom. The *devas* formed the thread which made the warp, Brahma the plank and Adisesha the rope. The song seems to indicate a horizontal loom.[85]

Irfan Habib has made the point that the ordinary loom meant for simple weave was practically incapable of further development until the coming of Kay's flying shuttle in the first half of the eighteenth century.[86] Such a statement would hold good if one were talking in terms of mechanization only, but is no longer tenable when other types of innovations are considered. For instance if patterned weaves could be produced on a horizontal loom, it would to a considerable extent revolutionize the technique. While only the plain tabby weave could be woven on an ordinary loom, the weaving of fancy designs and patterns would be possible only on a patterned loom or on a draw loom. While tracing the history of the draw loom Joseph Needham[87] states that the Chinese had developed the essentials of a draw loom between the first and the fourth centuries, although the invention came to Europe only around the fifteenth century. He also indicates that it might have existed in 'India from very early times since India was the home of cotton culture and cotton technology'.[88] However, Irfan Habib, while admitting that the draw loom had been invented in antiquity in China and perhaps also in the Middle East,[89] says that the earliest instance of its appearance in India, cited by Streynsham Master, was in 1679. Master observed at Ellur (Andhra) 'the manufacture of carpets on upright looms with coloured weft threads woven in accordance with patterns set on paper.'[90] Master says that these were woven by Muslims in the Persian manner.

It is possible to suggest on the strength of inscriptional evidence relating to South India that the patterned loom in India can be dated from the eleventh century onwards. A reference to *achchutari*[91] occurs in 1001 of the period of Rajaraja Chola I, from Tiruvottur, North Arcot district. The word *achchu*[92] by itself means 'mould' or 'print' but when combined with the word *tari* (loom) it refers to the process by which the threads are tied together to form certain sequences and then the heddles are lifted by hand in the weaving of the pattern. A further reference to the *achchutari* is to be found in the period of Rajaraja III[93] (thirteenth century). Further innovations in the production of the figured weave were made in the Vijayanagar period.

Textile Trade

There was brisk internal as well as external trade in textiles. Inland trade was carried on mainly through pack bullocks. Textiles or cotton were also either carried on the head (*talaikkattu*) or in bags suspended at both ends of a long pole and slung over the shoulder (*kavadi*).[94] In the weekly *santa* or fair held in the Andhra country the unit of sale was a bag or a sack.[95] The common wooden cart was a cheap means of transport and carts were loaded with gingili vegetables and also cotton and sarees. An inscription from Kotyadana in Andhra dated 1147 gives the tax rates on the head load and cart load of *chire* as well as Saliya *chire* being sold at the weekly fair. The rates are 1 *visa* on headload and 1 *adduvu* on every cart load.[96] Cloth was in fact taxed at so much per cart load or head load. Another unit of sale was the *pudavai kattu* or a bundle of sarees.[97]

From very early times many regions in the South seem to have been leading textile manufacturing and trading centres. In the Tamil country there were several major weaving centres. While those catering to the internal demands were linked to the *peruvali* or grand highways, those supplying the export markets were connected to the nearest ports. For instance in the Tanjavur district, Shiyali, Arantangi, and Kumbakonam[98] taluqs were cotton growing areas and weaving centres and these were linked to Chola ports, as is evident from references to 'the highway leading to the *pattinam*'[99] (probably Kaveripumpattinam) in the inscriptions. In Ramanathapuram district, at Tirupattur as well as Sivagangai[100] taluqs, cultivation of cotton and the existence of cloth merchants (*aruvai vanigar* or *chilai chetti*) is mentioned. Madurai was a centre of cotton production and weaving[101] and also had a port, Korkai. Inscriptions from Tirunelveli, another important weaving centre, refer to cotton cultivation and the transport of textiles through the *pattinam*[102] or port. Chingleput again had numerous cotton production centres[103] and the outlet was Chaturavachagappattinam,[104] the flourishing port Sadras of the seventeenth century. Mamallapuram had been the Pallava port for Kanchipuram during the seventh–eighth centuries. Even later it continued as an active port and was known as Mallai. Mylapur was a flourishing port under the Cholas and is referred to in medieval inscriptions and literature. For instance a reference is made to the Nanadesi Valanjiyar community of 'Mayilarpil'[105] (*sic*) in an eleventh century inscription from Kottur near Ponneri, north of Madras. The *Periyapuranam*,[106] a religious work of the twelfth century, says that Sevasenan, a resident of Mylapur, became wealthy by participating in the flourishing shipping trade. Mylapur became known as San Thome when it became a Portuguese possession.

For the North Coromandel, Mottupalli was one of the most important ports during this period. The Kakatiya ruler Ganapatideva reduced the duties on all goods including silk yarn and silk cloth at Mottupalli in order to facilitate foreign trade.[107] The Venetian traveller Marco Polo (*c.* 1288–94) coming to India towards the close of the thirteenth century praised the delicate buckrams and muslins of 'Mutfili' (Mottupalli).[108] Ganapatideva's charter was confirmed and further elaborated by Anavota, the brother of Prolaya Vemareddi, in 1358 and, interestingly, the inscription was framed in both Telugu and Tamil, apparently for the convenience of merchants.[109] Terdal in Bijapur was an important textile manufacturing and trading centre. Thus there are references to the prosperous condition of the cloth merchants' corporation of Terdal and the sale of cotton, yarn and garments of novel designs (*navina mandana bahuvastradim*).[110] The evidence indicates that the manufacturing centres of cloth, especially of the export varieties, must have been located on the Coromandel coast.[111]

For the Karnataka region the major ports on the west coast were Saimur, Honavar, Batkal, Barkur and Mangalore.[112] A detailed reference to these comes from the account of Ibn Batuta pertaining to *c.* 1342–5.[113] He refers to Sandalur (Saimur) in the vicinity of Goa, Honavur, Abusarur (?), Fakanar (identified with Barkur), Manjarur (Mangalore), Jurfattan (Cannanore or Srikandapuram) and Dahfattan (Dharmapatam). Ibn Batuta comments that the clothing of the sultans of Honavar consisted entirely of silk stuffs and fine linen. Honavar itself was a centre for weaving[114] and it appears that textiles from surrounding areas like Arisakere, Halabidu, etc. in Hassan district were also brought to Honavar for trade. Bangalore, Mysore, Shimoga and Chittaldroog also produced different varieties of silks. The cotton textiles of Karnataka were, however, apparently inferior and do not find any mention in the inscriptions. Reference to the presence of Chinese silk in Karnataka ports comes from both literary and epigraphical sources. Somesvara and Harihara[115] refer to silk fabrics called *cheena* and *mahacheena*. Perhaps much of this silk was brought to Karnataka for re-export to other places.[116] Ibn Batuta alludes to the presence of Chinese junks in Cannanore. As late as 1429 an inscription from South Kanara refers to the sale and purchase of Chinese fabrics.[117]

The comments of foreign travellers are very valuable in gaining an idea of the popularity of Coromandel textiles abroad. Abdul Feda, an Arab traveller of the thirteenth century, comments, 'The Coromandel is celebrated by the reports of travellers. It is from there that they export muslin which has passed into proverb for its fineness.' Chau-Ju-Kua, a Chinese traveller of the same period, also refers to Tien-Chu (the coast of Madras) and the production of po-tie (muslin) here. He also refers to the export of cotton, cotton thread, silk thread and textiles, especially chintz and coloured silks, to Ta-tsin (Baghdad), Fu-nan (Cambodia) and other places.[118] Marco Polo said of the muslins of Mottupalli, 'In sooth they look like the tissues of a spider's web. There is no king nor queen in the world but might be glad to wear them.'[119]

Trade was actively encouraged through state patronage. Kulot-tunga I came to the throne in 1070 and is said to have abolished all customs duties at the ports to facilitate trade. Hence he was given the title 'Sungam tavirta Cholan' or Remover of Customs Duties. The poet Ottakuttar (1118 – 63)[120] lauds him for abolishing all customs which had been levied without fail 'even from the days of Manu'. In the thirteenth century the Mottupalli inscriptions of Kakatiya Ganapatideva as well as Anavota Reddi, dated 1245 and 1358 respectively,[121] record their *abhayasasana* (protective charters) issued to 'traders by sea, starting for and arriving from all continents, islands, foreign countries and cities.' The writer condemns the practice of former kings who are said to have confiscated the goods of ships attacked by storms and driven ashore. All customs were abolished except a fixed duty called *kapasulka* which amounted to one-thirtieth on all exports and imports. The record of Anavota gives the rates as 2 coins (*ruka*) on 100 cloth pieces being brought from the southern side and 3 coins (*ruka*) on 100 cloth pieces being imported from the northern side. On cloth meant for export the rate was 3 per every 100 pieces. These rates are not very different from

the ones given in the Tirukkalukkunram inscription, which also
belongs to the middle of the fourteenth century. Here the rates given
are—2 *panams* for every 100 bales of cotton and 8 *panams* on every
pudavai kattu, besides the levy of 2 *panams* on every 100 *panams* worth
of oil sold, etc.[122]

In comparison to the export trade, internal trade in textiles was of
much less significance. The obvious reason in the eyes of the
majority of the travellers was that the Indian climate did not
demand much clothing[123] and the requirements of the people were
few and simple, except for the nobility which indulged in ornate
dresses. However, a more sophisticated explanation would be the
nature of socio-economic organization in this period. The existence
of powerful village assemblies and semi-autonomous regional
institutions seemed to have resulted in the institutionalization of
internal trade, to some extent by the creation of one or more
nagarams in every *nadu*.[124] Usually local looms were sufficient to meet
local requirements. There are however some instances of inter-
regional trade. In one such record of the late twelfth century from
Balagami,[125] the Kalachuri king Bijjana Deva says that the
Turuksha king offered him horses, the king of Sri Lanka pearls and
the Chola king milk-white cloth. A most significant inscription in
this   context   is   the   fourteenth-century   record   from
Tirukkalukkunram[126] which gives the rates to be levied on
merchants as contribution to the temple festival on the cloth they
took out of Chaturavachagan *pattinam* and the grain and oil they
brought into Sadras from the *pattinam*. The other port mentioned in
the inscription is most probably Masulipatnam, although grain may
also have been brought from the Gingelly or Orissa coast. This is a
clear instance of inter-regional coastal trading. Interestingly the
Malaimandalam *chettis* (i.e. of the Kerala region) are referred to in
areas of Tamil Nadu such as Chidambaram and Tiruvalanjuli.[127]
They dealt essentially in horses and are hence referred to as *kudirai*
(horse) *chettis* in all these inscriptions. The horses were basically an
item of import, although it is possible that the Malaimandalam
chettis partially exchanged these for Coromandel cloth. There are
frequent mentions in inscriptions to *peruvali* (trunk roads) such as
the Tanjavur trunk road, the Tirukkovalur merchants' trunk road
and the port trunk road.[128] While these might have been used for the
internal traffic in textiles, the majority of such trunk roads were
linked to the ports.

Commercial Organization

Textile trade was highly organized and was in the hands of merchant corporations. But within the limited area of their base, the weavers sold their own products at the local fairs, called *santa*.[129] The major merchant corporations operating in this period were the Tisaiayirattu Ainnurruvar, Manigramattar, Nagarattar, Valanjiyar, Anjuvannattar and the Pekkamdru. These were divided into two main categories, foreign or Nanadesi[130] merchants and local or *nadu, nagara* or *sthalada*[131] merchants. There is also sometimes reference to a third category called Ubhaya Nanadesi,[132] which is interpreted to mean those who operated commercially within the country as well as outside.

The Tisaiayirattu Ainnurruvar, literally 'the five hundred of the thousand directions' (indicative of the extensive range of their commercial operation) belonged to Aiyavole in Bijapur. The organization had wide ramifications spread over the entire South and seems to have exercised sòme control over the other corporations. The Aiyavole belonged to the Vira Banajiga caste (so called in Andhra and Karnataka but known as Valanjiyar in the Tamil country), and in several *prasastis* they claim descent from mythological figures such as Vasudeva and Baladeva, and are endowed with many virtues.[133] Inscriptions pertaining to the 'five hundred' have been found in Cuddappah and Chittoor in Andhra, Kolhapur in Maharashtra, Shimoga and other districts of Karnataka, and also places like Ramanathapuram and Tiruchirapalli in Tamil Nadu.[134] Their presence is referred to in Malayamandalam (Kerala region) and evidence is also found of their activity in Sumatra and Sri Lanka.[135] The earliest mention of the 'five hundred' is from Munusandai in Pudukkottai[136] in the ninth century and the last reference to this corporation seems to be in the Lepakshi inscription from Anantapur, dated 1680.[137] Next to the 'five hundred' of Aiyavole, the Chitrameli and the Manigramattar were the leading mercantile organizations.

Specialization in trade is indicated by the existence of independent associations of cloth merchants. In fact in Kanchipuram exclusive quarters were occupied by the cloth merchants (*kurai vanigar*).[138] A late Pandya inscription from Piranmalai concludes a lengthy statement on joint donations by all the merchant corporations with the signatures of the important persons and corporations.

Here the terms 'Jayangonda Cholamandala Chilai Chettis' (cloth merchants of Jayangonda Cholamandalam, also known as Tondaimandalam) and 'Kongumandala Chilai Chettis' are extremely significant.[139] Reference to cloth merchants as *chilai chettis* also comes from Dharmapuri,[140] pertaining to the thirteenth century. The *aruvai vaniya cheri* (cloth merchants' quarters) is mentioned in an undated record belonging to the period of Vira Pandya from Ramanathapuram district.[141] Similar references to cloth merchants' corporations can also be found in the Karanataka and Andhra regions. There is evidence of local and foreign cloth merchants' corporations making a contribution to the temple in a twelfth century epigraph from Shimoga district.[142]

Textiles, however, were not a monopolistic item of trade of a specialized merchant organization; they quite often formed a part of the general trade. Thus at both Mannargudi and Kulittalai[143] the merchants made a joint contribution to the temple by a fixed levy on the income derived from various items of trade. Here *pudavai kattu* (cloth bundle) is mentioned along with items like paddy, pepper, etc. The record pertains to the thirteenth century. In the period of Jatavarman Vikrama Pandya the merchants made a similar contribution on the sale of paddy and cotton at Velangudi.[144] In the fourteenth century, at Piranmalai, all the merchant corporations headed by the Tisaiayirattu Ainnurruvar[145] made a donation on all their commodities of trade per head load (*talai chumai*), per bag load (*pakkam*), a unit called *podi* (bigger bundle?), and cart load (*vandi*). Cotton (*parutti*), yarn (*nulu*), coarse cloth (*parum pudavai*), fine cotton cloth (*men pudavai*), *konikkai pattu* (?) and *pattavala* (patola silk) are given as the major items of trade. From the rates levied on each bundle or cart it is clear that head load was one-twentieth of a *pakkam*, a *pakkam* was one-tenth of a *podi*, and a *podi* one-fifth of a *vandi*.

In Andhra textiles sometimes formed a part of the general trade though more often it was in the hands of a specialized organization. A Kalachuri record from Managoli[146] in Bijapur says that the 'five hundred' made a donation to the temple through contributions levied on all goods, from rubies to cotton thread.

Certain clear conclusions can be drawn from the evidence presented on the organization of textile trade. It establishes first the importance of the mercantile organization in the medieval cloth trade. As one epigraph from Balagami puts it, they operated in

Chera, Chola, Pandya, Kamboja, Gaulla or Gauda, Lata, Barvara, Parasa and Nepala, trading in all commodities from precious stones to horses, spices and cloth. The corporations not only had their geographical control over the whole of South India, but in each region they were organized at all levels, from the Nagaram to the Nanadesis.[147] It appears that the Tisaiayirattu Ainnurruvar exercised some sort of control, or possibly had some jurisdiction over the other merchant corporations. It is stated that in 1279 in Krishnapatnam in Nellore district, the Anjuvanna *vanigar* Nanadesi *padinenthune samasta paradesigal* of Nadu, Nagaram and Malaimandalam met at the Ainnurruvar *Tirukkavam* (headquarters?) in Kolitturai.[148] In the Piranmalai record cited earlier the joint donation of all the merchant corporations like the Chitrameli, Manigramattar and others is headed by the Tisaiayirattu Ainnurruvar. Further, though cotton and cloth did form a part of the general trade of the merchant corporations, these were considered important enough to be vested in specialized textile merchants. While the inscriptional references to the *chilai chettis* indicate the possibility of a syndicate controlling the sale of cloth, it is extremely interesting that they also seem to have traded in all items connected with textiles. To illustrate the point an epigraphical record from Anantapur[149] of the period of the Telugu-Choda king Malladeva, dated 1162, states that the Nanadesi merchants of the four languages (Tamil, Telugu, Kanarese and Malayalam) of the Kubera lineage, consecrated the temple of Dasisvara by endowing to it a fixed fee on all articles in which they traded, including cotton, cotton thread and sarees. This is shown at greater length in a record pertaining to the period of Kakatiya Ganapatideva (1317)[150] in which a huge donation was made by the native and foreign merchants to a temple at Mattiwada in Warangal. The contribution or *ayam* is stated to have been levied, among other things, on *nulu, pattu nulu,* on *dasuri* and *pachchai pattu* (tassore and another kind of expensive silk), and on dyes like *nili, manjishta,* etc. Similar instances have been cited earlier. The evidence indicates the geographical extent of the leading mercantile corporations, pointing to some degree of horizontal commercial control, i.e. in terms of spatial trade organization. Similarly, the repeated references to the mercantile associations dealing in all items from raw cotton to textiles and dyes, are suggestive, to some extent, of vertical control. However the control exercised by these groups was far from being monopolistic and there is no doubt that yarn and textiles were also being bought and sold in the local fairs (*santa*) which were outside the purview of these corporations.

Every merchant organization had its own regiment, probably in order to combat the bandits who made transportation of goods unsafe. They are referred to as *senai angadigal*,[151] literally 'the merchants' army'. In fact quite often certain villages or areas were converted into *erivirapattinam*, a merchant settlement or town guarded by troops, which hence became the exclusive preserve of the merchant organizations. In Chittoor, during the period of Rajaraja I, the Ainnurruvar converted Siravalli into a 'Nanadesi dasamadi erivirapattinam'.[152]

Besides the functioning of these huge mercantile organizations, sometimes even ordinary weavers rose from the ranks to become merchants, although such instances are few and far between in this period. In little Kanchipuram, during the period of Rajaraja I (985–1016), Paramanadi Chetti, son of Nakkampandai of the weaver caste, belonging to Mayilapur, gave a gift to the local temple.[153] Similarly in Chidambaram during the period of Kopperunjingadeva, the Saliya chettis (the Saliya, as stated earlier, were the predominant weaving community during the Chola period) were provided with houses on condition that they supplied the necessary cloth to the temple.[154] The use of the suffix 'chetti' shows that these Saliya weavers must have been prosperous enough to function as merchants. A Kalachuri inscription from Belgaum district dated 1224 refers to donations by the Saliya *samayangal* (Saliya corporate organization) led by Kadidevayya Chetti.[155]

Another important factor in textile trade was the brokers. The term *taragu kasu* (brokerage fee) occurs repeatedly in later-Chola inscriptions[156] and there is a specific reference to a brokerage fee on textile trade, *kurai taragu ayam*, in an epigraph of the period of Rajaraja Chola III, belonging to the thirteenth century.[157] It is possible that these brokers were especially used in foreign trade since problems of communication and negotiations are more likely to have arisen in this connection where foreign traders would probably not have known the native tongue.

Taxation

All taxes relating to the weaving industry were paid to the state, unless their proceeds had been specifically granted to the temple by the state. To cite an instance, in Kanchipuram, during the reign of Vijaya Gandagopaladeva, a Pallava chief Kadavaraya gifted the tax on looms to the Jvaraharesvara Perumal temple.[158] Kulottunga Chola Sambuvaraya is also said to have donated the various proceeds of the village of Achcharapakkam,[159] including the tax on looms, to the local deity. Similarly Rajanarayana Sambuvaraya gifted the tax on looms within the four limits of the *tirumadaivilagam* for worship in the temple of Tiruppulipagava Nayinar in Pulipparakkoyil in 1343.[160] This suggests that even the tax levied on weavers within the precincts of the temple went to the state unless it was specifically endowed to the temple.

A variety of taxes was imposed on the handloom industry. The most frequently mentioned in the inscriptions is *tari irai*[161] (loom tax) also called *tari kadamai*.[162] Along with this, *per kadamai* was also levied.[163] *Magga dere* is the term used in Andhra and Karnataka to denote loom tax, though the records of the Chola kings belonging to the Andhra region refer only to *tari irai*.[164] Another tax mentioned in the records is *achchu tari*.[165] *Achchu tari* probably refers to the patterned loom as distinct from the ordinary loom. Another oft mentioned tax is the *tari pudavai*.[166] It is more likely that this was a general tax on cloth since *pudavai* in that period was loosely used to denote lengthy cloth of any kind.[167] Details of the taxes imposed at the local fairs or *santas* on *pudavai* are given in a twelfth-century inscription from Bhimavaram.[168] *Panjupeeli*[169] was the tax on cotton yarn. Cotton was taxed and is referred to as *parutti kadamai*.[170] Tax was levied on cotton thread (*nulayam*) and silk thread (*pattadai nulayam*).[171] *Kurai taragu ayam* (brokerage fee on textiles) is referred to in an inscription from Vedaranyam, dated 1251.[172] A tax called *kaibanna* or *bannige* was levied on the dyers.[173]

For the incidence of taxation on weavers evidence is rather limited for the early medieval period, though there is sufficient information for the Vijayanagar period. Loom tax was levied at Kovilpatti during the period of Jatavarman Srivallabha in 1129 on the twenty-four looms in the village of Solapuram, at the rate of 10 *panams* per loom per year.[174] The term *panam* occurs very rarely in the coinage of the Chola period. One such reference is the mention of *panam* in an inscription from Tiruvallikeni (Triplicane in Madras).[175] The *Mitakshara* of Vijnanesvara says that anyone who maimed breeding bulls was to be fined 100 *panams*[176] Since the fine for a minor offence could not have been very high, the value of a *panam* must have been lower than other coins like *varaham, madai*, etc. It is however impossible to have an idea of the value of the *panam*, except that since the loom tax averaged around 3 *panams* per year in the Vijayanagar period, 10 *panams* in this period just could not have had the same value.[177] Three inscriptions of the period of Hoysala Ramanathadeva[178] (mid thirteenth century) give the monthly tax on looms on an average as between 7 to 8 *kasu*, i.e. 96 *kasu* per year. It states that this was the reduced tax meant to placate those weavers who had earlier emigrated in protest against the high taxes. During the period of Jatavarman Sundara Pandya 6 *panams* per loom was the annual rate of taxation at Tirukkachchiyur.[179] If the value of the *panam* in the thirteenth century has any relation to what it was in the fifteenth and sixteenth centuries, then the tax rate appears to have been fairly high.

There are instances to show that the weavers protested against high taxation by emigrating and were successful in inducing the state to reduce the taxation rate. Thus during the period of Hoysala Ramanathadeva, in 1277, the Dandanayaka Ravideva made a report that the weavers of Kandaradittam in Tiruchirapalli had emigrated owing to high taxation and the king, on the basis of the report, reduced the tax to 8 *kasu* per month.[180]

The relative importance of the weavers in early medieval economy can be gauged by the attitude and policies of the state towards them. Not only did the state adopt a conciliatory stance in the face of protests by weavers, but it also offered them economic privileges and large-scale concessions. Thus the state reduced taxes in newly settled areas to attract weavers, and for the first two or three years granted total tax remission. During the period of Vikrama Chola in 1128[181] twenty families of weavers, at the rate of four families from five villages, were newly settled in Tirukkanapuram in Tanjavur district and granted special privileges, including tax remission. In Amritalur[182] in Guntur, the Mahamandalesvara Chintagupta Timmarajayya granted a charter (*sasanam*) exempting the weavers and other professionals from payment of tax for the first three years. In the period of Rajanarayana Sambuvaraya, there was remission of loom tax on the new settlers at Nerkunram in South Arcot.[183]

CHAPTER II

The Weavers, Society and the State

(Tenth to Fourteenth Centuries)

The weavers formed a part of the overall social structure of the age and their status and function in any particular region at a point of time was determined not merely by the nature of their economic situation but also by the nature of the polity, the ethos of the society in general and the values of the various social groups comprising it in particular.

The linkages between the Chola state, the functioning of village assemblies and professional bodies, and the various levels of interaction between the social groups and the state are complex and somewhat confusing. This is perhaps why pioneering historians of South India failed to resolve the apparent paradox between the Chola 'centralized state' and the 'village republics'. The American Indologist Burton Stein is, however, conscious of this compartmentalized mode of exposition—'The usual approach is to ignore in the section entitled "central government" what is conceded and admired in the section entitled "local government" . . . . When one is dealing with the Chola or Vijayanagar states of Medieval South India ... the political system at all levels must be reasonably consistent (or at least without contradiction) . . . .'[1] Viewed in this light the contradiction between the description of the Chola state as 'absolutist' (at one place Nilakanta Sastri even calls it Byzantian) and the local government as 'independent village communities or republics' becomes glaringly apparent.

Weavers and the Locality System

The theory of the village republics is a carry-over from British liberal-historicist and Indian nationalist traditions which believed in the existence of self-sufficient and self-governing 'village republics'.[2] But it is extremely doubtful that the *brahmadeya* or Brahmin villages (called *agraharas*) and the non-Brahmin villages (called *ur*) were really self-sufficient.[3] It is undeniable that service relationships, and in fact even the sharing of the grain heap, existed,[4] though services were more often paid in terms of a piece of land.[5] The minimum number of professionals to be settled in a new village is referred to in the inscriptions and the absence of the weavers in most of these lists is significant. For instance during the reign of Jatavarman Sundara Pandya I a *brahmadeya* village was founded in the Chidambaram taluq and 200 *velis* of land apportioned among 121 Brahmins. The village also made provision for settling the Vellalar (agriculturists) and pieces of land were allotted to various professionals—Vaidya (physician), Karnam (accountant), Tachchan (carpenter), Kollan (black-smith), Uvachchan (drummer), Navidan (barber), Kumbaran (potter), Padikappan (watchman), Jati Ambashtan (?), Purangali (?) and Vettiyan (village servant).[6] The settling of various professionals such as carpenter, mason and priest is also referred to in the village of Ravulacheruvu in Dharmavaram in Anantapur.[7] Thus these units mentioned in the records could not have been self-sufficient, since items like cloth and oil had to be brought in from outside. There are however a few records suggesting that the weavers constituted a part of the village community in these places. Appadorai has quoted two such instances. The Kurram plates of Paramesvaravarman I[8] (seventh century) refers to looms and Appadorai interprets this to mean that looms were included among the common property of the village. The record actually refers to taxes from looms along with oil mills, bazaars and even brokerage as being given to a donee. To interpret all these as being the common property of the village is very far-fetched. The other instance cited by Appadorai is a tenth-century inscription of Rajaraja I which refers to *anniyayavadandavirai*, interpreted by him as tax on unauthorized looms in the village.[9] This interpretation is again questionable. A reference is made in the Kanerese country to the granting of a site to a weaving community (*samaya pattagarage*) attached to the four hundred Mahajanas (village elders).[10] However in the majority of records the weavers do not seem to have constituted a part of the village community. This is also true of the oilmen. Nonetheless even the standard list of twelve functionaries said to constitute the village professionals (called *ayagars* in the Vijayanagar records) was a variable one. For instance in some lists the potter is left out but the goldsmith and the astrologer are included. It is possible to conclude from the evidence that the general omission of weavers and oilmen renders invalid the concept of self-sufficient village units.[11] The description of local self-governing units is more justified. The democratic nature of the village or *nadu* assembly and its effective functioning is testified to in several epigraphs. In 1268 the *nattar* of the Chengam area (North Arcot district), and those of the surrounding villages comprising the Mudalis, Chettis, Vanigar (petty traders), Sivabrahmana, Porkoyil Kaikkolar (the prefix *porkoyil* to the weaver caste is not quite clear) Manradi (shepherds), Vedar (hunters), Banar (a caste of washermen) and Paraiyar (untouchables, i.e. menials), assembled and laid specific charges on the representatives of Karikala Chola (Aditya II) in the regions of Perindaiyan, Arachanayakan and Ammatalvan for combining with a local potentate Karuppukkattinayakan and causing internal dissension. The assembly ostracized them and condemned them as illegal usurpers of power. All those who helped them or abetted them in any way were also to be ostracized and in fact killed, though the latter statement seems more a violent expression of disapproval than an active decision to punish by death.[12] Interestingly one of the officials whom the village assembly ostracized, named Ammatalvan, is mentioned in an inscription from Chengam itself in 1223 as having given a land as *devadanam* to the temple of Chengama Udaiyar.[13] This is just one out of numerous instances of the village *nattavar* or elders and big landlords coming together to make important decisions.

In contrast to the pioneering studies, Stein has tried to analyse Chola society and polity within the alternative framework of the segmentary state model. The theory propounds the existence of pockets of power, called segmentary zones, functioning virtually independently of the overall head at the centre, called the king, except for the peripheral foci of administration in each zone. 'Locality, social, economic and political systems' called *nadus*, which were self-regulatory though not self-sufficient, are identified as the crux of the structure. Thus Stein argues that the most important self-governing unit was not the village but the *nadu* administered by the *nattar* who constituted the dominant peasantry.[14]

Within each locality system there were numerous contradictions. These comprised the various communal and caste organizations, besides of course the more fundamental contradictions arising out of economic differentiation and stratification. There are repeated references to the eighteen *panas*,[15] caste and craft organizations which represented secondary contradictions within a particular set, and these were subsumed under the leading contradiction of the left-hand right-hand castes. However, even to assume the left-hand right-hand as clear-cut categories would be too simplistic since the two divisions represent only a paradigm[16] which assumed different forms in different regions under different situations. Thus in order to appreciate the precise nature of local government and the position of the weavers in it at a particular period or point of time, for instance the composition of the assembly (*sabha, ur, nagaram* or *nadu*) and the dominance of a particular group or groups in its policy decisions, all these internal contradictions have to be taken into account, plus their mutability.

The implications of the economic position of the weavers in the social sphere can be seen by examining the following aspects: (1) the nature and extent of weaver corporate organizations (2) the size and nature of the donations made by weavers to temples, including temple services such as the celebration of important festivals (3) individual as well as collective rights over land enjoyed by weavers, which in medieval times were an important status symbol (4) the conferring of economic and social privileges on weavers in recognition of their importance.

Corporate Organization

The weavers were organized in guilds called *samaya, sreni* and *mata*. Though the term 'guild' has been used here for the weaver organization it must be made clear that it is more as a matter of convenience: the South Indian guilds, though they were corporate bodies of artisans, did not perform the economic functions usually performed by medieval guilds in Europe, such as the maintenance of uniform standards in products and prices.

The members of the weaver guild usually belonged to the weaver caste and heredity formed an essential part of the professional guild. Thus there is reference to *samaya pattagara* (*pattagara* = weavers), the *saliya samayangal* and *seniya* (*seni* = *sreni*) *pattagara*.[17] The weaver guilds had an excellent local and regional organization and this was also true of some other prominent corporations of the time, such as those of the Banajigas or the Kammalar[18] (also called Pancalar). The Kaikkola guild of weavers is said to have been divided into four *tisai nadus*, eighteen *kilai nadus*, and seventy-two *nadus*.[19] The *mahanadu* was at Kanchipuram and the weaving communities of the surrounding areas secured their privileges only through representation to the Kanchipuram guild.[20] The supreme head of the guild was called the *Mahanattan* (alternatively he was also called 'Senapati' in some guilds). Reference is made to the donation of fifteen *kalanju* of *pon* (gold) for a perpetual lamp to a temple in Achcharapakkam by Pichchaidevan Kidandariyan, who is described as the Kaikkola Samaya Senapati.[21] The collective organization of the weavers at the regional level is shown by the epigraphic evidence from Coimbatore in which the Unmattur chief Vira Nanjaraja Udaiyar is said to have granted the tax on cloth bazaars (*sulai irai*) to the Kaikkola of Vadaparisvara *nadu*, Karuppu *nadu*, *nalur parru*, Perur *nadu*, Virasola Valanadu and Oduvanga *nadu* to the extent to which it was in force during the preceding two years (the rates are not mentioned).[22] The Devanga weavers also had a strong organization. They claim that they had their headquarters in four directions—Shakar (the community literature of the Devangas, such as the *Devanga Puranam*, does not give the location of this place but since Kasi or Banaras is claimed to be one among the four spiritual centres, it is likely that this caste headquarter is also located in Uttar Pradesh; this is also Thurston's assumption), Mudunur in Krishna district, Penugonda in Anantapur district and Padaividu in North Arcot district. These were further divided into *talangal*, *kattemanai* and *valanadu*.[23] The evidence that the organization was held together by cohesive ties is demonstrated by the interesting fact that even today the Telugu, Kanerese (of Kongumandalam) and Tamil-speaking Devangas (of the Madras region) look to the Hemakuta *mutt* in Bellary district as their religious headquarters.

The weaver organizations had their own rules and any violation of the code was severely punished, usually resulting in the expulsion and ostracism of the offender. A very interesting instance of this is provided from Mattewada, Warangal district, in the period of Kakatiya Ganapatideva. The deity Salesvara was consecrated by the Sale weavers who then pledged themselves to give a *visa* in the form of *ciravada gadayana* (a coin equivalent in value to the *varaha* or *pon*) to last as long as the moon and the sun, and 'any man who does not give this is a man who has pierced a tawny coloured cow by the side of the Ganges. He is outside the pale of the *samaya* .... a traitor to Siva.'[24] This sort of punishment was also common to other corporate organizations like that of the Pancalar, Chettis, etc.[25] The above inscription is interesting in that it also gives evidence of the guild territorial organization. It appears that Malli Chetti and Vanni Chetti were the overall heads of the caste organizations in these regions and the suffix *chetti* is a testimony to their prosperity and proof that they carried on trade. Apart from social ostracism the weaver guild, in certain cases, also imposed fines on the offenders. For instance during the period of Rajaraja I in 1005 the assembly (*urar*) of Vanapalli in Tiruchirapalli, including the Kaikkolar, imposed on three members of the Terinja Kaikkola *padai* a fine of thirty-five *ponkasu* for stealing from the local temple of Somesvara.[26]

Details of the working of the Kaikkola organization are given in a long copper plate inscription called the *Cholan Purva Pattayam*[27] preserved in Kanchipuram. Though technically an inscription, this record, by the nature of its evidence and style, is to be treated rather as a literary source. The document refers to the settling of the Kaikkolar (weavers), Vellalar (agriculturists) and Kammalar (artisans) in the Kongu country by Karikala Chola (actually Kulottunga III). The king is said to have summoned the heads of the weavers of Tondaimandalam and Shonapuri (Sholingapuram), i.e. the present Chingleput and North Arcot districts, to the Arunapurimandapam. A *Nattanmaikkaran* (headman) was appointed for every *nadu* and they were duly honoured by being given betel-leaf, a mark of status. They were told to settle disputes arising in their regions. If the crime was of a major nature, then it should be referred to the head of the Kanchipuram guild. Here several officials are mentioned—the *Talaimai Nattan* (overall head), followed by *Samaya Talapati* (guild commander), the *Karnigan* (accountant), *Samaya Sangati* and the *Samaya Ilandari* (the office performed by these two dignitaries is not clear). The record goes on to say that in the temple *tirtam* (holy water) and *prasadam* (food offering) should first be given to the *Nattanmaikkarar*.[28] Weaver organizations derived the requisite funds for their various activities, such as collective donation to temples, by levying a voluntary contribution from their members. In Srimushnam,[29] during the period of Sundara Pandya in the thirteenth century, the members of the local Kaikkola community made an agreement among themselves to make over to the temple of Tirunarayanisvaramudaiya Nayanar certain taxes on looms. This appears to be not so much the regular tax on looms collected by the state as a contribution on each loom levied by the organization itself.

Temple Donations

The weavers made individual[30] as well as joint donations[31] to temples during this period. The size and nature of the donations made to temples is an important index of the social status and economic prosperity of the weavers. These donations can be classified into the following categories:

(a) In terms of money for the maintenance of a perpetual lamp (*nonda vilakku*) or food offering to the temple.
(b) In terms of sheep for perpetual lamp.
(c) In terms of land (*tirunamattukkani, devadana*, etc.)
(d) In terms of temple service, setting up of deities and the celebration of festivals, etc.
(e) In terms of a proportionate share of the woven cloth, or on the sale of cloth, or contribution in terms of paddy by the weavers.
(f) In terms of money as *udirapatti*, which could mean crime expiation or money given to honour a hero or martyr.

The donations made in terms of money were either for the burning of a perpetual lamp (*nonda vilakku*) or for food offerings to the deity (*prasadam*). During the reign of Rajaraja I a weaver of Tiruvalakkoyil, a hamlet of Ponvilainda Kalattur in North Arcot, made a gift of *pon* for a twilight lamp in the temple.[32] The term used for the weaver is Kaikkolan. The donation for the lamp is specified as 5 *kalanju*[33] in a record of the period of Vira Rajendra, from Piramiyam in Coimbatore, stating that the gift was made by Kalikadinda Solakumaran of the Perumal-Kaikkolar.[34] In the same period a Kaikkola Senapati of Annur in Coimbatore made a gift of 1.25 *kalanju* for a lamp.[35] In the twelfth century in the Salem district a weaver made a gift of 1 *palanjalagai achchu*[36] for a lamp. Elsewhere a gift of 10 *varaham* is mentioned.[37] Money was donated not only for *nonda vilakku* but also for food offerings to the deity. A donation of 20 *panams* for this purpose was offered by Sokkan Pugalivandan, alias Narpatennayira-marayan, a Kaikkolan of Koduvayi in Coimbatore, during the reign of Hoysala Vira Ballaladeva.[38] The name 'Narpattennayira' suggests that the Kaikkolan may also have been a merchant, since like the Ainnurruvar this also indicates a merchant group. During the period of the Kongu-Chola king Vira Rajendra Deva a donation of 24 *achchu* for food offerings to the Idangainayaka was made by certain Kaikkolar and Senapatis of Annur in the same district.[39]

General donations of money were also made to the temples by weavers without specifying the nature of the offering. An epigraphical record of the period of Rajendra Chola (tenth century) from Udaiyarkudi in South Arcot refers to the gift of an umbrella containing 19,908 pearls surmounted by gold ornaments weighing 25.75 *kalanju* (!) presented collectively by the Kaikkolar.[40] This donation, by any standards, seems colossal. A gift of 450 *varaha panam* was made by the Saliya of Vikramapandyapuram (Tirupati) to the temple during the period of Vijaya Gandagopaladcva in the mid-thirteenth century.[41] When the donation was made by the *samasta praja* (entire population) of a village the contribution of the weavers was levied either from the guild, as in Mellacheruvu, Nalgonda district[42] (16 *cinna* or roughly 2 *panams*, 1 *cinna* being equivalent to 1/8 of a *panam*), or from each weaver's dwelling[43] (2 *annas* per house) as in Kokkireni, Krishna district. However in Manikyavalli[44] in Bijapur in a joint donation to the local temple by the *samasta praja* the weavers (Saliya *samayangal*) and the tailors' guild (Kottali *samayangal*) made their contribution at 5 *visas* (1 *visa* is equal to one single grain of gold or 1/16th of a *panam*) per head. From the size of the donations made by the weavers some idea can be gained of their standard of living. The collective contributions made by the weavers seem to be quite modest but individual contributions in some instances seem to have been rather large, although they are comparatively rare during this period. Apart from the individual donations for *nonda-vilakku*, one record from Tiruvallur in Chingleput of the period of Vira Rajendra states that a Kaikkola called Kannan Arasu made a gift of 9 *kalanju* of *pon* for the earring and 10 *kalanju* of *pon* for the necklace of Panaimulai Nachchiyar in the temple of Tiruppasurudaiya Nayanar.[45] Such donations are to be contrasted with the annual income of some of the lower functionaries of society. For instance two later-Chola inscriptions, probably of the thirteenth century, from Tiruvorriyur state that the Brahmins who recited the *Vedas* in the temple were paid 10 *nalis* of rice plus 1.5 *kalanju* of gold per annum,[46] while the person who supplied drinking water at a public place was paid 2 *kasu* per annum and a daily wage of one *kuruni* of rice.[47] Seen from this standard of comparison the size of the donations by some of the weavers does seem rather large. From the evidence it is clear that individual donations by the weavers ranged from 1.25 to 5 *kalanju* to 10 *varaha*. Only two other social groups seem to have equalled and often excelled weaver organizations in the size of their donations. These were merchant guilds like the Ayyavole and the agricultural caste, the Vellalas.[48] There are a few instances of the Kammalar or the Pancalar making donations of money[49] but not very many. On the strength of the evidence it is possible to locate the position of the weavers in the economic hierarchy next to the landed gentry, with the merchants figuring as the wealthiest group, though not necessarily the socially dominant one.

Monetary donations (or some other form of service) were also made in token of crime expiation (*udirapatti*). A fight between a Kaikkola, Kunjiramallan of the Adigan Paluvettaraiyar regiment, and a Vellala *kilavan* Nomban (the term *kilavan* means 'landowner' and also 'village elder') is referred to in an early undated record of Korajakesari (probably the ninth or tenth centuries) from Kilappalur in Tiruchirapalli.[50] In the fight the Vellalan was killed and the Kaikkola made as expiation an offering of ninety sheep for a perpetual lamp to the local temple. An instance of *udirapatti* being given in the form of land to the temple comes from Tirupattur in the period of Jatavarman Sri Vallabha in the fourteenth century. It is stated that the Kaikkolar of the *tirumadaivilagam* of the temple gave a land as *tirunamattukkani* to the temple in connection with the death by poison of the wife of a certain Sundara Pandya Bhattan in the temple.[51] *Udirapatti* could of course also mean donation in memory of a martyr.

Donations in terms of sheep or cows, most often for the maintenance of a perpetual lamp, were a common feature in the Chola period, though one rarely comes across this form of donation in the Vijayanagar period. It is interesting that ninety sheep was the number usually given for one perpetual lamp[52] and thirty-two cows and one bull for half a lamp.[53] Since these same figures are mentioned in all inscriptions, they appear to be the standard exchange value and did not actually mean the giving of so many sheep since efforts to calculate the livestock distribution of a specific region on the basis of these donations have resulted in improbable figures.[54]

Another form of donation was in the nature of a voluntary contribution levied on the profession. This could be in terms of a proportionate share of the cloth woven or on the sale of cloth, or merely a fixed contribution on each loom. In the eighth century the *srenipattagara* (literally 'guild of weavers') of Lakshmesvar in

Dharwar district made a donation in the form of a proportionate quantity of goods turned out by the weavers, i.e. one length on every forty lengths of silk cloth (*sampu*) woven.[55] In 1139 a corporation of tailors seems to have made a similar donation on almost all the items used by them, such as the ball of thread, saffron, cloth, etc.[56] A similar record of the same period comes from Shikarpur in Shimoga.[57] The Saliya *samayangal* of Puli in Belgaum gave a profit from every household 'on every piece of gold earned' to the deity Andhasura.[58] The record pertains to the period of a Kalachuri king and is dated 1224. At Mattewada in 1228, during the reign of Kakatiya king Ganapatideva, the Sales after consecrating the image of Salisvara resolved to contribute one *visamu* per *gadayana* (one *visa* is equal to 1/256 of a *gadayana*) on the sarees sold by the weavers.[59] A fixed contribution on each loom as donation to the temple is mentioned from Srimushnam in a record of Jatavarman Sundara Pandya dated 1310.[60]

The building of temples and shrines, the consecration of deities made of silver or bronze and the celebration of specific festivals in the temples by weavers are a reflection not only of their economic prosperity but also their ritual status. In fact often the consecration of an image by a donor would be followed by bestowing special privileges on him.[61] Araiyan Keyavitankan of the Tayatonga Terinja Kaikkolar community constructed in the period of Chola Parakesari at Kattumannar *koyil* in South Arcot district three shrines dedicated to Kuttar (Nataraja), Ganapati and Pichchar.[62] He gave along with this a gift of ten *kasu* for clothes for Kutta Perumal. In the thirteenth century, during the period of Maravarman Sundara Pandya, the trustees of the Arikesvaramudaiya Nayanar temple at Giriyambapuram in Tirunelveli, the Abimanabhushana Terinja Kaikkolar, granted 100 *kalams* of paddy from the *devadana* lands to the temple of Aramvalartisvaramudaiya Nayanar built at Kilur Kaderri by Kuttan Selvan, a Kaikkolan.[63] There are numerous instances of weavers consecrating images in the temples. At the Nagesvara temple in Kumbakonam in 990, the period of Rajaraja I, Devan Kuppan of the Viracholatterinja Kaikkolar set up a silver image of Tirukilkottalu Paramasvami and also made a cash endowment to provide for offerings and worship.[64] During the same period at the Uma Mahesvaraswami temple at Koneri Rajapuram, the Rajaraja Terinja Kaikkolar made a gift of a silver image of Siva and a copper image of *chaudesvara*.[65] The image of Tombarmalai, the deity of the Saliya, was set up by the wife of Saliya Nayaka[66] in the reign of Vikrama Chola at Perukalandai in Coimbatore.[67] Aludaiya Pillaiyar was installed by a Kaikkola weaver at the temple of Aludaiyan in Sirringur (South Arcot district) in the period of Kulottunga Chola II.[68] From the Andhra region in the reign of Kakatiya Ganapatideva (1228) comes the evidence of the consecration of the idols of Salisvara, Ganapatisvara and Sakalesvara at Ellamma Bazar in Mattewada, by the Saliya *janalu* of the entire surrounding regions meeting at the headquarters (*matiyasthala*) and gifting to the deity one *visamu* per *gadayana* on the sarees sold by the weavers.[69]

Another category of temple service was the undertaking of the celebration of specific festivals by the weavers. During the reign of Kulottunga Chola in 1221 the Kaikkolar of Tiruchchanur near Tirupati accepted the six *patti* of land given by *pokkaran* (treasurer) Pandiyadaraiyan and agreed to conduct the *Panguni* festival of Alagiya Perumal.[70] A record of the period of Ranganatha Yadavarayar (accession 1336–7) also from Tiruchchanur refers to the joint conduct of some festival (not specified) at the Alamelumangamma temple by the Kaikkolar and the Emperuman Adiyar or Devaradiyar.[71] At the Muktisvaram temple in Kanchipuram during the period of Vira Pandya (fourteenth century) an agreement was reached between certain persons to celebrate the festival of the deity on all the nine days in the month of *purattasi* (*navaratri* or *dussera*) for the 175 *panam* they received in addition to the 44 *panam* given by the Kaikkolar who had been conducting these festivals formerly.[72] The record shows that the weavers must have been prosperous enough to conduct festivals on such a large scale, though it does not explain why they later gave up conducting it themselves.

Temple donations on a smaller scale involved the construction of windows, door-posts and steps in the temples or specifically the construction of pillars. The reference to the setting up of windows, door-posts and steps collectively by the Kaikkola *perumpadai* in the Tisaiayirattu Ainurruvar *mantapam* of the Mahalingaswami temple comes from the reign of Rajaraja I. At Perukkalandai during the period of Vikrama Chola, Senittan, a weaver, made a gift of a door-post and pillars in the Adipurisvara temple. Construction of pillars in the Salesvara temple by the Saliya weavers comes from Nellore. At Tiruchirapalli in the late twelfth century the weavers constructed a flight of steps to the Meenakshi shrine of the Sundaresvara temple.[73]

Temple service was also sometimes in the form of donation of certain specific articles of worship. During the time of Kulottunga III, Avaniyarayan, a weaver of Vallalur in Coimbatore, donated a bugle, (*naraikkalam*), to the local temple.[74] Two records from Tiruvennainallur refer to the donation of *Kalasappanai* (vessel used for the sacred bath of the idol) by Nallarkunallan Kuttan in the Oppilananisvara temple and of a temple-bell, incense-brazier, chain lamp, and an *arati* plate (for waving the lamp before the deity) by Tirumalai Alagiyan alias Viragal Virapallavaraiyan, a Kaikkola Mudali, to the Kripapurisvara temple.[75] Both records pertain to the period of Pallava Kopperuningadeva in the early thirteenth century.

Religion and Caste Deities

Examples of donations and temple service as also a few other stray records provide an idea of the religious beliefs of the weaving communities. They were Saivites as well as Vaishnavites though Saivites were predominant. One indication is that most of the epigraphs pertaining to the weavers, especially regarding donations, are to be found in the Siva temples. Thus in Chingleput district alone, out of the seventy-six inscriptions relating to the Kaikkolas found on the temple walls of the main temples, sixty-three are in Siva temples and only eight in Vishnu temples. The Saivite affiliation of the Devanga and Jedara weavers in the Kanerese area can be perceived by their large participation in the Vira Saiva movement.

The Kaikkolar worshipped Siva, Parvati, Pillaiyar and Kartikeya, called Murugan. During the period of Rajaraja I a Kaikkolan constructed a shrine at Kattumannar Koyil to Nataraja (the dancing Siva) and Pillaiyar.[76] Reference to the installation of the images of Siva and Parvati with Pillaiyar in between by a Kaikkolan comes from Papanasam in the period of Jatavarman Sundara Pandya.[77] Pillaiyar was a favourite deity and references are found regarding donations to Kunichcha Pillaiyar, Vaduga Pillaiyar, Tirukkalvali Pillaiyar, Sengunta Vinayagar and Ganapati, another name for Pillaiyar.[78] Reference to the worship of Murugan is numerous because the Kaikkola weavers trace their descent from Virabahu, the divine lieutenant of Kartikeya or Murugan. Even to this day they celebrate the *sura-samhara* festival at which the birth of the nine Kaikkola warriors from Parvati's anklet is enacted by them. Kamakshiamman of Kanchipuram is the caste deity of the Kaikkolar and reference to the worship of *amman* is to be found in inscriptions and literature. The central figure in the *Cholan Purva Pattayam* is Kamakshiamman of Kanchipuram. The Sale Weavers worshipped Salisvara. Like the Kaikkola weavers they also worshipped Pillaiyar. The Saliya weavers of the Tamil country seem to have worshipped a peculiar deity called Tombarmalai.

The worship of *amman* or the mother goddess was popular among all weaver castes. As mentioned earlier, the caste deity of the Kaikkolar was Kamakshi *amman*. Chandesvari was the caste deity of the Togata weavers who styled themselves Ekangaviras. Chandesvaramma was also the special deity of the Devanga weavers. The worship of the mother goddess by the weavers, and in fact by many of the Sudra castes, is interesting. *Amman* worship gradually aquired an independent or dominant status, in contrast to the orthodox Saivite and Vaishnavite worship. Stein in his article 'Temples in the Tamil Country AD 1300–1750'[79] has codified the remarakable growth of *amman* temples during this period and the position of *amman* as the tutelary of powerful Sudra groups like the Vellalar. The position with regard to *amman* is also true of Murugan. To this day in South India *amman* and Murugan are the most powerful and popular deities among non-Brahmin sections of society.

It appears from literary as well as inscriptional evidence of this period that the Kaikkola weavers indulged in the practice of human sacrifice. The Kaikkolar and Kaikkola Mudalis of the Dharmisvara temple at Manimangalam are said to have carried out a human sacrifice at the *tirumadaivilagam* of the temple during the period of Yadavaraya in the fourteenth century.[80] The *Cholan Purva Pattayam* says that in Arunapuri, very near Kanchipuram, the deity as usual demanded a human sacrifice but that Karikala Cholar (Kulottunga III) resolved that henceforth human sacrifice was to be given up and only animal sacrifice was to be permitted. The work refers elsewhere to the practice of human sacrifice in Tiruvannamalai, and how the practice was ultimately given up by the thirteenth–fourteenth centuries.[81]

Weavers and Land

The estimation of the nature and extent of land donations by weavers has a special significance in the context of medieval society since land ownership was one of the most important status symbols. Land donation continued to be a form of endowment from the late-Chola to the late-Vijayanagar periods. The area of land is sometimes specified, thus making it possible to have an idea of the extent of landed power acquired by weavers. At Allur in Tiruchirapalli, during the regin of Chola Kopparakesari (early Chola, possibly ninth or tenth century), one of the Sundaranayanar Koyil Kaikkolar made a gift of ten *ma* of land.[82] During the reign of Uttama Chola, in Udaiyarkudi in South Arcot, Kali Karrali, a member of the Karikala Chola Terinja Kaikkolar, made a gift of half a *veli* and one *ma* of land to the temple of Tirumullurudaiya Nayanar at Mullur for the playing of music during *Sribali* service.[83] In the same period at Kanchipuram the Nagarattar are said to have sold 300 *kuli* (nearly one acre) of land to Achchan Senachchan of the 'Muttuvalperra' Kaikkolar regiment, who donated it to the temple of Terkkirunda Nakkar for food offerings to the Pillaiyar shrine within[84] In the reign of Kulasekharadeva I, two Kaikkolar belonging to Madurai gave two *veli* of land for lighting lamps in the Nelliyappar temple in Tirunelveli.[85] The practice of gifting lands to temples was prevalent among the more prosperous communities like the Pancalar[86] and, of course, the Vellalar.[87] One does not come across land donations among communities like the potters, drummers, etc., though small amounts of money are said to have been given to temples. But the largest (in terms of area) can be said to have been made only by those merchants who, individually or collectively, sometimes donated whole villages to the temple.[88]

The majority of lands gifted to the temple were in the form of *tirunamattukkani*[89] or *devadana*.[90] Any village or land gifted to the temple was called *devadanam* and when this grant was made for carrying on daily worship or for the celebration of festivals it was called *tirunamattukani*. In one instance from Dharwar the weaver community figures in a joint donation of land by the assembly to the temple. The record, dated 1062 of the period of the Western Chalukya king Somesvara, from the village of Mulgund, says that a gift of land was made for the feeding of ascetics in the *mata* of the Nagaresvara temple by the Chetti, Gammunda, one hundred and fifty Mahajanas, the Saliya 'fifty' and the Teliki 'thousand'.[91] Some times the donation by the weavers was not in the form of land but in the form of paddy. Thus one Kumaran Martandan, a Kaikkola of the Inanappiran Koyil in Kallidaikkurichchi, made a gift of paddy for maintaining a *kartigai* (Tamil festival in the month of *Kartigai*, corresponding with 15 November to 15 December) lamp.[92] He is also said to have given three groves of trees for other services in the temple. A similar gift of paddy was made by a Kaikkola called Annaparipala Tondaimanar from Pullur in Ramanathapuram in the thirteenth century.[93] In 1323, during the reign of Prataparud-radeva, the Sale weavers of Mattewada consecrated the image of Salesvara and decided to contribute one *addedu* (a grain measure) of grain per loom.[94]

The sizes of donations in terms of land made by the weavers are indicative of their rights over land. A particular donor of the period of Vira Rajendra Chola (eleventh century) is called Sengunra Kilan Nelvay Nambi Nayakar.[95] The term *kilan* stands for a landowner and village elder. Even by merely studying inscriptions which relate to weavers with land, it can be seen that rights in land could be acquired either by purchase or by the reclamation of waste land. During the period of Kulottunga Chola II the members of the Srikarana Chaturvedi Mangalam, a *brahmadeya* in the village Kavantadalam in Jayangonda Cholapuram, sold 380 *kuli* of land to Kaikkolan Isanadevan and his brother.[96] In another instance, in the reign of Vira Pandya in the fourteenth century, the temple authorities at Tirukkachchiyur sold the *kani-vilai* of the village Punniyam, originally purchased as *tirunamattukkani* from the assembly of Pulipakkam, to the Kaikkolar and Kaikkola Mudali of Tirukkachchiyur, consequent on the relinquishment of the right by earlier cultivators.[97] It is interesting that both the records cited above indicate the vesting of certain special rights over land in the village assembly as also individual purchase of land, as in the first case. In the second record the land is collectively purchased by the Kaikkolar and Kaikkola Mudalis.[98]

During the reign of Rajaraja II a weaver of Ravikulamanikkap-perunderuvu in Kanchipuram reclaimed certain lands for cultivation belonging to the *tiruvuragatimelerumar* (the assembly) and dug a small irrigation tank for 200 *kasu* and donated the produce from the land for food offerings to the deity.[99] In the Madurai district, during the period of Vira Pandya,[100] the Sthanathar (managers) of the

Vanisuramudaiy Nayanar Koyil gave as *kani vilai* to the Kaikkola Madevar Alagiya Chokkanar the land in Kilpidakaimattur because the heavily forested waste land had been turned into arable land by his efforts.[101]

The terms *kani vilai* and *kaniyatchi*, which occur so repeatedly in the records, merit special attention. The term *kani* appears to have been a generic term derived from the root *kan* meaning 'to see' or 'to mark,' which, in association with other terms, meant different things in different contexts. *Kani* in modern terminology means an area of land measuring 100 *kuli* (O. 33 acres). In the inscriptions we have reference to *kani parru* (land holding), *kani vilai* (sale of *kani* right). *uluvu kani* (cultivation right), *nir kani* (right to water), *kani vetti* (land given for free labour rendered in construction or public works) and *kaniyatchi*, which again can be interpreted as ownership or supervisory rights. *Kaniyatchi* has been interpreted as ownership rights over the land by Appadorai, Mahalingam, Noboru Karashima and Burton Stein.[102] However it is quite clear from the context in certain inscriptions that the reference cannot be to ownership rights. There is for example an instance where the *Uravar* gave *kaniyatchi* rights to the temple over the land in the area excluding specifically the holding of an individual landowner.[103] Sometimes when an individual donated land to the temple he was given *kaniyatchi* rights in perpetuity by the temple along with a lump sum (*mudal*) to clear the land and make it fit for cultivation. Similarly the term *kaniyalan* by and large seems to indicate a person holding supervisory rights over the land. Mahalingam's interpretation of the term as 'landowner' seems quite questionable from the contexts of its usage in the inscriptions. The interpretations and counter-interpretations of the term *kani* and associated terms have tended to make confusion worse confounded. In fact the same problem of definition also occurs in the case of the term *miras* which in the company period seems to have replaced the term *kani*.

Apart from rights obtained through purchase or reclamation, the weavers also received land from the temple or the village assembly for services rendered. There is one reference from Tirukkoyilur, of the period of Kulottunga Chola II, to the grant 1000 *kuli* of land, in addition to the 2000 *kuli* of land already being held by the Kaikkolar, by the temple authorities for their maintenance.[104] In Tiruvorriyur in the eleventh century, 2000 *kuli* comprised 1 *veli* , roughly 6.6 acres.[105] Since the same measure must have continued to prevail in the district in the twelfth century, it appears that the Kaikkolar were given for their maintenance nearly ten acres of land! In another example from the period of Rajanarayana Sambuvaraya (thirteenth century) the residents of Kalattur Parru in Chingleput gave Narayanseri alias Pundarikanallur, a hamlet, to a Kaikkola as *sarvamanya* or tax free grant.[106] This again not only indicates joint authority over the land but the fact that the Kaikkola must have rendered the residents of Kalattur Parru a valuable service for them to make such a grant.

There are several instances of weavers holding tenancy rights in land. The term usually used here is *kudi kani*. The residents of Vikramapuram, a weaver colony in Tiruvennainallur, were assigned 500 *kuli* of land for 25 *panam*, the sum they had to pay for obtaining tenancy rights, for the rearing of a flower garden for the deity.[107] In return they were also to be supplied with sustenance, clothes, etc. The record belongs to the period of Jatavarman Vira Pandya. In the fourteenth century, in the period of Jatavarman Sundara Pandya, the temple authorities at Tirukkalakkudi in Tiruppattur gave some lands on lease (*kuttagai*) to a Kaikkola, Uyyavandan Pandiyan alias Sundara Pandya Narasingadevan, and fixed the *melavaram* (the share of the landlord) to be paid by him to the temple.[108] Here the Kaikkola was clearly being given tenancy rights. There are however instances where the nature of the land right held by the weavers is not so clearly defined. Thus a record from Tiruchchanur dated 1221 in the Alamelumangamma temple (Tirupati) states that the Kaikkolar of the place accepted the six *patti* of land which was levelled and made suitable for cultivation 'through the investment of his own money' by *Pokkaran* (treasurer) Pandiyadaraiyan, son of Andar, and agreed to conduct the *Panguni* festival of Alagiya Perumal.[109] It is likely that the Kaikkola weavers had merely been entrusted with the grant and had responsibility of supervision over the celebration of the festival. It is also possible that the Kaikkolar were given tenancy rights over the land, and the donor himself might have belonged to this weaving community.[110]

The weavers seem to have invested the profits from their profession not only in land but also sometimes in straightforward usury. In the reign of Rajaraja I the *sabha* of Tiruvaduturai is stated to have secured a loan from a Kaikkola on the strength of a promissory note. At a later date the entire property of the Kaikkola seems to have been confiscated (*rajasvam*) by the state and the state demanded repayment of the old loan from the sabha.[111] Sometimes

the prosperous weavers, while not directly involved in moneylending, would donate a large sum of money to the temple. From the
interest on this certain services to the temple would be performed.
Thus in such cases it is the temple which gives loans out of the
donor's deposit.[112]

The size and donations made by the weavers in the form of cash,
land or other services to the temple, as well as the evidence of their
land ownership and moneylending activities proves that certain
weavers were in a fairly prosperous position. It is most likely that
this stratum of weavers was composed of those who catered mainly
to the temple and court and specialized in the finer varieties of cloth.

To state that economic power invariably led to social elevation
either by tacit or open consent on the part of society would be to
reiterate a truism. What is interesting however is the ways by which
an economically prosperous group sought to achieve this social
elevation and ritual recognition. In Hindu society this process has
been referred to as 'Sanskritization'[113] and in Muslim societies as
'Islamization'.[114] These two terms, however, subsume any number
of variables. In fact the so-called process of Sanskritization could
mean 'Brahmanization' and sometimes its exact opposite. For
instance in the case of most castes, social elevation meant a slavish
imitation of brahmanical practices such as the wearing of holy
thread and the adoption of *gotras*. But in the case of the Lingayats or
Vira Saivites it led to conflict with brahmanism and an outright
spurning of brahmanical practices.[115] While Brahmins cremated
their dead, the Lingayats buried them, and moreover in a sitting
posture! Thus the process of social elevation could take numerous
forms such as caste exaltation, either by imitating brahmanism or by
adopting completely contrary practices, or caste negation and social
protest. The effort to bolster their economic and social status was
made by the weavers in several ways: the demand for economic,
social and ritual privileges; the ascribing of mythological origins and
the claiming of brahmanical or supra-brahmanical status; participation in the *idangai-valangai* conflicts and schisms; and social protests
and participation in the Vira Saiva movement.

Privileges: Economic, Social and Ritual

The Madras Museum Copper Plates of Uttama Chola provide
ample evidence of the kind of economic privileges that were
conferred on weavers. The state seems to have accorded a very high

place to the weavers' organizations, entrusting them with grave responsibilities. Uttama Chola Parakesarivarman made a grant in his sixteenth year (985) to the temple of Uragam at Kanchipuram for celebrating the *sittirai tiruvila* of the deity. For this purpose 200 *kalanju* of *pon* was deposited with the residents, these being the two classes of Pattusaliyar residing in the four weavers' quarters of the city—Karuvulanpatti, Kamsahapatti, Atimanapatti and Eruvalich-cheri. This shows that the weaver organizations were considered reliable enough to be entrusted with money deposits. Some selected weavers were appointed as managers of the temple by Uttama Chola. The task of writing the accounts of the temple at Uragam was given to the weavers, who had to do it by turns. The income of the temple consisted of *kolmirai kuli* and *kolalavu kuli* collected at Kanchipuram (referred to as Kachchipedu in the inscription) on the produce from the lands at Kanchipuram and Tundanakkachcheri. Both pertain to tolls on articles measured by weight and capacity. Besides this the interest on paddy and money accruing on investments by the temple were to be apportioned for the several services in the main temple and the shrines, and the residents of two of the weavers quarters—Karuvulanpatti and Atimanapatti—were to be appointed to supervise and carry out the apportionment. In return for performing these important services the weavers were to be exempted from payment of taxes.[116]

The importance of the Saliya weavers under the Cholas is proved by the fact that they are referred to in the inscriptions as 'Choliya Saliyar'. During the period of Maravarman Vira Pandya the Saliyar of Chidambaram were granted 4 *veli* and 6 *ma* of land to construct their own exclusive quarters. They were expected to supply four new clothes every year to the image of the goddess Sivakamasundari on the day of the *tiruppudiyidu* for *parivattam* or *parisattam* (the head-dress of the deity) and five other small clothes for the shrine of Tirugyanasambandar.[117] Since this order was passed by Solakon, who is referred to as a Mudali, and not by the temple, the land granted must have belonged directly to the king because Mudali in this record has been used in the sense of 'state official.'

There is also some reference to privileges being conferred on the Kaikkolar during this period. In either the ninth or the early-tenth century a Tiruvottur inscription records a donation being entrusted to a Kaikkola, Ilanidaiyan, who is given the title *Pidaran*, meaning 'headman'[118] Economic privilege sometimes took the form of tax exemption, as in the Uttama Chola record. But the position of the weavers was not always high in all regions. In 1370, during the reign of Kampana Udaiyar, the Kaikkolar of Hattalikote obtained a charter from the Mahamandalesvara by which fines imposed on them for annoyance, theft, adultery, etc. were remitted and they were permitted to pay the customary tax of half a *gadayana* on their cows, which were to be allowed to graze freely. [119] For some reason which is not clearly indicated in the record it appears that the weavers in that region had been subjected to severe punishment in an earlier period. This inscription, however, is also extremely interesting for other reasons. Firstly the presence of the Kaikkolar, a weaver caste of Tamil Nadu, in the Mysore district shows their mobility. The reference to the Kaikkolar as cattle owners is also very significant because in medieval times cattle wealth was a primary index of prosperity.

Social privileges consisted of *sangu* and *tandu*, the right to blow the conch shell on all important occassions and the right to ride a palanquin, as well as the right to one's own flag and symbol. At Chintamani (Andhra) in 1231, the Devanga 'ten thousand' in the presence of their deity Ramayadeva and goddess Chandesvari are said to have been granted by the king the *panchavamne biruda* (all the privileges mentioned above) and also the right to the *yajnopavita*, the sacred thread worn by Brahmins. [120] In the period of Sambuvaraya Venrumankonda honours like *parivattam* and *odukku* (probably charge of temple store house) were conferred on a Saliya of Tirukkachchiyur who had made some donation to the Kachchapesvara temple. [121] Another instance of the conferring of *parivattam* and *odukku* by the temple comes from Anbil in Tiruchirapalli, in which the donor Achchiraman Kulottunga Pallavaraiyan, a Kaikkola Mudali (the name indicates a very high ranking military official) is said to have gifted for *prasadam* or food offerings to the temple a huge piece of land as *tirunamattukkani*. [122] The Kaikkolar or more specially the Kaikkola Mudali, i.e. the more prosperous and influential members of this community, figure as temple trustees in some regions during this period. The *Cholan Purva Pattayam* which pertains to the thirteenth century refers to their appointment as *kaniyalan* at several temples, especially in Kanchipuram, and also in the Kongu country; it also states that their income consisted of one-tenth of the total *manya* (revenue) of the temple, quite a large cut. [123] During the reign of Sambuvaraya in 1359, the Kaikkolar as temple trustees were deputed along with the Mahesvaras to make a settlement about some disputed lands in Tirukkoyilur on which taxes had not been paid.[124]

An idea of the status of weavers in the ritual hierarchy maintained in temples comes from the period of Yadavaraya (fourteenth century). In the Rajagopala and Dharmisvara temples in Manimangalam the assembly, consisting of 540 members plus the Sthanathar (temple managers), Adhikariyar (officials) and Mallunayakar, determined the order of ritual precedence of the *tirupalli eluchchi* (the waking-up ceremony of the idol). The state officials were to have first position followed by the Sthanathar, the assembly heads, the Vellalar, the Kaikkolar, the Devaradiyar, Malaiyantangal (?) Talaikariyan (could refer to the secretary), Ennaivaniyar (oil merchants), Agambadiyar (shepherds) and Navidar (barbers).[125] It is noteworthy that while the Vellalar, the dominant agricultural caste, are placed above the Kaikkolar, the oil-mongers and other professional groups are listed only after them. While in Manimangalam the Kaikkolar figure in order of precedence, at Tiruvorriyur they seem to have held a higher status because it was they as temple trustees who determined the ritual status here.[126] In 1265, during the reign of Rajanarayana Sambuvaraya, the Mahesvaras, Sthanathar, Nattar, Virachola Anukkar[127] and Kaikkolar of the Adipurisvara temple settled the order of precedence and the nature of the temple services to be performed by the Padiyilar,[128] Devaradiyar and Ishtabattaliyar. It is to be noted that all the three terms refer to dancing girls who also performed at this time various services in the temple.

An interesting aspect of temple service by the Kaikkolar is the association of their names with the Devaradiyar. For a long time the Kaikkola families had a tradition of consecrating the first girl born in the family to the temple. But while the Kaikkolar are said to belong to the *idangai*, the Devaradiyar belonged to the *valangai*. The *Cholan Purva Pattayam*, when it refers to the order of importance in which the Kaikkola guild members were to be honoured, says that the Devadasis were to be given one *kandangi chelai* (a type of sari) as well as the traditional betel leaf. In fact, the Devadasis or Devaradiyar are everywhere mentioned along with the Nattar, Talapati and the other members of the Kaikkola organization.[129] Epigraphical evidence of the association of Kaikkolar and Devaradiyar is numerous. To give just one example, a record from

Tiruvanakkoyil in Chingleput of the period of Jatavarman Sundara
Pandya (thirteenth century) registers the sale of house-sites to the
Devardiyar and Kaikkolar of the temple in the locality.[130]

A sub-sect of the Kaikkolar connected specially with temple
service were the Ponnambala-Kuttar, also called Nainar. These
were the temple minstrels and all the folk songs of the Kaikkola
community were composed and sung by these Nainar, The great
twelfth-century poet of this community was called Ambalakuttar
and because he sang a particular verse in the manner desired by
Vikrama Chola he is supposed to have been renamed Ottakuttar by
him.[131] A thirteenth-century record from Tirumanakkal in Tanjavur
registers the setting up of images in the temple by a Kaikkolan,
Karunakaran Kokkakuttan. A fourteenth-century record from
Sangramanallur says that a pillar in the Tandevesvara shrine of the
Cholesvara temple was the gift of Kaikkolan Pemman Ponnambala
Kuttan.[132] In the *Senguntar Tugil Vidu Tutu* the Nainar Ponnamba-
laper are mentioned as past masters in the art of magic and *tantra*,
and as singers of exceptional ability who earned 'the applause of the
gods'.[133]

It appears from the pattern of evidence regarding the grant of
privileges to weavers that in the tenth and eleventh centuries
weavers enjoyed considerable state patronage, as is evident from the
copper plates of Uttama Chola and other inscriptions. But the
actual evidence for the grant of social and economic privileges
between the twelfth and the fourteenth centuries is very limited. In
contrast the evidence for the grant of concrete social privileges
(*sangu, tandu*, etc.) is abundant in the Vijayanagar period. Thus
there appears to have been a definite improvement in the social
status of the weavers at the time of the Vijayanagar empire.

Origin Myths

While the acquisition of privileges was one tangible form of moving
up the caste hierarchy, ritual sanction was also achieved by such
means as claiming mythological origins and aspiring to a brahmanical or supra-brahmanical status. The tendency to claim mythological origins was present not only among the weaver castes but
among other professional castes as well.[134] The Kaikkola weavers
claimed their descent from Virabahu, the divine lieutenant of the
deity Kartikeya. The Devanga claimed to be Brahmins and traced

their origin from Manu and Devala Munivar—the son of Siva.[135]
Their attitude is best expressed in the verse of Sambalinga Murthy,
a priest of the Devanga weavers:

> Manu was born in the Brahmin caste
> He was surely a Brahmin in the womb
> There is no Sudraism in this caste
> Devanga had the form of Brahma.[136]

The Saliya also have a legend which is said to be found in the
Sthalapuranam of the Nallandai temple in Tanjavur. They believe
themselves to be descendents of Saliya, a low-caste man who did
some service for a saint called Visakar and became a *rishi* by his
grace. The Saliya wore the sacred thread and engaged Brahmin
priests.[137] Several references to Vishnu *gotra*, Atreya *gotra* and
Kasyapa *gotra* among the Saliya Srivaishnavas of the Tirumalai
temple are to be found in the records of Vijaya Gandagopaladeva
(mid-thirteenth century).[138] The Telugu Sale trace their origin to
Bhavana *rishi* who is said to have manufactured the thread from
Vishnu's navel and made cloth for the gods.

None of these legends can be dated accurately and one can only
say very broadly that they might have grown any time between
the twelfth and the seventeenth centuries. Moreover any origin
myth, being a part of oral tradition, keeps acquiring nuances as it is
passed down the centuries. Obviously the main point of interest lies
in the motive behind these mythologies rather than in their
authenticity. In their aspiration they are reminiscent of the
Suryavamshi and Chandravamshi origin myths of the Rajputs. The
purpose of such myths was two-fold—to serve as social codes of the
community's beliefs and rituals, and, more important, to provide
charters of validation for the low-caste group seeking respectability.

Legends about mixed castes are especially typical of occupational
groups like the weavers who tried to bolster their socio-economic
mobility through the acquisition of ritual status but could not find a
place for themselves in the established *varna* framework. For
example certain inscriptions refer to the evolution of a new caste, the
Ayogava, as a result of the upward movement on the part of the
weavers. These are stated to be the offspring of Brahmins married to
Vaishya women, an alliance described as *anuloma*.[139] Another record
quotes a Sanskrit verse which says that an Ayogava is born of the
union between a Kshathriya woman and a Vaishya, i.e. *Pratiloma*.[140]

They undertook to supply cloth for *upanayana*, the thread ceremony, and other domestic ceremonies, and also for the *dvijapatras*, the flag cloth to temples, etc. In 1128 twenty families of Ayogavas are stated to have settled down in Tirukkanapuram in Coimbatore district and secured the protection of the assembly and of the Srivaishnavas of that area.[141]

Weavers and the Idangai-Valangai *Paradigm*

The same desire for enhanced social status among the Sudra castes caused most of the conflicts and schisms between and within the left-hand and right-hand or the *idangai* and *valangai* groups. Just as the *varna* system marks a horizontal division of Indian society, or metaphorically of the human body, so the *idangai–valangai* classification marks a vertical division of South Indian society. This however excluded the upper castes, the Brahmins (the Kshatriyas as a social category are rarely to be found in the South), and was confined to the Vaishyas and Sudras. Each professional group claimed for itself social recognition and privileges and in this attempt it was challenged by rival caste groups. A professional caste which had registered its higher status by the obtaining of flags and symbols assiduously sought to prevent others from obtaining the same, thus leading to conflicts. These conflicts took place within the framework of the *idangai–valangai* categories. But it is noteworthy that during the Chola period they occur essentially as military divisions[142] or as broad communal divisions. The aspect of upward movement among professional castes and intense social conflict among them came about only in the Vijayanagar period.

Almost the entire mass of evidence relating to the *idangai–valangai* categories comes from the Tamil country. The *Cholan Purva Pattayam* says that Karikala Chola (Kulottunga III) brought Valanjiya *chetti*, the Kaikkola Kachchi Viran and the Kachchi Vira Vellalan to the Kongumandalam and here determined the *idangai–valangai* castes.[143] While the Kaikkola weavers have been classified as left-hand, the Saliya weavers have been categorized as right-hand. That the Kaikkolar belonged to the left-hand is also known from a record from Srimushnam of the period of Sundara Pandya (thirteenth century) which refers to the Kaikkola community which 'successfully practised the idangai creed'.[144] In fact the Kaikkola weavers, apart from worshipping their community deity Kamkshiamman, also worshipped the deity of the *idangai* castes, Idangainayaka. Thus in the reign of Vira Rajendra Chola the Kaikkolar and Senapati of Annur in Coimbatore are said to have made a donation of twenty-four *achchu* of *pon* to the Idangainayaka.[145] A reference to *valangai-idangai maganmai* is found in a record from Tiruvengadu in Tanjavur in the period of Vira Rajendra.[146] The same record also refers to *idangai-vari*. *Jati-Kanikkai* is mentioned in an inscription from Kanchipuram.[147] It appears from the numerous epigraphical records of this period that *idangai vari* was a tax levied by the state while *valangai-idangai maganmai* and *jati-kanikkai* could have been voluntary levies collected by the community for its general fund.

Instances of the *balagai* (*valangai*) and *yedagai* (*idangai*) are far fewer in the Andhra-Karnataka regions, though some epigraphical evidence is found of their existence. The *idangai vari* is said to have been collected from the Palli and other *idangai* castes at Padi in Chitoor district.[148] At Kayivira in Pekkundra in 1362, the *balagai* and *yedagai* castes co-operated in establishing a fair in the place.[149] Of the weaver castes of these regions, the Padmasale and the Seniyar are classified as *balagai* while the Devanga come under the *yedagai*. But by and large the two categories seem to have been operative only in the context of Tamil Nadu.

Weavers and Vira Saivism

In their clamour for social privileges, their creation of mythological origins and the left-hand right-hand conflicts, Sudra artisans like the weavers tried to overcome social and ritual barriers through exaltation of their own caste and the assumption of brahmanical status. These are of course the usual manifestations of the process of social elevation. But there are rare instances of social protest on the one hand and the assumption of supra-brahmanical status and even caste negation on the other. In the thirteenth century, during the reign of Kulottunga III at Tiruvennainallur, a Kaikkola weaver was martyred while fighting for the right to sing the *tevaram* (Saivite religious song) in the streets on festive occasions. His stand was apparently vindicated and special honours conferred on the martyred Kaikkola weaver.[150] A piece of literary evidence provides an instance of social protest and caste negation in the early fourteenth century. The Saiva saint Umapati Sivachariyar was the Rajaguru and an orthodox Brahmin. He was, however, converted by

Maraigyana Sambandar, the Sudra saint. As a result both partook of the *kanji* or rice starch from the Kaikkola weavers, though ritual orthodoxy did not permit a Brahmin to do this. Due to this action the Brahmins of Chidambaram excommunicated the Rajaguru and he was not permitted to attend the flag hoisting on the festival day. In fact traditionally the flag cloth was supposed to be supplied by the Kaikkolar. The Brahmins were unable to perform the ceremony till they had apologized to Gyana Sambandar and Umapati Sivachariyar and accepted the Kaikkola weavers' gift of the flag cloth.[151]

The Vira Saiva or Lingayat movement constitutes a striking instance of caste negation and, later, the assumptions of supra-brahmanical status and caste exaltation. The weavers and smiths as the leading Sudra artisans in society participated in large numbers in the Vira Saiva movement as well as the Srivaishnava or, more specifically, the Tengalai movement, both of which roughly began in the twelfth–thirteenth centuries (although Vaishnavism took on the aspects of a popular movement only in the Vijayanagar period). The Vira Saiva movement originated in the Kanerese country at Kalyani under the leadership of Basava in the twelfth century. The movement emerged in opposition to orthodox Brahmanism and Basava is described as an axe to the root of the tree of caste.[152] Unlike the brahmanical castes the Lingayats buried their dead, practised widow remarriage and did not observe any ritual pollution.

The social base of the Vira Saivite movement comprised trading groups such as the Banajigas of Ayyavole and others, shoe-makers, tanners, tailors, weavers and even some untouchables. The weavers in the textile production and trade centres like Bijapur, Belgaum and Dharwar were mostly Lingayats. Jedara Dasimayya, the famous Sudra saint who was a contemporary and follower of Basava, was a weaver by caste. At Allur in Dharwar district[153] an inscription is placed below three groups of sculptures and the first one depicts Jedara Dasimayya offering cloth to the idol. This incident is also narrated in the *vachanas* of Basava as Dasimayya having received the boon of inexhaustible treasure from the deity in return for his gift of cloth. Interestingly the other sculpture depicts Siriyala Chetti, who is said to have offered the cooked flesh of his son to Siva who came to him as a mendicant; and the third sculpture is that of a potter, Gumda, before whom Siva is depicted as dancing.

All these scenes are also narrated in the Vira Saiva *vachanas* and the themes are close to that of the sixty-three Nayanars of the *Periya Puranam* (twelfth century). Another famour Lingayat saint was Sankara Dasimayya who was a tailor by profession. Although in its origin the Vira Saiva movement began as a protest against orthodox brahmanism, it soon developed social exclusiveness based on the privilege of birth and cleanliness of profession, much along the lines of the brahmanical caste system. Thus the untouchables among the Vira Saivites could neither invest themselves with the sacred *lingam* nor perform the eight sacraments. In fact even the concept of physical pollution was revived. Second, the movement gave up notions of caste negation and reverted to efforts at exaltation. The Lingayats claimed superiority over all other social and religious groups and did not mingle or eat with them. As has been pointed out earlier while discussing the concept of Sanskritization, even the peculiar practice of burying their dead in a sitting posture was probably adopted in order to appear distinctive. Abdur Razzaq, in the course of his travels in the South, refers to the Djogis, 'said to be a caste of Hindus, who are commonly weavers. The people of this caste do not burn their dead and the women are sometimes buried alive with their husband's corpse.'[154]

The Tengalai movement in Srivaishnavism also brought within its fold many of the low Sudra artisanal castes. Ramanuja's philosophy does hold the idea of caste negation: 'If we descend below the four castes and come to the Chandalas, who, however lacking in virtue, are true worshippers of Vishnu, their servants' servants are my masters and their feet are mine to worship'.[155] But eventually the Tengalai Vaishnavites comprising mostly of Sudras also began to aim at covertly enhancing their status and establishing their superiority over the Vadagalai or orthodox Vaishnavites. However, these developments took place only during the period of the Vijayanagar empire, when the movement gained strength, especially under the leadership of Alagiya Manavala.

The study of the social condition of weavers during this phase enables us to arrive at several broad conclusions. Society was constituted of more or less self-governing but not self-sufficient units. The lack of self-sufficiency can be deduced from the absence of weavers and oilmen from the list of village artisans, although in some rare instances they do seem to have constituted a part of the village community. The Sale and the Saliyar were the dominant weaving communities and the Kaikkolar in the Chola period have mainly been mentioned in their capacity as soldiers and army commanders, although in peace time they seem to have pursued the weaving profession. The social status of the weavers can be gauged by the nature and extent of their donations to temples and the ritual and social privileges conferred on them. It can be seen that weavers of high quality cloth catering to the court and temple and also supplying export markets were quite prosperous and held many privileges. Towards the close of this phase came the Vira Saivite or Lingayat movement which gave artisanal castes like the weavers the opportunity to balance their actual status in society with their ritual status. The Vijayanagar period saw the intensification of this process: the increasing prosperity of the weavers and smiths, growing *idangai-valangai* conflicts and large-scale Sudra participation in the Tengalai movement.

CHAPTER III

Textile Centres, Production and Trade

(Fourteenth to Sixteenth Centuries)

The period of the Bahmani and Vijayanagar empires in South India witnessed a steady stream of travellers who described the political conditions, the economy and the society of the times. They left behind glowing accounts of the prosperity of the kingdoms and the flourishing trade in textiles and other commodities. Reference to the textile industry and trade have been made by Nicolo Conti the Italian (1414–19), Mahuan the Chinese traveller (1425–32), and numerous Portuguese travellers—Vasco da gama (1498–1524), Varthema (1503–8), Barbosa (1506–18), Tome Pires (1512–15), Domingo Paes (1520–2), Fernao Nuniz (1535–7), and Caesar Fredrick (1563–81). A few stray references are also to be found in the accounts of Razzaq the Arab merchant (1442–4) and Nikitin the Russian (1468–75). Their accounts constitute the major source of information for this period, apart from inscriptions and literary works.

The Weaving Communities

Certain changes can be perceived in the comparative position of the weaving communities. In Andhra and Karnataka, right from the Chola to the Vijayanagar period, the same communities dominated—the Sale, Jedara, Devanga, etc. But in the Tamil country the Kaikkolar gradually emerged as the leading weaving community, displacing the Saliyar who are mentioned in many inscriptions as 'Choliya-Saliyar'.[1] Thus after the foundation of the Vijayanagar empire there are innumerable references to Kaikkola weavers and only stray references to the Saliyar. It is likely that the Saliyar migrated further south because Barbosa refers to them as the dominant weaving community of the Malabar region.[2] He calls them 'Chaliens' and says that though they belonged to the upper castes their social status was low since they had but little money and clothed only the lower classes.

As in the earlier period, different professionals were assigned different streets in the city of Vijayanagar. The continuance of this practice is testified to by Abdur Razzaq.[3] Reference to 'the street of the Kaikkolar' comes from Madambakkam in the period of Devaraya in 1426.[4] An extremely useful inscription from the period of Krishnadeva Raya pertaining to the remission of tax on loom is located in the Kaikkola street at Tiruchchengodu,[5] itself a very important weaving centre in the Salem district. As in the earlier period, the weaver concentration was in the *tirumadaivilagam* of the temples.[6]

Textile Varieties

A variety of textiles was woven by the weavers and types of textiles were often named after the community engaged in weaving them. Thus brocaded silk is referred to as 'Devanga', in the *Varnaratnakara* of Jyotisvara Thakura[7] (fourteenth century) and 'Devanga Chira' (cloth) is again mentioned in the Varnakas or stock-lists of cloth compiled by the Gujarati writers of that period.[8] Similarly different types of Jedara silk are mentioned in the *Gurjararasavali*—Jedara Mathau (silk with sheen), Jedara Dadimasara (pomegranate coloured), Jedara Bhatigatu (patterned silk), etc.[9] The *Varnaratnakara* refers to *vichitra*[10] or variegated silk which the *Manasollasa*, an earlier text of the twelfth century, also mentions as an important textile variety. This corresponds to the chintz of European records. This is also taken to be the same as the Pintado of the Portuguese. The references to muslins are again numerous. This was the *chih-li-pu* of Mahuan, which, he says, was produced in Coimbatore *cam-pa-mei* and made up into pieces 4 feet 6 inches wide and 25 feet long. He also refers to the production of flowered and patterned goods, i.e. chintz.[11] The term 'sella' also stands for muslin. During the period of Achyutadeva Maharaya (1529–42) 'the merchants of the fifty-six countries' assembling at Omalur (Salem district) collected a voluntary contribution on their items of trade, such as *parutti* (raw cotton), *panju* (seedless cotton) *pattunul* (silk yarn) *salli cavaram* and *chichchilikattu*.[12] '*Salli*' stands for 'sella' and '*chichchili*' for 'chintz'. Sella is the salempores of the factory records, a cloth roughly sixteen yards in length which constituted a principal export item in the seventeenth century. The reference to sella also comes from a sixteenth-century inscription which says that the inhabitants of Balupuram (Dharmavaram, Ongole taluq, Guntur district) gave for the merit of Khan Ajam Khwaja Abdul Saheb (a local officer) a contribution of one *vam* on sella.[13] Barbosa in his account refers to the export to Pegu of silk cloth from Pulicat, called patola.[14] Fernao Nuniz, when describing the attire of king Achyuta Raya, says that he wore a skirt, doubtlet and cap of fine patola.[15] Domingo Paes refers to a variety of silk cloth called *soajes*.[16] The *Varnaratanakara* also refers to cloth varieties named after the region of production. Thus textiles from Kanchipuram were called *kanchivani* or *sachopakachi*, i.e. gold embroidered cloth. The coarser variety was just called *kachi*[17] (this is again another name for Kanchipuram). It also refers to cloth called *cholapatna*,[18] probably from Gangaikonda Cholapuram, and to *tanchera*, i.e. silk woven in Tanjavur. The term 'Molia' described in the *Jimanavaraparidanavidi*[19] stands for 'Morees'. In the description of Nagapattinam, given in the account of Tome Pires,[20] reference is made to several varieties of white and printed cloth—enrolados (?), which are thin as baftas (muslin), ballachos (from the Persian 'Parchah' or linen), printed cottons, tapechindes and sarassas—both of which were coarse painted cloth exported to the Malay Archipelago. Pires writes that Golconda produced white and dyed calicoes and bettilles. 'They make enough of these to furnish the world'. He also mentions the production of silken cloth at Calicut and the reference is most probably to fine calicoes and muslin. This description is substantiated by Pyrard who says that very fine white cloth and diverse types of printed and painted fabrics were woven at Calicut. Textiles from the ports were also brought to Calicut to be exchanged for horses from Ormuz and Aden.[21] Linschoten (1583–91) says in his account, 'there is excellent fair linen of cotton (calico, chintz, etc.) made in Nagapatnam, St. Thomas (San Thome) and Masulipatnam of all colours and woven with diverse sorts of loom works and figures, very fine and cunningly wrought, which is much worn in India and better esteemed than silk for that it is higher priced'.[22]

The same types of dyes, such as indigo, madder, kusumba and turmeric, that were common in earlier centuries continued to be used. Lac, from which red dye was made and which was also used for the printing of other colours and designs on cloth, was imported from Pegu. Barbosa refers repeatedly tó scarlet ingrain dye or the Kermes grain[23] which gave a fast red dye. This dye, however, had to be imported into Pulicat from Mecca through Jedda in the Middle East. The Chay root was also used for dyeing red and Methwold, writing in the seventeenth century, calls it a monopoly item of the king.[24] There are also numerous references by travellers to the Sapan wood or Brazil wood which yielded an inferior red dye. Thus Nicolo Conti says he saw them on the route from Chandragiri to San Thome and that they were also available in plenty in Malabar.[25] Ibn Batuta also refers to them.[26] The dyes were applied on the cloth by washing it in coloured water, and the application of coloured designs by means of the printed block referred to in the *Manasollasa* must obviously have continued during this period.

Extensive reference to textile designs is found in literary texts. Besides geometrical patterns such as circles and squares, repeated mention is made of flower designs. Some types of textile designs have been mentioned in the *Dhanabhiramam* of Nutanakavi Surana, pertaining to the mid-fifteenth century. It refers to *jalilu* (network design), *manchibommanchu* (sari border with pictures) and *gajapapallu (pallav* with elephant motif).[27] Other motifs popular from early times have been the Kalka or mango design and the tree of life motif.

Textile Technology

Information on the type of loom in use during these centuries is rather scarce but it would not be unreasonable to assume that technology may not have changed much from the twelfth-thirteenth centuries. But one very important inscription from Tirupati dated 1538[28] gives some remarkable information about the extent of specialization in different types of weaving. It records an agreement between the cloth and yarn merchants of virtually all regions of South India and states:

while we are assembling here ... in the course of weaving by handlooms, one-third of the *Sadisarakkudam* or *achchukkattu* should be drawn lengthwise and two-third of the cotton yarn should be used in cross-wise weaving. This mode of weaving *should be done only by the Muslims* (and not by the Hindus). As a reward for their services (in this style of weaving) they are authorized to collect the income from the gifted lands for their weaving...

Sadisarakkudam literally means 'a four cornered frame' and *achchukattu* means 'a bunch of cords'; and the description suggests a technological change from the earlier patterned looms to a draw loom. One obvious explanation for the merchants' injunction could be that the device was an importation that came in with the Muslims and hence was sought to be confined to them. In this case the reference must be to the weaving of brocades or embroidered carpets. Such carpets found some demand in the period of the East India Company. This inscription is remarkable not only for the extent of technological specialization which it indicates but for the evidence of the merchants' control over the productive processes.

The other references to weaving technology are from stray evidence provided by proverbs and folk-traditions. Such information, while giving some general idea about the method of weaving, cannot be ascribed to any specific period. That the loom was operated with the feet is indicated by the proverb which says, 'If a dog gets a sore on its head, it never recovers from it, and even so a weaver who gets a sore on his foot.' Thus, when plying shuttles in the weaving process the weaver always uses his feet in shifting the warp by treading on a press; hence a sore on the foot is synonymous with monetary loss. If this proverb could be roughly dated on the basis of its earliest occurrence in literary texts, it would be possible to have an idea of the period of introduction of foot treadles, a major innovation in weaving technology. Another proverb says, 'The Chetti lost by partnership while the weaver came to grief by isolation'. This makes it clear that weaving involved co-operative effort since it included processes like twisting and winding the threads, preparing the skeins etc. The proverb perhaps pertains to the seventeenth century when the chettis formed joint stocks.

One gradual development which is perceptible from the late-Chola period to the fifteenth – sixteenth centuries is the increasing specialization in the weaving industry. Earlier, reference has been made to the tax on dyers[29] and tailors,[30] but during the Vijayanagar period there are references to tax even on the carders, called *Pinja Siddayam*,[31] showing that they constituted a separate professional group.

Internal Demand

The development of certain factors during the period of the Vijayanagar and Bahmani kingdoms leads to the inference that domestic demand for cloth, especially fine cotton, must have gone up. The process of urbanization and the growth of the professional and artisan classes under state and temple patronage, which had slowed down with the decline of the Cholas in the thirteenth century, now began to revive. This, combined with the creation of a new bureaucracy, must have led to an increase in the demand for cloth. Of the lower classes it has been repeatedly stated by travellers that they wore very scanty clothing because of the climate. Abdur Razzaq says, 'The blacks of this country have the body nearly naked; they wear only bandages round the middle called *lankoutah*, which descend from the navel to above the knee. This costume is common to the king and to the beggar. . . . As to the Mussalmans, they dress themselves in magnificent apparel after the manner of the Arabs . . .[32] However a hundred years later, when describing the costumes of the upper classes, the nobility and the ladies, Paes and Nuniz exclaim on their elaborate apparel. Nuniz, after describing the rich attire of Achyutaraya, goes on to say, 'The king never puts on any garment more than once'.[33] The king himself must have contributed in no insignificant measure to keep the looms working! Nuniz says the king wore a doublet with a skirt attached to it, made of fine Patola silk, and a cap of rich brocade, and neither was worn more than once. From Paes's description of the Ladies of Honour, it can be seen that even women dressed in a similar fashion, including the way they wore the cap. The elaborate apparel of the horsemen and even the foot soldiers is also described by Paes.[34] It is to be noted that the size of the army under the Vijayanagar empire was considerable.[35] Thus one reason for the greater consumption of cloth seems to have been the strong Muslim influence on Indian costumes. Cloth was lavishly used in the decoration of fine buildings and Paes says, 'Let no one fancy that these clothes are of wool, because there are none such in the country but they are of very fine cotton'.[36] Apart from Indian cotton the Persian satins and damasks (Khanqabs) and the brocades of China were very popular with the nobility, and Paes and Nuniz refer to the lavish use of the Mecca velvet in the construction of tents and the decoration of buildings. While the prosperity of the kingdom and the lavish life-style of the upper classes led to increased demand for fine cloth, the demand for better varieties of textiles also came from a new section. The emergence of a new bureaucratic class, the Nayaks and Poligars or Palayakkarar (the representatives of the people in the cities and townships), must also have increased the consumption of fine cloth. This increase in the domestic use of fine cloth can however only be surmised and cannot be stated in terms of the actual volume. Since there were no technological improvements, the demand on the home front as well as for the export market must have been met by an utilization of the idle capacity of the looms, or by setting up of new looms.

It must be clarified that 'urbanization' has been used not in its modern sense but in a much more limited one. It is not being suggested that medieval township or, in particular, the weaving industry shook off agrarian links.[37] The merchant community which was such an essential feature of the town had strong connections with land. The best example of this is their numerous land donations, and in fact the donations of whole villages, and their position in some village assemblies.[38] The cotton industry certainly did not wholly move away from the village and in many parts it continued to be a part-time occupation of agriculturists. This is best perceived in one of the fifteenth-century poet Srinatha's verses which says that in Palnad the men were ploughing the field while the women were spinning.[39] Thus the emergence of temple-towns or commercial towns and the increasing demand for textiles is not being discussed in absolute terms.

The popularity of the Pulicat textiles in Gujarat and Malabar is evidenced by Barbosa. Pires refers to the Masulipatnam calicoes and muslins in Goa and says that all goods were gathered together there for export to foreign markets.[40] But the upper classes in Goa and Calicut also wore the Golconda muslins. The Kondavidu inscription of Nandindla Gopa gives a list of articles of inland trade. The list includes among other things dyes such as dammer and gallnuts, raw material like cotton, cotton-thread, etc.[41] In another instance, remission of customs on Sellapattu and Pattavali Pattu is made to the Nanadesis by the official authorities at Kanchipuram in 1586.[42] Both Sella and Patola are products of North Coromandel and they were, hence, obviously being imported into Kanchipuram.

The principal means of transport in inland trade was still the pack-horses, bullock carts, asses, head loads (*talaikattu*) and *kanchi-kavadi*[43] (a pole suspended over the shoulders with heavy sacks, containing the commodities of sale at either end of the pole). The naming of head loads as well as the *kanchi-kavadi* in the inscription indicates the importance of itinerant merchants or peddlers in the sale and purchase of goods. Mahuan[44] in his account of South India refers to the Kolings or Klings of Cochin who carried on their business like peddlers do in China. These Kolings or Klings are the South Indian counterparts of the Banjaras of the North.

The Export Markets

The foreign trade in textiles was perhaps of greater importance than the internal trade. To Pyreard writing around 1600 it appeared as if 'everyone from the Cape of Good Hope to China, man and woman, is clothed from head to foot' in the products of the Indian looms.[45] Without taking Pyrard too literally it is clear that he was struck by the popularity of Indian textiles abroad. The export of Indian textiles abroad was mainly in two directions. From the Coromandel coast, either from the port of Masulipatnam or San Thome (Mylapur), textiles were shipped to Achin, Priamam, etc. in Sumatra, to Bantam in Java and to Malacca. Malacca was a principal entrepot of trade. Here were brought the printed cotton cloths of Pulicat, and also Chinese silks, satins, brocades, damasks and Nankins. Barbosa, referring to the coloured cotton (chintz) of Pulicat and Mylapur, says that they were worth much money in Malacca, Pegu and Camatra (Sumatra). He also refers to the popularity of Masulipatnam Patolas in Pegu.[46] Caesar Fredrick substantiates Barbosa's statement by saying that the only commodity of San Thome for which there was demand in Pegu was 'the white cloth made of Bambast woven and painted, so that the more that kind of cloth is washed, the more lively they show their colours which is a rare thing. . . . Also from San Thome they load a great store of red yarn, of Bambast dyed with a root which they called Saia (Chay) which colour will never wear out.'[47] From Barbosa's account we further know that these textiles went right up to the Gulf of Siam, i.e. Patani, Singora, Tennasserim and Cambodia. The Chettis also took to these places the Cambaya (Gujarat cloths), Mecca-velvets, scarlet-in-grain cloth (cloth dyed with the Kermes which were, in the first place imported into Pulicat and then re-exported to these regions. From Malacca the ships went towards Ambam (Amboyna) on their way to the Moluccas or the Spice Islands. On their return trips from Malacca, Sumatra, Pegu and other regions of the Malay archipelago they took lac, mace, cloves, pepper (produced in Sumatra), benzoin, Brazil wood or Sapan, an inferior dye-wood.[48] Barbosa refers to merchant settlements 'Moorish and heathen' in as far as Tennasserim. In the countries of the Malay archipelago the patterned clothes of San Thome and Pulicat were in greater demand than the painted clothes of Masulipatnam in spite of the latter being artistically superior. Although the Masulipatnam muslins became the rage in England in the seventeenth century, even in this period the demand in the eastern markets was only for meticulous reproductions of cheap, stereotyped designs. The Pulicat· chintz which sold in these regions as Tape or Tape-sarassas were cheap and required little or no stitching since they were worn like sarongs.[49]

The other trade lay in the direction of Ormuz, Aden, Arabia Felix and Africa. The ships went from Ormuz to Socatra and Aden from the kingdoms of the Deccan and the country of Vijayanagar, through Goa, Calicut and Bhatkal. While cloth from Cambaya is repeatedly mentioned by the travellers, the bettilles (Masulipatnam muslin) and white cloth were exported from Calicut. Coromandel cloth and Malabar spices were exchanged for Persian horses, seed pearls, sulphur, musk, dried fruit and tankas.[50] From Aden the southern kingdoms imported Arab horses which were far superior to those from Ormuz; also rose water, raisins and other dry fruits, opium and madder, dye-wood, scarlet-in-grain, Mecca velvets, damasks, etc. In return they sold much fine cloth, especially the Golconda bettilles,[51] along with other Coromandel and Malabar products. Evidently the demand here, unlike in the eastern markets, was for the finer varieties of textiles.

Tome Pires explicitly states that there was no direct trade between the Coromandel coast and the Arab and African countries. The calicoes, fine muslins (mainly the Golconda bettilles) and the rice and sugar of the Coromandel coast were collected at Goa and sent from there to Ormuz, Aden and the African coast.[52] After Goa was taken over by the Portuguese, Vijayanagar exchanged its cloth and got its horses from Bhatkal. The balance of trade in the Red Sea commerce could not have been much in favour of the southern kingdoms because though they exported cloth, spices, etc. the import of horses, apart from other items, proved very costly. Thus Barbosa says that the Arab horses were priced at 500–600 cruzadoes and those of Ormuz cost around 200–300 cruzadoes.[53] The cruzadoes struck· by D'Albuqurque in 1510 were worth 420 reis or roughly 10 shillings of English money. Thus the cost of an Arab horse would be around £ 250–300 and that of an Iranian horse between £ 100–150. Marco Polo who wrote two centuries earlier also gives 500 dinars (roughly £ 300) as the cost of an Arab horse.[54] Barbosa also adds, like Marco Polo, that 'horses do not thrive in this country [Vijayanagar] and live therein but a short time. Horses [hence] bring in high prices by reason of the great need for them.'[55] The drain on the Vijayanagar exchequer can be gauged by the fact that the Portuguese demanded and received 30,000 cruzadoes to give Vijayanagar the exclusive right to purchase the horses![56] Again, while Golconda muslins were popular, all the contemporary accounts indicate that Gujarat textiles had a much greater demand, and that Bengal muslins were also purchased.[57] Hence the share of Coromandel textiles could not have been very large. In the African kingdoms, according to the description of Barbosa, there could not have been much demand for ordinary, let alone the finer, varieties of Coromandel textiles. Certain finer varieties of textiles were in demand in Cofala (Sofala) and Barbosa describes how the natives, not knowing the art of dyeing, unravelled the Cambaya cloth and wove it again, interspersing it with their own white yarn.[58] There might also have been some demand for Coromandel textiles in Abyssinia, known alternatively as 'Arabia Felix,' and called by the Portuguese the land of Prestor John, being the only Christian kingdom in Africa. Horses were exported to Vijayanagar and Golconda from its principal port Macua and it is likely that some textiles were sold in return. But by and large the demand for textiles in these regions was limited and a considerable part of it was met by Gujarat.

The Trading Groups

Till 1500, i.e. till the coming of the Portuguese, the entire export trade of South India was in the hands of the 'Moores', a term which included the Arabs, Khurasanis and the Deccanis. Barbosa refers to their settlements in Malacca and even Siam and Tennaserim. Of the traders at Malacca he says 'Many Moorish merchants reside in it, as also Gentiles, particularly Chettis, who are natives of Cholamandal and they are all very rich and have many large ships which they call Jungos [the Chinese junks]'.[59] Of the Paradesis (literally 'foreign merchants,' and in this category Barbosa includes the Arabs, Persians, Gujaratis, Khurasanis and Deccanis) he says:

In the days of their prosperity in trade and navigation they built in the city keeled ships of a 1000 and 1200 *bahars* (a weight equivalent to four hundred avoirdupois) burden . . . ten to fifteen of these ships sailed for the Red Sea, Aden and Mecca where they sold their goods at a profit, some to the merchants of Juda who took them on thence in small vessels to Toro and thence to Cairo, Alexandria and Venice, whence they came to our own regions [Spain, Portugal, etc.][60]

But the Portuguese managed to elbow out the Chettis and the Moores to a considerable extent, even if not completely. Writing around 1510 Barbosa, after describing the prosperity of the native merchants, says that they continued to thrive till the arrival of the Portuguese, after which time they either left off trading or functioned in a totally dependent and subordinate capacity. Barbosa was hinting at the gradual change in their status from independent merchants to merchant middlemen, first for the Portuguese and then for successive European Companies.

The entry of the Portuguese into South India began with the landing of Vasco da Gama at Calicut in 1498. The Portuguese viceroy at Goa, d'Almeida, decided to establish trade links with Vijayanagar for the first time in 1505. Within a few years the Portuguese held Diu, Daman and Cochin on the Malabar Coast and Nagapatnam and San Thome on the Coromandel coast. They established themselves in the Indies partly by war (like the wresting of Goa from Bijapur) and mostly by friendly commerce with the native powers of Vijayanagar, Golconda, etc. The alliances with Indian kingdoms were partly political and partly commercial. The manoeuvrings of the Portuguese can be seen at every turn in the course of the struggle between the southern kingdoms. In 1511, in response to an embassy sent by Krishnadeva Raya, Albuquerque promised to sell horses to Vijayanagar in preference to Bijapur, but in 1514 rejected these terms on the ground that such monopolistic privilege would destroy trade. A classic example of a political— commercial treaty is the one signed with Sadasiva Raya in 1547.[61] By this both parties pledged mutual aid against enemies. Monopoly of the purchase of Arabian and Persian horses was given to Vijayanagar in return for an annual sum of 30,000 cruzadoes and on the condition that transportation would be at the expense of Vijayanagar. The king of Vijayanagar promised to grant to Portugal the exclusive right to purchase the products of his empire. Of textiles it was said that:

All the cloths of the kingdom of Vijayanagar will not be brought over to the ports of Adil Shah, but either to Ankola or Onor (Honavar) and in the same way, the Governors will bind the Portuguese merchants to go there to purchase them and exchange them for copper, coral, vermilion, mercury, China silks and all other kinds of goods and the king of Vijayanagar will order his merchants to purchase them.

The last clause says that the king of Vijayanagar should not permit any Moorish ship to stop in his ports and, if any came, they should be captured and handed over to the Portuguese.

The textile trade of the Portuguese had four different directions— the trade with various parts of the Indian subcontinent, with parts of Africa, with South East Asia, and finally the export of textiles to Portugal. In Africa, Indian cloth was exchanged for slaves and the coarse blue salempores were used mainly to clothe the slaves. The cloth destined for the African market was also called balagate after the name of the place where it was produced, Balaghat near Cochin. This cloth was also called chindes or tapechindes (coarse printed cloth). In 1615 the Portuguese in India sent a consignment of 304 pieces of Balagate cloth, 7,818 pieces of bettilles (fine Golconda muslin), 445 pieces of coarse bettilles, 1,877 pintadoes (perhaps painted chintz) and 110 pieces of tapechiras. In 1616 the Golconda bettilles exported were to the tune of 25,290 pieces, while 17,060 pieces of chindes, 280 pieces of tapechindes and 1900 pieces of sarassas i.e. (cotton cloth patterned on the loom) were exported.[62] The reference to the Portuguese trade in textiles continues right into the 1630's, although the volume of their general trade had by then greatly declined.

The Portuguese established their trade monopoly by forbidding the ships of other natives to sail on certain reserved routes. Secondly they claimed the exclusive right to trade in certain commodities like pepper and saltpetre. Thirdly no Asiatic vessel could ply to any port or carry any cargo until fees had been paid and a pass (*cartaz*) obtained.[63] Even Akbar tacitly acknowledged the superiority of the Portuguese by getting passes which had to be renewed annually. The pass system was one of the most important causes of the decline of Portuguese power in the seventeenth century and, while it earned them a lot of ill-will,[64] it failed to stop effectively the Hindu or the 'Moorish' traders. Thus the clause in the Portuguese ordinance exempting from passes the native rulers with whom they had treaties was used by the native merchants, with the connivance of corrupt Portuguese officials, to continue their lucrative trade without much permanent damage.[65] The Portuguese also attempted a monopoly over the triangular spice trade. The Dutch acted as the principal distributors for spices. The position of the Portuguese in the commercial world seemed very secure because of the papal bull which divided world trade between Spain and Portugal. But the Portuguese power in India began to decline decisively from 1580 onwards, when Portugal came under the Spanish crown and the Dutch-carrying trade in the triangular commerce came to an end. Towards the close of the sixteenth century the Dutch started independent commercial activity and emerged as an important power in South India by the seventeenth century.

The success of the Portuguese and subsequently the Dutch and the English in capturing the Coromandel trade can to some extent be understood by the attitude of the native kingdoms towards trade. This is best reflected in the *Amuktamalyada* of Krishnadeva Raya (1509–29), in which he says:

A king should improve the harbours of his country and so encourage its commerce that horses, elephants, precious gems, sandalwood and other articles are freely imported into his country. He should arrange that the foreign sailors who land in his country on account of storms, illness and exhaustion are looked after. . . . make the merchants of distant foreign lands . . . attached to yourself by providing them with daily audience, presents and allowing decent profits.[66]

That such a policy was in fact adhered to is vouchsafed by Abdur Razzaq,[67] Barbosa and others. Barbosa says in his account that as soon as any of these merchants reached the city the king assigned him a Nayar to keep his accounts and look after his affairs, and a broker to arrange for him to obtain such goods as he had need of.[68]

Volume of Trade—Cloth Prices

The evidence regarding the volume of textile trade during the period of the Vijayanagar empire till the end of the sixteenth century is very slender and scattered, and some idea of the volume can be gleaned only from the factory records of the seventeenth century. Thus for the period prior to the establishment of the European Companies the travellers only indicate the extensive nature of the textile trade but do not always quantify it. However a rough attempt is being made here to quantify the volume of trade in textiles during this period. According to Tome Pires (1512–15), a Portuguese resident at Malacca, four ships sailed from the smaller ports of Southern Coromandel, each ship carrying in cargo between 12,000 to 15,000 cruzadoes in 'coarse kling cloth'. In addition one or two large ships left Pulicat, Coromandel's 'most important port' carrying between 80,000 to 90,000 cruzadoes[69] in cloth. If in a year of heavy trade two large ships did actually sail from Pulicat, then the total shipments from Coromandel to Malacca may have reached a total of 2,40,000 cruzadoes. At early seventeenth century prices of cloth in Pulicat[70] this total in cruzadoes would represent something under five million yards of cloth.

Some of the travellers have made a passing reference to the price of cloth but the information is so varying and disparate that no cogent picture emerges. Mahuan[71] writing in the beginning of the fifteenth century (1409) says that the price of cloth produced at Coimbatore (*cam-pa-mei*) called Chih-li-pu (*chihli*-muslin) measuring 4 feet 5 inches in width and 25 feet in length was 8 to 10 gold pieces per piece. He also says that raw silk was dyed several shades of colours and then woven into flowered patterned goods, each piece being 4–5 feet wide and 10–13 feet long, and was sold for 100 gold pieces! It is quite possible that he is referring to inferior muslin in the first instance and to the costliest variety of silk in the second, but by any standards the prices of the export varieties seem to have been high. Vasco da Gama who arrived in India about the beginning of the sixteenth century says that at Calicut a fine shirt was worth only 2 fanams (30 reis) which in Portugal fetched 300 reis.[72] Since £1 would roughly be equivalent to 400 reis, 300 reis would be around 15 shillings and 30 reis would be 1 shilling and 6 pence. Vasco da Gama's evidence indicates two things—first the fact that he was citing the price of the export variety of textiles, and second the enormous profits accruing from foreign trade in cloth. It appears from the evidence of both Mahuan and Vasco da Gama that they were describing the situation at the ports and citing the prices of the export varieties of cloth, which certainly must have been very high compared to the price of coarse cloth worn by the common people. Nuniz while describing the attire of Achyutaraya says that he wore a fine silk cloth called Pacholis, the reference most probably being to silk *patolas*, each piece of which cost 10 pardaos and that he wore a brocade cap wroth 10 cruzadoes.[73] The prices given are again very high.

Textile Ports

Of the ports during the medieval period, Abdur Razzaq says that the king of Vijayanagar had three hundred ports in his dominion, each of which was equal to Calicut![74] The statement is obviously an exaggeration but it does definitely indicate the flourishing condition of trade. For the textile trade the Coromandel coast is far more important than the Malabar coast, although there are specific instances of cloth being brought from the Coromandel region to the western coast for export to Ormuz and Aden. Thus Tome Pires says that the merchandise of Golconda and Vijayanagar was collected at Goa and the traders from East Africa, Aden and Ormuz purchased the calicoes from Pulicat, the bettilles from Golconda and rice from Goa.[75] Similarly horses were sent from here to the kingdoms of the Deccan and of 'Narasinga' (Vijayanagar).[76] Similarly in the agreement between Sadasivaraya and the Portuguese it is stipulated that the Portuguese would collect the textiles of the Vijayanagar empire from the ports of Honavar and Bhatkal (the Karnataka coast) and Vijayanagar would get its horses etc. from the same port. This was after Goa became a Portuguese possession. On the Coromandel coast the most important port at this time was Pulicat. Masulipatnam seems to have gone down in importance during this time because none of the travellers of this period—Razzaq, Nicolo Conti, and later Barbosa and Pires—refers specifically to Masulipatnam as an important port. However Robert Fitch, coming after the firm entrenchment of the Portuguese in India, says ships arrived at Masulipatnam from Pegu and Sumatra laden with goods.[77] The reason for the neglect of this port prior to the Portuguese could be the constant state of war that existed in this region, between the Bahmani and Vijayanagar kingdoms at first, and later between Golconda and Vijayanagar. Pulicat may have gained in importance since it was far removed from the storm centre.

In the Madras region Pulicat had greater importance than San Thome. San Thome, which as Mylapur was very important under the late Cholas, seems to have been a virtually deserted port by the fourteenth – fifteenth centuries. Thus Marco Polo (early fourteenth century) called it 'a little town having no great population, 'tis a

Map 2. Seaports in Medieval South India

place where few traders go because there is very little merchandise to be got there'.[78] Even Barbosa (1508–9), nearly two centuries later, calls Mylapur a deserted sea-port.[79] But according to Caesar Fredrick, writing in 1565, San Thome was 'one of the fairest ports in all that part of the Indies' and he refers to the export of chintz on a large scale from here to Pegu and Malacca. He also comments on the dangers of loading and unloading in so deep a harbour and the skill with which this was done by means of special barques.[80] This revival of San Thome can obviously be linked to the establishment of Portuguese factors there. But the position of the port changed again with the establishment of the Dutch at Pulicat and the gradual capturing of the textile market by them. Of Pulicat Barbosa says that it had many Moorish as well as heathen (Hindu) traders and was 'a very fair sea-haven'. He refers to the production and export of an abundance of printed cotton cloths from here to Malacca, Pegu, Sumatra and also Gujarat and Malabar.[81] Tome Pires cites Pulicat as one of the leading ports on the eastern coast.[82] The reference to Chaturavachagan-pattinam (the Sadras of the Europeans) as the principal port of the Kanchipuram region comes from the Vijayanagar period. Reference to the sale of cloth and export trade in textiles at Sadras comes from Tirukkalukkunram of the period of Kampana Udaiyer (early fourteenth century).[83] It is referred to as an important port for textile trade in another inscription from the same region of the period of Vira-Bokkara Udaiyar dated 1376.[84] This inscription also refers to a particular type of cess on the sale of sarees. Mahalingam has referred to this cess as customs duty and states that ten per cent was levied on the sale of cloth and two-fifths of a *panam* on every bundle of cloth (*pudavai kattu*).[85] But the tone of the inscription seems to suggest a voluntary contribution on the proceeds of the sales to the family deity by the Nanadesi merchants. In fact this kind of donation is found in many inscriptions.

Among the other ports on the Coromandel coast, Nagore and Nagapattinam are important. Tome Pires (1514) in his list of the ports of the Coromandel coast refers to Nagore as a leading port.[86] This was a port a few miles away from Nagapattinam. Caesar Fredrick, writing in the later part of the sixteenth century, also says that Nagapattinam was 'a country of small trade'.[87] So apparently in the sixteenth century Nagore served as the port for the textiles produced in the Tanjavur region and nearabouts. But once the Portuguese set up their factory at Nagapattinam in the early seventeenth century, it became an active port.[88] Among the other ports on the Coromandel coast, Pires in his comprehensive list includes Cuddalore, Pondicherry, Tranquebar (Tarangampadi), Karikal and Adiramapattinam. He also refers to Tirumullaivasal (near Madras).[89]

A fair idea of the customs duties charged at these southern ports can be gleaned from the travellers' accounts. Abdur Razzaq says that a duty of 2.5 per cent was collected at Calicut.[90] Writing around the 1560's Caesar Fredrick says that the customs at Cochin amounted to 4 per cent.[91] But the increasing influx of European companies must have enhanced the rates, for the king of Cochin specifies that charges on foreigners would be 8 per cent. Robert Fitch (1583–9) referring to the charge at Goa after the Portuguese takeover says it was 8 per cent.[92] Horses were the costliest item of import in the sixteenth century and on them the customs duty was between 5 and 7 per cent.[93] The charges in the southern ports are to be contrasted with the rates prevailing elsewhere. Thus both Abdur Razzaq and Nikitin[94] say that the customs duty at Ormuz was 10 per cent, which was 'very high'. Tome Pires says that at Pegu the duty was 11 per cent.[95] At Malacca 6 per cent was the official charge but to this must be added presents to the Shah-*bandar* (Port official), Lasamane (Chief admiral), Tumunguo (the chief magistrate), and even to the Bemdara (Bemdara was the highest official of the Malaccan kingdom).[96]

Organization of Textile Trade

During the fourteenth–fifteenth centuries, and to some extent in the early sixteenth century, textile trade continued to be in the hands of indigenous merchant guilds, although instances are not wanting of weavers selling their own products at local fairs. Details of the role of merchant guilds in the textile trade of these centuries are available from inscriptional evidence relating to all parts of South India. The privileges of the Ayyavole guild are referred to in a record from Anantapur district dated 1451.[97] The 'merchants of the fifty-six countries' are referred to in the sixteenth century in Coimbatore.[98] In Salem during the period of Achyuta Raya (1529–42),[99] the same guild made a *maganmai* or voluntary contribution to the deity on items like cotton, cotton yarn, sarees, chintz and Sella cloth, among various other items. In 1531 in

Animala in Cuddappah district[100] the Vira Balanja (also referred to as Banajiga or Valanjiyar) of Ayyavole levied a *maganmai* for donation to the temple on items like cotton, yarn, cloth, etc. The most significant epigraphic evidence showing the continued hold of the indigenous merchant guilds over textile organization and trade comes from Tirupati in 1538, the period of Achyuta Raya, in the inscription already cited in the context of loom technology.[101] It registers an agreement between the cloth and yarn merchants of Tondaimandalam, Puramandalam and Ulmandalam (the last two terms refer to foreign and native merchants because *pura* means 'outside' or 'foreign' and *ul* means 'within' or 'indigenous') and the lease-holders of certain areas, essentially port-towns like Vidhura-*pattinam* and Magadha-*pattinam* (*pattinam* refers to a port-town). The merchants specify a particular type of cross-wise weaving and say that this kind of weaving should be done only by the Muslims, and for this purpose the Muslim weavers are allotted the income from certain lands. A fine of twelve gold Varahas (around forty-eight rupees in terms of the seventeenth century rupee) was to be imposed on any weaver violating this rule! Finally the inscription concludes that this order is to be communicated 'to every Hindu Village and Muslim dwelling, every cloth merchant and agent (broker) for strict observance and application in Tirupati, Kanchipuram and other parts of the South.' The inscription is invaluable for it proves several things clearly: the continued existence of specialized and powerful merchant guilds, like that of the cloth and yarn merchants cited above, in the sixteenth century; the wide territorial extent of the merchant guilds; and the influence of merchants on the process of production. Since the merchants seem to have been in a position to control even the technique of weaving, it is likely that some form of putting-out system existed because such authority can be explained only in terms of a system of advances.

The remission of customs duties on the Nanadesi merchants is referred to in the period of Venkatapatideva Maharaya (1586) from Kanchipuram.[102] Among the articles brought in by the Nanadesi merchants are mentioned Sallapattu (Sella) and Pattavalipattu (Patola). All these inscriptions indicate that in the sixteenth century textile trade continued to be in the hands of merchant guilds, and in fact the Ayyavole guild and its connection with the textile industry continued till the late seventeenth century.

A merchant group which is not referred to in any later-Chola record, but which finds repeated mention in all the travellers' accounts from the fifteenth century onwards, is that of the Klings. The earliest reference to them is in the account of Mahuan (1451).[103] The latter refers to five classes of people in the kingdom of Cochin—the Brahmins, the Muhammedans, the Chettis who were the wealthy class, the Kolings (Klings) whom he refers to as commission agents, and the Mukuas (in whom are supposed to be included all the lower classes and untouchables). Mahuan also adds that the merchants (the reference is clearly to the Klings, an itinerant community) of this country carry on their business as do peddlers in China. Ibn Batuta refers to another community 'Suli' (Choolia)[104] which is also mentioned along with the Klings by the travellers. He refers to them as the natives of Quilon and Cochin and says that they possessed considerable wealth, enough to purchase a shipload of cargo or send a vessel filled with cargo. Tome Pires (1512–15) refers to the Klings as the merchants of the Coromandel coast and says that they were the largest and most powerful trading community in Malacca: 'There are also the great Kling merchants with trade on a large scale and many junks. This is the nation which brings the most honour to Malacca. These have the bulk of the trade in their hands'.[105] In fact he even refers to Coromandel cloth as 'Kling cloth'. Castenhada, a Portuguese traveller who visited India between 1528 and 1538, refers to Klings as Quelins and says that they came from Kalinga.[106] It is clear from the accounts of Pires and Castenhada that the Klings functioned as independent merchants. But when Peter Floris refers to them in the seventeenth century it is again in the sense in which Mahuan refers to them, i.e. as itinerant merchants and probably agents of big merchants.[107] This description shows the fall in their status with the coming of the companies.

In the light of the evidence presented so far regarding merchant organizations in relation to textile trade, it seems relevant now to analyse the theory presented by Burton Stein. Stein postulates the thesis that the powerful merchant guilds, acknowledging only the symbolic overlordship of the Chola kings, declined with the establishment of a centralized bureaucracy under the Vijayanagar kings.[108] His theory assumes a very close link, in fact a partnership, between the Sudra peasantry who, according to him, dominated the assemblies of the 'nuclear core regions,' and the merchant guilds, with the latter in a 'subordinate role'. These assemblies were made up of those 'who produced many of the commodities sold and consumed the largest part of the goods bought;' the theory also assumes that by the fourteenth century the village assemblies as well as the merchant guilds had declined.

The first assumption is drawn entirely from the Chitrameli guild. In fact the merchant guilds by virtue of their economic power also acquired considerable land and, far from being subordinate to the local elements, even tended to dominate the village assemblies.[109] Moreover the demand for the products of the merchants came not merely from the local agrarian groups but was much more widespread. Nothing but very brisk internal and foreign trade can account for the wide geographical extent of the merchant guilds and the commodity-production practised by them, for instance the repeated references to horse merchants (*kudirai chettis*),[110] cloth merchants (*chilai chettis*),[111] etc. Stein, however, dismisses their activity as 'a certain amount of trade carried out by the itinerant merchant associations like the Ayyavole body in which a few necessities such as salt and iron and a diverse collection of luxury items were exchanged'. Kenneth R. Hall goes so far as to say that 'commerce was institutionalised to mitigate its more harmful effects', that the *nadu* was the basic peasant marketing region and that the *nagaram* served as its nuclear market, implying that trade had no independent existence outside the agrarian set-up.[112] This conclusion regarding the character of commercial organization in medieval South India is not borne out by actual inscriptional evidence on the range and functions of mercantile guilds during the Vijayanagar period.[113] The sixteenth-century Tirupati inscription cited earlier, in which the cloth and yarn merchants of a number of regions imposed certain specifications on the weavers, shows the continuing influence of the mercantile corporations. In fact inscriptional reference to the Ayyavole guild continues right down to the seventeenth century.[114] Stein's thesis on the decline of the merchant guilds therefore does not seem tenable.

The Genesis of the Weaver-Merchant or Master-Weaver

In spite of the existence of merchant guilds it is clear that trade in textiles was not entirely in their hands, as I have said earlier. The system of weavers selling their own merchandise in their immediate locality or in country fairs continued. The *Amuktamalyada* refers to these large numbers of weekly fairs.[115] In the fourteenth century at

Tirukkalukkunram (Chingleput), a consolidated tax of seventy *panams* was charged to the Kaikkola weavers on the cloth taken by them to Chaturavachaganpattinam (Sadras) for sale and on the commodities brought back by them on the orders of Kampana Udaiyar.[116] A Belur inscription of the fourteenth century (1382)[117] gives a list of the twenty-seven towns which held fairs and the list includes Udayagiri, Adoni, Kanchi, Padaividu and Sadras. The other towns which held fairs were Vijayanagari, Hastinavati, Dorasamudra, Gooty, Penugonda, Chandragiri, Malavay, Mangalaru, Barakuru, Honnavuru, Chandravura, Araga, Chandragutti, Annigere, Huligere, Nidugallu, Chimatanakallu, Tariakallu, Anaviddasari, Kalheya, Telakalambi and Singapattana. The weavers have themselves been given the title 'Chetti' in some records. The title 'Chetti' affixed to the names of weavers shows they must gradually have risen to the rank of merchants. Again, the Kaikkola weavers are referred to as one of the 'Kasayavargattar Pala Pattadaiyar' (merchant communities) in a sixteenth-century record from Vilichai Kulattur (Chingleput district).[118]

The rise of individual weavers to the status of merchants is indicative of a very significant development—a growing differentation in the ranks of the weavers. This is clearly proved by a fifteenth—century record from Kunnattur (Chingleput district)[119] of the period of Harihara Raya which states that one 'Narpattennayira' Solakumaran who had set up an image in the temple was given the privilege of *parivattam* and a site with the stipulation that he should pay 4 *panams on every loom* set up therein. The nature of the gift, i.e. the setting up of an image which is a very expensive form of donation, suggests the prosperity of the weaver. The subsequent stipulation indicates that this weaver had emerged as a kind of master-weaver employing artisans under him. It is significant that the inscription points to the operation of several looms at a single weaving site.[120] The prefix 'Narpattenayira' before his name is the nomenclature of a trading group and indicates that he was also a weaver-merchant. The existence of master-weavers is also proved by an inscription from Velpamadugu (Gooty taluq, Anantapur district)[121] dated 1526 of the period of Krishnadeva Maharaya. It says that Lingarasa of Dharasura (a local official) issued orders to Chettis, *senabovas* and local and foreign merchants residing in Velpamadugu, fixing the rate of taxes in the new bazaar street. While no taxes were to be levied for the first three years, in subsequent years 3 *panams* were to be levied on a loom, and if ten looms were kept by a single family only nine were to be taxed. A detailed survey of the annual produce of the kingdom of Alamkonda[122] in Rayalasima gives the different sets of rates on looms meant for weaving cloth of different colours and on looms on which only white cloth could be woven. It gives the looms of Gurivi Chetti as 65, those of Kunigiri Lingi Chetti as 100 (!) and those of Viraya as 16. The information pertains to the period of Vira Narasimharaya (the last decade of the fifteenth century). In the instances mentioned above at least two of the master-weavers were merchants and the concentration of a large number of looms in very few hands is extremely interesting. In the seventeenth century as also in the subsequent period the master-weavers had an important dual role to play. On the one hand they served as the East India Company's instrument for the exploitation of the weavers, and yet on the other hand their interests were ultimately bound up with those of the weavers. Hence when the competition of British textiles threatened their very existence they lined up with the weavers.

The Middlemen

Another important group in the organization of textile trade was the brokers or middlemen. The reference to brokers in the textile trade comes as early as the thirteenth century. *Taragu Kasu*, repeatedly referred to in the inscriptions, pertains to brokerage fee. Did the broker function in an independent commercial network or was he a part of the bureaucratic set-up? Mahuan in his account clearly refers to two categories of persons, both of whom participated in the export trade in textiles. Thus he says, 'Chettis are merchants who are called in when anything is to be sold and who are retained by the king to conduct his trading transactions ashore and afloat.' Describing a transaction in detail he says that when a ship arrived from China the king's overseer went on board with a Chetti and made an invoice of the goods, and a day was settled for valuing the cargo. On the day appointed the silk goods, more especially the Khinkis (embroidered silks, the Persian Khanqabs), were first inspected and valued. When this was decided, all joined their hands, whereupon the Weinaki (broker) said: 'the price of your goods is now fixed and cannot in anyway be altered.'[123] Thus Mahuan is referring to the official valuer as well as to the broker. Barbosa writing in the sixteenth century says[124] that when any foreign merchant came to the city the king assigned a Nayre (Nayar—a caste in Malabar) to serve him, and a clerk and broker to arrange for him to obtain such goods as he had need of. Barbosa appears to be referring to the broker as part of the bureaucratic set-up. But Varthema (1503–8) and Caesar Fredrick (1563–81) both give very similar descriptions of the participation of brokers in commercial transactions and their evidence points to the operation of brokers in an independent capacity. Varthema says that when the merchants wished to sell or purchase they always did this through the Cortor or the Lella, i.e. the broker. The buyers and sellers agreed upon a figure by silently touching fingers under a sheet of cloth.[125] Caesar Fredrick describes the same details and says that the reason for such a silent and secretive transaction was that they did not want to disclose the price to other merchants who eagerly came to watch the proceedings.[126]

Taxation

Some evidence is available for the incidence of taxation on weavers in the period from the fourteenth to the sixteenth centuries. In the Table an effort has been made to tabulate the information on taxation of weavers, especially concerning looms. The majority of the information comes from the Tamil region. The inscriptions from Andhra and Karnataka regions help substantiate the findings arrived at by studying the figures available steadily over a period of time from the Tamil country. The inscriptions make it clear that taxation was annual. The only isolated instances of monthly tax come from the reign of Saluva Narasimha. The basic scheme of taxation does not seem to have been very different from the earlier period. The most frequent reference is to the loom tax called *tari irai* or *tari kadamai* in the Tamil country and *maggada hana* or *maggadere* in the Andhra and Karnataka regions. There is also reference to *Per kadamai* or profession tax. This is variously referred to on the different communities as Kaikkola-*kadamai*, Seniya-*tari*, Saliya-*tari*, etc. The inscriptions refer to tax on ordinary thread (*nulayam*) as also tax on silk thread (*pattadai nulayam*). The sale of cloth was also taxed, assessment being based on a percentage of the profits obtained by the sale of cloth. The weavers also paid *vasal vari* or house tax. A new tax connected with the weaving profession

Rates of Taxation in the Handloom Industry
(Fourteenth to Sixteenth Centuries)

Source	King	Dynasty	Period	Name of Place	Taluq	District	Nature of Tax	Rate of taxation (annual)	Tax in terms of rupees (approx.)	Remarks
A.R.E., 170 of 1933	Kampana Udaiyar	Vijayanagar	End of fourteenth century	Tirukkalukkun-ram	Chingleput	Chingleput	Consolidated tax (kattukkutagai) on the Kaikkolar	70 panams*	17	If a sum of 3½ panams is taken to be the average charge per loom, then 70 panams constituted the tax on 24 weavers in the Tirukkalukkunram area which was an important weaving centre.
A.R.E., 221 of 1929–36	Harihara Raya	,,	Fourteenth century	Kunnattur	Chingleput	Chingleput	Loom tax (tari-irai)	4 panams	1	
A.R.E., 293 of 1910	Bukka II	,,	1404–5	Pulipparkkoyil	Madurantakam	Chingleput	Loom tax (tari kadamai) on Kaikkolar profession plus tax (per kadamai) on Kaikkolar	2 panams 2 panams	1	
A.R.E., 364 of 1908	Virupana Udaiyar (Virupaksa I)	,,	Beginning of fifteenth century	Vayalur	Kanchipuram	Chingleput	Loom tax	3 panams	3/4	

Source	King	Dynasty	Period	Name of Place	Taluq	District	Nature of Tax	Rate of taxation (annual)	Tax in terms of rupees (approx)	Remarks
A.R.E., 294 of 1910	Vijaya Raja I	"	1418	Pulipparkkoyil	Madurantakam	Chingleput	Remission of house tax (vasal vari) on Kaikkolar	6 panams	1½	
							Tax on sale of cloth (tanduppudavai)	40 panams	10	
A.R.E., 59 of 1914–5	Devaraya II	"	1429	Tiruvaigavur	Papanasam	Tanjavour	Loom tax on each Kaikkola weaver with one working loom	4 panams	1	These rates were fixed by the assembled residents of Parantakanadu, the Valangai 98 and the Idangai 98 sects. This was necessitated by the ruin of the economy of the country by the Kannadigas (Hoysalas?).
							Kaikkola with loom that did not work	2 panams	1/2	
							Saliya weavers for each loom	9 panams	2½	
							Lace loom in working order	3 panams	3/4	
							Lace loom not in working order	1½ panams	1/6	
A.R.E., 272 of 1912	Devaraya II	"	1436	Nerumbur	Chingleput	Chingleput	On silk thread (pattadai nulayam)	2 panams	1/2	
A.R.E., 252 of 1916–7	Mallikarjuna	"	1463	Srimushnam	Chidambaram	South Arcot	Loom tax collected from Kaikkolar living in tirumadaivila-gam of temple	20 panams		Since on an average the loom tax was 4 panams per individual, 20 panams were apparently levied from five weavers.

Source	Ruler		Date	Place		District	Nature of tax	Amount	Value	Remarks
A.R.E., 201 of 1923	Virupana Udaiyar (Virupaksa II)	"	Late fifteenth century	Tiruppulivanam	Kanchipuram	Chingleput	Consolidated tax on each loom	5 *panams*	1¼	The weavers of Tiruppulivanam had deserted owing to their inability to pay the previous tax. Hence the tax was revised to 5 *panams* with the assurance that no other tax would be collected from the weavers.
A.R.E., 318 of 1909–10	Saluva Narasimha	"	1484	Tirukkachchiyur	Chingleput	Chingleput	Loom tax (monthly)	¼ *panam* per month = 3 *panams* annual	¾	This and the following evidence are the only instances of monthly tax on looms.
S.I.I., xvii, no. 221	Saluva Narasimha	"	1486–91	Tiruvakkarai	Villupuram	South Arcot	Loom tax (monthly)	½ *panams* monthly 6 *panams* annual	1½	
L.R., vi, 324–8	Saluva Narasimha	"	1486–91	Alamkonda	—	—	Loom tax for weaving coloured cloth (patterned cloth) / Loom tax on loom for weaving white (plain) cloth	½ *ruka* monthly 6 *rukas* yearly / ¼ *ruka* monthly 3 *rukas* yearly	1¼	The *ruka* of the Andhra country is the same as the *panam* of the Tamil country.

Source	King	Dynasty	Period	Name of Place	Taluq	District	Nature of Tax	Rate of taxation (annual)	Tax in terms of rupees (approx.)	Remarks
A.R.E., 62 of 1934–5	Saluva Narasimha	"	1490–1	Tellaru	Wandiwash	North Arcot	Consolidated tax on the Kaikkolas of Tellaru, a *devadana* village	32 *panams*	8	A.R.E., 72 of 1934–5, a late Pandya Inscription towards the end of the fourteenth century gives the number of looms at Tellaru as 12. Therefore the charge per loom was 2¾ or 3 *panams*.
A.R.E., 247 of 1916	Vira Narasimha	"	1504	Srimushnam	Chidambaram	South Arcot	Loom tax of each Kaikkola weaver	3 *panams*	¾	Weavers deserted due to heavy taxation. Therefore the tax was reduced to 3 *panams*.
							Loom tax on each loom of the Chettis	3 *panams*	¾	An interesting instance of a merchant owning looms which were apparently operated by weavers working under them.
A.R.E., 409 of 1913	Krishnadeva Raya	"	1513	Aragal	Attur	Salem	Loom tax	3 *panams*	¾	To encourage rehabilitation of deserted villages, all taxes were reduced. 3 *panams* constitutes the reduced tax.

Reference	Ruler		Year	Place	Town	District	Tax	Amount	Value	Note
L.R., lxi, 23–4	Krishnadeva Raya	,,	1523	Kotakonda			Loom tax	½ *varaha*	1¼	According to an inscription of the period of Devaraya II (*A.R.E.*, 172 of 1916) 10 *panams* = 1 *varaha* but usually 15 *panams* = 1 *varaha*.
S.I.I., ix pt 2, no. 516	Krishnadeva Raya	,,	1526	Velupadige	Gooty	Anantapur	Loom tax	3 *panams*	¾	
A.R.E., 140 of 1915–6	Krishnadeva Raya	,,	1509–29	Tiruchchengodu	Tiruchchengodu	Salem	Loom tax	3 *panams*	¾	
A.R.E., 364 of 1912	Acyuta Raya	,,	1532	Devakipuram	Arni	North Arcot	Tax on silk thread 1½ *panams* (*pattadai nulayam*)		⅙	
A.R.E., 2 of 1913	Sadasiva Raya	,,	1561	Pillaipalayam (Big Kanchipuram)	Kanchipuram	Chingleput	Loom tax	5½ *panams*	1½	

mentioned for the first time in the sixteenth century is the tax on carders (*pinja siddhayam*)[127] the evidence for which comes from Devasamudra Hobli, Malakalamuru taluq, Chittaldroog, of the period of Sambuvaraya (dated 1557). Evidence shows that the tax was made collectively and not individually. Further, the preference was to levy a consolidated tax rather than a variety of cesses. At Srimushnam twenty *panams* were being collected from the Kaikkolar living in the *tirumadaivilagam* of the temple. Evidence from Tirukkalukkunram and Kulattur of the fourteenth and sixteenth centuries respectively shows that taxation was not only collective but also made into a consolidated tax, probably in order to render collection easier. As in the Chola period, evidence for the fifteenth–sixteenth centuries shows that the tax on looms was collected by the state and that in fact assessment and collection of all professional taxes on the communities was the duty and prerogative of state officials; it had nothing to do with the temple except when it was specifically assigned to the temple by the orders of the king's official (Mahapradhani), as in the instance from Tirukkoyilur in 1445.[128]

On the basis of the evidence provided it is possible to conclude that the loom tax (which virtually constituted the consolidated tax on the weavers) varied very little over a period of two centuries. On an average it seems to have remained constant at 3 or 4 *panams* per loom per year. It seems to have gone upto 5½ – 6 – 6½ *panams* only after the period of Krishnadeva Raya, i.e. after the 1530's. Even during the reign of Krishnadeva Raya there seem to have been attempts to increase the tax rate but this had to be revised to the old rate of 3 *panams* due to protests and desertions by weavers.[129] In fact whenever weavers felt that taxes were unduly high they protested through their organizations and compelled the state to bring these down. That economic protest was a very effective instrument is proved by several instances. Harihara II, for instance, was faced with a strike by the weavers of the Agastyesvara temple in Olakkur, which successfully paralysed all temple activity.[130] Subsequently the weavers had to be conciliated.[131] The rate of taxation during the reign of Virupana Udaiyar (1465–85) was rather high—5 *panams*.[132] As a result there were repeated strikes and *en masse* desertions by the weavers. The *valangai* and *idangai* organization also united in the face of oppressive taxation and determined the tax rates, as testified by the inscription from Srimushnam.[133]

The attitude of the state in general was to interfere as little as possible with the local structure and to adopt a favourable attitude towards protests by the weavers. The benevolent attitude of the state is reflected in numerous charters and edicts. All newly-settled areas were exempted from payment of tax for the first two or three years. Thus an inscription from Tiruchchengodu (an important weaving centre of the Salem district) of the period of Krishnadeva Raya refers to the founding of a new village called Samasamudram[134] by Sama Nayanar, agent of a Triyambaka Udaiyar, who was governing Mulavay. The Kaikkolar, Chettis and other professionals (*rasavargam*) were exempted from payment for the first two years but were to pay 3 *panams* in subsequent years. Tax exemptions were also made in the event of natural disasters, invasions and plunder of the countryside. Thus Devaraya II reduced the tax on looms in Srimushnam because the inhabitants had suffered exorbitant taxation and plunder under 'the rule of the Kannadigas' (Hoysalas?).[135] An Arabic inscription in the fort of Adoni (the kingdom of Bijapur) of the period of Ali Adil Shah dated 1574 says that the weavers and the grocers of that area were to be exempted from tax for a period of twelve years because political disturbance and change of government had disrupted the economy.[136] The attitude of the state towards weavers and other professional classes is also reflected in the innumerable charters of protection and assurance (*nambikkai pattayam*) granted by the state to weavers and other artisans.[137]

CHAPTER IV

The Weavers, Society and the State
(Fourteenth to Sixteenth Centuries)

The period of the Vijayanagar empire is regarded as a landmark in terms of the changes in the conception and organization of the state. Scholars have tended to look upon the Chola period as 'the golden age' of local self-government while conversely characterizing the Vijayanager empire as a 'warrior state'[1] with powerful feudatories and officials who left no room for the functioning of local assemblies as well as more or less autonomous caste and professional organizations. To view the Vijayanagar empire as a watershed in these terms is to create an artificial break in the process of social history. Local institutions continued well into the sixteenth century and the guilds continued to function and did not decline or decay. In fact instead of imposing a new officialdom at every level and disrupting the existing political and social order, the Vijayanagar kings attempted a rapprochement with local elements, and this was done through royal influence and patronage. Thus effective alliances were forged between caste and sectarian leaders on the one hand and the ruling class on the other.[2]

Hence in order to understand the position of weavers in contemporary Vijayanagar society it is essential first to place them in the context of the general functioning of village assemblies in relation to overall state policy, second to view the interaction between weavers and other social groups (especially as reflected in left-hand right-hand conflicts), third to understand the extension of state patronage to them through the grant of privileges, and finally to study their ritual role in temples and their participation in the heterodox movements of the time.

Weavers and The Ayagar System

It would be essential to discuss the nature of the *ayagar* system if the actual position of caste and local assemblies in the Vijayanagar period is to be properly understood. *Ayagars* were village functionaries who were remunerated for their services to the village community either in terms of tax free lands (*manyam*)[3] or a share of the grain heap.[4] The term *ayam* itself means fee or remuneration. These functionaries were generally twelve in number.[5] But this was not a rigid figure and the composition of the *ayagars* and their number in every village depended on the exigencies of that particular village. The *ayagars* usually included a watchman, a barber, an astrologer, a potter, a washerman and possibly the smiths, though not every village had a goldsmith. The weavers only rarely formed a part of the village functionaries. The chief of the village functionaries was the headman, called *Gauda* in the Andhra country and *Pidaran* in the Tamil country.

The village headman was sometimes appointed by the representative of the king[6] and sometimes by the collective village assembly itself.[7] With regard to other officials, the only instances where the state is mentioned in connection with the appointment of local functionaries seem most often to be when a particular office was an object of dispute between two parties.[8] An instance of the appointment of a village astrologer by the royal representative is available but from a much later period (1631),[9] by which time of course the entire conception of the functioning of village assemblies had become attenuated on account of a variety of factors. But by and large it does appear as if the state put its stamp of approval on the choice of village functionaries rather than that it actively appointed them, except in the case of the headman whose position was important—he would not only be the village head but also the representative of the state in the village.[10] The *ayagars* functioned during the Vijayanagar period as village officials rather than as servants of the government.[11] Hence the theory of the decline of village assembly would be true not so much of the heyday of the Vijayanagar empire but of the late sixteenth century when it had ceased to be a powerful political factor.

Weaver Corporate Organization

It has been clarified that the continued existence of powerful caste organizations of the weavers rests on the continued functioning of village assemblies and other local caste bodies in the Vijayanagar period. Evidence of the continued activity of weaver guilds right upto the sixteenth century is available from epigraphic and literary sources. The reference to a grant at the *Devanga Pallala-matam* (Devanga weavers' meeting place) in Kapistalam (Papanasam taluq, Tanjavur district) in 1542 shows the continued functioning of the Devanga weavers' craft organization.[12] In 1554 the Kaikkolas of Jambai (South Arcot district) made an agreement among themselves to contribute to the maintenance of a *matam* (corporate organization or guild).[13] Similarly in 1584 at Tirupati some activity (not specified) seems to have taken place at the Kaikkola-*mantapam*.[14] A late sixteenth-century record from Pattamadai (hamlet of Seramadevi in Tirunelveli) refers to a temple donation by Sattam Tondan, one of the Nattu-Saliyar. It appears that the donor was a local head of the Saliya guild organization.[15] Contemporary literature also refers to the guilds. A reference to the guilds of weavers (weaver of ordinary cloth) and the weavers of silk cloth is found in the *Amuktamalyada* of Krishnadeva Raya.[16]

I have earlier mentioned that the weaver organizations had their own code of conduct and that any violation of this code was severely punished. Not only did the weaver guilds have their own code of conduct and settle disputes arising within their guild, they also arbitrated in temple disputes in the capacity of Sthanathars. During the reign of Vira Sayans Udaiyar, in the Muktisvara temple at Attur (Chingleput), a gift of land, free of taxes was resumed by the temple authorities. Taxes were assessed thereon and, as the tenants could not pay them, a meeting of the Kaikkolas and Kaikkola-*mudalis* was called.[17] It appears that the Kaikkolas held a position of considerable importance in the temple and were hence asked to arbitrate to settle the issue. Similarly, during the period of Kumara Kampana Udaiyar (fourteenth century), in the Vadagirisvara temple at Tirukkalukkunram, a sum of 850 *pon* (gold) was found to be missing from the temple. The thief was captured and the Kaikkolar, Kaikkola-*mudalis* and Ponnambalakkuttar arbitrated in the case, imposing heavy fines on the offender.[18] These are interesting instances of the judicial powers enjoyed by weavers outside their own guild organization.

Temple Donations

The size and nature of temple donations was throughout the medieval period an index of the economic prosperity and social status of any community. Donations continued to be both individual[19] as well as collective,[20] though instances of individual donations were rare. As already discussed, during the Chola and late-Chola periods donations to the temples seem to have been chiefly for the setting up of perpetual lamps (*nonda-vilakku*) by the gifting of money or sheep to the temple. During the Vijayanagar period the form of donation was essentially in the nature of food offering (*prasadam*) and large-scale feeding of the disciples, apart from grants of money and lands to the temple which continued throughout.

During the reign of Ariyana Udaiyar (fourteenth century) the Kaikkolar living in the Tirumadaivilagam of Brahmapurisvara temple at Perunagar (Chingleput) are said to have made a collective gift (not specified) to the deity.[21] In 1366 the Kaikkolaru of Madivala (Bangalore district) attached to the 'fine temple' (name not given) combined with the Mahajanas and temple trustees in making a collective gift of paddy to Sri Rudra Mahesvara of Chitrameli Parukalan-Dirukkavanam, residing in the temple Tamaraikkirai in Rajendra Chola Valanadu.[22] Similarly in 1425 (in the reign of Devaraya II) the Kaikkolar of Valuvur (Wandiwash, North Arcot) made a collective gift of money for a lamp to the temple of Tiruvayanisuramudaiya Nayanar.[23] These records are a further proof of the fact that the weaver caste and craft organizations continued to flourish during the Vijayanagar period and co-operated in social matters. A record from Kallidaikurichchi (Tirunelveli district) dated 1597[24] states that a contribution of 10 *panams* per loom was levied by the Kaikkola Mudali Nayanars of the village and similar contributions were levied by other village professionals for conducting festivals in the temple of Nandiyappar. In the sixteenth century at the Sitaramasvami temple in Dharmavaram (Ongole, Guntur district), the spinners made a collective contribution of 2 *dha* (?) on every *ratam* (spinning wheel) and the weavers 1 *vam* (?) on Sella (inferior, very low quality muslin).[25] Some records also refer to joint construction of temples by the weaver communities. Thus the Kaikkolar of Ambasamudram constructed a temple in 1507 for Annivinodisuramudaiya Nayanar and Bhutalavira Rama Pillaiyar, and were in return granted the hereditary right of receiving a garland and endowed with many incidental privileges.[26]

There is one striking difference in the nature and size of donations

between the Chola and the Vijayanagar periods. While in the Chola
period nominal donations of money or sheep by individual weavers
are innumerable, there is hardly any reference to nominal individual
donations in the Vijayanagar period. The only instances of
individual donations which occur in the Vijayanagar period are
major donations like the gift of land, the setting up of deities or the
construction of temples, and in every case the donation was
reciprocated by high honours and privileges conferred on the donor.
In 1398, at the time of Virupaksha I, Venaudaiyar, one of the
Kaikkola Mudalis of the temple of Tiruvannakkoyiludaiya Nayanar
is said to have made a gift of land in the hamlet of Uttamasolavilagam to the deity. It is said that Uttamasolavilagam was originally
granted to the temple for worship and repairs by Vira Kampana
Udaiyar.[27] It is thus possible to infer that the land was bought up by
the Kaikkola Mudalis and subsequently a part of it gifted to the
temple. The donor was apparently wealthy and powerful, for he was
a landowner and the title Mudalis enjoyed by him reflects his social
status. At Ponnur (Wandiwash, North Arcot) in 1383 Magadarayar,
a Kaikkola, reconstructed with stone the *maha-mantapa* of the temple
of Parasarisvaram Udaiya-Nayanar, in recognition of which he was
given land and privileges by the trustees of the temple.[28] In another
instance from Kunnattur (also in the Chingleput district)
Narpattenayira-Solakumaran, a Kaikkola who had set up an
image of Chokka-Nayanar in the Tirunagesvara temple, was given
the privilege of *parivattam* (the head-dress put for the god) and a site
with the stipulation that he should pay 4 *panams* on *every loom* set up
therein.[29] The same privileges were also accorded to his descendants. The donor was again clearly a man of considerable wealth
since he seems to have owned several looms and probably employed
workers under him. In 1506 at Melacheval (Tirunelveli district) the
Kaikkolan Keralan Martandan (this shows the migratory pattern of
the community and the presence of the Kaikkolar in Kerala) reconse-
crated the temple of Udaiyavar which had been deserted during
Muslim occupation. Presumably as a recognition of his service he was
made the accountant of the temple and given 4 *nali* of cooked rice every
day from the *prasadam*.[30] In an instance of individual donation from
Aragal (Salem district) during the period of Achutaraya (1532)
Kannan, a Kaikkola of Kaliyur who had instituted a car festival (*ter
utsavam*) in the temple, was granted a house, a loom, a piece of land and
certain specific privileges in the temple by the temple trustees. These

same privileges were also guaranteed to his descendants.[31] As all these instances of individual donations prove, the donors in every instance enjoyed a lot of power. This is clear from the size of the donation or temple service performed, which invariably resulted in social and ritual privileges being conferred on the donor. This further makes clear one very significant fact—that differentiation among the weavers was increasing. While a few wealthy weavers seem to have made major donations to temples, donations of nominal amounts by ordinary weavers were entirely absent. Secondly the evidence shows a shift in the form of donations from money for perpetual lamp and the donation of sheep in the Chola period to the institution of festivals and disbursement of *prasadam* in the Vijayanagar period. This can especially be perceived in the donations made to Tirupati,[32] for instance, though there are a few earlier instances of donations being made in terms of food offering even in the thirteenth century.[33]

The donations made by weavers during the Vijayanagar period are once again to be contrasted with the donations made by other communities. The merchants were of course the largest donors, though their donations, were as usual essentially in the form of *maganmai* or contribution of the profits on their items of trade.[34] The Pancalar or Kammalar (i.e. the smiths) are another community mentioned frequently in the records of this period in connection with donations to temples. The smiths of Udayagiri, Nellore, Koratur, Gandavaram, Allur, Kovur and several other regions are said to have endowed to the deity Kamatesvara of Dharamkota the *palayan-payindi* of Amaravaram in the year 1490.[35] This was probably a communal cess levied upon members of the community. Elsewhere the smiths are said to have made a collective gift of land to an individual, Buddhasane. Apart from the considerable size of the donation, equally significant is the fact of corporate ownership in land.[36]

Standard of Living

It would be appropriate to attempt at this point an understanding of the standard of living of weavers and other artisanal groups. Some indication of this has already been provided by the nature and size of the donations made by them. This shows the merchants as the most prosperous group, followed by the weavers and the smiths.

Since most of these professionals paid their taxes in cash it is clear that the flow of money was not low, although the peasantry paid their tax more often in kind than in cash. Besides money, paddy also constituted a standard of value. Artisans like weavers and smiths seem to have come within the middle strata of society, as distinct from the rural poor or low-caste artisans like potters and leather workers on the one hand and merchants and the bureaucracy on the other hand. It is possible to form only the most tentative conclusions regarding the consumption pattern and life-style of the weavers. According to a popular oral tradition the fourteenth-century weaver-poet Tiruvalluvar accidentally discovered the efficacy of starching yarn while consuming rice gruel. While the weavers seem to have been able to afford rice, it appears that the poorer sections could afford to eat only rye or *ragi*. This interesting fact is brought out by the Kannada saint and poet of the early sixteenth century, Kanakadasa, who wrote the *Ramadhanya Charitre* in the form of a conversation between *ragi* and rice. While at the beginning rice is proud and haughty because it is the food of the upper classes, it is eventually humbled by *ragi* which forms the staple food of the majority of the people. In fact *ragi* is respectfully addressed as 'Sudranna', literally 'Sudra elder brother'. Since Kanakadasa himself belonged to the Kuruba or shepherd caste it is clear that rye was the food of the poor.[37] However according to Vasco da Gama rice appeared to be in abundance. Corn, according to him, was very cheap and bread which sold at 3 *reals* at Calicut, was sufficient for a man's daily sustenance.[38] Manchana's *Keyurabhirama* composed in the fourteenth century indicates that barter was quite common. It narrates the story of an oil-mongers's son who was willing to sell his oil for an equal measure of rice, although the prevailing rate was seven measures of rice for one measure of oil.[39]

Vallabharaya's *Kreedabhiramamu* of the fifteenth century describes the same region as Manchana's work, i.e. the eastern Deccan. The work is about the travels of a rich merchant and his Brahmin friend in Ekasilanagaram (modern Warangal). The author says that the two friends ate a meal comprising high quality rice, ghee, pulses, curds, fruits and sweet dishes for one *ruka,* a *ruka* being equal to a *panam* (very roughly 0.15 or 0.16 of the seventeenth-century rupee).[40] This seems fairly expensive if seen in terms of the salaries paid to the lowest professionals in the temples. This was one or two *panams* annually, besides a share of the *prasadam* and sometimes a *vetti* or *pudavai.*[41]

Although hardly any regular figures are available to determine the income of weavers during this period, it is possible to arrive at a very rough estimate of the weavers' income from a reference found in Vasco da Gama's account. Commenting on the cheapness of commodities at Calicut he says that a 'very fine shirt' which in Portugal fetched 300 *reis* was worth only 2 *panams*, equivalent to 30 *reis*. Now, asssuming the cost of stitching and transportation to be equal to the cost of weaving, the weaver can be said to have produced half a fine shirt per day, or one *panam* worth of labour, since roughly three to four yards can be woven in a day on an ordinary loom. Assuming that the weaver weaves about three yards per day or the equivalent of one shirt, working 276 days a year he would produce 138 fine shirts a year, or 276 *panams* worth of labour. This would be his gross annual income. From this must be deducted the cost of yarn, the cost of bleaching and dyeing, and the cost of transportation. If the cloth is not sold directly in the market but through a middleman, his commission has to be deducted. It is being assumed that the weaver did not have to incur any expense on the spinning of thread because this was done by his household, as also on associated processes like carding, combing, twisting and winding the yarn. A further reduction has to be made from gross sales revenue of a depreciation charge on the loom, and finally of the tax paid by the weaver. From the Tax Table it seems unlikely that the weaver paid more than five· *panams* per year as loom tax (besides other taxes) not exceeding three to four per cent of the gross sales revenue. If all the items mentioned above were to amount to sixty per cent on a very rough estimate, the weaver must have made at least eight *panams* per month. This was the position for the weaver of fine cloth, and it is likely that the income of the coarse-cloth weaver was much less. So far as the ordinary weaver was concerned, although he was better-off than the poorer sections of society, it is quite clear that a single meal costing one *ruka* such as that described in the *Kreedabhiramamu* would have been beyond his means.

Weavers and Land

Weavers continued to have connections with land in the Vijaya-nagar period. In the Chola period services to the temple were reciprocated by the grant of lands. In 1383 at Ponnur, Magadar-ayar, a Kaikkola was given land with certain privileges by the temple in appreciation of his construction of a *mantapam* in the temple.[42] In 1532 a weaver who instituted the car (*ratha*) festival at the Karivaradaraja Perumal temple in Aragal (Salem district) was given land, a loom and certain ritual privileges by the temple authorities.[43] There are also numerous references to weavers acquiring land as *kaniyatchi*. Thus two Kaikkolar, Kuttadundevar and Puluginapperumal, the sons of Kalingarayar, were conferred land as *kani* in Kariyandal (Tiruvannamalai, North Arcot district).[44] In another record from the same area the statement regarding confirmation of *kaniyatchi* is followed by the remark that 15 *panams* was the *chandesvarapperuvilai*. Both these records appear to be instances of long lease or purchase of land by the weavers.[45] During the period of Bukkana Udaiyar twenty *ma* of land in the *tirumadaivilagam* which had been lying waste since the days of Sambuvaraya was sold to the weavers for settlement.[46] Two points in this record are noteworthy: that the land was cultivable waste land and that it was collectively purchased by the weaver community. In 1428 the Kaikkolar of Nerkunram (South Arcot district) are said to have been given the *kaniyatchi* right of the village Vadagarai-Tayanur in return for the amount of thirty *panams* given by them to the Uravar.[47] This again appears to be an instance of the conferment of supervisory rights in land rather than the actual conferment of land upon the Kaikkolar. However, one inscription from Tirukkoilur is very ambiguous on this point. The record, dating around 1550's,[48] registers an order of the king (the ruler of Travancore, Udayamartanda Varman) granting land belonging to the temple as *kaniyatchi* to Marttandan, a Kaikkola. Perhaps the king exercised some control over the temple land because the record says that it had originally been granted by him to the temple in 1531. Collective purchase of house sites by the Kaikkolar is referred to from Kanchipuram in 1364. The record states that with the sanction of Koppannangal, the executive officer of Kampana Udaiyar at Kanchipuram, the authorities of the Rajasimhesvara temple at Kanchipuram sold some houses in the north row of the *sannidhi* street to the Kaikkolar and the Kaikkola Mudalis against payment of 150 *panams* made by them, which was deposited in the treasury. It further states: 'These houses and gardens attached to the house may be sold or mortgaged by them.'[49] In 1536, during the period of Achyutaraya, Nami Chetti is said to have constructed a *mantapa* in the Govindarajaswami temple in Tirupati (Chitoor district) on the land which he purchased from the Kaikkolar.[50] The land was apparently held collectively by the Kaikkolar because no individual owner is mentioned. In another significant record from Puliyur dated 1563 (Sadasiva Raya),[51] the Sthanathar of the Brahmapuris-vara temple made an agreement that they would cultivate certain lands of the Kaikkola Mudalis of Puliyur and pay taxes on them to the temple treasury. Ownership of land by the weavers is also indicated by the records which refer to donation of land by the weavers to the temple. Thus in 1398, at the time of Virupaksha I, Vena Udaiyar,[52] a Kaikkola Mudali, made a gift of all lands in the hamlet of Uttamasola-vilagam to the temple of Tiruvanakoyiludaiya Naya-nar. Another record dated 1404 refers to the purchase of land at Pulippakkam by the same Venaudaiyar.[53] A similar gift of land was made by a Kaikkola of Madurai in 1478.[54] In yet another instance a gift was made by a section of the Kaikkolar of a share of their lands to another section for the services the latter had to render in the temple.[55] A sixteenth century record from South Arcot mentions Kaikkola tenant cultivators. The managers of the Ramalingesvara temple and Kudama Nayaka, the agent of Surappa Nayaka, issued an order to the Kaikkolar giving lands in Marangiyur (Tirukkoyilur, South Arcot).[56]

Privileges—Economic, Social and Ritual

The economic prosperity of the weavers, evidenced by their ownership of land and the numerous donations made by them to the temples, led to the conferment of economic and social privileges by the state in recognition of their enhanced importance in society. To this was added ritual recognition by the temples. Economic privileges took the form of appointment as temple managers or trustees, accountants and treasurers of the temple. As temple trustees they even seem to have had considerable right over the sale and purchase of temple house sites and land. In 1410, during the period of Bhupati Udaiyar, the Sthanathar and Kaikkolar of Valuvur (Wandiwash, North Arcot district) purchased land for the Brahmapurisvara temple at Valuvur.[57] At Tirupparkadal (Wala-japet, North Arcot) in 1469, the period of Kampana Udaiyar, the Maharudrar, Sri Mahesvaras and Kaikkola Mudalis who were the trustees of the Tirupparkadal Udaiya Nayanar are said to have sold a number of houses belonging to the temple to meet the expense of taking the deity in procession.[58] In another instance from Devakipuram (Arni) in the same district, the Kaikkola Mudalis as trustees of the temple made a gift of land and a house in the temple (*devadana*) to an individual in 1523.[59] In 1533 in the same region the Kaikkola Mudalis acting as trustees of the Brihadamba temple granted the right of supervision of temple lands to an individual.[60] The more affluent members of the weaver community not only functioned as temple trustees but also as temple managers[61] and also held the responsible position of accountants in several temples, especially in the Tirunelveli area (a highly productive cotton tract). For example Keralan Martandan was appointed as the accountant of the temple he renovated. Another instance of the appointment of a weaver as accountant comes from Kallidaikurichchi in 1525. At Giriyamba-puram in 1566 the same man, Kaikkolan Perrapan, was put in charge of the accounts of three temples.[62] The appointment of a weaver as the headman (*pidaran*) of a village comes from Elavanasur (Tirukkoyillur, South Arcot) in 1555. Vengappayan, the *pradhani* of Surappa Nayak, is said to have made the Kaikkola Mudali Gangarayan the *pidaran* of the village and he was also allowed to own a tax free loom.[63]

   Tax reduction or tax exemptions on the weavers were sometimes in the nature of an economic privilege conferred on them. For instance the Kaikkolar of Tirukkalukkunram were exempted from a number of taxes like *karpura kanikkai* (price paid for cultivation rights over temple lands), *Adhikara chodi* (dues paid to officers), *pattadai nulayam* (tax on silk thread) *attai sammadam* (annual contribution), etc., while during the reign of Saluva Narasimha, the Kaikkolas of Kunnattur were exempted from all taxes.[64] In another interesting instance from Velpamadugu (Gooty taluq, Anantapur) in 1526, during the reign of Krishnadevaraya, it was decreed that at Velpamadugu the rate of tax was to be 3 *panams* per loom and if ten looms were kept by one single family, only nine were to be taxed. [65] This is clearly an instance of an economic privilege being conferred on a wealthy master-weaver. Tax exemption as a privilege was also enjoyed by the Pancalar and in a greater degree by the barbers in the Andhra country. Here they were frequently exempted from tax and also had privileges conferred on them during the Vijayanagar period, especially in the time of Sadasiva Raya.[66] But tax exemption was not always indicative of an economic privilege. Very often it was granted in new settlements and served as an inducement to attract weavers[67] and other artisans, or constituted tax reduction in the face of economic protests[68] by the weavers.

Social privileges essentially meant the conferment of *sangu* and *tandu* or *dandu* (the right to blow the conch shell and the right to ride the palanquin on all important occasions). It could also mean the right to whitewash homes or have a double storied house, to sport their own insignia or even to wear certain types of clothes. Among the Kaikkola caste of weavers the Kaikkolar of Kanchipuram were apparently the first to secure the privileges of the use of *sangu* and *tandu* on all good and bad occasions because all inscriptions from other regions state that the weavers in these areas obtained these privileges on the pattern of the weavers in Kanchipuram, or that the head of the guild at Kanchipuram by the name of Aramvalartta Nayanar accorded them these privileges. Thus the Kaikkola weavers of Tirvennainallur, Tiruttalur, Tirukkoyilur and Brahmadesa[69] (all in South Arcot district) are said to have got similar privileges on the model of the Kaikkolar of Kanchipuram as per the decision taken by the Aramvalartta Nayanar[70] in consultation with Kongurayar and Kachchirayar.[71] Another professional caste that held privileges equal to the weavers was that of the smiths. A record of the reign of Harihararaya (1336–57) refers to the conferring of social privileges on the smiths.[72] A record from Amaravati dated 1437 says that they were entitled to the various royal insignia like a leather musical instrument, a golden musical instrument, *sangu* and *tandu*, *garudadvaja* (banner), etc.[73] The almost equal social importance enjoyed by the smiths as well as the weavers was perhaps one reason for such frequent conflict and rivalry between these two groups.[74]

Ritual privileges were an even more important aspect of social acceptance and recognition for the professional castes, including the weavers. At Kunnattur during the period of Harihararaya (end of fourteenth century) a weaver, Narpattennayira Solakumaran, who had set up the image of a deity in the temple was given a weaving site and also *parivattam* (head-dress of the god).[75] In 1433, during the reign of Devaraya Maharaya, a Kaikkola, Kulandai Andar Amarakonar, was given the *tirumukhakani* at the temple of Tiruvagisvaram-udaya-Mahadeva in Tiruvagisvaramadam (Wandiwash, North Arcot). It is said that Aramvalartta-Nachchiyarmishta Kandamanikkam, the temple dancer and sister of the Kaikkola, personally interviewed King Devaraya on behalf of the temple and procured a copper plate grant from him, making the

sarvamanya gift of the village. In return for her services the temple
conferred some privilege on her brother and granted her one *padakku*
of grain every day and two *panams* per month.[76] This record shows
the continued association between the Kaikkolar and the Devaradiyar and incidentally confirms the very interesting observation
made by Domingo Paes that the Devaradiyar or temple dancers
were the only women to have direct access to the king.[77] In 1506,
when the Kaikkolar of Ambasamudram constructed a temple for
Bhutalavira Rama Pillaiyar, they were given the hereditary right of
receiving a garland from the temple.[78] Elsewhere, especially at
Tirupati, a weaver, in return for his donation, was given the
privilege of a share in the temple *prasadam*.[79] While these are ritual
privileges conferred in recognition of a donation or service, in certain
temples the weavers held a position of such importance that they
themselves determined the ritual ranking of others. Thus at the
Adipurisvara temple at Tiruvorriyur it was the Kaikkolar themselves who, along with the Nattar and the temple trustee,
re-examined the old dispute which began in 1265 about the order of
precedence and temple duties of the Ishtabattaliyar, Devaradiyar
and the Padiyilar.[80] In 1368, during the reign of Kampana
Udaiyar,[81] certain disputes about ritual precedence regarding these
three categories of women engaged in temple service were determined by the Kaikkolar and, at the beginning of the fifteenth
century,[82] in the reign of Harihararaya, the final decision over the
dispute was given.That the Kaikkolar should have arbitrated in an
issue of such importance is indicative of their ritual status in that
temple. At Kanchipuram the Kaikkolar, as in the Chola period, held
positions of ritual significance. Kopanna, the minister of Kampana
Udaiyar (fourteenth century), gave the Kaikkolar and Kaikkola
mudalis of the Kailasanatha temple in Kanchipuram the right to
mortgage and sell their honours—their precedence (*mudalmai*) in the
receipt of betelnut honour (*adaippam*), their service to the deity
(*tevar-atimai*) and their proper place in temple ranking (*ataivu*.)[83] The
Kaikkolar also held a position of equal importance at Tirupati. In
1337 the task of conducting the celebration of an important festival
(not specified) at the Alamelumangamma's temple at Tiruchchanur
was vested in the Kaikkolar and the Emperuman Adiyar (temple
dancers).[84] The Kaikkolar figure as the temple servants in
innumerable inscriptions from Tirupati and as such they were
entitled not only to remuneration but also a share in the *prasadam*.

The remuneration to the Kaikkolar in the Tirupati temple between 1400–1500 ranged from one *panam* per service to three *panams* per major service.[85] To this was added a share of the *prasadam*. Their role in the Tirupati temple was enhanced when, in the fourteenth–fifteenth centuries, the Tamil or Prabhandic school of Vaishnavism began to gravitate towards Tirupati while the Bhasya or orthodox school became concentrated at Varadaraja temple in Kanchipuram.[86]

It is noteworthy that the Saliyar, the dominant weaving community under the Cholas, hardly figure in the records of the Vijayanagar period. Whether it is with reference to the weaving profession or the acquisition of social and ritual honours it is only the Kaikkolar who find mention. This makes it quite clear that by the Vijayanagar period the Kaikkolar had replaced the Saliyar as the dominant weaving community in the Tamil Nadu region. In the Andhra–Karnataka regions, however, the Sale and the Devanga continue to find mention, though the references to Devanga are more numerous from 1500 onwards.

Weavers and the Idangai-Valangai

From the evidence of the various privileges conferred on weavers, especially the Kaikkolar, it becomes very clear that there was an upward movement among them, for the social privileges accorded to them, such as *sangu*, *tandu*, etc. are more numerous in the Vijayanagar period than in the Chola period. It is essential to note that this upward mobility was not an isolated phenomenon among just one narrow section of South Indian society but comprised several of the influential professional groups: the tanner, the oilmen and, more especially, the Kammalar or Pancalar (the groups of five smiths). these groups aspired for social and ritual recognition and this reflected in their large-scale participation in the Vira-Saiva or Lingayat movement and in the Tengalai-Vaishnavite movement. It is also reflected in an equal degree in the right-hand left-hand ferment in society, in their acts of co-operation as well as in their conflicts and schisms.

During the period of the Vijayanagar empire further dimensions were added to the *idangai-valangai* classification. Sociologists have tended to describe the categorization as a root paradigm which had varied application at different points of time in different regions. It is quite clear that in the Vijayanagar period the left-hand right-hand divisions had nothing to do with the army since the Muslim invasions and the rise of the Sangama dynasty had resulted in the disbanding of the Chola army. In the fourteenth century the categorization is said to be based on economic grounds. According to Abbe Dubois[87] the classification was based on the struggle for precedence between the followers of the old established handicrafts and innovators who came from outside. Thus it is held that in the Kanchipuram area the Saliyar, the predominant weaving community under the Cholas, were classified as *valangai* while the Kaikkolar, whose professional importance arose only during the Vijayanagar period, are classified as *idangai*. But this explanation is not feasible because even as soldiers in the Chola regiment the Kaikkolar were still classified as *idangai*. Another explanation is that the division of society into *idangai* and *valangai* represented the struggle between landed, stable, agricultural groups on the one hand and the rapidly increasing, mobile urban and artisan groups on the other.[88] But even if the Vellalar are considered as *valangai* (although most often they do not figure in these categories at all) other agricultural castes like the Pallis were included in the *idangai* category. Nor would it be true to say that all the artisan classes belonged to the *idangai* as the Padmasale (weavers), Rangare (dyers) and Kumbhara (Potters) figure as *valangai* in the Karnataka region. That there was no logical basis for the division of castes into *idangai* and *valangai* is proved by the fact that while the men of the Chakkiliyan and Palli castes belonged to the left-hand, the women of their caste were classified as right-hand.

The most plausible explanation is that the *idangai-valangai* schisms during the Vijayanagar period were due to the desire for higher status among the lower castes (comprising all the Sudra castes) and the attempts by the higher category of non-Brahmins (sometimes referred to as the Sat-Sudras) to preserve their status. This had been achieved through the process of Sanskritization, by assiduously keeping others out. A certain social mobility is always present in any society but there is no doubt that the upward movement of professional castes, the clamour for privileges among them and the resultant conflicts were much more intense and violent during the Vijayanagar period than during the Chola period. But, following the analogy implicit in the terms, the left-hand right-hand constitutes a vertical division of the human body, just as the caste system is supposed to symbolize a horizontal division of the human body; since what is divided is a single and complete human body, the metaphor expresses conflicts as well as underlying unity.[89] Thus the issue of the *idangai-valangai* castes has to be studied from different facets. The position of the weavers within the major *idangai-valangai* contradiction[90] has to be studied in terms of, first, the elements of co-operation and conflict within the *idangai* and the *valangai* categories separately; second, the elements of conflict between certain elements of the *idangai* and *valangai* categories; and third, instances of co-operation among the *idangai* and *valangai* categories in opposition to other elements like the landlords or the tax officials. The last aspect of course would make the *valangai–idangai* categories themselves part of a broader contradiction within society.

To take up the first proposition, i.e. the position of the Kaikkola weavers[91] as a part of the large communal organization of the *idangai* castes, the weavers were bound not only by the rules of their own caste and craft organization but by the broader code of the *idangai* category. Thus in 1399 the *idangai* community of Tiruppukkuli (Chingleput) made a *sarvamanya* gift of the *idangai vari* to maintain a lamp in the temple and in their record the Kaikkolar are specifically stated to be *idangai*.[92] A record from Chandragiri (Chittoor district), states that the *idangai* community of the region met in the *Idangainayaka mantapa* and made a *sarvamanya* gift of a village to their deity.[93] Similarly in 1434 the village of Tirumangalam in Sangattukkottam was given as *sarvamanya* to meet the expense incurred for the blowing of trumpets by the *Idangaiyar* on the occasion of the Tiruppuram festival in the shrine of the goddess Kamakshiamman in Kanchipuram.[94] In 1457, during the reign of Mallikarjuna, certain dues like *idangai vari* and *jati kanikkai* collected from the residents of Tirupparambur and its hamlets by the *idangai* Nattavar and Vanniyar were assigned as *sarvamanya* for lighting a lamp to the goddess Kamakshiamman in the temple mentioned above.[95] But another record, also of the period of Mallikarjuna, gives a different idea regarding the tax *idangai vari*. This records the remission of the *idangai* taxes on a new settlement of the Kaikkolar at Kunnathur (Chingleput) by Mahamandalesvara Saluva Narasimha and the communication of this order to the Kaikkolar through the officers of the king.[96]

Inspite of these instances of co-operation among the left-hand castes there are examples of conflict between two or more of the elements constituting the *idangai* category. The origin of the conflict was always over privileges. In 1503, during the reign of Saluva Narasimha, Ambikamakkilavan Aramvalartta Nayanar (of Kanchipuram), agent of Narasa Nayaka, bestowed on the weavers of Tribhuvanamadeviparru, Naduvukaraiparru and Nenmaliparru (Tiruvandarkoyil, Pondicherry State), certain privileges like the use of *sangu* and *tandu* on all good and bad occasions 'as the weavers of the country situated on the bank of the Pennai river (Tondaimandalam) were privileged to have.' The record significantly adds that those who objected to this right should undergo the punishment fixed for it as per the records at Seliyanganallur.[97] More explicit evidence of the conflict over privileges comes from Vriddachalam (South Arcot) during the reign of Sriranga (1572–85).[98] The record registers an agreement entered into by the Vasal-*mudali* of Kongarayar, Nayanar Kachchirayar and the Nattavar of Idaiyaru, denying the privilege of using *pavadai, parivattam,* etc. to the artisans (*kammalar*) i.e. the smiths, which was enjoyed by the Kaikkolar of Padaividu, Senji and Tiruvannamalai.

The conflict over privileges at another level was between the *idangai* and *valangai* castes. Conflicts usually arose over issues such as the ritual ranking in temples, the allocation of symbols and honours, etc. To quote Abbe Dubois

Perhaps the sole cause of the conflict is the right to wear slippers or to ride through the streets in a palanquin (*tandu*) or on horse-back during marriage festivals. Sometimes, it is the privilege of being escorted on certain occasions by armed retainers, sometimes that of having a trumpet sounded in front of the procession, or being accompanied by native musicians at public ceremonies. Perhaps, it is simply the particular kind of musical instrument suitable to such occasions that is in dispute, or it may be the right of carrying flags of certain colours or of certain devices during these ceremonies.[99]

During the reign of Vijaya Bhupati Raya at Tiruvannamalai, an order stated that all distinctions between the *idangai* and *valangai* were to be obliterated and that in future the Kaikkolar of the *idangai* were to enjoy all the privileges such as *sangu, tandu, aanai* (right to ride an elephant) *chamaram* (the fans), etc. enjoyed by the *valangai* in the region.[100] One *valangai–idangai* conflict in South Arcot during the reign of Ariyana Udaiyar lasted over four years, though its origin is shrouded in mystery.[101] At Malayampattu in North Arcot one such conflict led to loss of lives on both sides.[102] In a rare instance at Tiruppukkuli in Chingleput in 1399, the *idangai* community made a collective gift to the deity with a special stipulation by the Kaikkolar that the Sanketi Samayakkarar may not interfere. This is one of the few instances where opposition was directed against the Brahmins.[103] More often the *idangai–valangai* disputes over privileges took place between professional castes among the Sudras with a somewhat similar status in society. A significant case in point are two records pertaining to the periods of Achyutaraya (dated 1549) and Sadasiva Raya (who ruled between 1542–76, but the record is not dated) from Tiruvamattur, South Arcot. The first record states that the Ilaivanigar, i.e. the betel-leaf merchants (they must have belonged to the *valangai* like all the merchant communities) had erased an inscription on the wall of the Tirukkamisvara temple relating to certain social honours and privileges enjoyed by the Kaikkolar. As a protest the Kaikkolar and the Devanga left the village. The matter was enquired into and the issue decided in favour of the Kaikkolar, so that a fresh copy of the inscription was made, based on the copper plate kept in Kanchipuram.[104] The follow-up record pertaining to the period of Sadasiva Raya says that in the time of Surappa Nayaka the Ilaivanigar agreed to accord the same privileges and rights to the Kaikkolar which they had enjoyed earlier before the inscription granting them the privileges was effaced by a group of the Ilaivanigar. The order was now re-engraved on the temple walls.[105] The record is also significant on several grounds. It shows that the weaver castes acted in solidarity in certain altercations over privileges and, probably, the spirit of co-operation between the Kaikkolar and the Devangas was also enhanced by the fact that they both belonged to the *idangai* community. Secondly the Kanchipuram copper plate preserved at Kanchipuram is stated to be the ultimate authority for the bestowal of privileges on the Kaikkolar. It substantiates the point that the headquarters of the Kaikkola community was at Kanchipuram. The *valangai–idangai* conflicts continued right into the seventeenth–eighteenth centuries and was in fact exploited by the Dutch and the British to gain control over the textile industry and trade.

As stated earlier, the *idangai–valangai* is a vertical division of the human body, just as the caste system is supposed to be a horizontal division, and since what is divided is a single and complete human body the metaphor expresses conflict as well as underlying unity. Throughout the Vijayanagar period one comes across various examples of co-operation among the *idangai* and *valangai*, especially against oppressive taxation. A record from Jambai, South Arcot, after referring to ninety-eight *valangai* and ninety-eight *idangai* groups states that the weavers made a voluntary contribution for the construction of a *matam* (guild meeting place) for their community.[106] In another record the ninety-eight sects each of the *valangai* and *idangai* are said to have met at Korkai (Mayavaram, Tanjavur district) during the reign of Devaraya II (1427) and declared, 'they did not tax us according to the yield of the crop but levied the taxes. . . unjustly. . . . We were about to run away. Then we realized that because we of the whole country (*mandalam*) were not united in a body, we are unjustly dealt with. Hereafter we shall but pay what is just.' They go on to fix the rates of taxes on different sections.[107] Two records dated 1429 from Elavanasur[108] and Vriddachalam (South Arcot district)[109] give in detail the agreement among the *idangai* and *valangai* to resist unjust taxation and to socially ostracize those who violated this agreement. This is followed by a detailed list of taxes to be paid by the various professional castes.

Weavers and Heterodox Movements

The clamour for privileges, the claiming of mythological origins and the *idangai–valangai* schisms and conflicts represent only particular dimensions of a complex social situation in which an attempt at upward mobility and Sanskritization was taking place, not only among the weaver castes but also among other leading professional castes like the Kammalar or the Pancalar (the smiths) the Teliki (oil-pressers) and others. The cause for this is to be found in the renewed vigour of the urbanization process,[110] the growth in exports and the state patronage to crafts, as evidenced by the *Amuktamalyada*.[111] Thus a situation had developed where certain professional castes 'exerted a profound influence upon medieval society, enjoying a rank and social power which was far greater than that accorded to them by the legal and social texts of the period.'[112] These castes sought ritual recognition not only by exalting their own caste and acquiring social privileges but by large-scale participation in the Lingayat or Vir-Saivaite and the Tengalai-Vaishnavite movements, and in fact certain southern school Brahmins (Tengalai Srivaishnavas) can be identified as former Sudras from their manners and customs.[113]

The largely non-*dvija* or non-Brahmin composition of Tengalai

Vaishnavism can be seen by the number of sectarian leaders in it who belonged to the Sudra caste. The movement which began in the post-Ramanuja period had Srirangam and Tirupati as its nuclei in the fourteenth-fifteenth centuries while the Bhasya or the orthodox Sanskrit school of Vaishnavism shifted its centre from Tirupati to the Varadaraja Perumal temple at Kanchipuram. The first Jiyar at Srirangam, Kuranarayana, and later Pillai Locacarya and Alagiya Manavala, strengthened the Tengalai movement, i.e. the Prabhandic or Tamil school of Vaishnavism, by offering discipleships to the Sudra servants of the temple. There were several non-Brahmin disciples of Ramanuja like Pillai Uranga villi Dasar, who was a *malla* by caste (professional wrestlers), or Pattina Perumal. Ramanuja Dasar, another disciple, was a sculptor belonging to the Kammalar caste, while Nambi Eru Tiruvadaiya Dasar was a *shanar* (toddy tapper).[114] It is even believed that Kandadai Ramanuja Dasar, the non-*dvija* (Sudra) Vaishnavite saint of the fifteenth century who held a position of great importance and patronage at Srirangam and Tirupati, was a brother of Saluva Narasimha. Though this relationship may or may not be true, it is a fact that Saluva Narasimha extended greatest patronage to these two temples.[115]

The Kaikkola weavers held a position of considerable importance at Srirangam. The Koyil Kanakkan was a Vellalar while the ritual of offering a coconut to the deity was done by the Kaikkolar. Sudra functionaries called Sattada Mudalis (holy men who do not wear the sacred thread) performed important ritual functions at both Srirangam and Tirupati.[116] The Kaikkola are mentioned as important functionaries of the Tirupati temple along with the Kammalar or Pancalar in a record dated 1544.[117] The Kaikkola weavers were in charge of the *matangi* and *perantalu vesham*. In the *matangi vesham* a Kaikkola worked himself into a state of divine intoxication and then a metal wire was passed through the middle of his tongue without causing any harm.[118] In the *perantalu vesham* a Kaikkola dressed up as a woman and rode around the town on a horse, distributing the *prasadam*, *kumkum*, saffron-paste and flowers. In view of the fact that in Tirupati, during the Vijayanagar period, the emphasis seems to have shifted from mere grants or burning of perpetual lamps to food offerings, the distribution of *prasadam* had a crucial significance, and it is noteworthy that this important task was given to the Kaikkola caste. Tengalai Vaishnavism also had a large following among the Padmasale caste of weavers of the

Andhra–Karnataka region. Their guru was the Tatacharyar.[119] The Saurashtrar or Pattunulkaran weavers who virually replaced the Kaikkolar as the dominant weaver community of Tamil Nadu in the seventeenth century were predominantly Vaishnavites and, right into the nineteenth century, were involved in litigation in law courts claiming *dvija* status. The large-scale incorporation of Sudra professionals in the Vaishnavite movement can be seen by the creation of *ramanujakutam* (free feeding house)[120] by Saluva Narasimha. This was mainly managed by the Sudra disciples of Ramanuja. Although Kanchipuram was gradually becoming a stronghold of Vadagalai (orthodox) Vaishnavism, even here non-*dvijas* continued to hold a position of importance in certain temples. They also continued to play an important part on the occasion of *Sura Samhara*.

Professional castes like the Palli and the Kammalar performed equally significant ritual roles. The Palli caste has an important role to play in the annual function of the Parthasarathi temple in Triplicane. At Sriperumbudur in Chingleput, they enjoy the privilege of accompanying the idol during procession on the ground that they once sheltered the idol from a Muslim raid. They are also allowed to draw the car of the idol at Kanchipuram, Kumbakonam and Srivilliputtur in Ramanathapuram. The Kammalar or smiths enjoyed many such privileges. A sixteenth-century inscription from Udayagiri states that one Kontayyadeva Maharaja, a chief of Udayagiri, performed the *ratha* or car festival of the idol Raghunatha Nayakalu and prescribed the ceremonies to be followed. According to this, dancing girls were to accompany the deity in the *ratha* while a member of the Panchanamuvaru (smiths) wearing a head gear and a cloth loosely wrapped around the waist went in front of the car with a chisel, a nail and a sickle in his hands.[121]

The rising social importance of Sudra professionals and their quest for ritual recognition is also reflected in the proliferation of *amman* temples between 1300 and 1750. In this context the temple statistics worked out by Stein become very interesting. Stein cites the section on Sudras in the Baramahal records, which make it clear that the religious activity of the Sudra castes, both agricultural and artisan, pertained to clan and place tutelaries, mainly goddesses called *amman*. He uses the 1861 census and other sources of information to arrive at the conclusion that the priests in these *amman* shrines were mostly Sudra called *Pandarams*, recruited from the Vellala and Palli castes.[122] At Kanchipuram, the *ratha* (car) festival in honour of Kamakshiamman was arranged by the Kaikkolar. Thurston, giving a descriptive account of the festival, says that some of the car pullers had two cords drawn through their flesh, about twelve inches apart.[123]

In conclusion, certain very significant points emerge from the mass of evidence presented. Society during the period of the Vijayanagar empire was in a state of flux. This was because of the renewal of urbanization and temple activity under the patronage of the Vijayanagar kings, and on account of the overall prosperity of the empire. As a result there was an upward movement among most of the Sudra professional groups such as the smiths, the weavers and the oil-pressers. But the economic power and social privileges gained by the weavers and other leading professionals was hardly in accord with the low place allotted to them in the ritual hierarchy. In medieval South India the battle against caste took the form not of caste negation but of caste exaltation. Like the Rajputs in the north who claimed to be Suryavamshis and Chandravamshis, the Kaikkola weavers ascribed their origin to Virabahu, the mythological lieutenant of Lord Kartikeya. Similarly the Devanga weavers of the Andhra–Karnataka region claimed descent from Manu and Narada. They also laid claim to the Brahmanical status and wore the holy thread. Thus what was happening among the weaver communities and other professionals like the Kammalar in medieval South India was to an extent the reverse of the Bhakti movement in the North. The leaders of the Bhakti movement in the North during the thirteenth–fifteenth centuries, like Kabir (a weaver), Dadu (a cotton carder), Namdev (a calico painter), Raidas (a barber) and Nanak (a petty grocer), all belonged to the artisan community. They spearheaded the movement for equality with the upper castes not by seeking mythological origins or claiming ritual privileges but by a total negation of caste.[124] Ramanand, the teacher of Kabir, said 'Let no man ask a man's caste or with whom he eats. If he shows love to Hari, he is Hari's son'. Kabir himself rejected caste in several of his devotional verses—'it is needless to ask of a saint, the caste to which he belongs. For, the priest, the warrior, the tradesmen, all the thirty-six castes alike, are on a search for God. The barber has sought God, the washerman and the carpenter. Even Raidas was a seeker after God'.[125] In an even more thought-provoking verse Kabir, after proclaiming his weaving profession, says, 'of the earth and the sky the Lord hath made a loom. And the sun and the moon, the warp and the woof. . .And I, the weaver realized the Lord within my own home. Sayeth Kabir, when the loom breaks; then the thread merges in the thread of the world. They who wear *dhoties* of $3^1/_2$ yards and 3 fold sacred cords, and display rosaries on their necks. . .they are the cheats of Banaras, not the saints of the world.'[126] The verses of Nanak and Dadu express similar sentiments. Thus the process of caste exaltation and the assumption of a brahmanical or supra-brahmanical status is absent in the north. Unlike the Lingayats or the Tengalai Vaishnavites, most of the leaders of the Bhakti movement in the north reject the entire idea of caste. But in the south, while Basava the Vira-Saivite saint and Ramanuja the Vaishnavite leader expressed ideas of caste negation, their followers adopted techniques of caste exaltation. The Lingayats claimed superiority over Brahmins and, to emphasize the point, adopted peculiar practices like the burial of their dead in a sitting posture, while the Tengalai Vaishnavites contended with the Vadagalai for caste superiority and ritual recognition.

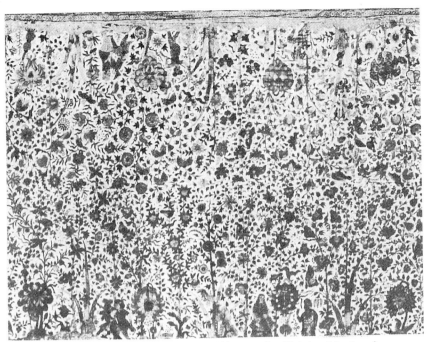

Bijapur wall-hanging dated around 1640—a medley Christian, Islamic and Hindu figures

Vishnu and Lakshmi at the centrepiece with scenes from the *Bhagavatam* in surrounding panels

An Islamic Kanat of the seventeenth century from Golconda

The Pandavas at the end of their exile, offering worship to Lord Narayana. A scene from the *Mahabharata*

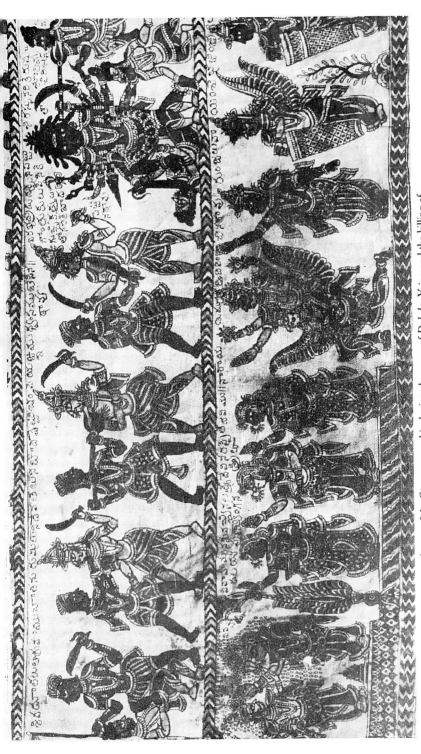

A part of the *Sivapurana*, this depicts the scene of *Daksha Yajna* and the killing of Daksha by the 'Shivadhoota' or Shiva's army

Bijapur wall-hanging dated around 1640—a medley of Christian, Islamic and Hindu figures

CHAPTER V

Textile Production, Organization and Trade

(Seventeenth Century)

The seventeenth century was a period of fluctuating fortunes for the weavers. The European companies figured largely on the commercial scene and their impact was especially felt on the handlooms, which was one of the principal items of export from South India. At the beginning of the century only the Portuguese had a sphere of influence in South India, but by the second decade of the century both the Dutch and the English had entered the commercial fray and Portuguese power had began to wane. While the Dutch dominated the first half of the century, the English had definitely emerged as the main commercial power in the south by the end of it.

The native political scene was no longer dominated by the Vijayanagar kingdom or the Bahmani sultanate and its successor states. The authority of the once-powerful Vijayanagar kingdom was now confined to Vellore and its vicinity, and it was the powerful Nayakas of Madurai, Tanjavur and Ikkeri who determined and shaped policies. The successor states of the Bahmani sultanate were also beset by internal factionalism and internecine warfare, and they declined and collapsed during the course of the seventeenth century.

The fate of the handloom industry in the seventeenth century has necessarily to be studied against the background of the nature and consequences of the interaction between the weavers, the merchants, the East India companies and the native powers.

Portugal had been the first European nation to get a foothold into India by displacing the Arabs. They held Goa, Diu and Cochin on the Malabar coast, and Nagapatnam and San Thome on the Coromandel coast. The commercial interest of the Portuguese was essentially concerned with the export of pepper and spices from Cochin in the Malabar coast and the Malay Archipelago, and Coromandel textiles were used as the principal article of barter in the spice trade. However in 1580 when Portugal passed into the

hands of Spain, all cordial relations with the Dutch ceased. The
Dutch utilized the situation created by the defeat of the armada to fit
out expeditions of their own. In 1605 the Dutch pinnace 'Delft'
anchored at Masulipatnam and established a factory there under
the leadership of Pieter Yassacx Eyloff. Settlements were also
established at Nizamapatnam, Tegnapatnam or Devanamapattinam
(Fort St. David) and Pulicat (Fort Geldria). By 1600 the English
East India had been established. In 1611 the 'Globe' brought the
first English traders to Nizamapatnam and Masulipatnam and in
1619 these entered into a partnership with the Dutch at Pulicat. By
the 1620's the alliance between the English and the Dutch had
broken down due to mutual suspicion. From Pulicat the English
moved on to Armagaon (1626) and Madras (1640). By the 1620s the
Danes had also secured trading rights from the Nayak of Tanjavur
and had established settlements at Tranquebar or Tarangampadi.
Thus the struggle for a commercial empire in South India in the
seventeenth century was mainly among these powers, the French
having entered the scene rather late, only in the eighteenth century.

Textile Centres and the Location of Weavers

Availability of raw material and transport were still the primary
considerations in the establishment of textile centres and this meant
the continuation of traditional centres. Clusters of weaving villages
gradually emerged as important textile towns in the course of the
fifteenth–sixteenth centuries, i.e. the pre-company period, and the
earliest factories were in fact established here. Undoubtedly, new
weaving villages emerged into prominence depending on the
demand generated by the companies for a particular variety of cloth,
but by and large the companies established their factories within the
nucleus of the textile centre surrounded by weaving villages. The
best example of this sort of development is provided in the account
of Daniel Havert (1671–85).[1] He says that at Warangal (then a
town) and twelve villages thereabouts which lay seventy-two miles
north-west from Masulipatnam (the site of the Dutch factory), the
weavers produced bettilles, arral (?), common sarongs and also finer
sorts of cloth. At Ellur and eight villages thereabouts, about twelve
miles from Masulipatnam, they wove fine salempores, percalles, and
unbleached bettilles. At Mustabad and ten villages thereabouts
which lay at a distance of roughly twenty miles from Masulipatnam

were woven blue tapechiras boolongs, negro cloth (the reference is to the coarse salempores) madapollams (this is itself the name of a weaving centre) and every kind of blue cloth. The other nuclei of textile production with their clusters of weaving villages were— Linga with ten weaving villages; Mangalagiri with fourteen weaving villages; Maliporo with twenty-two weaving villages; Ventapollam with twenty-four weaving villages, etc. As is evident from Havert's description, every traditional textile centre which was also a flourishing commercial town of the medieval period was ultimately taken over commercially and linked to the factory town established by the Dutch, i.e. Masulipatnam which was nearly equidistant from these textile centres.

Havert gives a similar breakdown, though not quite so detailed, of the textile centres and their surrounding cluster of weaving villages for South Coromandel.[2] In the Tanjavur area, Nagapattinam, Tranquebar (subsequently a Danish settlement) Trimelevas (Tirumullaivasal), are referred to. Havert also comments upon the significance of Porto Novo as a harbour and says that in the time of the Moors it was called Muhammad Bandar. Sadras, Kanchipuram, Madurantakam and other places are dealt with in connection with the establishment of the Dutch factory at Pulicat.

The policy adopted by the companies in the location of their factories is indicated by the letter in the *Consultations* of Fort St. George in 1677 in which the Agent and Council take credit for the fact that their factory at Madapollam was 'so well seated' since it 'lyes [*sic*] among the weavers'.[3]

Localization based on textile specialization, however, constituted a limited sphere of operation. The locality could meet the needs of a limited internal market through the medium of local fairs. Streynsham Master has commented on the weekly fair held at Ventapollam.[4] It is quite clear that this was much more than a village fair, since textiles from the surrounding weaving villages were brought here and sold. But this system was insufficient from the point of view of long-distance trade in textiles. Hence the establishment of textile centres especially for export varieties had to be determined by the distance between the weaving centres and the points of shipment as well as the actual cost of shipping from the Coromandel coast to the Malay Archipelago, England and other European countries. This seems evident from the fact that all the European factories were established on the coast. Even though

Madurai was an ancient weaving centre, no attempt was made to establish a factory there. While some of the Company settlements like Masulipatnam or San Thome were also, conveniently, tradition-al weaving regions, places like Vishakapatnam (Waltair) were chosen purely from the point of view of shipment and cotton from the Godavari region, and Tegnapatnam (Fort St. David) was 'imported' into Vishakapatnam to meet the requirements of the weavers.[5]

In the seventeenth century there was a partial shift in the dwelling place of the weavers. The majority of them were probably no longer settled in the temple premises because very few inscriptions of this period locate them within the temple square. Among these a record from Perungulam in Srivaikuntam[6] (Tirunelveli), which is dated 'kali 70' and is in seventeenth-century characters, is inscribed on the south wall of the Meyakkutta Perumal temple. It ascribes the construction of the shrine to Valudinayakapperumal Ulagamulu-dum Nikkacheydan, a Kaikkola tenant of the temple of Tiruvaludis-varam who was also the temple treasurer. Grant of land and ritual honours to Kaikkolar are again mentioned in two records, one dated 1632[7] and the other also of the seventeenth century,[8] inscribed on temple walls at Pallikondai in Vellore and Tevaiyur in Perambalur (Tiruchirapalli). A joint registration of a gift to the deity Palesvaras-vamin by the Kaikkolar comes from Tiruppulisvara temple in Ponneri, Chingleput.[9] The record is dated 1679. It does definitely indicate that the Kaikkola weavers were settled either on the temple premises or in the temple square. But unlike the earlier period quite a few of the records pertaining to weavers in the sixteenth–seventeenth centuries have been located in public places in the village rather than in the temples. An inscription pertaining to the period of Ariyappa Gaundar which relates to the Kaikkola weavers is inscribed on a stone located in the middle of the *kudiyana* (literally 'farmers') street in the village of Vilichai Kulattur in Chingleput. A charter given to the weavers of Kaliyapettai in Kanchipuram by Angalgu Krishnappangaru, the agent of Kasturi Rangappa (1620–30), is inscribed on a slab fixed in the middle of the village.[10]

One feature which seems to have struck European travellers was the mobility of the Coromandel weavers. The only prerequisite for the weaver to settle down in a place seems to have been the availability of shady trees. However, mobility was not an enduring characteristic of the South Indian weavers since it is obvious from the evidence of the earlier centuries that they moved only in times of acute distress or as a mark of protest against enhanced taxation. The mobility of the weaver in the seventeenth century would seem to indicate unsettled conditions. The tendency towards migration could be the result of invasions or political oppression. Thus in the *Consultations* of 28 September 1675 it is stated that Madanna's forces had captured the English Company's merchants and the weavers had fled to Gingi.[11] Famine and scarcity of food also led to the migration of weavers.[12] The European companies also did their best to attract weavers to their settlements. The idea behind this step was to make the procurement of cloth easy and minimize their dependence on intermediaries. The English company wrote in its general letter to Fort St. George, dated 15 December 1676: 'We find the Dutch have their dyers and painters (i.e. the weavers of chintz) on the coast and we know no reason why we may not have our business as well as they...'[13] They were offered inducements like paddy at cheap rates, lowering of customs and taxes, higher wages, etc. That this policy was fairly successful is proved by the records which refer to the migration of weavers and washers to the Portuguese, English and Dutch settlements.[14] In a letter from the English factors at Pulicat to the Company in 1622 they wrote that 'many weavers and painters have voluntarily offered to follow the English wherever they go.'[15] In 1634, when the English began negotiating with the Golconda rulers for a settlement at Mallavol (near Masulipatnam), weavers and other people immediately began to settle there and the population doubled, 'so fast do the poor people flock hither from Moorish tyranny.'[16] Similarly the Dutch factors in their letter of 1615 also claimed that their presence at Narsapur had attracted weavers to their neighbourhood. The letter goes on to say that like the weavers and painters, blacksmiths, carpenters, goldsmiths, tailors and other craftsmen were also attracted to Narsapur.[17] The significance of the letter lies in the fact that it offers a possible explanation for the reduced number of inscriptions relating to weavers and other craftsmen in the temples by pointing out that at least some artisans migrated to the European settlements. The available evidence indicates therefore that in the seventeenth century there was a certain shift in the dwelling places of those weavers who provided for the export market, from the temple premises to company settlements on the coast.

Textile Varieties

The types of textiles which were in demand in the indigenous market do not seem to have changed much from the earlier period. Ordinary cotton cloth for local consumption was woven in the locality itself. The native aristocracy, besides the use of silken and cotton *patolas* and the finer varities of muslin, was also attracted by certain varieties of English cloth like broadcloth, scarletts and aroras. For a time the Company even brought vast quantities of these cloths in the hope of vending them in exchange for Indian calico.[18] Broadcloth was given in part payment for fine percalles, moorees and ginghams. But this market was extremely limited[19] and the English ended up merely giving them as presents or *peshkashes* to win the goodwill of merchants and local officials.[20]

The textile varieties meant for the export market had however a much greater significance in view of the particularity of the various markets where Indian textiles were sold. The painted calicoes of Coromandel, the tape-chindes, the sarassas and sallaloes, i.e. different types of coarse muslin and chintz, were the only cloths in demand in the Malay Archipelago, and the particularism of the eastern markets was a great headache to the companies. To quote Peter Floris: 'But a great oversight hath been committed in the bespeaking of the pattas, dragons, sallalos, etc. for they have all of them, a little narrower edge and the upright Malay cloth must be without it. ... I had never believed it, that so small a fault could cause so great an abatement in price.[21] The tapechindes and coarse blue salempores were the varieties in demand in West Africa and spelt the badge of slavery for the blacks. In fact they came to be referred to as slave cloth.[22] It seems possible to deduce that because of the nature of demand in these markets, some of the weaving villages producing varieties such as Kanakagiri, Nellai, Anantagiri, Kambamet, Siyapalli, Palliwanchi[23] and others in the vicinity of Naglewanch came within the purview of the Dutch company.

The same vegetable dyes continued to be used for colouring the cloth. Indigo was the most commonly used dye. The price of cloth and the earning of the weaver were considerably influenced by the price not merely of yarn but also of indigo. The best indigo came from Surat, but on the Coromandel coast Naglewanch is supposed to have produced good indigo. Some indigo was produced at Dabhol, and Wengurla in Bijapur is referred to as a dyers' village in the Dutch records.[24] In 1614 the Masulipatnam indigo cost 12 pence per pound while the Surat indigo cost 13½ pence.[25] While the Sarkhej indigo usually ranged between 15 rupees to 20 rupees, Biyana indigo was much more costly.[26] Anthony Schorrer gives the price of Masulipatnam indigo as 2.43 pagodas, i.e. a little under 10 rupees. The indigo available in South Coromandel was much inferior. Besides indigo the Company records also refer to *kusumba*, *manjishta* and *sapan* or brazil wood. However, some attempt seems to have been made to use unacceptable colours made of spurious dyes such as green and orange, and the companies found themselves compelled to return all such cloth.[27]

The designs or motifs produced on cloth began to undergo some change as a result first of the Turkish and later the European influence. By and large the inspiration for the themes depicted on South Indian textiles during this period came from the mythology and religious symbols of Hinduism, the Deccani, essentially Bijapuri, school of painting, the Persian Safavid tradition of art as well as its modified version, the Mughal art, and with the coming of the European companies, Christian themes and European secular themes.

The themes most popular with the Hindu weavers were from the epics, *Mahabharata* and *Ramayana*. Other popular themes were Sivalila, the divine play of Siva, the Bhagavatam or the story of Krishna and the *Bhagavad Gita*, the depiction of Lord Krishna's counsel to Arjuna, etc. The finest depictions of these are in the kalamkari textiles. The kalamkaris were sometimes divided into compartments separated by decorated pillars. The most common motifs used were the tree of life, the betel leaf motif, the temple dome or *gopuram* and a sort of *chakra* that is a floral design encased within a circle. Floral designs and flowering shrubs were extensively used to fill blank spaces and for the borders. The monkey, the peacock and the deer were popular subjects while in the niches or alcoves shown on a painting one could find the figures of gods like Ganesha. One very interesting feature of the depiction of women in these paintings is that they are shown wearing the traditional sarees with decorated blouses. Paes, Nuniz, Methwold and other European observers have commented on the heavy jewellery worn by the women and this can be seen in the painted textiles, where they are shown wearing heavy bracelets, chains, etc. The men are shown in the traditional *dhoti* with *angavastra*. They are also shown wearing turbans similar to the one Paes and Nuniz describe the Vijayanagar kings and their officials as wearing.

Textile designs influenced by the Deccani, Mughal and Persian schools are quite different. Depiction of drinking scenes is not uncommon. These paintings are most remarkable for their flora and fauna. The depiction of male costumes in these correspond closely to those worn at the Mughal court, especially the girdles and the turbans with heavy plumes. The costumes of the women are essentially Deccani. One of the most beautiful aspects of Islamic art is the brilliant tints in flowers and fruit. Although the tree of life is a common motif, its depiction in the Muslim style by the weavers is quite different. A single tree with an extremely slim trunk would be shown bearing very heavy flowers and fruit of totally unrelated species. These would be interspersed with bamboos and single stem plants, the plants bearing one gigantic flower with fantastic forms and colour painted purely imaginatively. Varieties of birds are also shown. The hues achieved in these flora and fauna principally by means of chay gives them a brilliancy and glow that is unsurpassed. The chay root for getting a bright red was a great favourite with Indian weavers. The best chay was produced at Tambreve near Petapoli[28] and the king of Golconda is said to have had a monopoly over all red cloth. The use of beeswax as resist was a special technique used in South India. The wax-coated cloth was dipped in a solution of fermenting myrobalan, indigo, lime and soda, and an alum solution was applied to fix the colours.

Some of the originality and creativity of the weavers seems to have been lost gradually in the course of the seventeenth century when the European companies made them work 'to the perfection of the pattern,' based on company musters. If the ultimate product was not to their satisfaction the company would reduce payment to the weavers. Nevertheless the weavers and painters continued to exercise their imagination, although the effect was not always aesthetically pleasing. The European influence on art commingled with native themes and motifs, leading eventually to a fantastical hotch-potch of patterns. Among the Christian themes occurring in South Indian wall hangings is that of the mother and child being adored by such well known saints as Francis Xavier and Ignatius Loyola. Later such secular or everyday themes as a gentleman riding a horse or hunting with his dogs are to be found. However, very few of the themes of these fabrics were purely European. In some of the paintings the figures are depicted with wings, an influence of medieval Christian Europe. The influence of the Renaissance in Europe is also to be seen in the costumes of gentlemen, especially the frilled ruffs around the necks and their hats. These purely European characters are intermingled with natives in brightly coloured Deccani costumes and in between are the usual exotic flora and fauna typical of the Persian style. In a few of these paintings women are for the first time shown wearing full-length gowns in the European fashion.

The Indian penchant for mixing the European musters with native tastes seems to have resulted in serious problems for the European companies. The Europeans were averse to green trees on a red background dyed by chay or the copying of colours from nature, producing a garish effect. Accordingly they instructed their factors in India that 'those which you shall send we desire may be with more white ground and the flowers and branch to be in the middle of the quilt ... whereas now most part of your quilts come with sad red grounds which are not so well accepted here.' [29] Two outstanding examples of such admixture of designs are the two huge wall hangings from Bijapur dated around 1640, displayed in the Victoria and Albert Museum in London. The scenes are a remarkable medley of the Indian tree of life, tigers and gentlemen in European costumes with their dogs.[30] The degeneration of Indian textiles is shown in two nineteenth-century textiles which depict rows of bicycles alternating with the tree of life and the depiction of currency notes on an otherwise traditional design.[31]

Textile Technology

It is an undisputed fact that in the seventeenth and eighteenth centuries India was the major exporter of textiles to England and other European countries. It was only in the early nineteenth century that the industrial revolution in Britain altered India's position.

In spite of the fact that for more than five hundred years India had been an exporter of textiles, economic historians, taking their cue from contemporary political economists, have tended to attribute this merely to wage differentials[32] rather than to a competent technology. As the author of an anonymous tract written in the seventeenth century put it, 'as much labour may be had there for two pence as in England for a shilling.'[33] Palsaert, who came to India in the same period, made a similar observation.[34] But actual technological data, although very limited, indicates that in various aspects of the textile industry—preparation of the yarn and thread, dyeing and weaving—the indigenous technology was superior to that of Europe.

Indian thread, especially when spun by the spindle, was very strong and durable and was exported to England for the benefit of the linen industry.[35] In the context of Indian textile technology Irfan Habib's numerous scholarly articles on the subject seem to suggest that the really important changes either came in with the Turkish invasions or in the seventeenth century from the west. Habib's evidence suggests that the *kar-chob* or the square wooden frame initially used in embroidery came into use only around the seventeenth century, when it is referred to for the first time.[36] However, as stated earlier, the *sadisarakkudam* referred to in the Tirupati record[37] is very similar to the *kar-chob*. Habib has ascribed the draw loom to the seventeenth century as well.[38] He links this innovation to the vertical loom and says that while the draw loom had been invented in antiquity in China and the Middle East, in India the earliest instance of its use occurs only in the seventeenth century. In 1679 Streynsham Master observed at Ellur (Andhra) the manufacture of carpets on upright looms with coloured woollen weft-threads in accordance with patterns set on paper.[39] Habib accepts the view of Master that this was a recent innovation from Persia, and says that it was only as a result of Persian influence that the vertical loom, 'otherwise a stranger to India,' was employed in the weaving of carpets. But as has been conclusively proved earlier, the vertical loom was in fact the earliest and most primitive loom in existence.[40] Nor was the draw loom a late seventeenth-century invention since the Tirupati inscription, as already discussed, does suggest a draw loom in which the heddles were lifted by a mechanical process rather than by hand.

The tie-and-dye technique which produced the *bandhini* and *patola* sarees was known in India since the twelfth century. Indians also employed excellent dyeing techniques and their vegetable dyes produced such fast colours that they were exported to England.[41] However, with silk material the Indian dyers were unable to produce certain colours so that silk dyers and throwsters had to be brought in from England to instruct the Indian weavers. In 1681 two silk dyers were appointed at Fort St. George for dyeing in black and other colours.[42] Similar appointments were made at Qasimbazar in Bengal.[43] However these dyers were not of much service and the experiment had to be given up.[44]

It also appears that there was a marginal alteration of Indian looms due to the demands of the European market. There is a reference in English company records to *en masse* alteration of looms in Wooriar Pollam (Udaiyarpalayam in Tiruchirapalli district) to meet the demand of the Company for a specific variety of longcloth and salempores.[45] Similarly the Company caused three hundred looms 'to be altered to a better sort' at Fort St. David for the weaving of salempores.[46] Very often the number of warp threads (*punjams*) was increased or decreased to weave cloth suitable to the export market.[47] In the *Consultations* of 1672, Kasi Viranna, the chief merchant of the English East India Company, claimed that the *punjams* of the looms at Madras had been altered from four to ten for the weaving of longcloth, salempores, moorees and percalles.[48]

It can be concluded from the available evidence that a competent technology went hand in hand with low wages in contributing to the popularity of Indian textiles abroad. As the directors of the English East India Company wrote to their Agent and Council in Bengal: 'We have always found any new commodity dearer by almost half first than it is after your workmen are well practised in the making of it.'[49] It was the combination of technical excellence and low labour costs that led to the massive exports to Europe and the firm faith of contemporary thinkers that Indian calico was more valuable than English bullion.

The Internal Demand and Trade in Textiles

Descriptions of the attire of the common people are not usually found in Indian literary sources or travellers' accounts. While these were too much a part of the everyday scene to interest indigenous writers, foreigners' accounts were limited either to a description of the costumes of the aristocracy, as with Paes and Nuniz, or to an account of the bizarre. The growing Muslim influence on Indian costumes which generated a demand for more and better varieties of cloth was commented upon by Nuniz and Paes in the sixteenth century. This change in costume styles can be perceived in many of the sixteenth and seventeenth century paintings. From brief descriptions given in a few other accounts it seems likely that more cloth was also worn by some other sections of Indian society as a result of Muslim influence, both Persian and Turkish. Methwold[50] for instance describes the *devadasis* (courtesans) wearing a sari of either calico or silk, as well as what he calls 'waistcoats' covering the upper portion of the body, with sleeves upto the elbows. The description fits the blouse usually worn by Indian women. Methwold says that both men and women were 'civilly clothed'. The men are described as wearing a loose white calico cloth around their shoulders (the traditional *angocha* or *angavastra*) and then cloth from the middle downwards, the description fitting the four-yard *dhoti*. He says that, alternately, men also wore a coat attached to a cloth reaching down to their ankles (i.e. the doublet and skirt), which again shows the Muslim influence. It can however be assumed that no great change could have taken place in the dress of the poor, whose costumes obviously continued to be extremely scanty. Methwold's description does however suggest that domestic consumption of cloth must have gone up, although this would apply predominantly to the North Coromandel where the Muslim influence was very strong.

Coarse cloth for local consumption was produced virtually everywhere and the cloth was sold at weekly fairs called *santa*, the North Indian equivalent being the *haats*. Streynsham Master, the Governer of Fort St. George in the 1680's, refers to the sale of textiles at the local fair held every Wednesday at Ventapollam in Krishna district. Master says that people came from Masulipatnam and elsewhere to the fair. One can presume that the weaving villages referred to by Master, like Bhimavaram and Vipparla,[51] and the numerous weaving villages mentioned by Havert, held similar fairs. Buchanan, writing in the beginning of the nineteenth century, refers to these weekly fairs. He says that at Waliuru in Mysore cloth was woven for the local market as well as for export. While the cloth meant for local consumption was sold at these fairs the export variety cloth was usually commissioned by merchants.[52] Buchanan says that at Gubi, a place close to Kolar, coarse cloth called *chire*, the local word for sari, was woven and about a hundred pieces were sold at each weekly fair.[53] So far as ordinary cloth was concerned, therefore, localities were self-sufficient, but there is no doubt that besides the quantity sold in local fairs a fair amount of inter-regional trade in textiles did exist.

Compared to the plethora of records which deal with the foreign, especially Company, trade in textiles, the sources for internal trade are very limited. With the decline of Vijayanagar, royal patronage of temples and the practice of inscribing the activities of the various social groups on temple walls also declined. Thus very few epigraphic records relating to internal trade are available for the seventeenth century.

Some reference to the internal cloth trade is found in the *Attavanavyavaharatantram*,[54] a late-seventeenth or early-eighteenth century administrative manual in the Telugu language which provides a detailed schedule of revenue rates. It says that among other things woollen goods (produced in Chittaldroog and other places in the Mysore region), silk, cloths, trousers and indigo were brought by sea to Balaghat. From the north (perhaps Bijapur) to Balaghat were brought cotton and shawls. Chittaldroog and Jarimela-sima exported woollen blankets. The price of a blanket is given as between one and ten *varahas*. Cotton produced in Adoni (Andhra) was sold in Kolar (Mysore). Silk and cotton goods and thread made in Dharmavaram, Tadapatri, Adoni, Gooty and Bellary were sold in Srirangapatnam and other places in Karnataka at a profit of twenty-five per cent. The tract also makes the interesting statement that while no tax was levied on cloth or thread sold in the place of manufacture, presumably at the weekly fair, duty or *sunkam* had to be paid if the cloth was going to be taken out, and the weavers usually sold the cloth to merchants who paid the duty on it.

Travellers' accounts also make some reference to the internal trade in textiles. Peter Mundy, for instance, says that Burhanpur exported chintz and red *salu* (sallalo), a variety of coarse muslin, to Bengal.[55] Buchanan's account, although it belongs to a later period, also gives a fairly comprehensive idea of the internal trade in textiles. He says that Hyder Ali and Tipu Sultan had forbidden trade with the lower Carnatic (Madras) and other areas, but it was still considered worthwhile to smuggle cloth out of Waliuru and other places because of its cheapness. Thus the merchants of Walajapet (North Arcot) sold spices and other commodities in the Mysore region and Mysore textiles in the Madras region. But Waliuru itself produced insufficient cotton and it was imported from Hubli, Karwar or 'northward' (this could be the East Godavari region) and brought via Hospet. Buchanan refers in great detail to the silk and cotton cloths woven at Bangalore and to their export to the west coast, to Burhanpur and other places in the region, and also to Madras and Tanjavur.[56] Bangalore is one clear instance where the domination of the European companies seems to have led to a decline in the demand for the particular variety of silk cloth which was its specialization. To quote Buchanan: 'nor will the English officers ever demand the native goods so much as the Mussalman Sirdars did. The manufacturers of this place can never, therefore, be expected to equal what they were in Hyder's reign unless some foreign market can be found for the goods.'[57] Buchanan says that he received musters of silk and woollen cloth from native merchants seeking a market in England.

Interesting cross-references to the native trade in textiles are occasionally to be found in the company records. This was in the context of companies entering the sphere of what they termed 'country trade'. William Nicholas, the English agent at Surat, suggested to his superiors at Bantam as early as 1616 that there was 'cento per cento profit' to be made by taking raw silk, benjamin and other items from Surat to Masulipatnam—which was then in the hands of the native merchants.[58] Commenting on the flourishing state of the internal trade in the hands of indigenous Indian merchants, the factors at Masulipatnam remarked in their letter dated 24 September 1628: 'Believe me, Sir, if any profit could be made there [at Bengal], these Masulipatnam Moors would not leave these profits to us but gain these profits themselves with their small vessels.'[59] Ysbrantz, the Dutch agent at Masulipatnam, wrote that it would be cheaper if the Dutch bought these goods from the native merchants rather than if they fetched it themselves. It has been estimated that most coastal vessels engaged in the predominantly textile trade between Cambay and Goa were owned by Indian merchants.[60] The Dutch nevertheless managed to acquire an effective share in internal trade. A letter of the Dutch company in 1641 refers to the exchanging of Coromandel cloth for pepper at Cannanore and also states that they were 'very much in need of cloth [from Surat] for our country trade.'[61] The English participated in the trade between the west and east coasts by exchanging pepper for Coromandel cloth, and the Dutch factors remark that if the English continued to bring down prices by providing the coast of Coromandel with more spices than they need, their inland trade would soon be at a loss.[62]

As the cost of water transport was relatively low, a substantial part of the cross-country trade in textiles was carried on along the coast. But textiles were also transported in carts along highways linking important centres. Trunk roads led from Surat to Burhanpur. The trunk road linking Hyderabad and Masulipatnam passed through Kolar. From the town of Tenara, a road led to Madras. There was also a direct road from Vijayawada to Madras. The route taken by Tavernier and Thevenot provides an idea of the system of roadways.[63] A letter of the Dutch factors written in 1615 says that goods from Masulipatnam to Pulicat were transported by being loaded on nine hundred oxen and nine hundred *sirbary* or coolies.[64] The word *sirbary* literally means 'head-load' and the same term occurs very frequently in inscriptions where the word used is *talaicumai*. Apparently the load was carried on the heads of the coolies. Besides this, goods were also transported in carts. It has been held that wheeled traffic was absent in the South, in contrast to Gujarat and Bengal.[65] This is however a misconception and South Indian inscriptions as well as travellers' accounts[66] refer to the transportation of cotton, yarn and cloth, apart from salt, pepper and other commodities, in carts.

Foreign Trade in Textiles

The nature of the foreign demand for South Indian textiles was varied because a large volume of textiles was demanded in markets with tastes and requirements very different from each other. While the demand in the Malay Archipelago was for the painted calico of South Coromandel and tapechindes and sarassas, the consumption pattern in Europe was a changing one: it moved from a demand for calico for curtains and coverlets to bettilles as fashion wear, and for calicoes as utility items of clothing.

During the Vijayanagar period South Indian textiles had a market in the islands of the Malay Archipelago such as Banda, Amboina and Malacca, and also in Persia and the Middle East. As said earlier, there was also some demand in Arabia Felix and Africa for Indian textiles, although this was supplied primarily by the west coast.

In the early decades of the seventeenth century the primary market for Coromandel textiles was still the Malay Archipelago. The competition among the rival nations was intense because the

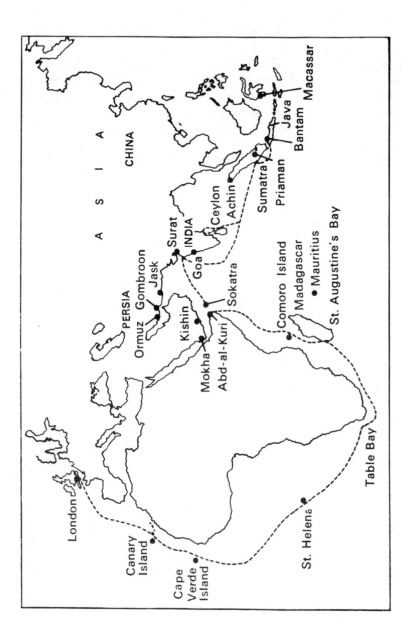

Map 3. The Direction of East India Trade in the Seventeenth Century

Moors, the Portuguese, the Dutch, the Danes and the Chettis were all in the commercial fray for the triangular spice trade, whereby Coromandel cloth was sold in the East Indies, and spices sold at great profit in the Middle East and Europe. In the 1630s textiles accounted for about forty-three per cent of the total value of Dutch exports from India, and the bulk of them was sent to South East Asia where they made a profit of 125 per cent. Their closest competitors were the native merchants or Moors, whom they regarded as their 'greatest competitors in commerce'.[67] Commercial rivalry created a situation where anything the weavers produced was bought up. A letter from the agent and council at Batavia to the English East India Company in 1626 laments the obstruction of their purchase of textiles at Pondicherry by the Danes, and at Masulipatnam by the Dutch.[68] At the same time the Spice Islands became glutted with cloth, causing a fall in prices. The situation in the Spice Islands is best described by Peter Floris,[69] a Dutch merchant turned English agent,[70] who says of Patani in 1612:

four years ago there was such a vent in them that it seemed the world has not clothings enough to provide this place as was needful ... and that now it is so overcloyed. ... But the cause why the same lyeth now so underfoot is this—that the Portugals bring the same quality of clothing in Moluccas heretofore as they have done, hereupon followed by the Hollanders who have not only filled Bantam and Java but also all the islands of Molucca, so that they [i.e. the Portuguese] have no utterance at Malacca. Besides this, there may be some ships of the Moors which trade for Tennasserim and provide Siam; besides this two Portugals and a Moorish ship have found out a new haven this year called Tarang and this year arrived a Gujarati ship and another from Nagapatnam at Keda bringing the lawns overland and so overfilled it that no man ever saw the like; and to all these we come with 200 packs, the rumour whereof being sufficient to cause the price not to rise these ten years. [!]

Floris says that where four years ago he had made three hundred to four hundered per cent profit, now he could not make five per cent.

The Indian merchants, both Moors and Chettis, offered stiff competition to the Europeans in what has been termed 'inter-Asiatic' or 'country trade', i.e. both the Red Sea trade as well as the trade with the Spice Islands. The historian Van Leur has shown that the share of Asian merchants in Coromandel trade was a sizeable one.[71] According to his figures in 1620 the tonnage of European ships in oriental waters averaged between 12 and 14 thousand, while Chinese and Siamese shipping amounted to 18,000 tons and

Coromandel native shipping around 10,000 tons. Anthony Schorrer gives a detailed account of the trading of the Masulipatnam Moors in 1615. He says that their ships sailed to the coasts of Bengal, Arakkan, Pegu, Tennaserim, Achin, Priamam, Kheda and Pera, laden with all sorts of cotton cloths, cotton yarn (both red and white), glass, iron, tobacco, shells, etc. From there they brought back goods which they took right upto Cochin, sailing all along the coast. They also sold rough Coromandel cloth in Ceylon and the Maldives, bringing in return cinnamon, coir and precious stones.[72] The names of certain individual merchants, both Moors and Hindu Chettis, figure in company records as great trade rivals in the Indian ocean. A Dutch record which gives Malaya Chetti's original name as Asappa says that in the early seventeenth century Malaya and his brother Chinanna had a splendid trade with Pegu, Tennaserim, Kheda and Pera, and also Pulicat and the ports around the South point of India, Gingee, Tanjore and Madurai. Till around 1644 they both made a profit of twenty and thirty per cent by providing the company with guinees, sail cloth, rambustin, bolatins, tapechiras, madapollams, painted cloth and indigo, and on their own account they shipped still larger quantities across the sea.[73] The Dutch in their chagrin seem to have referred to these indigenous merchants as 'pirates'. For instance in their letter of 14 December 1652 they accuse the Portuguese of intriguing with 'that pirate Beri Rama Chetti' to capture Dutch vessels in the gulf of Sind.[74] Reference to the participation of Mir Jumla and Mir Kamaluddin occurs repeatedly in both the English and the Dutch records. In fact the Dutch found that Mir Kamaluddin sent to Persia large cargoes of cloth and sapan wood (red dye) purchased from the Dutch themselves, and all that the Dutch could do was stop the sale of sapan wood to him.[75] The traders of Nagapattinam, both Moors and Chettis, are supposed to have been particularly enriched by their trade with Achin as well as with Mocha and the Persian gulf. Some of the Chettis are also mentioned as having entered into some sort of partership with the Portuguese.[76] The English factors observed that in 1627 not one single Christian vessel came to Mocha, but several native vessels did.[77] They are said to have traded in sashes, allejaes, fine dutties, *chaddar* (bedsheets) and cotton wool, with Mocha, Jedda and Cairo. In fact the Dutch sought to combat native trade competition by increasing the duties at Malacca to ten per cent and by refusing passes. Indian ships found sailing for Achin, Malacca,

Kheda or other places were seized. The Dutch company's orders to its servants was in fact 'to burn the Moorish vessels'.[78] But the Dutch finally had to admit that there was no use in forbidding Moorish trade since they could always use the land route to Persia via Qandahar and Mocha.[79]

The companies met with little success in their efforts to build up their Red Sea trade with Persia and Gombroon.[80] In 1634 the English Company decided to invest 20,000 pounds in gold, either coin or bullion, for trade with Persia. They believed that they could invest even triple that sum because, 'witness the abundance of rich bales that was yearly bought by the Moors etc. about Golconda and transported on your ships from Gombroon'.[81] The English company therefore decided to invest 10,000 pounds in textiles for Gombroon, raising 5,000 pounds from the transportation of freight goods. The trade with Persia was however systematically hindered by the Mughal administration at Golconda, which claimed a monopoly over all the fine-piece goods and ordered that the weavers should work only for the government.[82] The Dutch, as an alternative, secured their painted cloth from Pulicat and Pondicherry while the English set up their factory at Armagaon. But the markets at Basra and Gombroon were again ruined by the competition between the Dutch and the English. The agent and council at Grombroon wrote to the president and council at Surat in 1647: 'The markets here are very bad and likely to be worse since a Dutch ship is daily expected from Masulipatnam. There is no demand for longcloth—the so-called guldars [broad cloth][83] are found to be but nimguls which are but half as long as the guldars and so more suitable for Basra. The Chelalos are so bad that there is no offer for them and the brown salempores are too coarse to tempt buyers.'[84]

As textile trade in the Malay Archipelago reached a bottleneck, efforts were made by the European companies to explore other avenues of trade. The silk trade between China and Japan suggested strong possibilities. Apart from the restricted trade privileges accorded to the Portuguese at Macao, the Chinese seaboard was closed to foreigners and consequently Chinese silk, so much in demand in Japan, could be purchased only on neutral territory. No Japanese vessel could directly enter Chinese port: a single Portuguese ship came annually to Japan from Macao carrying canton silk.[85] Both the Dutch and the English hoped to obtain a share in this lucrative trade. In July 1612 the Dutch sent a consignment of silk and silkwares from Patani to Japan and, six months later, silk and other Chinese goods were being sent to Japan from Siam also.[86] But the silk trade did not develop probably because the other neutral entrepots were more convenient for both the Chinese and the Japanese.[87] It is noteworthy that when a similar situation of glut in textiles occurred in the European market in the 1680's, the possibility of trade with Japan in Bengal silk was mooted.

It was the Portuguese who first began sending Indian textiles to Europe. They exported the textiles of Balaghat—sarassas and tapechiras and the fine and coarse bettilles of Golconda, besides many other varieties. The figures available till the 1630s show that the volume exported was considerable. To give just one example, 7,818 pieces of fine Golconda bettilles were exported in 1615 but 25,290 pieces in 1616.[88] The Goa customs list of 1630 which included 112 different commodities indicates that the private cargoes that year were made up chiefly of a wide range of Indian textiles. It has been calculated that almost 4,500,400 yards of cloth were sent to Portugal in 1630.[89] In 1631 the Portuguese ship 'Bom Jesus de Monte Calvario' carried textiles, spices and gems, and textiles comprised the largest part of the cargo.[90] Textiles accounted for about 43 per cent of the total value of Dutch exports from India to Europe where they made between 65 to 160 per cent profit.[91]

In 1621 the English East India Company made a tentative effort to send Coromandel textiles to England and in 1623 the council at Batavia wrote to the Company that the great quantities of 'long calico' sent to Europe by the Dutch from Masulipatnam gave them the idea of sending some fine calicoes to England, but noted with regret that they did not sell.[92] The Company persisted with its efforts and when King James I asked the Directors of the Company what vent they had for the great mass of calicoes that came yearly, they replied, 'much of it is very useful and vendes in England, whereby the prices of Lawns, cambrics and other linen cloth are brought down.'[93] The world's lawns and cambrics came from the cities of Lyons and Cambrai, from where England usually imported its linen. However in the early stages calicoes were in demand in England only as table cloths, coverlets, napkins and wall hangings, and this limited demand was met by the Surat factory. Secondly a major part of the textiles was re-exported to Africa. There was an expanding demand for coarse blue salempores and Guinea cloth, i.e. striped or chequered calico sold in Guinea. Tapechiras and sannoes were used as barter for slaves on the West African coast and as loincloths for slaves when they reached the New World.[94]

The first indications of the existence of a European market for Coromandel cloth comes in 1647 when President Ivy at Fort St. George wrote to the Company that they would 'rejoice to learn that, the Persian, and Bantam markets having been fully stocked with coast clothing, a quantity has at last found its way to England and they yielded considerable profit.'[95] The cloth was also intended for re-export to other European countries. In 1650 the English East India Company wrote to the president and council at Surat that the Coromandel textiles 'are more preferred before any of the Surat clothing, because they fit best for France and other foreign lands.'[96] In 1658 the Company exported to England from Fort St. George 84,000 pieces comprising of long cloth (50,000), salempores (20,000) and other types including muslins, 14,000. In 1659 the Company specified over 90,000 standard pieces, namely longcloth 50,000, salempores 30,000, and other varieties 11,000. A standing order was also given to provide roughly 100,000 pieces in future years.[97]

The Eurpoean market for Coromandel textiles was dominated by the European companies and the Indian merchants do not seem to have played any role in this trade except as middlemen. The English–Dutch competition for the European market was already under way by the 1620s–30s, by when the Portuguese trade had begun to wane. There was an enormous growth in the volume of textile exports to Europe by both the English and the Dutch. In 1642 the Dutch had shipped between 8,000 and 10,000 pieces of Guinea cloth from Coromandel to Holland. In 1682, forty years later, 23,500 pieces of Guinea cloth were shipped from Masulipatnam to Holland, together with an additional 40,000 pieces from the various factories in Coromandel.[98] Similarly the English Company's export of Coromandel textiles to England totalled 18,225 pieces in 1638–9.[99] In 1664 the total volume of calicoes exported by the English Company stood at well over a quarter of a million pieces and their value accounted for about seventy-three per cent of the entire trade of the Company. In two decades, i.e. by 1684, the calicoes exported to England by the English Company stood at more than a million-and-a-half-pieces and the relative share of textiles to total output had also increased to eighty-three per cent.[100] The English Company, writing to its factors, says: 'The Hollands East India Company have lately had a court of sales and we find that they have sold long cloth at near 4 Pounds per piece, and salempores at 400 shillings per piece and moorees, percalles and other fine cloth at greater prices. We, therefore, desire that you send us a proportion of each of these sorts.'[101] The enormous profit made by these companies can be seen by the fact that, even around 1677, they were purchasing the fine salempores at 1.35 pagodas per piece, i.e. half a pound, and long cloth around the same price.[102] In spite of the transportation charges etc., the companies must have made a profit of 300–500 per cent.

The calico craze reached its peak around the 1680's. A letter from the Directors in 1680 to Fort St. George states, 'there is nothing so difficult but may be effected where the material silk and mid-wife labour are so cheap as with you ... Encourage the ingenious and first imitators of staple commodities of the usual production of Italy and France which pick our pockets while they come from thence, but would fill his Majesties and subjects purses if we could buy them from India.[103] The European demand for calico was more than doubled by the fact that fashions in high circles changed very rapidly. As the Company put it: 'Note this for a constant and general rule ... that you change the fashions and flower as much as you can every year, for English ladies and they say the French and the Europeans will give twice as much for a new thing not seen in Europe before though worse, than they will give for a better of the same fashion worn the former year.'[104]

Calico became utility item for all classes when, instead of merely being worn on the outside, its possibility as a soft and light inner garment began to be realized. This started off the demand for calico shifts, izzarees, diapers, and also calico stockings.[105] In 1682 the Company, placing an order for 200,000 shifts at Fort St. George, specified that some should be of the coarser cloth, i.e. blue salempores or ordinary white, for seamen and ordinary people; others 'middling white' for citizens and 'middle sort of people'; and fine cloth for the ladies.[106]

In the last phase of the seventeenth century the calico export began to decline. The aim of the rival companies was to 'overbuy and under-sell' each other. This resulted in the company warehouses getting overstocked, a glut in the market, and decline in prices. This situation occurred in 1672–3, 1675–6 and throughout the eighties of that century.[107]

While on the one hand European competition ruined the prospects of profits, on the other hand interlopers and private traders constituted the enemies within. Every agent in every factory complained about private traders poaching on company trade and destroying the market for their goods by selling the same goods earlier. Private traders vitiated the entire policy of country trading. But it is most interesting that the same agents and factors who at the official level had to grapple with the problem of private trading were themselves not free from the sins of private trade. Greenhill, Chambers, Winter, Streynsham Master, Pitt, Mohun and Mainwaring, to mention only some names, all left India under clouds of dishonour thrown up by their private ventures. The situation in the Dutch company was equally chronic. A hilarious instance is given in the *Dagh Register* where Dutch agents seem to have played musical chairs over the question of private trade. In May 1632 Arent Gardenijas replaced Isbrandszoon at Masulipatnam; the latter was dismissed for indulging in private trade. In September of the same year David Peterszoon superseded Gardenijas for precisely the same reason. But in June 1633 of the following year Isbrandszoon was recalled to replace Peterszoon, who was accused of indulging in private trade![108]

The East India companies adopted stringent measures to check interlopers. The accounts of goods in each ship were to be examined to determine the real owners. The commander of ships were to forfeit forty pounds for any private goods they carried from the bay or the coast. Similarly all goods of interlopers were to be confiscated and out of this the commanders and seamen who had helped in seizing the ship were to have one-third of such goods.[109] These measures seem to have been successful in checking the menace of interlopers because after 1680 the references to private trading are fewer and the company claimed that all interlopers had been effectively suppressed.[110] However the English East India Company was subsequently to realize that the ending of private trade did not really solve all their problems because, with the accession of William, the competition of rival companies in the East India trade became wholly legal.

Towards the end of the seventeenth century protests began in England against the export of Indian calicoes. It was widely believed that the sale of Indian goods was achieved at the expense of the indigenous wool and silk industries, resulting in the displacement of hundreds of weavers.[111] The riot of the Spitalfields silk weavers broke out in 1697. Another pressure group was the mercantilist lobby which argued that the import of Indian calico meant the drain of bullion from England.[112] The result of all the lobbying was the passing of the Act of 1701 prohibiting all Indian printed and painted calicoes.

The factors leading to the ban on Indian calico were much more complex than appeared to contemporary observers. Was calico capable of substituting for wool in the English market or did Indian calico displace the French and Dutch linen imports into England? How did the growing linen industry of England react to the threat of competition from Indian calicoes? Some of these queries the contemporary thinkers sought to answer in their own way. Sir Josiah Child, in a tract published in 1677, remarked: 'The India goods are so different in their qualities from the product of our country, and the main of our manufacture, that it is absolutely impossible they should ever do them any injury.'[113] The argument that the utility of the Indian calicoes lay in cutting down the import of cambrics, lawns and other linen from France and Holland, was used as early as 1664 by Thomas Mun.[114] The argument regarding the drain of bullion from England was reversed by the defenders of the East India Company without shifting from the mercantilist logic of 'money begets money and trade increaseth money'.[115] The bullion export was not to be thought of in terms of a drain since Indian manufactures were purchased very cheaply, because of cheap labour, and then re-exported to Spain, France and other countries, bringing into England three times the amount of bullion expended in the East India trade.

The largest impact of the import of calicoes should have been on the English linen industry, but as late as the 1650's the English linen industry was still in its infancy. To the linen manufacturers the import of Indian calicoes did not seem a threat at all. In fact they vigorously protested against the attempt by the woollen and silk manufacturers to ban Indian calicoes because the Indian cloth provided employment to hundreds of linen drapers, dyers, printers and silk throwsters in England.[116] But, although the long-term impact of Indian calico import seems to have escaped contemporary observation, it was nevertheless there. From 1670 onwards the import of raw cotton yarn and thread from the Coromandel and raw silk from Bengal was steadily increasing in order to feed the English linen industry.[117] It was perhaps this that later gave the English textile manufacturers the strength to impose curbs on Indian calicoes. Indian weavers seem to have protested against the export of cotton yarn in some rare cases, the Surat weavers being a case in point. They refused to meet the demands of the English Company unless the export of raw cotton from the area was immediately stopped.[118]

As things stood in 1700 it was in all probability the protest of certain sections of the woollen and silk manufacturers which brought about the ban of 1701, irrespective of the fact that calico could hardly substitute for wool. The ban was not particularly effective because the government admitted in 1721, on the eve of the second prohibition act, that 'more calicoes are worn in England that pay no duty than are painted and worn here that do pay duty.' The export of Indian calicoes and piece goods into England continued right till the 1820s, though it never touched the peak achieved in 1680.

Organization of Textile Production and Trade

THE MASTER WEAVERS

To a large extent the weaving villages continued to be far flung, though weavers of certain specialized varieties were concentrated in some towns—notably Company settlements such as Masulipatnam, Narsapur or Pulicat. Some efforts were also made to establish *karkhanas* for weavers, washers and dyers. Frequent reference to the English East India Company's weavers and washers or bleachers is to be found in the Fort St. George Records.[119] Daniel Havert refers to the dyers workhouse at Tegnapatnam or Fort St. David and Pulicat or Fort Geldria.[120] But such instances are rare. On the other hand there was the weaver who produced and sold his own cloth. But the most common practice was that while in slack seasons the weaver produced at his own risk and sold in the weekly fairs, the same weaver also wove for the export market: for this his goods were commissioned by merchants. The commissioning of cloth by merchants' middlemen was in fact the usual practice. As K. N. Chaudhuri puts it: 'To attempt to characterize a craftsman as one kind of specialist trader is to ignore all reality. A situation in which the industrial producer sells directly to the consumer is likely to be a limiting case of an extreme kind.'[121] Marx's observation that in all pre-capitalist societies 'commerce ruled industry'[122] can be

regarded as axiomatic. In producing for the market it was essential
to have an up-to-date knowledge of the varying demands of the
markets, and also a fairly large capital outlay involving commercial
risk. Both these factors rendered inevitable the presence of merchant
middlemen and to some extent their penetration into production in
the process of what Marx calls 'exploitation through trade.' This,
according to Marx, could take two roads. The weaver himself could
turn into a merchant and small-time entrepreneur, in what he calls
'the truly revolutionary way', or it could be the merchant who
dominated production with the logical possibility of eventually
turning into an industrial capitalist.[123] The emergence of the master
weaver is characteristic of the first path. The genesis of the master
weaver in the context of an expanding market for textiles and the
growing economic stratification among the weavers has already
been discussed. Their emergence did not, however, alter the
handicraft nature of production and the weavers merely acted as
middlemen, either in an independant capacity or on behalf of the
company. The system of cloth production under one roof was
unsuitable in the Indian context. The Indian loom was not a
complex or costly device beyond the reach of a craftsman of modest
means. Moreover the Coromandel weaver was a very mobile
craftsman who required little more than the shade of a huge tree to
set up his loom, thus rendering redundant the establishment of a
manufactory which would involve the expense of upkeep and
supervision. The system of distributing the advance among the
weavers had the added advantage of making it possible to involve
not only the artisan but also the members of his household in
production. Given the disadvantages of the manufactory system in
the Indian situation, the rise of the master weaver is still an
indisputable fact. While in the Vijayanagar inscriptions the suffix
'Chetti' follows the caste name of the weavers, in the company
records the term used is chief weaver, master weaver or weaver-
merchant.

It was the Dutch who had the largest dealings with the master
weaver in the initial period. The Dutch had more liquid capital at
their disposal *vis-a-vis* the English, and it was therefore possible for
them to go into the weaving village itself instead of being dependent
on merchant middlemen. In the detailed break-up of the weaving
villages catering to Draksharama (Decheron, the site of the Dutch
factory in North Coromandel), the Dutch record gives the numbers

of weaving households in each village as well as the number of looms.[124] The average ratio of weaving households to looms works out to 3:4. For instance at Pithapuram and Thuni there are said to have been 600 weaving households in each village and about 800 looms; Kesavaram, a smaller village, had 60 weaving households and 80 looms; while Amalapuram and Nagaram had 900 weaving households and 1,200 looms. The evidence indicates the existence of weavers owning several looms. The Dutch records also contain direct reference to master weavers.[125]

Some scattered reference to the operation of master weavers comes from English Company records, especially in the context of the great left-hand right-hand caste war of 1654–5. In his charges against the Brahmin intermediaries Venkata and Kannappa, the English agent Greenhill accused them of causing trouble in the Black Town by creating a rift among the painters (i.e. the weavers of chintz) and inciting the 'Cooly' (worker) Painters against the Chief Weaver'. The Brahmins in their turn state that although 'Chinna-wand Chetti', a painter (the suffix 'Chetti' is again used for the master weaver), failed to fulfil his contract made with the Brahmins on behalf of the company, Greenhill employed him on a further contract.[126]

Like the Dutch the English also made some attempts to place their orders directly through the head weavers, thus eliminating the middlemen who tended to take a sizeable cut. On 16 November 1694 the English Company signed a contract with the Salawar weavers for unbleached cloths and the amount of 207 pagodas was impressed on the chief weaver as advance. A similar contract for striped bettilles was made with the chief weaver of the Janrawar caste of weavers. The same record mentions another master weaver, Ponnambalam, who also secured a contract to supply cloth.[127] In all these instances the master weavers acted not independently but as agents of the Company.

Some master weavers, however, began as independent merchants, competing with the Company. Thus in the Fort St. George *Consultations* of 1693[128] the factors lamented that the Company's merchants had been outwitted by two 'merchant weavers', Namashivaya and Bussaporte (Basappa Reddy), who gathered all the weavers of that part of the country so that the Company's merchants could not get their goods till their business was done and all the looms were changed to the Manilla sort of cloth. These two

master weavers were brought into the English Company's fold along
with some others by being made chief merchants of the Company.
Thus the Company report dated 1694 refers to the appointment of
Namashivaya, Bussaporte, Porpactum and Ramakrishna, all master
weavers, as chief merchants of the Company.[129]

Hamilton Buchanan, in his highly investigative account of
Mysore and the surrounding regions, provides details of the different
organizational methods of the master weavers. He says that the
master weavers kept between two to five servants who were paid by
the piece.[130] Perhaps they were also paid time wages because he says
that workmen who were employed to weave cotton cloth with silk
borders made a *panam* or eight pence daily. Time wages usually
ranged between six and eight pence a day.[131]

The master weavers under the companies had a dual role to play
in the set-up of the production organization. While on the one hand
they represented the company's interests, they also on the other
hand represented the weavers. When the weavers were pushed too
far they led the weavers' opposition to the company, as Kalatri, the
chief painter, did in 1662.[132] It appears that the revolt was provoked
by Kalatri, the master weaver, being dismissed by the company. But
gradually, in the course of the eighteenth and nineteenth centuries,
the master weaver began increasingly to act as the henchman of the
company and to coerce the weavers working under him.

Indian Merchants

Weavers usually worked on a system of advances made by the
merchants. This was quite different from the 'putting out' system
since the advance was usually in cash and not in the form of yarn or
other material. Methwold says in his account: 'The next tribe is
there termed a committy and these are generally the merchants of
this place, who by themselves or their servants travel into the
country, gathering up calicoes from the weavers and other commodities which they sell again.'[133]

Merchant guilds dealing in yarn and cotton cloth continued to
figure in the textile market. The powerful merchant guilds of the
earlier centuries continued into the seventeenth century. The
evidence for their operation is however extremely limited, partly
because there are very few inscriptions pertaining to this period and
partly because the company records make but the vaguest of
references to them. The Ayiravar Nagarattar, a powerful merchant

guild, is said to have made a grant of *maganmai* or religious toll on their merchandise to the Arunachalesvara temple at Chengam in Tiruvannamalai in 1691.[134] The medieval guild of Ayyavole continued to trade in yarn and cloth even in the seventeenth century. An inscription from Narayanavanam in Chittoor district in Andhra dated 1620 records the gift of tolls on various articles of merchandise such as cloth, pepper and jaggery by the Ayyavole.[135] Their survival well into the seventeenth century is also proved by the inscription from Lepakshi (Anantapur district, Andhra) dated 1680. The record states that the lords of the Ayyavole, both *paradesa* (dealing in foreign trade) and *svadesa* (dealing in indigenous trade), led by their chief Prithvi Chetti Rayani Bhaskaranna, in consultation with the local caste organizations—among them the *tantuvayins* (weavers), *vastra-bhedakas* (cloth-dyers) and *vastra-rakshakas* (tailors?)—fixed certain rates on pack-bullocks, looms, etc. as *maganmai* for the benefit of the deity Nanjundesvara.[136]

The Choolias also continue to find mention in the seventeenth century. A Dutch record of 1652[137] says that when they declared war on the Portuguese, the Mudaliyar of Alican (a place apparently very close to Tiruchendur) with a number of Choolia 54 (the association of a number with a mercantile organization was an old practice) merchants along with a number of Moorish merchants came over to the Dutch. The *Diary and Consultations* of Fort St. George of 1686 refers to the arrival of the ship of a 'Chooliar' from Achin to the Madras Port.[138] In 1687 the English East India Company hired ships from some 'choolar' merchants.[139] The Kling and Choolia merchants, however, seem to have lost the prosperity they enjoyed in the fifteenth-sixteenth centuries. While Tome Pires and others refer to them as wealthy merchant communities, a contrary picture of them in this period is presented in the account of Peter Floris—'The Tsulias and Calynders . . . bringeth a corge or less of diverse sorts, running with this through all the country, giving the goods so cheap that it is to be admired at, only to receive a copan (seven pence) for to buy rice for their bellies.'[140]

One feature of the seventeenth century in the context of merchant organization is that generally merchants are mentioned in their individual capacity rather than as part of a mercantile corporation. Secondly, the dividing line between independent merchants and merchants acting on behalf of the Company is very thin. In several cases a merchant functioned in both capacities, such as Malaya and his brother Chinanna, Kasi Viranna, and various others. But in the Company records certain Indian merchants are distinctly mentioned as their rivals and competitors. An effort is made here to list such names, with the exception of such well-known personalities as Malaya and his brother, and the merchant-noble Mir Jumla.

In a letter written by Pieter Gilles, the Dutch agent at Masulipatnam, to his company, all the prominent Hindu and Muslim merchants in that region are listed. Among the Moors appear—Khwaja Nizam, Khwaja Hassan Ali, Mirza Ishaq Beg, Mir Qasar and Khwaja Araby. Among Hindu merchants—Happa Vohra, Rabidas, Narasimha Ramachetti, Cangoe (Ganga) Chetti, Daughy (Dorji) and Jarem Saha.[141] Raghava Chetti is another merchant mentioned by the Dutch at Pulicat in 1627 as having been put into prison by them because he refused to discharge his debts, either to the company or the company's merchants. He retaliated by escaping to Armagaon and placing himself under English protection.[142] It was Mir Kamaluddin, the famous Muslim merchant, who negotiated with the Dutch on behalf of the Sultan of Golconda at Masulipatnam in 1629.[143] The Hindu merchants operating in the Porto Novo—Cuddalore region are named as Tendatie Chetti, Ariecaltsie Chetti and Komaty Chetti.[144] At Ventapollam in 1632 the English records mention Commer Bampa, an old merchant who brought musters in the hope of doing some business with the Company.[145] The Dutch also make incidental reference to Indian merchants in other company settlements. For instance in 1637 they note that Vendorda Tacendas, a rich merchant resident at Goa, was captured by the Portuguese when he was trading in Bijapur.[146] Kesara Chetti was another leading merchant in South Coromandel who eventually became a middleman for the Dutch East India Company.[147] Similarly Seshadhri, Varadappa and Koneri Chetti, including of course Malaya and Chinanna, functioned as independent merchants. They were in fact so powerful politically that they even commanded forts, while at times they functioned as merchant middlemen for the Dutch Company.[148] Chinanna, when he turned against the Dutch, raised an army and unsuccessfully besieged Fort St. Geldria.[149] Malaya was at this time acting in the capacity of the Governor of Udayagiri, and the Dutch records comment on Udayagiri being 'entrusted to a man who was only fit to sit behind the counter of a small shop.' Another famous figure was Kasi Viranna, referred to as Casa

Verona by the Europeans, who was originally a Muslim with the name of Hasan Khan. Of another merchant Mirza Mohammed operating in Pulicat, the Dutch records state that he was very influential and close to Haqueekat Khan, the governor.[150] Some prominent independent merchants are also mentioned on the Malabar coast, such as Narasimha and Ratnasamy Mudaliyar, operating in Wengurla;[151] and Malappa Malo, the great Cannanore merchant who was very close to the Governor Surappa Nayak and without whose help no textiles or rice could be bought in Cannanore.[152] The frequent reference to 'Malabar pirates' found in both the English and Dutch records[153] was most often applied to enterprising Indian merchants. Thus Beri Rama Chetti is referred to as 'that pirate' by the Dutch, and Narasimha and Ratnasamy Mudaliyar are said to have come 'accompanied as usual by the pirates from Malabar'.[154] The company records make it clear that they faced stiff commercial competition from these indigenous merchants.

However many of the native merchants found that it was more profitable and less risky to act on behalf of the companies rather than make voyages on their own. The emergence of these merchant middlemen of the company, besides of course a whole accompanying strata of intermediaries, accounts for the decline of the medieval mercantile guilds. Thus in the majority of cases the merchants either branched off independently or acted within the framework of the companies. In the organizational set-up of the companies their function was fourfold. In a region like the Coromandel where weavers were widely scattered, merchants and other intermediaries were needed to purchase cloth and act as links between weavers and the company; second, they supervised weavers and minimized the companies' risks by taking on bad debts; third, they ensured quality control by providing weavers with musters and seeing that they 'worked to the perfection of the pattern'; and finally merchants even saved the companies the necessity of laying out vast sums of money by making the initial advances themselves. The companies were in fact in debt to many of their chief merchants.[155]

The middlemen between the weavers and the companies existed at several levels. There were first, the chief merchants for each region assisted by smaller merchants. (In 1654 Timmanna, the chief merchant at Fort St. George, was paid a salary of six pagodas per month, which was considered princely).[156] Below them were the

Egyb or brokers, each region having one or more head-brokers assisted by subordinate brokers. The cut of the head-brokers was one per cent on coarse cloth and 1.5 per cent on fine cloth.[157] Sometimes the office of *dubash* or interpreter was also held by the broker,[158] but most often it was a distinct profession. The salary of an interpreter at Bancoolen towards the close of the seventeenth century was ten dollars per month.[159] The records also refer very often to the 'braminy' who acted as go-between, like Ramabhadra or Muttappa Mudaliyar for the Dutch,[160] or Vira Raghavayya in the 1670s and Chandrasekharayya in the 1680s, who acted on behalf of the English East India Company.[161] Their income seems to have ranged from four to ten pagodas a month. These Brahmins may have combined the office of broker and interpreter. Frequent reference is also made to an intermediary who is alternately called *vakil* or *mulla*. The term *mulla* must have come because most of them seem to have been Muslims. The duty of the vakil was to point out the implications of any company policy on native laws and customs.[162]

Taxation

Not much information is available on the nature of taxation on the weaving industry during this period. The seventeenth century company records merely indicate that the tax on weavers was fairly heavy. In 1607–8 the Dutch factors say that at Petapoli the weavers were so overtaxed that they intended to run away, but the Dutch paid up their taxes, thereby obliging them to work for the company.[163] A *farman* of Shah Jahan applicable to Pipli, and in fact to the entire trading on the Bay, says that the tax on cotton, linen, woollen and silk cloths was two per cent of the price of the cloth calculated at bazaar rates.[164] It is possible that the rate of taxation for the Coromandel coast was not very different. A variety of taxes seem to have been imposed on the textile industry, such as tax on cotton, on the loom and on cloth stamped on the loom (*chappa dalali*, literally 'stamping plus brokerage'). The evidence for these taxes comes only from the eighteenth century. As in the Vijayanagar period, the loom tax referred to as *tari irai* was universal. A number of records from the Salem district pertaining to the period from 1791 to 1835 refer to the taxes on looms and cotton in the context of their abolition in Salem.[165] In 1793 in the Ramanathapuram district the loom tax was between 3 to 4 pagodas per year. During the period of Tipu Sultan loom tax in Mysore was between 24 to 60 *panams*, i.e. between 2 and 4 pagodas.[166] In the seventeenth century it appears from the occasional reference that the *chappa dalali* amounted to between 11 and 13 per cent and was paid by the merchants,[167] but the Salem records clearly show these as being levied upon the weavers.[168] Besides the loom tax, house tax, referred to as *vasalvari* in the Vijayanagar inscriptions, continued to be levied. It also appears that there was a curious custom of compelling the weavers to buy grain at a fixed rate, considerably above market charges.[169] Mention is also made in the Dutch records to the *guddam* tax, but the nature of this tax is ambiguous.[170]

It is not possible to determine the incidence of taxation on a continuous time scale as was done for the Vijayanagar period because of a paucity of information. But it is likely that the loom tax in the seventeenth century averaged around 2 to 4 pagodas, i.e. between 30 to 60 *panams*. Allowing for the devaluation of the *panam* from the fourteenth to the seventeenth centuries—from 10 *panams* a pagoda to nearly double—it is still clear that taxation had increased. However, as in the past, collective protest was effectively used by weavers' organizations to oppose excessive taxation, the best example being the strike in the Black Town when around 1686 the company imposed wall tax.

CHAPTER VI

The Weavers, Society and the East India Company
(Seventeenth Century)

The seventeenth century saw the heyday of the Honourable East India Companies. Like the proverbial camel in the Arab's tent, the East India companies had come to stay. They became an inevitable part of the politics and economy of South India, finding their way into the society and even the vocabulary of local people. The 'kumbini', as the local populace called it, was not to be ignored. As with the rest, the spinners and weavers, the washers, the dyers and the once powerful textile-merchant guilds had their links with the company factories. Of course there were also those merchants and weavers who operated independently of the company, but their proportion was small.

The Weaving Castes

The position of the various professional weaving castes was in a state of flux and one major indication of change was the mobility of the weaver castes, though in certain areas the traditional castes continued. The Kaikkolar were still heard of in the Tamil country. Inscriptional reference to the Kaikkola guild comes from Chingleput in 1679.[1] Another very interesting reference to them comes during the caste disturbances that took place towards the close of the seventeenth century. In the *Diary and Consultations* of Fort St. George on 15 January 1708[2] it was recorded that both the left-hand and the right-hand castes had complaints against the 'Kaicullawarr' weavers because they were very fickle and sometimes declared in favour of one caste and at other times of the other. The Devanga weavers continued to be important in the Andhra and Karnataka regions. At the Venkataramana temple in Arsikere (Hasan district) they are mentioned along with the Billimagga, another weaving caste, in an eighteenth-century inscription.[3] They are also referred to in many seventecnth-century epigraphic records, including the important Lepakshi inscription.[4] The Salewar are referred to in one Company record dated 1694 as ancient inhabitants of the Tamil country with whom a direct contract was signed for the delivery of coarse and fine unbleached neckcloths. The Salewaru seems to indicate the Telugu Sales but since they are referred to as ancient inhabitants they were probably the Saliyar, the earliest weaving community to be mentioned in the Chola inscriptions. Another weaver caste with whom the Company is said to have entered into direct dealings in the same record was the Janrawars who are said to have 'lately come from Kaveripakkam'.[5] This was apparently one of the groups which had become mobile in search of economic opportunities. Their immigration into the Tamil country from Andhra five years earlier is also recorded in the *Consultations* of 1689–90:

The President, having for several years, used his utmost endeavours and interest in this and other countries to invite and bring as many of the several castes of weavers to inhabit and settle their families and trade in this town . . . having been long treating with the Janrawar (inhabiting Canerese and Telegu districts) a fine caste of weavers, persuaded near fifty families of them to come hither. To whom, after having viewed and allotted them ground in Peddanaikapetta separate from other castes of weavers . . . and other conveniences for their trade and worship, gave them a cowle [charter].[6]

Apart from these traditional castes the weavers also come to be known by their specialization, and perhaps these specialized groups formed new castes. For instance the Caingaloon weavers were those who wove cloth destined for the Malay Archipelago: the word 'kain' in Malay means cloth and 'gulong' means rolled. The supply of gold thread to the Caingaloon weavers at Armagaon is referred to in a Company letter dated 1629[7] and they were also involved in the major left-hand right-hand flare up in the 1650s.[8] Similarly the Mambaloom 'painters' are also referred to,[9] i.e. those who specialized in the production of painted chintz. The Mooree weavers produced superior cotton cloth used as a base for chintz making.[10] The name seems to indicate that they were Muslims. One new caste of weavers emerged in the South, especially in Madurai and nearby areas, in the seventeenth century. These were the Saurashtras or the Pattunulkarar.

The Saurashtras claim to have a long history of migration. According to their tradition their earliest home was the Saurashtra region. In the Mandasor inscription dated 473[11] a class of silk weavers called Pattavayaka (the Sanskrit equivalent of 'Pattunul-karar') are said to have constructed a temple to the Sun God in 437 and renovated it forty years later. The record praises them as excellent weavers of silk and skilled in archery,[12] and states that they originally immigrated from Lata, Gujarat. After this evidence there is no documentary or epigraphical information to trace their further migration into South India. However the various stages of their emigration from Saurashtra as far as Madurai is covered in a unique folk tradition known as *Bhovlas*.[13] This was a sort of question and answer session which took place between the bride and the groom at the time of their engagement. According to this tradition the Saurashtras emigrated from Somnath towards Nagardesha (Lata, South Gujarat) Devagiri (Daulatabad), Vijayanagar and Madurai. Apart from these major places a number of others are also mentioned, mainly pilgrimage centres, but these point to efforts at self-glorification rather than to the actual facts. There is one very striking aspect about these stages of migration that make them historically plausible. Somnath was the first to come under Muslim attack (the invasion of Mahmud Ghazni) and the regions subse-quently mentioned all came under Muslim sway at one time or another. More practical proof of the migratory pattern of the Saurashtras is the peculiarity of the Saurashtran dialect, called Patnuli. This is a mixture of Marathi, Kannerese, Telugu and Tamil. The caste's ethnic affinities also lend credence to these traditions regarding their origin.[14] An epigraphical reference to the Pattunulkaran comes from Pattiavaram[15] near Kumbakonam, Tanjore district. The extent to which they replaced the Kaikkolar as the dominant weaving caste in the Tamil country cannot be gauged since the company records begin to refer to weavers by their mode of textile specialization rather than by their caste nomenclatures.

Standard of Living

An ancient proverb of the Pattunulkarar weavers says 'If you have money, *dipavali*, if not, a *potaro* [bamboo reel for winding yarn].'[16] The saying is apt for the fortunes of the weavers were constantly fluctuating from conditions of near prosperity in times of European competition to starvation in times of famine. There was considerable stratification among the weavers. The 'cooly' weavers and painters seldom rose above the poverty line and could not even put the cloth on the loom without an advance.[17] In times of famine they had also to be supplied with rice.[18] The master weavers on the other hand employed artisans and some became merchants themselves, competing with the company in the internal and external trade. Any estimate of the standard of living of the weavers *vis-a-vis* other social classes must remain a highly tentative one because of several limitations: inadequate data on the incomes of weavers and other social groups; the disparate information on paddy prices, which are neither steadily available over the years nor continuously available for a specific region; the artificial level of cloth prices maintained by the East India companies through their contracts with the merchants.[19] Keeping all these limitations in view one can still attempt a very broad and tentative study of the standard of living of the various social groups.

The earliest reference to the wages of artisans comes from the account of Methwold (1621–2).[20] He says that the average artisan was paid 3 pence a day and there was very little variation in the wages of the lower class of artisans. This works out to an income of roughly Rs 3 per month. This was the standard wage of the weavers, the smiths and others. A domestic servant was paid between 4 shillings 6 pence and 5 shillings per month, i.e. around Rs 2. Methwold says that a palanquin bearer was paid no more. A Dutch record of 1652 states that a weaver was paid 3½ fanams (or *panams*) for the production of a Guinea cloth (35 yards).[21] Since a weaver working on an ordinary loom can produce between 3 and 3.5 yards in a day, he may be estimated to produce around 26 pieces of Guinea cloth in a year if he were to work 276 days in the year, i.e. his monthly wages must have been approximately Rs 3. Compared to the weaver the diamond workers in the mines were paid much less, for according to Tavernier (1641–67) they earned only Rs 0.75 per month.[22] Streynsham Master (1680) on the other hand gives the wages of a miner as nearly Rs 4 in money and corn. He also gives the wages of the washerman as Re 1 per month and of servants as ranging from Rs 3.50 to Rs 7.[23] Thomas Bowry (1669–79) gives the wages of a peon (not much higher than a domestic servant) as Rs 2 per month.[24] That wages did not go up much over the years is demonstrated by the fact that in 1737–8 the monthly wage of Rs 5 demanded by the Bombay weavers was considered a high figure.[25] In 1790 a weaver at Vishakapatnam earned Rs 4 per month, and at Cuddalore the earnings of the weavers ranged from Rs 3.50 to

The Price of Paddy and Rice in the Seventeenth Century at Uneven Intervals of Time

Year	Region	Price	Price in Rupees	Quantity	Quantity In Kgs.	In Maunds	Price per Maund in Rupees	Remarks	Source
1655	Masulipatnam	1 panam	0.07	48 measures of paddy 30–52 " " "	60	1.6	0.04	The company complains that although the market rate was 48 measures for one panam they could get only 30–32 measures for the same.	E.F.I., 27 December 1655, p. 40
1673	Madras	3 sols (3 pence)	0.10	5 pounds	2.31	0.06	1.87		Travels of Abbe Carre, vol. II, p. 598
1676	Madras*	2 pagodas Rs 16	7 16	1 candy of paddy 1 candy of rice	740 740	20 20	0.35 0.80		The Diary of Streynsham Master, vol. II, 1 Jan. 1677, p. 96
1678	Madras	6 pagodas 33 panams 16 pagodas 22 panams	around 24 around 58	1 garce of paddy 1 garce of rice	4000 4000	108 108	0.22 0.54		Ibid., 23 December 1678, p. 150
1687	Ballasore	Re. 1	1	7 maunds of rice	259	7	0.14	The price here is stated to be very cheap while famine rates were prevailing at Masulipatnam.	Dispatches from England, 12 Oct. 1667, p. 93
1680s 1688	Masulipatnam Masulipatnam	5 pagodas 12 pagodas	16.25 39	1 candy of paddy ibid.	740 740	20 20	0.81 2.00	In this year Masulipatnam was hit by the worst famine of the century.	Letters to Fort St. George, 13 March 1668, p. 25
1688	Madras	1 pagoda	5.25	36 mercall of paddy	360	9.7	0.33		Ibid., p. 39
1689	Madras	1 panam	0.07	3.5 pounds of paddy	1.5	.04	1.75	Famine price of paddy.	Ibid., 16 July 1689, p. 37

Year	Place	Price		Quantity				Remarks	Source
1692	Madras	24 pagodas	78	1.75 garce of paddy	7000	189	0.41		Diary and Consultation, 23 December 1692, p. 11
1693	Madras	1 pagoda	3.25	25 mercall of paddy	250	6.8	0.48		Ibid, 18 March 1693, p. 60
1694	Madras	1 pagoda	3.25	13–14 mercall of paddy	130–140	3.5–3.7	0.93–0.89	This constituted company fair price in time of famine.	Ibid., 20 Sept. 1694, p. 100 and 19 Nov. 1694, p. 150
1696	Madras	1 pagoda	3.25	7 mercall of paddy	70	1.9	1.71	Madras region badly hit by famine.	Ibid., 26 Nov. 1694, p. 154
1696	Madras	1 pagoda / 23 pagodas	3.25 / 75.75	20 mercall for land paddy / 1 garce for sea paddy	200 / 4000	5.4 / 108	0.60 / 0.70	Says fear of Marathas robbing the country initially brought more grain into the market, cheapening the price. The letter uses two peculiar terms—paddy and land paddy. Not defined in Hob.-Job.** Says price of sea paddy has risen since land paddy has become scarce. Perhaps the chief distinction lay in the mode of transportation of the paddy.	Letters, 20 June 1696, p. 57
1698	Madras	1 pagoda	3.25	70–100 mercall of paddy	380–400	10.3–10.8	0.32–0.30		H.D. Love, Vestiges of Madras (1640, 1800), vol. I, p. 43
1700	Madras	1 pagoda	3.25	38–40 mercall of paddy	4000	103	0.03		
1733	Madras	25 pagodas	81.25	1 garce of paddy	4000	103	0.03		Love, vol. I, p. 252
1784	Madras	80 pagodas	200	1 garce of paddy	4000	103	2.41	The day that advice was received of peace with Tippoo, the price of rice fell from 115 to 80 Pagodas per garce.	Hob.-Job.**, p. 364

* The Diary and Consultation of 25 January 1676, p. 78, gives the price of Bengal rice as Rs 0.50 per maund and compares it with the price of Milan rice in London which was 18–22 shillings (i.e. Rs 7.50) per maund. The factors comment that considering the enormous difference in price, it is cheaper to import rice from the Bayor, the Coromandel Coast.

** Hob-Job = Hobson-Jobson, A Glossary of Colloquial Anglo-Indian Words.

Rs 5.25 per month. During the same period a sepoy in the army was paid only Rs 7 per month.[26] A hundred years earlier, in 1694, a sepoy was paid Rs 8 and the record states that previously his wage had been only Rs 2.[27] It is extremely interesting that Buchanan (1807) describing the situation at the turn of the century should state that while a weaver of fine cloth could make as much as 8 pence per day (around Rs 6.66 per month), a weaver of ordinary cloth earned 2 pence per day (Rs 2.50 per month),[28] precisely the same figure Methwold gave two centuries earlier. Buchanan, however, comments that the weavers were much better-off than those engaged in agriculture. Roughly during the same period spinners were paid much less, only 1 to 1.25 pence per day.[29]

As with the incomes of the weavers, the cloth prices paid by the company also show only negligible variation. The price of ordinary long cloth always averaged around 25 pagodas per corge and that of Salempores 14 pagodas per corge[30] right from 1675 to 1700, irrespective of pressures on the production front due to famines, wars, etc.[31] In contrast to the wages of weavers and cloth prices, the price of paddy, which constituted and still constitutes the staple diet of the common people in South India, shows considerable fluctuation. In the Table an effort has been made to show the fluctuations in paddy prices from 1675 to 1700. Even from the limited evidence available it is clear that the price varied considerably spatially, from region to region and also over the years. In times of famine the price of paddy shot up by nearly 400 per cent. During the 1688 famine a maund of paddy at Masulipatnam cost Rs 2, while the wages of a weaver ranged only from Rs 2.50 to Rs 3 per month, and that of other classes was even lower. In 1694, again a time of famine, wages remained constant at Rs 2–3 per month. Paddy sold at Madras at Rs 1.8 per maund, while the price of cotton thread at the same time was around Rs 5 per maund.[32] Even from the limited examples cited it is clear that wages lagged far behind the prices of necessities. Wars, however, had at times a peculiar effect on paddy prices. In a letter from Fort St. George dated 20 June 1696, the agent says that they had stored up about 100 garce of paddy (4,000 kg) and 40 garce of rice, since paddy was being sold at 20 mercall (200 kg) per pagoda because 'the fear of the Marata army coming to rob the country hath induced the farmers to bring their paddy hither in considerable quantities for sale.'[33] But this constitutes an unusual occurrence and by and large both wars and famines[34] did tend to inflate prices.

The position of weavers in the economy has to be judged in terms of the cost structure, the market price of cloth and their own income. However the information on the price of cotton, yarn, dyes and the cost of bleaching is so scattered and disparate that it does not really provide an idea of the cost structure. Moreover the interacting effects of various components of costs is too complex to be analysed properly—for instance the effect of the price of foodgrains on the price of cloth. While Oxenden commented from Surat in 1663 that the merchants varied the prices of cotton goods depending on the scarcity or abundance of crops,[35] it was conversely believed that cloth actually became cheaper because the weavers worked twice as hard in order to earn more and compensate for the dearness of provisions.[36] It seems more correct to assume that the price of cloth did not fluctuate much because the merchants were already tied to fixed contract prices. Hence the increase in costs was met by cutting down the weavers' price, resulting ultimately in the emigration of weavers and shortfalls in supplies.

In 1672–3 when the price of cotton was 15 pagodas per candy[37] (it is stated that earlier in 1659 it had been 9 pagodas per candy), and paddy was being sold at 5 to 6 pagodas per candy in the Madras region and at 2 pagodas per candy at Masulipatnam,[38] the price of unbleached salempores was 12 to 14 pagodas per corge (a bundle of twenty pieces). From 1673 to 1681 the price of salempores registered very mild fluctuation, remaining more or less constant at 14 pagodas per corge, and the paddy price fluctuated between 5 to 6–6½ pagodas per garce. Even in March 1693, paddy was being sold at 25 mercalls per pagoda and the price of salempores ranged from 10 pagodas and 25 *panams* per corge to 14 pagodas per corge; but in late 1693 and 1694, the price of paddy increased to 13 to 14 mercalls per pagoda; by November 1694 it was 7 mercalls per pagoda and the weavers had begun to leave the Madras region and move southwards in search of cheaper paddy.[39] While the prices of paddy and cotton shot up during times of famine, the price of cloth was artificially regulated by means of the contract. The merchants compensated for the squeeze from above by pushing the weavers below the level of subsistence. A report prepared by George Morton Pitt towards the close of the eighteenth century[40] shows that while in average years the percentage share of the weavers was thirty-five, in famine times when the price of cotton and thread rose it fell to as low as ten per cent for the coarse varieties. The consequences of the short-sighted policy of the company were the flight of weavers, starvation deaths and even change-over to other professions.

Famines occurred with great frequency throughout the seven-teenth century. Famine broke out at Masulipatnam in 1630–2. Price of cloth soared, cloth became scarce and the factors wrote to Bantam: 'the major part of both weavers and washers are dead, the country being almost ruinated [*sic*] ... occasioned by the great dearth of rice and other grain.'[41] In 1647 famine raged in the Madras region as well as at Masulipatnam. The factors at Fort St. George reported that 3,000 had died at Madras while San Thome and Pulicat lost five times that number: 'People gave themselves for slaves to any man that will but feed them.'[42] Ivy, the President at Fort St. George, wrote to the president and council at Surat: 'How violent the famine hath been here is not to be credited ... here is not above one-third of the weavers, painters and washers living of what were formerly. This hath made cloth 15 per cent dearer ... ' . Ivy also reported that cloth was very scarce and shortfalls in supplies were expected to last three years.[43] In 1659 famine again broke out at Masulipatnam and continued until 1661.[44] In 1673 there was a severe famine at Madras. In 1688 famine recurred at Masulipatnam and Madras and can be termed the most severe in the entire century. The price of paddy increased by 400 per cent.[45] The last decade of the century again witnessed a famine in 1694–5 at Madras.[46] Grain was imported into Madras from the Godavari delta, from Visakhapatnam, from Ganjam and even from Bengal.[47] Many merchants indulged in the dubious practice of making a profit out of grain. So also perhaps did the East India company, which managed to store up more than 100 garce of paddy and 40 garce of rice.[48] This was the time when weavers no longer worked for a wage but for payment in paddy, which was given in advance.[49]

Weaver Corporate Organization

DONATIONS

In many respects the social position of weavers in the seventeenth century stands in sharp contrast to their position in the earlier phases during the Chola and Vijayanagar periods. From the few rare inscriptions of this period it appears that weavers' guilds did survive into the seventeenth century but that they were no longer a privileged group. Lack of royal patronage had destroyed much of their importance, if not their initiative,[50] and the petty kingdoms of the Nayaks and poligars (Palayakkarar) which arose in the seventeenth–eighteenth centuries failed to offer the weavers and other artisans the sense of security they had enjoyed earlier. The numerous records endowing them with social and ritual privileges in the heyday of the Vijayanagar empire are virtually absent in this period. Instances of individual or collective endowments by weavers are noticeably rare. Nevertheless they were made, and contrary to the theory that local and caste organizations ceased to exist from the Vijayanagar period onwards, one finds the survival of weaver and merchant guilds and even local and caste assemblies right into the seventeenth century.

Reference to a collective donation by the weavers' guild comes from Tiruppulivanam, Chingleput district, in the year 1679,[51] by when Vijayanagar rule had officially ended. (Sri Ranga III, who was virtually the last ruler of Vijayanagar, died in 1672). The people of the *nadu* and *desam* of the Kaikkola guild made a provision for midday offerings and worship to the god Palesvarasvamin. Yet another record from Kaliyapettai, Chingleput district, registers a cowle (charter) given to the weavers of Kanchipuram by Angalgu Krishnappangaru, the agent of Kasturi Rangappa Nayakar (1620–30) and the founder of the village after the death of his master.[52] The weavers also made several joint donations to temples in co-operation with merchant guilds and other professional groups. In 1680, at the initiative and leadership of the Ayyavole, one of the most ancient guilds in South India, a joint gift was made to the god Nanjundes-vara of Lepakshi-Sthala[53] in which the Tantuvayin (weavers) and Devanga (Telugu weavers) contributed certain fixed rates on looms. Similar contributions were also made by other specialized castes in textile production like *rajakas* (washermen), *vastra-bhedakas* (cloth dyers) and *vastra-rakshkas* (tailors), as well as professional castes like the potters, barbers, etc.[54] Similarly in 1745, again under the leadership of the Ayyavole, all the professional castes of Arsikere who were adherents of Vira-Saivism made a joint donation to the temple of Siva—an *addedu* of grain being paid by the shops of the cloth-sellers, tailors, goldsmiths and grain dealers, and for each loom of the Billimagga and Devanga.[55] In another instance from Koratagere (Maddagiri taluq, Tumkur district), the Devanga weavers made a joint contribution at the rate of 1 *hana (panam)* per house for Kamatesvara Durga Mahakali under the leadership of the Pancalar.[56] The record is dated 1656. The only instance of weavers casting images and setting up deities in the temple, an expensive form of temple service, come from Kadiramangalam, Kumbakonam taluq, Tanjavur district.[57] In 1789 the weavers of Kadiramangalam had new images of Draupadi–Dharmaputra cast for the temple and made an agreement to contribute 1/8 of a rupee per year for the worship.

Some rare instances of individual donation also exist. Valudinayakaperumal Ulagamuludum Nikkachcheydan, a Kaikkola landowner, constructed the temple of Mayakkuttan in Perungulam, Tirunelveli district.[58]

There are a few instances of grants of land being made to weavers by the temples in recognition of their service to the temple. In 1632 the Kaikkola-Mudalis of Pallikondai, who performed for the Uttara Ranganathasvami temple the service of bearing the image of the god in procession, were given a hereditary grant of some land and a portion of the *prasadam*.[59] The Kaikkolar of Valikandapuram in Tevaiyur, Perambalur taluq, Tiruchirapalli district, were given 200 *kuli* (0.66 acres) of wet land for the service of bearing the deity Sribali Nayaka.[60]

THE FIGHT OVER PRIVILEGES

The quarrels between the various castes over the question of privileges extended into this period. These disputes continued to be contained in the root-paradigm of the *idangai* and *valangai*.

Interestingly, in the few epigraphical records pertaining to the Kaikkolar in this period, they are referred to as 'Senguntar', the alternative caste name[61] by which they prefer to be known in present times. This seems to suggest that the Kaikkolar became downgraded socially and it is extremely significant that even now the term 'Kaikkalavar' is a term of abuse in the Tamil country. The social degradation of the Kaikkolar in this period is however only a surmise which cannot be substantiated in terms of actual evidence in this period. However, only social degradation can account for such a rigorous attempt to change their nomenclature and glorify themselves. A copper plate from Rasipuram (Salem district)[62] gives a long panegyric of the Senguntar community, referring to all their legendary exploits.[63] In another record known as the Morur Kangeyar copper plate,[64] the Senguntar of the *idangai* are said to have performed a great act of sacrifice; as a reward they were paid annually 12 *panams* from contributions levied by all communities like the oilmen, the artisans, etc. The Pattunulkara weavers are, for the first time, mentioned in the inscriptions in connection with a fight over privileges. At Kumbakonam during the period of Tirumalai Nayak, a quarrel broke out between the Pattunulkara (literally silk weavers) and the Chettis over the question of precedence in the matter of receiving betelnut on marriage occasions. The issue was resolved by determining that a cloth, some betel leaves and nuts, were to be given to the goddess and then to the Chettis and Pattunulkarar simultaneously.[65] The record makes a very significant point—that the Pattunulkara weavers had emerged in a predominant position in the Tanjavur region. Social privilege did not merely mean the claiming of certain symbols of ritual precedence, but sometimes even extended to social legislation. An extremely interesting example of social legislation comes from Honnavalli (Tiptur taluq, Tumkur district) in *c.* 1600.[66] The record states that the various castes of Honnavalli village such as the Devanga weavers, the washerman and the potters, made some regulations about women who lapsed from marriage. The inscription is cryptic since it offers no explanations for a legislation of this sort, but it is nevertheless a proof of the continued activity of caste organization and local assemblies in the seventeenth century.

The only attempts at claiming a brahmanical status among the weaver castes were made by the Pattunulkara weavers, which again indicates that they were probably economically on the ascendant during this period. In 1704 in Madurai on the occasion of *Avani Avittam* (an auspicious day in the year when the holy thread is changed) eighteen Saurashtra 'Brahmins' were arrested by officials at the behest of Brahmins for performing rites forbidden to them. When the issue came up before Rani Mangammal, she resolved it in favour of the Pattunulkarar or Saurashtras.[67] If this evidence is reliable then this record provides an interesting example of sanskritization in this period.

However, as in the earlier periods, the main antagonists of the weaver castes in the social sphere were not the Brahmins but the other Sudra castes. The seventeenth-century traveller Fryer makes a very penetrating comment on the attitudes of the various castes:

But the most insolent were the artificers; as the engravers, refiners, goldsmiths, carpenters, and the like, who behaved themselves not only disrespectfully to their superiors but tyrannically to those of a viler rank, as the husbandmen and labourers. Whereupon they jointly conspired their ruin, and with that their own slavery, taking the Moors to their assistance who not only reduced the usurpers to composition, which was that they should be accounted the scum of the people and as base as the Holencores [scavenger caste] and not be permitted to ride in a palanquin at their festivals . . . but on horseback which they count as high disgrace; but they [the Moors] also took power into their own hands which, though despotic, the gentus endure.[68]

Left-Hand Right-Hand Conflicts and the Company's Contract for Cloth

The left-hand right-hand conflicts and social tensions generated as a result of the clamour for social privileges among the lower castes took on a new complexion during the seventeenth century. In the Vijayanagar period all such conflicts had centred around the temple and had mainly involved precedence in temple honours and ritual recognition. But in the seventeenth century all conflicts between the left-hand and the right-hand castes were invariably related to the company and its interests, and the scene of many of these caste fights was the Black Town which lodged the weavers, merchants and other artisans affiliated to Fort St. George. The company faced the task of legislating and regulating the affairs of the entire Madras region. Thomas Pitt, the Governor of Fort St. George in the closing years of the seventeenth century, once said in desperation: 'I never met with so knotty a villainy in my life, nor even with anything that gave me so much trouble and perplexity as this [the left-hand right-hand factionalism] has done.'[69] Pitt ultimately had to resign his governorship because of his failure to handle the left-hand right-hand issue properly.[70] He was however not the first to leave under a cloud over this same issue. President Ivy and his successor Greenhill had been equally harassed by the problem. Greenhill was in fact personally involved in the quarrels.

The first major left-hand right-hand conflagration occurred in 1650–2. The company's chief merchants, the Brahmins Venkata and Kannappa who had held office under Ivy (1646–7), were sought to be replaced by Seshadri and Koneri Chetti who had originally held this post under Greenhill. The Brahmins had the support of the president, Baker. Accusations and counter-accusations were hurled by both the parties and the entire Black Town population, of which the weavers, painters (weavers of chintz) and washers formed a sizeable part, was dragged in. The weavers took advantage of the insecure position of the Brahmin chief merchants in Greenhill's regime to decamp with the advance made to them. As a punitive measure Rudriga and Timmanna (supporters of Seshadri), the brokers, were imprisoned while the Brahmins went unpunished because of Baker's intervention. In 1651 the first caste war broke out in the Black Town and following this Baker made his award on 5 November 1652, determining the various streets through which the left-hand and right-hand castes could pass with regard to their weddings and funerals;[71] any violation of this was punishable by a fine of one thousand dollars.

By 1653 tension had again begun to mount, fanned by the Brahmins on one side and the Komatis on the other. The Beri Chettis took a stand against the Komatis[72] due to the competition for the company's contract for cloth. The Brahmins declared that Timmanna and Rudriga tried to persuade the 'Mooree' and 'Caingaloone'[73] weavers to put themselves under Seshadri's protection, but only the Mooree weavers joined him. Seshadri provoked a left-hand right-hand quarrel by inciting the Moorees to take their funeral procession through the west gate, which was forbidden to them. The painters also eventually joined Seshadri. They were persuaded by Seshadri to quit the Black Town in protest. Precisely the same accusations were hurled by Greenhill and his supporters at the Brahmins. In a document titled 'Charges against the Brahmins by the painters, weavers and others inhabiting Chennapatnam', the Brahmins were accused of creating a rift among the painters and winning the support of the cooly painters. As a result with their support the Brahmins got themselves appointed *samaya mantris*, i.e. head of all the right-hand castes in Madras. This statement is extremely interesting since it shows that the painters were classified as right-hand. So were the Kavarai, a caste of weavers mentioned by Abbe Carre.[74] Other weavers like the Kaikkolar were classified with the left-hand. On the incitement of the Brahmins a section of the weavers left the Black Town in protest.[75] After the painters came to town again, a quarrel was sought by the Brahmins with a goldsmith for tenanting the same house as them in spite of his low birth.[76] The Caingaloone weavers also seem to have been victimized by them. The Brahmins also played a double game with the Beri Chettis, sometimes siding with them and sometimes opposing them. The Brahmins as *samaya mantris* collected 100 pagodas from the inhabitants of the Black Town and levied a contribution from the washers. When a fight broke out between the Pallis[77] and the painters the Brahmins supported the Pallis, upholding their right to take out their marriage and funeral processions, limiting the Balijawar to the Komati street.[78] The quarrels lasted till 1654 when the courts decided in favour of Greenhill, recalled Baker for his partisan attitude and dismissed the Brahmins.[79]

The East India Company, by virtue of its jurisdiction over the artisan and merchant population of the Black Town, was compelled to get involved in caste questions and social issues. In 1672, the president of Fort St. George determined the proportion of contribution (in paddy) to the temple (not specified) by the various castes.[80] Anyone who violated the regulation had to pay to the company a fine of 12 pagodas. The company seems to have respected caste feelings and the records show that a washerman's street was made alongside the potter's street, separated by the Gentu Street (Brahmin street).[81] The company conceived of the extremely interesting idea of winning over the Black Town population by forming a joint corporation, with members from the East India Company as well as the local population. The dispatch from England dated 1687[82] expounds this idea in a masterly manner:

If you could contrive to form a corporation to be established of the natives mixed with some English freemen. . . . we might give the members of that corporation some privileges and pre-eminences by charters under our seal that might please them (as all men are naturally with a little power) . . . and it is not likely but the heads of your several castes, being made Aldermen and some others Burgesses, with power to choose out of themselves yearly their mayor and to tax all the inhabitants for a town hall or any public buildings for themselves to make use of . . . and wise governments may so manage such a society as to make them proud of their honour and preference and yet only ministerial and subservient to the ends of the government. [!]

The company further made the wise injunction that in the nomination of aldermen, no two members of the same family or of the same caste were to be appointed, but 'to mix the castes that you might always hold the balance.'[83]

This idea of forming a grand corporation of the various castes did not work. The only time the castes worked in harmony was when the company sought to impose a tax for meeting the military expenses on the Black Town population. The castes combined to the detriment of the company's interests and organized a strike against the enhanced taxation.[84] Otherwise, caste tensions continued, resulting in the second major flare up in 1707. The main issue was the competition between the left-hand and right-hand merchants for securing an exclusive trade contract with the company for the procurement of textiles. The right-hand merchants had so long held exclusive contract for cloth, and when in 1694 the company sought to give Mooda Verona's place to Japa Chetti, a merchant of the left-hand caste, the right-hand caste merchants protested.[85] The company, however, finally chose to form a joint stock consisting of both left-hand and right-hand merchants. Timmappa and Allingall from the right-hand caste and Basappa Japa Chetti and two 'weaver-merchants', Namashivaya and Bussporte from the left-hand castes,[86] were made the company's chief merchants.[87]

In 1696 the company was called upon to settle the quarrel between a goldsmith and a 'cooly chetti' employed by the Dutch as their merchant in Tegnapatnam.[88] The minor caste tensions of the 1690's combined with the major issue of an exclusive contract for textiles to produce the great caste war of 1707. The issue began when the right-hand castes attempted a massacre of the left-hand castes on 26 June 1707, following a dispute between the two groups about taking wedding processions through certain streets.[89] Thomas Pitt wrote to Sir Edmund Harrison on 8 December 1707 explaining the origin of this quarrel which was seemingly based on such a petty issue:

The grounds of these dissensions and what led the right-hand castes into this hellish conspiracy, I find to be that it had firmly been practised among them that the left-hand caste could not make any bargain or buy any goods unless one of the right-hand were joined with them to direct their shares, so that they governed the trade as they thought fit and the company's investment fall generally under their management. . . To break the neck of which I put up papers upon the sea gate and other public places to encourage all merchants indifferently to bring in goods to be sorted out by the Company's masters. The left-hand castes (who are the only merchants that can serve you in this method) being intimidated by threats of the Right. . . were prevailed upon by the assurance of our protecting and defending them. The Right-hand upon seeing their designs defeated and that the reins of trade were no longer in their hands, fell upon this barbarous attempt to regain it, industriously spreading false rumours amongst the poor and ignorant people to cause them to desert us.[90]

The significance of Governor Pitt's statement can be seen by the fact that the dispute between left-hand and right-hand castes over marriage processions immediately followed the sale of the company's broadcloth to some merchants of the left-hand and the purchase of textiles from the merchants by the company at the seagate.[91] On 20 August all the right-hand castes left the Black Town, taking with them the washerman caste, the *mukuva* or fishermen caste, and some of the artisans. Colloway and Vincatte acquainted the company's board of enquiry that the factions were 'more upon their making the investment for the company than that of the streets' and till these disputes were over nothing could be done. The Kaikkolar caste of weavers as also the oilmen caste played a peculiar role in these quarrels, sometimes siding with the right and sometimes with the left which led to bitter complaints against them. They were compelled to make their final decision and they declared for the left-hand castes.[92]

Thomas Pitt, who was then governor, failed to settle the issue of the left-hand right-hand castes effectively, leading to his resignation.[93] The factionalism between the two groups essentially over the question of the company's contract for cloth but apparently over flags and symbols recurred sporadically and in spurts throughout the eighteenth century—in 1725–30, 1749 and 1786.

From the evidence presented so far on the social position of weavers in the seventeenth century, it seems quite plausible to conclude that their position had undergone great vicissitudes since the heyday of the Vijayanagar empire. While they still retained some initiative and some bargaining power, their prospects were gloomy. They were steadily being drawn into greater and greater dependence on the company for their survival.

The period of magnanimous donations to temples, of acquisition of economic, social and ritual privileges from the state and the temple was over, and the weaver community records of the seventeenth century striving so desperately at self-glorification read more like an apologia. It must be noted that the East India Company had a demoralizing effect not only on the weavers but on the majority of artisan castes. Their administration had long-time detrimental effects not only on handlooms but on handicrafts in general. The position of weavers in the seventeenth century reflects what can be regarded as the beginning of an eclipse for South Indian handlooms and weavers which has lasted over two hundred years.

CONCLUSION

This study has endeavoured to trace the vicissitudes of the weaver communities in the light of the changing fortunes of the handloom industry in medieval South India. The position of the weavers has been studied with reference to three distinct phases. The first phase, from the ninth to the thirteenth centuries, was characterized by flourishing trade conditions, powerful guilds, village assemblies and caste-based armies. The second period, from the fourteenth to the sixteenth centuries, was the period of Vijayanagar domination. This period witnessed renewed urbanization, the growth of trade under royal patronage and commercial wars between the Golconda and Vijayanagar kingdoms. Towards the end of this period, i.e. the close of the sixteenth century, Portuguese power was established at Goa. The opening decades of the seventeenth century witnessed keen commercial competition among the Moors, the Portuguese, the Dutch, the English and the indigenous Hindu merchants, the Chettis. This was the phase in which whatever the weavers produced was bought up and they were in a strong bargaining position *vis-a-vis* the companies. The middle decades were distinguished by the great commercial struggle between the Dutch and the English. In the closing years of the century, Dutch power was clearly on the wane and the English East India Company was gradually working towards a commercial monopoly. But the last decade of the seventeenth century, which witnessed the triumph of the English East India Company in India, also saw the victory of protectionist interests in England and the passing of the first of the prohibitory laws against the import of Indian calicoes.

In the framework of this periodization an attempt has been made to analyse the socio-economic position of the weavers. In the period of the Chola and Vijayanagar empires the weavers, like other professional groups, formed a part of the temple complex, but they catered not only to the needs of the temple and the locality but also to the foreign demand for textiles. Two types of economies existed side by side—one which met the demands of the immediate local market by the sale of cloth by the weavers themselves at the local fairs, and the other which catered to the export market and had wide ramifications composed of a chain of textile traders organized at various levels. The same distinction could be perceived in the variety and price of cloth which ranged from cheap, low-quality common wear to extremely expensive export varieties. Evidence indicates that the weavers of superior cloth, catering to the court and the export market, were economically very well-off in contrast to the ordinary coarse cloth weaver.

State taxation seems to have been imposed at every level of the textile industry. Taxes on cotton yarn, thread, sales tax on cloth and profession tax are mentioned. Yet taxation was perhaps not so heavy because the various categories of taxes were most often consolidated into one tax under the head of a capital tax on looms. Where the strain of taxation was felt to be heavy the weavers restored the equilibrium by coming together and striking work. There are numerous instances of effective economic protests by the weavers, both in Chola and Vijayanagar times. The state on its part adopted as pliable an attitude as possible towards the weavers, yielding in the face of economic protests and offering commercial concessions and tax remissions in new settlements.

The Vijayanagar period did not witness any major changes in the textile organization and trade. Merchant guilds did not decline, nor was the local administration drastically overhauled. The changes which crept into the system of textile organization were gradual and came about in the late sixteenth–seventeenth centuries rather than with the foundation of the Vijayanagar empire. The most important development during the late sixteenth century was the rise of Portuguese power in South India. The Portuguese strengthened their control through a policy of political partnership either with Vijayanagar or Golconda alternately, and established their commercial monopoly by adopting the system of cartazes or passes. They sought and obtained exclusive contracts for trade in textiles and spices. Following the Portuguese, the Dutch and the English companies in the seventeenth century sought to capture the triangular trade and, later, expanded the directions of the export trade in textiles. The share of the indigenous merchants in this trade is a widely debated issue ranging between extreme viewpoints among historians such as those who hold that the Portuguese and other European companies destroyed Asian shipping and others like Van Leur who believe that native shipping and trade accounted for a considerable percentage of the overall trade. Evidence does strongly suggest that the share of Asian merchants in the export trade, especially inter-Asiatic trade, was considerable. But by the end of the seventeenth century the English East India Company had virtually established a trade monopoly and the effects of this could be seen in the eighteenth century, which witnessed the ruin of many great indigenous banking houses.

The status and role of the various weaving castes in contemporary medieval society reflected the ups and downs of their economic condition. In the Chola period the main weaving community of the Tamil region were the Saliyar while those of the Andhra and Karnataka regions were the Sale, Jedara and Devanga weavers. But in the Vijayanagar period the Kaikkolar, who had essentially functioned as a military group under the Cholas, emerged as full-fledged professional weavers and replaced the Saliyar in the Tamil country as the dominant weaver community. This change-over to weaving was most probably the result of the disbandment of caste armies after the death of Rajaraja Chola III (early thirteenth century). Another notable feature of the Vijayanagar period was the mobility of the weaver castes. The Kaikkolar of the Tamil country settled in the Andhra and Karnataka regions while the Devanga weavers moved into the Kongu country from Karnataka. The motive was usually economic betterment, although migration could also be caused by factors like famines or Muslim oppression, as in the case of the Pattunulkaran caste of weavers who moved from Gujarat to Madurai in stages.

The medieval period was a period of urbanization and temple activity under the patronage of the Vijayanagar kings, and the overall prosperity of the empire was marked by an extension of production, increase in trade and the cheapness of essential commodities. Society was in a state of flux and there was an upward movement among most of the Sudra professional groups. The weavers, as an important artisan group, were leading beneficiaries of the commercial prosperity of the empire. Textile trade till the sixteenth century was to a great extent in the hands of the merchant guilds, but there was considerable economic mobility among the weavers, so that some of them joined the ranks of the merchants while others became master weavers, employing workers under themselves. The weavers formed their own corporations with codes and regulations and any violation of these rules was punished by social ostracism. The status of the weavers in society can be measured in terms of the size and nature of the donations made by them to the temples, their ownership of land, and the social and economic privileges extended to them by the state and the temple. The extensive donations made by weavers (they figure in the inscriptions as donors next only to the merchants) is proof of their having been an important and prosperous professional group in medieval society. The temples reciprocated by bestowing on them certain ritual honours and extended to them the privilege of *sangu* and *tandu* (the right to blow the conch shell and the right to ride the palanquin) which were important status symbols. But the economic power and social privileges gained by the weavers and other leading professionals like the Kammalar (smiths) was hardly in keeping with the low place allotted to them in the ritual hierarchy. They tried to overcome these caste and ritual barriers through the creation of origin myths, intensification of the left-hand right-hand schisms and conflicts, and participation in the medieval heterodox movements. The upward movement on the part of the weavers manifested itself in caste exaltation on the one hand and social protest on the other.

With the establishment of the rival European companies in the seventeenth century the lives of the weavers no longer revolved around the temple but around the European factories and the Black Towns. The squabbles of the left-hand and right-hand castes invariably involved the crucial question of who was to secure the Company's contract for cloth. The weavers gradually began losing their bargaining power and independence as they worked on a system of advances provided by the companies' merchant middle-men. Their creativity also suffered since they were compelled to copy mechanically the musters provided to them. Economically they were much worse off. In times of famine the paddy was cornered either by the company or by the provision merchants who had a contract with the company. While grain prices soared during famine, the income of the weavers remained fixed by the company contracts, resulting in the death and destitution of weavers. The turn of the century saw the passing of the first prohibition act against Indian calicoes, and the cotton revolution in England dealt the handloom weavers a great blow. This study closes with the ban of 1700, a warning of the shape of things to come.

Rewind Forwards

The Indian textile industry has a continuous history dating back to the pre-Christian era. Weaving communities of South India such as the Senguntar (Kaikkolar), the Saliyar, and the Devangar, can boast of a hoary tradition, with their ancestors playing a prominent role in the economic and cultural life of the South in the great temple building era of Pallavas and Cholas. In today's age of rapidly changing lifestyles and technology explosion, the continuance of the traditional weaving communities in the handloom industry, is a remarkable feature of the South Indian cultural fabric.

Continuance of weaving communities does not mean that the process of survival has been smooth. The Democles' sword remains suspended over the handloom weavers, many of whom live constantly on the poverty line. 'It is the grave pit, not the loom pit' (*tarikuzhi alla, chavu kuzhi*) quoted a weaver when I asked him about the condition of the handloom industry in his area. I was in Gugai area of Salem district, an ancient cotton textile centre, the year was 1986. Coarse carpet weaving on pitlooms was even then prevalent in this area. My presence was due to an official assignment by the Handloom Board, then under the Ministry of Commerce, for a project on 'Weaver Folk Traditions in South India', commenced in 1985 and completed in 1988.

In the course of my interviews with the weavers in Tiruchirapalli, Salem, Thanjavur, and Madurai districts, I was startled to find that they expected me to act as a medium of communication between them and the *sarkar* at Delhi. They expressed fears about the 'New Textile Policy' framed in 1985, especially the onslaught of the powerlooms in the handloom sector. Some of them complained about political interference and the malfunctioning of some cooperatives. The caste *sangha*s of the weavers presented petitions they had drafted to the Handloom Board. I took these petitions back to the office of the Development Commissioner of Handlooms along with the folk traditions and loom songs that I had been asked to collect. I was told that my job was to collect folk traditions and not listen to the weavers' petitions.

My report on 'Folk Traditions' in which I had willy-nilly included some of the petitions, lies among other unpublished reports in the Ministry of Textiles. However, I continued to go back to the weavers, particularly in Salem, which is my maternal hometown. Some of the recent researches were presented by me at the special panel on handlooms at the Congress of Traditional Sciences and Technologies organized by Peoples' Popular Science and Technology (PPST) at Chennai in 1996. In the workshop held with weavers and textile manufacturers, it became clear that big-time cloth manufacturers and merchants especially those dealing in silks were prospering while subsistence weavers were being pushed below the poverty line. I was told by a weaver from Erode, '*kadar kadarudu*', a pun on the word kadar which is the Tamil word for khadi. While the word kadar represents home-made cloth, *kadaral* in Tamil means lamentation. In other words, the weaver was trying to tell me that handlooms were in its death throes.

The handloom industry in the course of the twentieth century, especially in the post-independence era, suffered not due to the competition of the mills of Lancashire or Manchester, but by India's own powerlooms. The penetration of powerlooms has been such that block-printed mill imitations are available even of such inimitable textiles as Andhra *kalamkari*s and the Madurai tie-and-dye sarees called *chungdi*s. The recommendations of the Kanungo Textile Enquiry Committee of 1952 reiterated the support to powerlooms, a clause the mill owners exploited to get the maximum benefit. Kanungo stated in his report:

For ordinary cloth, the pure and simple handloom is and must be a relatively inefficient tool of production. With the exception of those items which required an intricate body pattern, there seemed to be no variety of fabric which the handloom industry could produce in a better quality or at a lower price. A progressive conversion of handlooms into powerlooms through organised effort over a period of fifteen to twenty years is therefore, recommended.[1]

Nityananda Kanungo calculated that about fifteen yards per year would be the average requirement per person and this could be met by replacing ten handlooms with one powerloom. The report led to violent protests by weavers from Kanchipuram and they led a 'hunger march' (*pattini pattalam*) under the leadership of their union head Parthasarathy.[2]

The Santanam Committee appointed by the government of Tamil Nadu in 1972 proposed that excise duty on powerlooms should be brought on a par with that on handlooms. It further proposed that certain export sectors should be reserved for handlooms in the already existing markets in the European countries, particularly England as well as the United States. The committee suggested that Latin American and African countries should be explored in terms of their market potential for Indian handlooms. However the Santanam Committee was probably the last effort to stem the tide against handlooms. Subsequent committee reports have been clearly tilted in favour of powerlooms. A census survey of handlooms by the Development Commissioner of Handlooms in Tamil Nadu commenced in 1995 and was published by the Handloom Board, Government of India, New Delhi in 1997. The next survey according to the information provided by the Ministry of Textiles, is due in 2006–7.

The New Textile Policy framed in 1985, was a major milestone for the Indian handloom industry. Under the Reservation of Articles of Production Act, twenty-two items were reserved exclusively. It further stated that 'any power-operated loom violating this law is liable to various penalties including confiscation of goods made by powerlooms, fine and imprisonment of the producers'.[3] Unfortunately there was a wide gap between policy and implementation compelling the handloom weavers to threaten to go on 'satyagraha' since it was 'a matter of life and death' for them.[4] Writing about the Seventh-Five-Year Plan, a memorandum submitted by the Tamil Nadu Handloom Weavers' Co-operative Society Limited stated that the plan provided only Rs 53 crores towards grants and subsidies for the controlled cloth, Janata cloth and other handloom varieties resulting in an allocation of only 0.002 per cent. The petition pointed to the enormous growth in unauthorized powerlooms, which produced cheap polyester yarn mixed textiles in large quantities, pricing handlooms out of the market. The petitioners also pointed out that merchant–weavers with powerlooms used the limited number of handlooms they had to claim government subsidies and then went on to produce these 'reserved' items on their powerlooms. The 1985 Reservation of Articles Production Act had set aside twenty-two items earmarked exclusively for handloom weavers but the Act was wholly ineffective in preventing the powerlooms from creating the same items at a lower cost and selling it in the 'grey-market'.

In early 1990s, a series of surveys of the handloom sector were undertaken as a prelude to the Mira Seth Committee Report. The most important of such efforts was the Development Commission's report, *Compendium of Handloom Schemes* published by the Ministry of Textiles, Government of India in 1993. One of the startling facts brought to light was that 45,921 powerlooms constituting 30 per cent of the total number of powerlooms (which stood at 155,395) were unregistered and unauthorized. Some traditional handloom weaving communities like the Devanga Chettiars of Gugai in Salem district, enjoyed the concessions or subsidies offered to the handloom sector while surreptitiously operating powerlooms. A related report[5] published by the Ministry of Textiles points out that the handloom sector provided employment to more than 30 lakh weavers' households, with about 103 lakh weavers. The statistics, however, indicate only male weavers by and large, since women weavers were rare except in the North-Eastern region. The report estimated that while the handloom sector provided nearly 20 per cent of the total cloth production and brought in about Rs 1500 crore of export earning annually, the majority of weavers lived below the poverty line.

The Indian textile industry today is clearly caught on the horns of a dilemma. In the past, Indian handlooms had been signifiers of Indian culture and the hand-woven fabrics of India made Indian cotton 'king' in the world. Daniel Defoe, the celebrated author of *Robinson Crusoe*, wrote that after the Revolution of 1688 when William and Mary landed in England, they were resplendent in Indian calico. Yet Indian textiles today are caught between the devil and the deep sea. Modernization and cost effective production lies in the direction of powerlooms and jetlooms while pristine culture and Indian aesthetics is best reflected in handlooms. While unique Indian handloom varieties like *mashroo, telia, jamdani,* and *ilkal,* along with the weavers of these fabrics made their way to the Festivals of India, their domestic market had shrunk drastically. Cloth was woven only when it was commissioned since weavers could not run the risk of trying to market their own cloth. Handlooms had become so prohibitively expensive that synthetic textiles were more easily found even in the weaving villages.

Today, individual weavers and co-operative societies survive on subsidies. Every effort has been made by the Government of India to set aside certain varieties exclusively for the handloom sector. The introduction of the 'Janata cloth' aimed at taking handlooms to the homes of the poor and the working class. Nevertheless the compulsion seems to be towards pacing out handlooms in the face of the ubiquitous presence of powerlooms and jetlooms. This trend is clearly reflected in the deliberations of the Tamil Nadu state draft committee on handlooms circulated on 30 December 1996.[6] While continuing to exercise concern about the condition of weavers, the report reflects changing perceptions about future handloom policy. On the one hand it shows that besides having 628 mills in the organized sector, Tamil Nadu has 2,30,179 power-looms in contrast to 4,29,000 handlooms, a ratio of 1:1.86. The reality on the other hand is quite different. The official powerlooms figure does not include the unregistered powerlooms that could nearly double the official figure. The committee clearly states that a 'Powerloom Development Corporation' should be set up to facilitate the process of conversion of handlooms into powerlooms.[7] A corpus fund would be created to provide financial assistance to weavers for 'modernizing' and converting their looms. The reason offered for pacing out handlooms was that Tamil Nadu was a surplus producer of yarn and hence a substantial quality of the yarn produced had to be sold outside the state to textile centres like Bhiwandi, Ichalkaranji, and so on. This would no longer be necessary once more handlooms are converted into powerlooms with a much higher turnover.

The priorities for the millennium have been outlined in the latest textile policy released by the Tamil Nadu government:

In an increasingly globalized economy, industries will have to be more market-driven than ever before. Therefore any strategy designed to meet this objective will have to start with the markets and work backwards.... The unifying themes which will therefore run through this process will be greater measures of 'Market-orientation' and 'value addition'.[8]

The policy makers have clearly spelt out the need for reducing the subsidies given to handlooms. The *Report on Textile Policy* published by the Handlooms, Handicrafts, Textiles and Khadi Department in 1998 states:

Due to low value addition, low productivity and increasing costs of raw materials and labour, handloom fabrics have traditionally suffered a cost handicap in the market compared to similar products produced by powerlooms. This is particularly true in the case of simple, plain weave fabrics like dhoties, lungies, towels, plain sheeting and plain sarees. Therefor, to offset this inherent handicap, subsidies have traditionally been given to the handloom sector.... It is estimated that the annual subsidy in Tamil Nadu is of the order of Rs 70 crores. Despite such support, the economic condition of the weavers producing low value fabrics has not improved. In fact, as noted earlier, there continues to be a steady attrition in the number of handloom weavers.[9]

The latest Textile Policy of Tamil Nadu in its final form came out in 2000.[10] On the one hand the report offers some sops to the handloom sector such as reducing the 2 per cent sales tax on hank yarn and stricter enforcement of the 1985 Act on Reservation of Articles for Production, but on the other hand most of the existing subsidies were clearly being withdrawn. Recognizing the domination of the powerloom sector in the handloom industry, the Tamil Nadu Government Report estimates a total of 17 lakh powerlooms (including a rough idea of the unregistered ones) in the country in 1998. The policy makers point out that while exports of fabrics and made-ups of the powerloom sector in 1996–7 was Rs 5603 crores (54 per cent of the national total), the comparative figure for the handloom sector was Rs 1780 crores (roughly 17.2 per cent of the national total) only.

The Satyam Committee report concretized many of the steps indicated in the Textile Policy of 1998. The committee recommended the repeal of the Handloom Reservation Act, Hank Yarn Obligation Act, and withdrawal of fiscal assistance to handloom workers. The main thrust of the recommendation was the phased integration of handlooms into the powerloom sector. The South India Handloom Weavers Organising Committee reacted to this with a series of protests, agitations, and country-wide marches against the Satyam Committee recommendations. The Handloom Weavers Association pointed out that more than 3.5 crore people in the rural sector were dependent on handloom weaving for their livelihood. Handloom had also managed to hold its ground in the face of new technological and industrial challenges. The handloom sector produced 4000 million square metres of fabric in 1989–90, which rose to 7000 million in 1999. Handloom exports amounted to Rs 341 crores in 1990, which shot up to Rs 2010 crores in 1999. Armed with facts and figures in their favour, handloom weavers' organizations joined forces with cotton farmers and textile and garment workers to resist globalization culminating in a grand protest march in April 2000.[11]

Weavers' co-operatives that have been a seminal feature of the handloom industry have also passed through many vicissitudes. Co-operatives came up to fill the vacuum caused by the decline of the powerful medieval corporations of the weavers. In the colonial period the weavers were alienated from their temple towns and moved into the 'Black Town' area of the British, whether it was Fort St George in Madras Fort St David in the Kanchipuram region or the 'Black Town' area around Masulipatnam. Relocation in these craft areas meant for the 'black' artisans and merchants of India, dependent entirely on the largesse of the British, led to the loss of community identity and economic independence. The formation of handloom weavers' co-operatives in the pre-independence era was a major thrust in the direction of bringing some kind of cohesion into the economic life of the weavers.

The first attempt to bring handloom weavers into an economic association was the Co-operative Union of Kanchipuram started in 1905. This was followed by a number of such societies coming up in the 1920s. It is estimated that during 1926–7, there were 52 weavers' co-operative societies.[12] A spate of weavers' co-operatives were also started in the early 1940s obviously in order to meet war exigencies. During the world war the societies were used primarily to produce gauze, bandage cloth, and mosquito nets for soldiers.

The Textile Enquiry Committee which submitted its report in 1954 estimated that roughly 1.5 million weavers were employed in the handloom sector.[13] This figure could be higher, perhaps 1.8 million, if one included the part-time workers engaged in weaving.[14] Details of total number of weavers presently employed in the handloom sector is provided in the Textile Policy Report issued in 1998. According to this, handlooms accounted for about 23 per cent of the textile production of the country and employed more than 30 lakh households and about 100 lakh weavers. Despite the decreasing importance of handlooms in the textile production of the country, handloom weaving continues to be the sole means of sustenance for many rural families, next in importance only to agriculture. Protection to the handloom sector through the formation of co-operatives therefore became vital for the survival of lakhs of families dependent on the loom for their daily living.

The weavers' co-operatives were based on the principle of maximization of benefits from handlooms both to the nation and to the weavers. Co-operatives would ensure quality of the fabrics and also enable the revival of handloom varieties like telia, kotni, or mashroo through sustained training of weavers in these dying traditions. Equally important, weavers were brought into the co-operative fold in order to take care of their primary needs—easy availability of yarn at reasonable rates, credit facilities, and the ensuring of a steady income through regular marketing outlets.

In the early years of its inception the co-operative movement was comparatively weak. The main cause was the lack of financial cushioning which most co-operatives so badly required. Credit facilities were too little and reached the weavers rather late. Wide fluctuation in yarn prices caused them great hardship and there were no means of ensuring that finished products would find a ready market. In fact handloom sales survived on festival time rebates. A survey undertaken in 1934–5 showed that out of the twenty-nine weavers' co-operatives in Tamil Nadu only fourteen were functioning.[15] Some of the societies especially in Salem were hijacked by master-weavers who got into the management and diverted funds to themselves. Siphoning off of society funds was a major factor behind the failure of co-operatives in both Uraiyur (Saurashtra Weavers' Society) in Tiruchirapalli and in the Devanga Chettiar dominated co-operatives in Salem. Another major problem for the handloom sector was the existence of bogus and defunct co-operatives. The author herself in her extensive tour of co-operatives in South India came across many which functioned only at one-third of their number. This was specially true of many Tamil Nadu co-operatives in Salem, Tiruchirapalli, and Madurai.

The year 1935 however was crucial for the Tamil Nadu co-operative sector in the creation of a new institution. The Tamilnadu Handloom Weavers Co-operative Society is an apex institution for the primary weavers co-operatives societies. Registered in August 1935, it has taken care of the needs of both silk and cotton weavers. Yarn was purchased by the society from the co-operative spinning mills which constituted sister concerns of the handloom co-operatives and sold to the primary societies through special depots. The apex society also distributed raw silk, dyes, and chemicals to the primary societies besides proving sales outlets. In 1938, weavers of Kudlu, Shiribagilu, Madhur, and Kasargod met under the leadership of the freedom fighter M. Umesh Rao and founded the Kasargod Weavers' Co-operative Society. Kasargod and Chirakkal can boast of being possibly the oldest weavers' societies in Kerala.

The war years witnessed an overall improvement in the handloom industry, for weavers both within and outside the co-operatives. Foreign outlets were opened to the weavers with the slowing down of textile production in war torn countries like England. But two developments in the transitional years of independence, especially in 1946–97, brought distress to co-operatives. One was the abolition of controls on textiles resulting in acceleration in production and sale of mill cloth and the other was the imposition of surcharge on free yarn. In 1948 the surcharge was abolished after repeated appeals by co-operatives to the government.

Co-operative societies improved their position in the 1950s. The number of weavers' societies rose from 1,092 in 1950–1 to 1,191 in 1952–3 in Tamil Nadu and Andhra Pradesh (before Andhra became a separate state). The number of looms within the fold of the primary societies also increased from 1.76 lakhs to 2.12 lakhs. The Tamil Nadu co-operatives in 1953 boasted of 2.29 lakh weavers as primary members. However in terms of percentages, this was less than 50 per cent of the total number of weavers in Tamil Nadu. More than two-thirds of the weavers continued to work for master-weavers.

The Madras volume of the 1961 census carried a special report (part XI A) on the condition of the handloom industry in the State. The census stated that Tamil Nadu ranked first in handloom industry employment, at both household and non-household industry levels. Handloom industry accounted for a fifth of the total workers in the manufacturing sector of the state in 1961. Khadi seemingly did not gain much ground in South India, the number of workers in this sector constituting less than 1 per cent with the bulk of the weavers in the general category of handloom weaving.[16] The weavers seemed to have been mostly outside the co-operatives. In Salem which ranked first in terms of its contribution to the handloom industry, production was dominated by master-weavers working within the framework of caste sanghas. The most important master-weavers and merchants in this region were the Devanga Chettiars who were migrants into the Kongu country (comprising mainly Salem, Coimbatore, and Dharmapur districts) from Andhra and Karnataka.

The Santanam Committee in its report of 1972, highlighted the fact that handloom weavers preferred to work for master-weavers despite less favourable terms of service. The report stated that while the number of looms within the co-operative fold were 139,039 (with the highest number 32,638 in Salem), those outside co-operatives being employed by master-weavers were 416,947. According to Santanam:

Only 30% of handlooms in Tamil Nadu are under co-operatives and the bulk of the remaining 70% are working for private producers. Even now many weavers prefer to work for master-weavers because the weaver is able to get advances and other assistance in times of need, as at the time of marriages and funerals.[17]

In order to benefit weavers through the co-operatives system, the role of the apex body was strengthened with a view to bring more weavers into its fold. In 1971 the apex society had had a membership of 1221 with a paid up share capital of Rs 43.25 lakhs.[18] In 1975 this amount stood at Rs 122.23 lakhs but the number of members had fallen to 965. In accordance with the renewed efforts to promote handloom co-operatives, societies came up in Salem, Coimbatore, Kanyakumari, South Arcot and North Arcot, Tiruchirapalli, Kanchipuram, Tanjavur, Srivilliputtur, and Tiruchendur. Besides supplying yarn and dyes, the centres also provided training in designs. The gradual phasing out of the Janata cloth scheme had resulted in unemployment among the weavers and therefore co-operatives also endeavoured to provide part-time employment to weavers.[19] In the year 1975 Handloom Development Corporation was started in most of the southern states.

In the course of my fieldwork in the weaving areas of South India during 1985–6 when the New Textile Policy was framed, I encountered mixed reactions from individual weavers, co-operative societies, and master-weavers. Considering that most of the weavers continued to operate outside the co-operative sector, there was a lot of scepticism about the efficacy of the co-operative system itself. Anekal Co-operative Society in Karnataka showed that out of the forty looms installed, twenty-four were idle looms and the total number of weavers registered were just twenty.[20] The only success stories in the co-operative sector in Karnataka is from the South Canara region, that is Irkal, Bannihatti, Gadag, Ramadurg, Mangalore, Udupi, and Mijar.

The weavers co-operatives are also going through an acute crisis in Andhra Pradesh. A case study of the Sai Baba Society in Ponduru, Srikakulam, an ancient textile centre is symptomatic of the malady that has hit co-operatives. The society was established in 1930 and by 1960 it had 2000 members on its rolls. The co-operative set up its sales depot and invested its profits in shares in spinning mills, thereby ensuring availability of yarn to its weavers. In a recent survey, Pankaj Sehsaria reports:

Today, membership has fallen to less than 200 people with regular work being made available to not more than 20. No payment has been received from APCO [Andhra Pradesh State Handloom Weavers Co-operative Society] since Nov. 1998 and total dues stand at Rs. 14 lakhs.... A working capital crunch has forced it to halve its monthly production from nearly Rs 2 lakhs last year to about one lakh today....[21]

The situation of weavers in Andhra today is bleak. Bad debts caused to a large extent by non-payment by Andhra Pradesh State Handloom Co-operative Society Limited (APCO), no working capital, idle looms and under employment, drastic fall in production—this is the general state of the co-operatives. In 1991, newspapers reported starvation deaths and suicides by the weavers of Andhra Pradesh. A graphic feature story in the *Frontline*[22] recounts the mass suicides by handloom weavers in Dubakka, Medak District of Andhra in 2001. The previous government headed by Chandra Babu Naidu seemed determined to restore co-operatives to their past record of efficiency and success. This purpose would be best served if the state government can ensure both accountability and efficiency on the part of APCO.

The weeding out of bogus or idle co-operatives became a major target of the government initiatives based on its findings published by the Ministry of Textiles as *Compendium of Handlooms Schemes* in 1993. The Ministry also declared that its major goal would be to bring about 30 lakh weavers with seven and a half lakh looms within the co-operative fold.

Since the 1990s the government has also focused on bringing women of the weavers' caste into the weaving sector. It should be noted that traditionally women (except in the hill areas) did no weaving but only spinning which was entirely women's occupation. In 1990–1, as a result of the efforts of the government, out of the total of 190 weavers' co-operatives set up in the state of Tamil Nadu, 10 were organized exclusively for women with a special financial assistance of Rs 10 lakhs per society for implementing benefit schemes for the women. The high powered central government committee on handlooms which submitted its report in 1996 further introduced welfare schemes for women. Apart from insurance and general medical benefits, maternity benefits were increased from Rs 500 to Rs 2000.

Weaving co-operatives were to be complemented by the creation of larger number of spinning co-operatives. The establishment of spinning co-operative mills was started in 1975–6. The 1993 scheme envisaged the setting up of new mills of 255,000 spindles along with the modernization of existing mills. The National Co-operative Development Corporation (NCDC) was to constitute the primary agent for the implementation of the above schemes.

It was stated by the 1993 Handloom Commission Report that the creation of idle looms and 'on-paper' co-operatives was primarily because of the absence of support structures; and adequate monitoring and auditing of co-operatives on a more rigorous and frequent basis. The support structures for co-operatives were envisaged in 1993 as 300 Handloom Development Centres (HDC) and 500 Quality Dyeing Units (QDU). These were to take care of the following requirements of the weavers:

a. Adequate arrangements for ensuring supply of yarn of the requisite quality and counts.
b. Providing facilities for quality dyeing and training in improved dyeing practices.
c. Creation of a market network for the textile products of co-operatives.
d. Generating adequate working capital to sustain long term production as well as the setting up bodies which would provide loans to the weavers.

e. Setting up design development centres with the necessary infra structure to disseminate these designs to the primary societies of the weavers.

Credit facilities have essentially been provided by National Bank for Agricultural and Rural Development (NABARD). In addition to this, funding for weavers has also come from Tamil Nadu Backward Classes Economic Development Corporation (TABCEDCO). The 1993 Hand-loom Schemes also came up with something new called 'Margin Money' for weavers. Weavers below poverty line could avail a cash assistance of Rs 2000 per person with a ceiling of one lakh 'Margin Money' per society. In addition to these credit plans, the government also started thrift fund and group insurance schemes for workers in the handloom sector.

Time alone can tell whether languishing weavers' co-operatives has received a new lease of life as a result of these measures. The picture might be clarified by the report on handlooms currently under preparation by the Ministry of Textiles in co-operation with the office of the Development Commissioners of handlooms from the centre and the states due to be published either towards the end of 2006 or in 2007. However in an interview on 23 December 2001 by the author, the Deputy Director of Weaving at the Chennai Weavers' Service centre, G. Parandamaiah estimated that the salaries of weavers working within the co-operatives, stood at between Rs 50 to Rs 70 (these figures may be on the more optimistic side) while the weavers working under master-weavers marginally made a little more, between Rs 60 to Rs 80.

The 1998 Co-operative Societies' Report clarifies the present position of weavers' co-operatives in a nutshell. The co-operative sector has survived till date on the strength of its powerlooms and not handlooms. According to the Tamil Nadu government survey undertaken in 1997, handlooms constitute a mere 20 per cent within the co-operative sector while powerlooms constitute 78 per cent. Composite or organized mill sector can be said to constitute 2.5 per cent.

At one time, handlooms were almost synonymous with cottons. This was true of most of the celebrated textile centres of the South which had black soil or red ferruginous loamy soil. Whether one is thinking of Madurai, Kanchipuram, Coimbatore, or the cotton belt of Andhra Pradesh centring around Kakinada in East Godavari (Bhimavaram) and Ongole (Dharmavaram), the association of textiles was only with cotton. It was only Karnataka which produced raw silk or tussar fabrics. Sericulture was a latecomer in the Tamil country having been introduced by the

British in Kanchipuram only in the nineteenth century. Therefore cotton yarn constituted the essential raw material of the handloom industry.

It is strange but true that cotton yarn no longer sustains the handloom industry and in the near future pure cotton yarn may become a thing of the past. The fading of the cotton yarn due to the tough competition offered by viscous yarn/polyester fibre formed a major plank at the discussions of the draft committee which framed the 1999 New Textile Policy of Tamil Nadu. It was pointed out in the report that Tamil Nadu was a major producer of cotton and cotton yarn as well as the leading state in its export. In 1995 it was estimated that 40 per cent of the total yarn produced in India came from the mills of Tamil Nadu. In terms of spinning capacity, the installed spindleage in the state was 32 per cent, that is 10.09 million spindles out of the total capacity of 31.25 million spindles in the whole country. The cotton spinning mills in Tamil Nadu also account for 42 per cent of cotton yarn exported from the country.[23]

What the draft committee report begins with, is a representation of Tamil Nadu as the traditional stronghold of cotton.[24] The projection into the future is however dismal. Spinning mills in Tamil Nadu are beginning to close at an alarming rate. Cotton production in the region has declined considerably with the annual production averaging around six lakh bales. Very often the state has to buy its cotton from other cotton-ginning areas like Punjab, Gujarat, Haryana, Madhya Pradesh, and Maharashtra. Ironically, while on the one hand the State continues to export cotton, it has to import cotton at times for its own requirements.

The new textile policy of the state suggests remedial measures on a war footing. The cotton policy of the State envisages the following measures:

a. Establish a state level advisory committee on cotton with representatives from the department of agriculture, agricultural universities, farmers, industry, and trade.

b. Cotton crop should be accorded the status of a plantation and be exempted from the operation of the Land Ceilings Act. If this is done, textile mills could undertake corporate farming of cotton.

c. Expansion of cotton production in the rice fallows of Kaveri and Tamraparni river basins. The ground level survey of cultivable wastes to be undertaken in order to introduce cotton production in suitable tracts.

d. The task of reducing contamination in cotton to be entrusted to the Tamil Nadu Pollution Control Board which would set up common treatment plants.

In a recent interview, M. Sonkusley,[25] the Director of the Weavers' Service Centre at Chennai, commented on the efficacy of the following measures laid out for sustaining cotton textiles. He said that the declining trend of cotton continued despite all efforts primarily because cotton production was not cost-effective compared to polyester or viscose fibre. Secondly, he believed that in so far as cotton yarn is concerned, Pakistani cotton that is long staple yarn is much finer as compared to the Indian cotton which is comparatively coarse, and therefore dominates the market.

Polyester cotton is at present growing very popular. In so far as the silk sector is concerned except for traditional areas like Kanchipuram, silk weavers in areas like Bangalore tend to use an admixture of art silk or polyester yarn along with pure silk threads. Filature silk is also gaining increasing popularity. A rough comparison between the figures of 1989–90 and 1990–1 provided in the *Draft Committee Report* of 1996, reveals the dramatic increase in polyester yarn production in Tamil Nadu in just one year:

Table 1: Yarn Production

Yarn production (million kg)	1989–90	1990–1	1989–90	1990–1
	All India		Tamil Nadu	
Cotton yarn	1639	1795	473 (28.9%)	529 (29.5%)
Polyester yarn	272	328	46 (16.9%)	63 (19.2%)
	(16.9%)	(19.2%)		

Note: The figures in brackets indicate the percentage share of Tamil Nadu in the all India volume of yarn production. Source: A rough comparison between figures of 1989–90 and 1990–1 was provided in the *Draft Committee Report* of 1996.

Nalli Kuppusami Chettiar who represents 'Nalli Sarees' commented on the pathetic situation of cotton weavers among his own Saliya community as well as among the Senguntar and the Devanga communities. Most weavers have taken to the production of polycott sarees. Alternately firms like Nallis which are specialists in silk are providing gainful employment in the silk sector to many traditional weavers.[26]

Nalli Kuppusami also spoke about the changing quality of silk yarn.[27] While Indian silk yarn is used for the weft, the warp yarn is imported from China. Chinese yarn has several advantages:

a. The yarn is of even quality, being two deniers six threads. One cocoon consists of three deniers of yarn.
b. The yarn being multi-voltane, provides a special sheen to the silk.

c. Most important, Chinese silk yarn is cost effective for the Indian silk
    producer.

Policies on textile designs have also undergone a sea change over the
last millennium. The dilemma of the central and state governments in
the context of traditional designs versus consumer demands has resulted
in ambivalent attitudes towards indigenous knowledge systems in the
sphere of designs. Traditional floral and geometrical patterns were woven
into traditional colours which combined to produce textile designs which
were cultural signifiers. Consumerism and computerization are thrusting
on the weavers designs which may reflect popular tastes but is at variance
with patterns reflecting their cultural ethos and aesthetics. The use of
computer-aided designs (CAD) by handloom weavers has resulted in
setting another major trap for themselves. Unlike traditional designs many
of which could be woven only on the handloom, the 'received' designs
from craft centres could be easily created by the powerlooms at half the
cost. As a consequence a grey market was created in which powerloom
owners produced and marketed chungdi design sarees as chungdi
handlooms. A survey undertaken in 1993 showed that while one kilo-
gramme of hank yarn could yield only ten metre of handloom cloth, the
production reflected 1.206 million more of handloom cloth proving the
existence of a grey market.[28] Evidence revealed that 20 per cent of the
hank yarn was used to produce handloom imitations with the now easily
copied computer designs.

It is interesting that complaints about the dilution of purity in designs
go back to the late nineteenth and the beginning of the twentieth century
when European demands compelled the weavers to churn out block-
printed cultural collages such as bicycles in a row followed by the tree of
life, sometimes inset with the face of the imperious British queen Victoria.
Natesa Shastri wrote in *Journal of Indian Art* in 1889:

Take any Madura or Kanchipuram cloth and look upon the borders and see
what art you find in it.... Can the machine do this? It can perhaps make one
pattern and be turning that out for endless time. A weaver can every third day,
turn out a new pattern. But all of them have declined. As plain and white washed
mud walls are to the grand structure of the Mahabalipuram rathas or
Kanchipuram gopurams, these pieces of machine-made cloths are to our own
hand-made cloths.[29]

The concerns of Natesa Shastri continue to exercise the minds of
weavers, textile designers, and governmental, craft centres even today.

The Crafts Council of India, Madras Craft Foundation (MCF) Non Governmental Organizations (NGOs) like the Dastkar as well as design and craft departments attached to the Weavers' Service Centres set up by the government, have tried to fulfil task of supplying weavers with designs. The report of the 'High Powered Committee on Handlooms', brought out in 1996 states as its primary objectives :

a. Development of new designs which bring out the strength of hand-looms, including designs for renewal of heritage for domestic and international markets.
b. Services of reputed private and foreign designers may be availed of.
c. CAD should be increasingly used.
d. Commercial viability of the designs should be kept in view and closely monitored through market feedback.

This report however seems to hang on the horns of a dilemma in its endeavour to reconcile heritage designs with computer aided ones. When the Festival of India euphoria was on, that is in the 1980s, G. Ramulu, a master-weaver from Puttapakka, Andhra Pradesh, who had won the Craftsman Award for his telia design which had reached the Paris Festival, told me that his winning design had been inspired by the Japanese designer Issey Miyake.[30] It is ironical that a weaver coming from the heartland of tie-and-dye designs, the cluster of villages led by Pochchampalli, should claim that he drew inspiration from the Japanese tie-and-dye produced by Miyake.

A survey report on textile designs by S. Rangarajan, Technical Advisor, Indian Handloom Export Promotion Council, submitted in 1996, is perhaps one of the best recent studies on this theme.[31] He attributes the dilution and/or disappearance of traditional designs to the loss of traditional patronage as well as changing lifestyles and consumer demands dictated in many cases by Western fashions. The whole design tradition now stands on its head by craft centres, CAD workshops, and well-meaning NGOs. Designs instead of originating in the minds of the weavers and forming and reflecting an entire cultural ambience, now reflect the ideas and aspirations of graduates coming out of National Institute of Designs (NID) or National Institute of Fashion Technology (NIFT) located in Ahmedabad, Chennai, or institutions abroad. The major problem with CAD is its intrinsic quality of symmetry. To quote Rangarajan on the attitudinal problems of design graduates and computer designers:

They are impressed by its (weavers design tradition) lesser qualities like minute workmanship and intricacy of ornament and miss its main virtues like its infinite modulations in colour and texture and asymmetric decorative variety. These they consider forgivable defects resulting from a primitive consciousness or technical incompetence.[32]

Asymmetry used skilfully by the Indian has constituted a major strength of the handloom industry in contrast to the monotonous symmetry produced by the machine. Design suppliers using CAD have to keep in mind this factor. Rangarajan also points out that 'saris, curtains, bedspreads etc. are all produced with the same structure and design, dress materials printed with designs meant for quilt covers, blouse materials meant for cattle trappings'.[33]

Equally crucial to the survival of the handloom industry is the weavers' own native memory regarding certain traditional textile varieties like jamdani, *himroo*, or telia. Certain designs can be produced only on these fabrics which need to be produced only on the handloom. Secondly the brocaded design appropriate for jamdani would be inappropriate for telia. The latter is adaptable only to the tie-and-dye variously known as *ikat, patola, kotni*, or chungdi in different parts of India with minor variations in technique. These varieties of cloth with their intrinsic patterns or designs had given to Indian textiles the primacy they had enjoyed in the past. Designs like *panna hazara* which are exclusively used for brocades such as *jamewar* and jamdani, necessitate changes of shuttle in every pick, an operation that is possible only if the loom is being operated manually. Design centres, whether of the government or private NGO sector, need to be sensitized to the fact that if handlooms were to hold their own against powerlooms and justify their continued existence in a era of jetlooms, they can do so only by producing that, both in terms of textile variety and designs, which the powerlooms can never hope to imitate.

Handlooms can be designer-ware in a sense in which powerloom products can never be. This can be explained in one word as 'exclusivity'. Nalli Kuppusami who has been forced by circumstances to shift in a large measure to CAD dictated by consumer demands told me that his grandfather had a clientele which was interested in the possession of sarees which would be exclusively for themselves. He points out that the maximum length that could be woven on a traditional hand-loom was eighteen yards. Therefore no more than three women could wear the same type of saree throughout the world.[34] Powerlooms and CAD have led to the virtual disappearance of this quality of exclusiveness.

To argue in favour of preservation of traditional designs and exclusive handloom varieties is not to deny the imperative need for commercial viability if handlooms are to survive. The concluding remarks of Rangarajan's report is worth quoting in this context:

India's handloom designers must have a training which equips them to combine two things. They must know how to draw upon India's own rich heritage and they must know how to adapt the inspiration obtained from this heritage to current living needs of other countries and the new era of twenty first century warp of life.[35]

In this age of technological revolutions, what place can traditional pitlooms, horizontal looms, and vertical looms occupy? Prima facie, handloom weavers struggling to weave three and a half to four metres per day appear an anachronism when thousands of yards are produced by the fastest of machines almost in the twinkling of an eye. Yet handlooms are indispensable as the cultural signifiers of India. It must not be forgotten that Gandhi made the charkha or spinning wheel the symbol of India's freedom struggle. Therefore handlooms have survived and can continue to flourish in the next millennium only if they follow the principle of appropriate technology.

Many of the national textile policy framers today seem inclined to believe that the survival of handlooms in their present form is impossible and their conversion into powerlooms is inevitable. This trend comes through very strongly in the textile policy framed by the government of Tamil Nadu. The proposal tabled by the high powered committee on textiles states that conversion of handloom into powerloom was to be brought about by the financial aid and support of two agencies—a Corpus Fund for Loom Modernization; and the Powerloom Development Corporation. To quote the policy makers on this theme:

We must allow conversion of Handlooms to powerlooms. Tamil Nadu is at present surplus in cotton yarn production. A substantial quality of yarn ... is now sold outside the state in centres such as Bhiwandi, Ichalkararji, Calcutta, Delhi etc. We should encourage conversion of handlooms to powerlooms so that more yarn can be consumed within the state and value added cloth is produced. Financial assistance may be given to the existing handloom weavers to acquire powerlooms which will not only help the weavers improve their income but also make cloth available to the public at lower rates.[36]

What is noteworthy is that conversion of handloom into powerloom is actually not possible. The fundamental difference lies in the fact that while handlooms are wooden, powerlooms are made from cast iron.[37] Therefore in effect the so called conversion will mean 'junking' hundreds of thousands of handlooms.

The handloom will however have to be retained if a serious effort is to be made to revive unique weaves like jamdani, himroo, jamewar, telia etc. Handlooms alone can provide the necessary flexibility in weaving these delicate and gorgeous fabrics. To quote Rangarajan:

Even after the loom is set up and the weaving process has begun, corrections and changes in design can be effected easily by the weaver in contrast to power-loom weaving where no manual intervention is possible. In fact designs which involve change of shuttle in every pick and even part of a pick, can be produced on a handloom.The tie and dye and jamdani techniques for instance, are supreme examples of such techniques unique to handlooms. Random insertions of different types of yarn, use of slubs, fancy yarns, wadding threads and so on, are operations which are routinely performed on a handloom, but cannot be easily reproduced on a powerloom. It is because of the ease with which designs can be played around with on a handloom that even large mills use handlooms at the design stage.[38]

Technology is however very much a part of the traditional handloom industry. However technological inputs have been most effective only when the initiative has come from below, that is from the weavers or master-weavers themselves. These grassroot initiatives have been specially facilitated by award schemes introduced by the National Research Development Corporation (NRDC). For example as far back as 1985 when the New Textile Policy had just come into force, S.P. Subramanian, an ordinary weaver from the Devanga weaving community of Uraiyur, an ancient textile centre in Tiruchchirapalli, invented the *korvai* loom. This was a significant technical innovation. Traditional border designs like *thalambu* could be created on a saree only by using a number of working hands in the weaving process. Subramanian's invention comprised a separate box attached to the sley box. A small shuttle in this box automatically weaves a *korvai* border on the saree. Where the earlier process needed two full-time weavers, the 'Espeyes Korvai Loom' of Subramanian needs only one weaver and thus reduces labour input by 50 per cent.[39] The indigenous *jala* or *adai* looms used by handloom weavers are still preferred to the jacquard for weaving intricate *zari* designs. Nalli Kuppusami Chettiar pointed out that as someone born into the Padma Saliyar weaving tradition he still uses the adai in case of *chinna pettu* or traditional single border designs.[40] *Kuttu* is another technique in which the body and border of a saree is interlocked, a technique that is slow and appropriate only for the pitloom with a jala being used in weaving the *pallav* and a lattice dobby for weaving the border.[41]

Marketing and the commercial viability of handlooms, has been one of the primary target areas of textile specialists and policy makers in both the centre and the various states known for their textile production such as Gujarat and Tamil Nadu. This concern was voiced by Mani Narayanaswami who was the first Development Commissioner of Handlooms. However it was N.P. Seshadri, the man who did much for handlooms who put this issue in perspective, justifying the international fairs and Festivals of India meant for boosting India's arts, crafts and culture, especially handlooms:

By organising handloom pavilions and airs, it is hoped to dispel the commonly held view that handloom products are coarse and of limited utility and project that these are fashionable, durable and are capable of meeting all needs from clothing the peasant with his plough to draping the trendy teenager at the discotheque sporting his guitar. The idea is to present the handloom industry as a modern, commercially viable and forward-looking industry, capable of holding its own, against the mechanised textile industry.[42]

As the country enters the new millennium it has done so not only with an explosion of infotech and globally spread industries with competing technology but also with the uniquely Indian, culturally distinct handlooms. The road to survival has been a Herculean task for both the handloom weavers and the Indian policy makers. As government after government comes out with report after report, the most recent one being the Satyam Committee and Meera Seth Committee reports, the phasing out of handlooms is seen as inevitable even as the members recommend elaborate measures for its protection and survival.

After the great Coromandel famine when thousands of weavers died in Andhra and Tamil Nadu, Alfred Chatterton is said to have commented that the Indian handloom industry has survived because the weavers have learnt to live on less and less. True then, true now, but with this important difference. The weavers all over South India have bonded themselves together for their war against mindless mechanization,[43] for their right to a way of life which has been theirs for over two thousand years.

Notes to Introduction

1. Paiyampalli is located in Tirupattur taluq. See *Ancient India*, 1964–5 and *Indian Archaeology—A Review*, 1964–5 and 1967–8. Also see K.S. Ramachandran, *Archaeology of South India: Tamil Nadu* (Delhi, 1980), pp. 36–7. Phase I, A, layers eight and nine to which the circular potsherds and bone awls pertain, has been roughly dated at 1300 BC

2. Adichachanallur is in Tirunelveli district. The site was excavated around 1900. I am grateful to Mr K.S. Ramachandran of the Archaeological Survey of India (New Delhi) for providing me with this evidence. The evidence can be dated between the second century BC and first century AD. Evidence of cloth wrapped around pottery in the Nilgiris is discussed in J.W. Breeks, *An Account of the Primitive Tribes and Monuments of the Nilgiris* (London, 1837). This evidence pertains to about the fourth century AD.

3. *Silappadikaram*, ed. P.V. Somasundaranar (Madras, 1969).

4. *Manimekalai*, ed. P.V. Somasundaranar (Madras, 1971).

5. *Silappadikaram*, canto v, stanzas 16–17; canto xiv, lines 205 to 210.

6. *Arthashastra*, ed. R.P. Kangle, 2 vols. (Bombay, 1963), book ii, chap. ii, sec. 29, line 115.

7. *Porunararrupadai* in *Pattupattu*, ed. P.V. Somasundaranar (Tirunelveli, 1971), verse 383.

8. Ibid., verse 393.

9. Ibid., verse 155; verse 383, line 12; verse 393, especially lines 14–15.

10. *Atharvana Veda*, 10/7/42, cited in Moti Chandra, *Prachin Bharatiya Vesh-bhusha* (in Hindi) (Prayag, 1950), p. 14.

11. *Rig Veda*, 6/9/2–3, cited in ibid., p. 15.

12. *Agananuru*, ed. P.V. Somasundaranar (Madras, 1974), lines 133–5.

13. *Narrinai Nanuru*, ed. A. Narayanaswami (Madras, 1967), stanza 247, line 4.

14. See for instance Irfan Habib, 'Notes on Indian Textile Industry' in *Essays in Honour of Prof. S.C. Sarkar* (New Delhi, 1976), pp. 181–2.

15. *Purananuru*, ed. U.V. Swaminathan (Madras, 1971), verse 125, line 6; verse 326, line 5; also *Narrinai*, verse 353.

16. *Atharvana Veda*, 10/7/42, cited in Wilhelm Rau, *Weben und Flechten in Vedischen Indien* (Wiesbaden, 1971), p. 19. The transliteration of the verse is:

Puman enad vayati udgrnati
Puman enad vijabharadi naghe
ime mayukha upa tastabhur divam
Samani chakrus tasarani otave.

17. *Purananuru*, verse 274.

18. See R.E.M. Wheeler, 'Arikamedu, an Indo-Roman Trading Centre on the East Coast of India', *Ancient India*, no. 2, July 1946, p. 34.

19. See *Indian Archaeological Review 1964–5*, ed. A. Ghosh, p. 25.

20. *Silappadikaram*, canto v, 32–3.
21. *Manimekalai*, verse 28, line 39.
22. *Silappadikaram*, canto xvi, lines 205–18.
23. I. Mahadevan, 'Corpus of Tamil Brahmi Inscriptions', in R. Nagasamy, ed., *Seminar on Inscriptions* (Madras, 1968), no. 64, p. 60.
24. Aruvai Vanigar Elavettanar's poetry figures in *Nqrrinai Nanuru*.
25. Herodotus, vii: 65, cited in D. Schlingloff, 'Cotton Manufacture in Ancient India', *J.E.S.H.O.*, vol. 17, 1974, p. 81.
26. *Periplus of the Erythraean Sea: Trade in the Indian Ocean*, ed. Wilfred H. Schoff (New York, 1912), p. 59.
27. E.H. Warmington, *The Commerce Between the Roman Empire and India*, (Delhi, 1974), p. 175.
28. Pliny, xii: 84 and vi: 101, cited in ibid., p. 274.
29. *Periplus*, 62, p. 195.
30. Ibid., 59.
31. Ibid., 60.

Notes to Chapter I

1. *Economic Atlas of the Madras State*, National Council of Applied Economic Research (New Delhi, 1962), p. 103.
2. The Kasakudi plates of Nandivarman II—730–96, *S.I.I.*, vol. ii, pt. 3, no. 73—refer to the availability of *sengodi* (*plumbago zelanica*), whose root served as a powerful caustic in the Kanchipuram region. The records also refer to *kusumba*, i.e. safflower, (*E.C.*, vol. vii, Sk. 112), *manjishta* or madder and *nili*, i.e. indigo (*H.A.S*, vol. xiii, pt. ii, no. 14).
3. *E.C.*, vol. xii, Ml 31 from Tumkur and *E.C.*, vol. x, cb. 2 from Kolar district, both in Karnataka, and copper plate 18 of 1917–18 from Anantapur in Andhra.
4. *A.R.E.*, 286 of 1910 from Tiruvanakkoyil, dated 1339; Rangacharya, *Inscriptions of the Madras Presidency*, 3 vols. (Madras, 1919), vol. ii, pp. 1360–1. No. 996 from Kapistalam, dated 1542; *A.R.E.*, 201 of 1936–7 and 41 of 1922–3 from Tiruvamattur, dated 1550, etc.
5. Veman Shivram Apte. *Sanskrit-English Dictionary*, ed. Gode and Kasre (Poona, 1957), p. 1547.
6. *S.I.I.*, vol. xi, pt. i, no. 97, dated 1062, and *E.I.*, vol. viii, no. 22E, dated 1224.
7. *S.I.I.*, vol. x, no. 533, dated 1323; *S.I.I.*, vol. x, no. 507, dated 1314; *H.A.S.*, vol. xiii, no. 30, dated early fourteenth century.
8. *T.T.*, vol. i, nos. 70, 71 and 72, etc.
9. Edgar Thurston, *Castes and Tribes of Southern India* (New Delhi, 1976), vol. vi, p. 278.
10. *A.R.E.*, 400 of 1964–5 from Jinnur, and *E.C.*, vol. vii, Hl. 40 from Balagutti.
11. *E.I.*, vol. xxix, no. 19. The reference to the Jedara caste of weavers in the Tamil country occurs only from the seventeenth century onwards. See H. D. Love, *Vestiges of Madras* (London, 1913), vol. i, p. 547.
12. *A.R.E.*, 388 of 1911–12 from Sattravada; 400 of 1965–6 from Jinnur, etc.
13. *A.R.E.*, 269 of 1913–14 from Chidambaram.

Notes 193

14. *S.I.I.*, vol. iii, pt. 3 no. 128, p. 264. The Madras Museum Copper Plates of Uttama Chola from Kanchipuram; vol. v, no. 223 from Chidambaram of the period of Rajendra Chola; *A.R.E.*, 538 of 1916–17, of the period of Kulasekharadeva, from Seramadevi.

15. *A.R.E.*, 187 of 1927–8, from Perukalandai, of the period of Kongu Chola Vikramadeva; *S.I.I.*, vol. vii, no. 103 from Tiruvottur of the period of Ethiroli Chola, and *A.R.E.*, 132 of 1915–6, from Ettiyatali, of the period of Maravarman Kulasekharadeva, the beginning of the fourteenth century.

16. *A.R.E.*, 253 of 1907–8, Tiruvidaimarudur; *S.I.I.*, vol. vii, no. 451 from Achcharapakkam.

17. *A.R.E.*, 278 of 1911–12 from Tillaisthanam, and 228 of 1911–12 from Kumbakonam.

18. *A.R.E.*, 144 of 1928–9 from Tiruppalanam, and 627 of 1909–10 from Koneri Rajapuram.

19. *A.R.E.*, 300 of 1909–10 from Tirukkachchiyur.

20. *A.R.E.*, 286 of 1910–11 from Tiruvanakoyil, and 218 of 1910–11 and 276 of 1912–13 from Nerumbur and Pulipparapakkam.

21. *Itti Elupatu* of Ottakkuttar published with a commentary by Thiru Murugavel in the *Sengunta Mithiran*, serialized in June-July 1970. The work refers to the various military exploits of the Kaikkolar called Senguntar because of the curious hook-like weapon (*kuntam*) which they carried. See specifically stanzas 5 to 17.

22. *Vira Narayana Vijayam* contained in *Sengunta Prabanda Tirattu*, ed. Sabapati Mudaliyar (Madras, 1926). Although this work cannot be dated, its events refer to the period of Parantaka I (907–55) because Vira Narayana is one of the names of Parantaka. See *S.I.I.*, vol. ii, pt. 3, Udayendiram Plates of Prithvipati Hastimalla which refer to Parantaka Vira Narayana.

23. Senguntar was the special name (*sirappu peyar*) given to the community, while Kaikkolar denoted their occupational name (Kai + Kol = hand + loom rod and refers to the plying of the weaver's craft). This professional name was the one used in everyday parlance. In fact it was the practice of most castes to have two names. For instance the Shanar of Tirunelveli preferred to be known by their special name Nadar, rather than Shanar which denoted their profession, toddy tapping.

24. *Adi Diwakaram* (of Diwakaram Munivar), ed. Thandavaraya Mudaliyar (Madras, 1892).

25. *E.C.*, vol. iv, chap. 97 from Hattalakote and *E.C.*, vol. ix, Bn 66 from Madivala.

26. *A.R.E.*, 68 of 1958–9 from Yalamari.

27. The legend is found in the Tamil version of the *Skanda Puranam*, written by Kachchiyappa Sivachariyar, ed. Kuppuswami Nayakar (Madras, 1907).

28. *A.R.E.*, Nos. 5 and 7 of 1943–4 from Nandivaram.

29. *Devanga Puranam* of Mambala Kavirayar, ed. Sadasivayya (Madras, 1893).

30. Edgar Thurston, vol. vi, p. 265.

31. In fact the *idangai-valangai* classification of the various castes originated as military groups under the Cholas. (*A.R.E.*, 56 of 1912–13) Apart from *idangai* and *valangai*, the Chola inscriptions also refer to the *munrukai padaiyinar* (*A.R.E.*, 189 of 1895–6). The caste based army is discussed by K.S. Vaidyanathan in his article 'The Members of the Ancient South Indian Army (Senai); Their Assembly and Functions'. Quarterly Journal of Mythic Society, vol. xxxii, no. 4.

32. T. N. Subramaniam, *South Indian Temple Inscriptions* (Madras, 1957). The glossary defines *tirumadaivilagam* as quarters around a temple but in *A.R.E.*, 1921–2,. pt. 2, it is translated as temple square.

33. The reference to weavers as being settled in the *tirumadaivilagam* comes from Musiri (*A.R.E.*, 311 of 1968–9), Tiruvanakkoyil (*A.R.E.*, 286 of 1910–11), etc.

34. *S.I.I.*, vol. ii, pt. 3, no. 94.

35. *S.I.I.*, vol. ii, pt. 4, no. 128—The Madras Museum Copper Plates of Uttama Chola.

36. *S.I.I.*, vol. viii, no. 569.

37. *Jivaka Chintamani*, ed. P. V. Somasundaranar, (Madras, 1972), 1320 and 2477. This work belongs to the tenth century and its author is Tiruttakkadevar.

38. *S.I.I.*, vol. iv, no. 813 from Kanchipuram.

39. *E.C.*, vol. ix, N1 3, Kulottunga Chola, 1121.

40. *S.I.I.*, vol. i, no. 64.

41. *E.C.*, vol. viii, no. 33.

42. *E.C.*, vol. xi, Hr 87. Of this, the editor Lewis Rice quotes the belief that this type of shawl woven in Chittaldroog could be rolled up into a hollow bamboo (!)

43. For some illustrations, refer to B. Shivaramamurthy, *Amaravati Sculptures in the Madras Government Museum* (first to third centuries, the period roughly divided into three phases) (Madras, 1956), p. 101, plate v, figures 15 and 17; plate vii, figure 14. Also see the table on p. 35.

44. *Silappadikaram* canto v, stanza 16–17 and *Manimekalai*, verses 28 and 39.

45. R. Champakalakshmi, 'Tanjore Frescoes in the Brahadisvara Temple', *J. I. H.*, Golden Jubilee Volume, (Kerala, 1973), chamber 9, figures 13 and 14.

46. *S.I.I.*, vol. ii, pt. 2, no. 66.

47. *E.C.*, vol. v, Ak.no. 40.

48. *E.C.*, vol. v, B1 no. 236.

49. *Manasollasa* of Someshwar, the western Chalukya king of the twelfth century, Gaikwad Oriental Series, no. 84, pt. ii, verses 17, 18 and 19.

50. Ibid.: 21.

51. Ibid.: 24—*chakrareka suramyani*, 26—*chatushkona surekani* and *bindu yutani*.

52. Ibid.: 28.

53. *Jivaka Chintamani*, 71 and 1307.

54. Ibid., 923, 2090, 2444 and 3046.

55. The reference to Coimbatore as a leading textile centre is to be found in the account of the Chinese traveller Mahuan (fifteenth century) who refers to Coimbatore as Campamei. George Philips, 'Mahuan's Account of Cochin, Calicut and Aden,' *Journal of the Royal Asiatic Society of Great Britain and Ireland*, 1896, p. 345n.

56. *S.I.I.*, vol. v, no. 283.

57. *E.C.*, vol. viii, no. 33.

58. *Andhra Pradesh Government Archaeological Series*, vol. ix, no. 15.

59. *H.A.S.*, vol. xiii, no. 14.

60. *H.A.S.*, vol. xiii, glossary of terms by P. Sreenivasachar.

61. *Yajnavalkya Smriti* with the commentary *Mitakshara* by Vijnanesvara (1070–1100) tr. by J. R. Gharpure, Hindu Law Text Series, 2 vols., pts. 1–3 (Bombay, 1938), pt. ii, chap. viii, stanza 186.

62. *E.C.*, vol. vii, Sk 112 from Talagunda.

63. *E.C.*, vol. v, B1 236.

64. *H.A.S.*, vol. xiii, pt. ii, no. 14 from Mattewada.

65. *Mitakshara*, stanza 186.

66. Ibid.

67. *E. I.*, vol. xix, no. 4 from Kolhapur of the period of Silahara Gandaraditya dated 1135.

68. *Mitakshara*, stanza 186.

69. *Manasollasa*, verse 19.

70. Ibid., verse 20.

71. *E.C.*, vol. v, Bn 119.

72. *A.R.E.*, 197 of 1912.

73. *E.C.*, vol. ix, Cp 66.

74. I. Habib, 'Changes in Technology of Mughal India', paper presented at the Symposium on Technology and Society, Waltair, 1979, pp. 35–6.

75. *English-Sanskrit Dictionary*, ed. Monier Williams. The Sanskrit equivalents given for chintz are *vichitrapatam, chitrakarpasam*, etc.

76. I. Habib, Technology Symposium, p. 36, identifies vichitra with painted calico while Moti Chandra in his article on 'Costumes and textiles in the Sultanate Period', *J. I. T. H.*, no. 6. 1961, identifies it with printed calico—refer pp. 21, 27, etc.

77. *Manosollasa*, verse 21.

78. *Adaikalapantu* in *Tiruvachagam*, ed. P. Ramanatha Pillai (Madras, 1953), stanza 8.

79. *Sripindanajukti* with the *vritti* of Malayagiri, Devachand Lalbhai Jaina Pustakoddhara, (Bombay, 1918), verse 574, p. 157.

80. *Abidana Chintamani*, ed Dr. Hargovind Sastry (Varanasi, 1964), p. 227, pt. iii, no. 575.

81. *Nannul* by Bhavanandi Munivar, Kandikai's commentary ed. by the collective editorial board of Saiva Sidhanta Publication (Madras, 1972), stanza 24. Bhavanandi is said to be the contemporary of Kolottunga III—*S.I.I.*, vol. iii, no. 62 and also *S.I.I.*, vol. xiii (Pandavas), p. 123. I cite the relevant portions of this verse: *panjitan solla, panuval ilayaga .... kadire madiyaga ...* '.

82. The use of the kadir or spindle is a partial confirmation of Irfan Habib's belief that the spinning wheel came to India only in the fourteenth century (see I. Habib, 'Technology Symposium', pp. 14–15 and also his other articles on technology). For a further discussion on this point see Viyaya Ramaswamy, 'Notes on Textile Technology with special reference to Medieval South India', *I.E.S.H.R.*, April–June 1980.

83. See introduction for reference to vertical looms in Vedic India.

84. *E.C.*, vol. vii, Sk 145 from Kollu Mathada.

85. I am grateful to Pulavar C. Raju of Erode for giving me the Tamil text of this folk song. Since the poem cannot be dated, it is not being used as positive evidence of the use of horizontal looms in the twelfth–thirteenth centuries. It merely shows that horizontal looms were in use and since the basic structure of looms changed very little over the centuries, it would be natural to assume that this type of loom functioned in the medieval period.

86. I. Habib, 'Notes on the Indian Textile Technology in the Seventeenth Century', *Essays in Honour of S.C. Sarkar*, pp. 182–3ff.

87. Joseph Needham, *Science and Civilization in China*, 7 vols. (Cambridge, 1953–9), vol. iv, pt. 2, sec. 27, p. 124.

88. Ibid., pp. 102–3.

89. I. Habib, 'Notes on the Indian Textile Technology', pp.183 ff.

90. Streynsham Master, *Diaries*, ed. Richard Temple, 2 vols. (London, 1911), vol. ii, p. 171.

91. *S.I.I.*, vol. vii, no. 98.

92. *Tamil Lexicon*, 6 vols. plus supplementary, Madras, 1936. The word *achchu* is a generic term used in innumerable contexts with regard to the loom. It could mean the reed instrument for pressing down the threads of the woof, or the comb like frame in a loom through which the warp threads are passed or the weaver's plank (*achchu palagai*), but the terms *achchtari, achchkattu* and *achchkatti* indicate the patterned loom and one who specializes in figured weave. In the inscriptions the term *achchutari* is distinctly referred to separately from the common *tari*, which denotes the ordinary loom.

93. *S.I.I.*, vol. i, no. 64. This inscription also refers to *Saligaitari* (a loom used by the Saliya weavers ?); *paraitari*, which probably refers to the loom for weaving plain cloth because *paraituni* refers to coarse cloth, and *tusagaitari*, probably coarse carpet weaving.

94. *S.I.I.*, vol. xx, no. 299; vol. xv, no. 211, etc.

95. *S.I.I.*, vol. x, no. 239 from Achanta in Godavari dist. Also *E. C.*, vol. ii, no. 327, etc.

96. *Selected Telugu Inscriptions*, pt. i, no. 22.

97. *S.I.I.*, vol. vi, no. 41. Also *S.I.I.*, vol. vii, no. 21. *Pudavai* need not necessarily mean women's wear since in those days it was broadly used to denote cloth of any kind.

98. *S.I.I.*, vol. xiii, no. 16 from Tiruvenkadu of the period of Rajaraja I; vol. viii, no. 21 from Tiruppunavasal of the thirteenth century and vol. viii, no. 22 from Tiruvalanjuli of the same period.

99. *S.I.I.*, vol. xiii, no. 16 from Tiruvenkadu cited earlier.

100. *S.I.I.*, vol. viii, no. 442 a late Pandya inscription and also vol. viii, no. 177 from Kalaiyarkoyil of the period of Kochchadaipanmar Sundara Pandya. See also *A.R.E.*, 507 of 1958–9 from Velangudi of the thirteenth century.

101. *S.I.I.*, vol. iv, no. 37 from Madurai.

102. *S.I.I.*, vol. v, no. 446 and 448. The reference to *pattinam* comes from the same volume, no. 450. The inscriptions belong to Tirunelveli proper, *pattinam* refers to a port-town.

103. *Economic Atlas of the Madras State*, pp. 103 ff. Taluqs like Saidapet Madurantakam and Kanchipuram had the type of red ferruginous (loamy) soil best suited to cotton cultivation. For inscriptional references see the list with map on weaving centres.

104. *A.R.E.*, 170 of 1933–4 from Tirukkalukkunram of the fourteenth century.

105. *A.R.E.*, 256 of 1913–14.

106. *Periyapuranam* verse: 2932, cited in K. V. Raman, *Early History of the Madras Region* (Madras, 1957), p. 165. Mylapur, however, appears to have declined from the thirteenth century onwards because Marco Polo, the thirteenth-century traveller, says, ' 'tis a place where few traders go because there is very little merchandise to be got there.' (*The Voyage of Marco Polo*, ed. and tr. Yule (London, 1938), book ii, p. 395).

107. *E.I.*, vol. xii, no. 22.

108. *Marco Polo*, p. 395.

109. *A.R.E.*, 380 of 1926–7.

110. *Indian Antiquary*, vol. xiv, p. 19. Also *Karnataka Inscriptions*, ed. R. S. Pancha-mukhi, B. R. Gopal *et al.*, Dharwar, 1941, vol. v, no. 22.

111. Refer to the map on textile centres. Moreland also expresses a similar opinion: 'The impression left by the narratives of travellers and merchants is that both in Gujarat and on the Coromandel coast, the bulk of the cloth exported was woven in the immediate vicinity of the ports.' W. H. Moreland, *India at the death of Akbar*, [Delhi, 1962], p. 171.

112. Muhammad Husayn Nainar, *Arab Geographers' Knowledge of Southern India*, (Madras. 1939), pp. 139 and 143. Also *Marco Polo*, book ii, p. 395.

113. *Rehla* of Ibn Batuta, ed. Mehdi Hussain, Gaikwad Oriental Series, no. cxxii, Especially refer to the map on p. 184 tracing his route.

114. *E.C.*, vol. v, Hn no. 66.

115. *Manasollasa*, verse: 20 and *Basavarajadevara Ragale* by Harihara, book ii, 11–13, p. 49; cited in S. Gururajachar, *Economic and Social Life in Karnataka*, Prasaranga (Mysore, 1974), p. 70.

116. *Foreign Notices of South India*, ed. Nilakanta Sastri (Madras, 1939), pp. 222–3. *Periplus*, 56 and 64, says that silk cloth was exported from Nelcynda and also that raw silk yarn and silk cloth were brought on foot through Bactria from Thiral to Barygaza and were exported to Damirica by way of the river Ganges. Nilakanta Sastri interprets this as a reference to Chinese silk passing through the Karnataka coast for re-export.

117. *S.I.I.*, vol. vii, no. 196 from Mudalidure refers to *Chinambara vikraya krayikarin*.

118. *Foreign Notices*, p. 214 and 148.

119. *Marco Polo*, book ii, p. 395.

120. *Vikrama Cholan Ula* by Ottakuttar in the *Muvar Ula*, ed. U. V. Swaminathan. Adayar Library Series (Madras, 1946), verses 25 and 26.

121. *E.I.*, vol. xii, no. 22 and *A.R.E.*, 380 of 1926.

122. *A.R.E.*, 173 of 1932–3.

123. See the travels of Nicolo Conti and Abdur Razzaq in R. H. Major ed., *India in the Fifteenth Century* (New Delhi, 1974 reprint), pp. 22 and 17. Razzaq's statement is rather exaggerated, 'The blacks of this country have the body nearly naked; they wear only bandages around the middle called lankoutah ... . This costume is common to the king and to the beggar .... '

124. This forms a crucial argument in Kenneth Hall's thesis, *Trade and State Craft in the Age of the Cholas* (New Delhi, 1980).

125. Lewis Rice, *Mysore Inscriptions*, no. 39, p. 76.

126. *A.R.E.*, 170 of 1933–4.

127. *A.R.E.*, no. 322 of 1936–7 and no. 196 of 1927–8.

128. *A.R.E.*, 363 of 1907–8 from Tanjavur, *S.I.I.*, vol. vii, no. 911 from Dindivanam and vol. xiii, no. 16 from Tanjavur. The reference is probably to Nagapattinam.

129. *S.I.I.*, vol. v, no. 65 from Bhimavaram in Godavari district, of the twelfth century. Also *S.I.I.*, vol. x, no. 239, etc.

130. *A.R.E.*, 15 and 16 of 1917–18 from Hemavati in Anantapur dated 1162.

131. *A.R.E.*, 342 of 1912–13 and *E. C.*, vol. vii, Sk 118 Balagami.

132. *I.A.* vol. x, p. 185 ff., from Dambal in Dharwar.

133. *E.C.*, vol. vii, Sk 118 from Balagami, dated 1054. Also see Lewis Rice, *Mysore Inscriptions*, no. 38 from Balagami in Shimoga district.

134. *A.R.E.*, 200 of 1937–8 from Animala and 342 of 1912–13 from Basinikonda; *E.I.*, vol. xix, no. 4 of the Silahara king Gandaraditya *E. C.*, vol. vii, Sk 118; *S.I.I.*, vol. viii, no. 422 from Piranmalai and *A.R.E.*, 286 of 1964–5 from Kulittalai.

135. *A.R.E.*, 78 of 1963–4 from Krishnapatnam; *A.R.E.*, nos. 406 and 407 of 1914–15.

136. K. A. Nilakanta Sastri, *Cholas*, p. 596.

137. *A.R.E.*, copper plate 18 of 1917–18 mentions Akkanna and Madanna, the Brahmin ministers of Golkonda.

138. *A.R.E.*, 609 of 1919–20.

139. *S.I.I.*, vol. viii, no. 442.

140. *S.I.I.*, vol. vii, no. 583 and *A.R.E.*, 165 of 1968–9.

141. *S.I.I.*, vol. xiv, no. 94 from Edirkottai.

142. *E.C.*, vol. vii. Sk 118 from Balagami.

143. *S.I.I.*, vol. vi, no. 41 of the period of Kochchadaipanmar Sundara Pandya, and *A.R.E.*, 88 of 1914–15 of the period of Jatavarman Vira Pandya.

144. *A.R.E.*, 507 of 1958–9.

145. *S.I.I.*, vol. viii, no. 442. The rates are as follows:

commodity	unit of sale	rates of contribution
cotton		
(*parutti*)	per *vandi*	10 *kasu*
	per *podi*	2 *kasu*
	per *pakkam*	1 *kasu*
	per *talaichumai*	$^{1}/_{2}$ *kasu*
yarn		
(*nulu*)	per *vandi*	20 *kasu*
	per *podi*	5 *kasu*
	per *pakkam*	2½ *kasu*
	per *talaichumai*	2 *kasu*
coarse sarees		
(*parum pudavai*)	per *podi*	10 *kasu*
	per *pakkam*	5 *kasu*
fine sarees		
(*nen pudavai*)	per *podi*	20 *kasu*
	per *pakkam*	5 *kasu*
	per *talaichumai*	5 *kasu*
konikkai pattu	per *podi*	2 *kasu*
(a special type of silk)	per *pakkam*	1 *kasu*
	per *talaichumai*	1 *kasu*
patola silk		
(*pattavala pattu*)	per *talaichumai*	30 *kasu*

146. *E.I.*, vol. v, no. 3A

147. *A.R.E.*, 342 of 1912–13 from Chittoor district. In *E. C.*, vol. vii. Sk 118 from Balagami, cited earlier, the divisions of the merchant corporations are mentioned as eighteen *pattana*, thirty-two *veloma* and sixty-four *yoga pitas*. In the Tamil country, the divisions of the Five Hundred are referred to as eighteen

pattanàm, thirty-two *velapuram* and sixty-four *kadigaitavalam*. *(S.I.I.*, vol. viii, no. 442 from Piranmalai). There are innumerable inscriptions dealing with mercantile corporate organizations but only a few have been used here as examples.

148. *A.R.E.*, 78 of 1963–4 from Krishnapatnam.
149. *A.R.E.*, nos. 15 and 16 of 1917–18,. Appendix C.
150. *H.A.S.*, vol. xiii, no. 14.
151. *S.I.I.*, vol. vii, no. 855; *T.T.*, vol. i, no. 100 etc. Numerous instances of such armies maintained by the merchant corporations are cited in R. Narasimha Rao, *Corporate Life in Medieval Andhradesa* (Waltair 1967).
152. *A.R.E.*, 342 of 1912–13.
153. *A.R.E.*, 460 of 1919–20.
154. *A.R.E.*, 308 of 1913–14.
155. *E.I.*, vol. xviii, no. 22E.
156. *A.R.E.*, 309 of 1968–9 from Tiruchirapalli of the eleventh century.
157. *S.I.I.*, vol. xvii, no. 452.
158. *A.R.E.*, 228 of 1910–11.
159. *S.I.I.*, vol. vii, 454 and 455 Achcharpakkam in Chingleput. Also refer *A.R.E.*, 333 of 1935–6 from Potladurti in Cuddappah district, etc.
160. *A.R.E.*, 218 of 1910–11. Also of 1910–11.
161. *S.I.I.*, vol. viii, nos. 7 and 8 of the period of Rajaraja I; vol. viii, no. 117 of the period of Rajendra; vol. viii, no. 123 of the period of Kulottunga I, etc.
162. *S.I.I.*, vol. v, no. 410 from Tirunelveli proper.
163. *A.R.E.*, 218 of 1910.
164. *E.C.*, vol. vi, Hs. 97 from Kudakkuru in Mysore district; *E.C.*, vol. ix, copper plate 66 from Yeliyur and *A.R.E.*, 628 of 1920–21 from Amritalur in Guntur district. For the levy of *tari-irai* in Andhra by the Cholas, see *A.R.E.*, 64 of 1958–9 of Vikrama Chola's perliod from Mundalapundi in Chittoor district.
165. *S.I.I.*, vol. vii, no. 98 of the period of Rajaraja I (1001) from Tiruvottur in North Arcot and *T.T.*, vol. i, no. 99 of the period of Vira Ballala dated 1310.
166. *A.R.E.*, 182 of 1916–17 of Vira Rajendra (1067) from Kunimedu in South Arcot district. Also *S.I.I.*, vol. v, no. 176; vol. vii, no. 4, etc.
167. In *S.I.I.*, vol. iii, pt. 4, no. 151; *tarippudavai* is interpreted as the cloth on each loom.
168. *S.I.I.*, vol. v, no. 65.
169. Reference to *panjupeeli* comes from *S.I.I.*, vol. v, no. 301 from Nilikkottai in Madurai dated 1192. Also *S.I.I.*, vol. viii, no. 177 from Ramanathapuram district, etc.
170. *S.I.I.*, vol. vii, no. 936, thirteenth century Pandya inscription from Tirukkoyilur in South Arcot district.
171. *S.I.I.*, vol. vii, no. 109 of Rajanarayana Sambuvaraya from Tiruvottur. Also *A.R.E.*, 68 of 1958–9 from Yalamari in Chittoor and *E.C.*, vol. ix, copper plate from Bangalore. Tax on silk thread is referred to in *A.R.E.*, 170 of 1933–4 from Tirukkalukkunram.
172. *S.I.I.*, vol. xvii, no. 452.
173. *E.C.*, vol. ix, Cp 66 from Virupakshapuram Hubli in Bangalore.
174. *S.I.I.*, vol. xiv, no. 221.
175. *S.I.I.*, vol. viii, no. 543.

176. *Mitakshara*, book ii, p. 236.
177. For the tax rates during the period of the Vijayanagar empire, see taxation table under Chapter III.
178. *A.R.E.*, 311 of 1968–9 dated 1261 from Tripattavellur; 152 of 1928–9 dated 1267 from Nattamangudi and 203 of 1928–9 dated from Kandiradittam, all from Tiruchirapalli district.
179. *A.R.E.*, 300 of 1909–10.
180. *A.R.E.*, 203 of 1928–9 and 152 of 1928–9.
181. *A.R.E.*, 508 of 1922–3.
182. *A.R.E.*, 628 of 1920–1.
183. *A.R.E.*, 218 of 1934–5.

Notes to Chapter II

1. Burton Stein, 'The State And The Agrarian Order' in Burton Stein ed., *Essays on South India* (New Delhi, 1975), p. 73.
2. T.V. Mahalingam very correctly points out that *agrahara* villages were not peopled exclusively by Brahmins because they also had need of the essential services, including cultivation of the land and artisanal products, and similarly Brahmin priests may have been a part of the *ur. South Indian Polity* (Madras, 1967), p. 349. For Sudra professionals settled in a *brahmadeya* village, see *S.I.I.*, vol. ii, pp. 527–8—The Tandantottam Plates of Nandivarman II.
3. *S.I.I.*, vol. ii, pt. 2, no. 66 of the period of Rajaraja I from Tanjavur. This however need not necessarily point to the jajmani system but may merely indicate payment in kind.
4. *A.R.E.*, 376 of 1954–5, Sundara Pandya, thirteenth century, Peruntalaiyur, Coimbatore district.
5. *A.R.E.*, 306 of 1958–9; 308 and 309 of 1958–9, all from South Arcot, also refer to the founding of *brahmadeyas* along the same lines.
6. *A.R.E.*, 5 of 1952–3.
7. *S.I.I.*, vol. i, no. 151, p. 155. See A. Appadorai, *Economic Conditions of Southern India, 1000–1500*, 2 Vols. (Madras, 1936), vol. ii, p. 475.
8. *E.I.*, vol. iv, pp. 137–8.
9. *E.I.*, vol. xiii, no. 15, p. 187.
10. *E.I.*, vol. vi, no. 13.
11. The significance of the fact that at least two of the commercially important items—cloth and oil—were brought from outside is observed and stressed by Pavlov, *Historical Premises for India's Transition to Capitalism* (Moscow, 1979), pp. 51, 111, etc.
12. *S.I.I.*, vol. viii, no. 118.
13. *S.I.I.*, vol. vii, no. 120. However, since a gap of forty-five years exists between the first and the second inscription, this identification is by no means certain.
14. Stein's model of the segmentary state, originally borrowed from Aiden Southall's *The Alurs of Uganda: A Study in Processes and Types of Dominations* (Cambridge, 1953), has been presented by him in *Peasant State and Society in Medieval South India* (Oxford University Press, 1980). Earlier versions of the

model are to be found in many of his articles—'Integration of the Agrarian System of South India' in R. E. Frykenburg ed., *Land Control and Social Structure in Indian History* (Madison, 1969); 'The Segmentary State in South Indian History' in Richard Fox ed., *Realm and Region in Traditional India* (New Delhi, 1977); 'The State and the Agrarian Order in Medieval South India' in Burton Stein ed., *Essays on South India* (New Delhi, 1976).

15. Eighteen *pana* is a conventional number and is used as early as the period of the *Jatakas* (Jat. vi, pp. 1,427, cited in R. L. Majumdar, *Corporate Life in Ancient India*, third edition, Calcutta, 1969). A detailed list of the eighteen *pana* is given in *A.R.E.*, copper plate 18 of 1917–18, pt. ii, pp. 174–5—pancala (smiths), kumbalika (potters), tantuvayin (weavers), vastrabhedaka (cloth dyers), tilaghatika (oil mongers), kurantaka (shoe makers), go-rakshaka (cowherds) etc. The eighteen *pana* are also referred to in the Karnataka region in *H.A.S.*, vol. xiii, nos. 30 and 53 where they are called the eighteen *samaya*.

16. Arjun Appadorai refers to the various facets of the paradigm in his thesis, 'Left-hand—Right-hand Castes in South Indian History,' (unpublished, Chicago, 1973).

17. *E.I.*, vol. iii, no. 15 from Ron; E.I., vol. xviii, no. 22 E from Hubli and *S.I.I.*, vol. xx, no. 11 from Lakshmisvar.

18. *S.I.I.*, vol. viii, no. 442 from Piranmalai refers to 18 pattinam, 32 velarpuram and 64 kadikaitavalam. That exactly the same divisions existed in the Andhra region is proved from an inscription from Chittoor district (Basinikonda), which refers to the 4 tisai nadu, 18 pattinam, 32 velarpuram and 64 ghatika sthana of the Tisaiayirattu Ainnurruvar. The pancala guild organization is referred to in detail in *E.I.*, vol. iii, pp. 67–9.

19. The corporate organization of the Kaikkolar is discussed in the *Sengunta Prabanda Tirattu*, ed. Sabapati Mudaliyar (Madras, 1926).

20. See *A.R.E.*, 473 of 1921–2, *A.R.E.*, 291 of 1928–9 from Tiruvennainallur and Tirukkoyilur.

21. *S.I.I.*, vol. vii, no. 451.

22. *South Indian Temple Inscriptions* ed. T.N. Subramanyam (Madras, 1953), no. 219 B 2949–21. It is not possible to date this inscription though it might pertain to the thirteenth–fourteenth centuries. The regions also cannot be identified.

23. *Devanga Puranam* by Palanisami Pulavar (Coimbatore, 1971), gives a comprehensive account of the history of the Devanga and their territorial organization. This information is based on ancient texts like the *Devanga Puranam* of Mambala Kavirayar.

24. *H.A.S.*, vol. xiii, nos. 10 and 13. Another record from Lakshmesvar, (*S.I.I.*, vol. xx, no. 11) of the reign of Srivallabha i.e. late eighth century or early ninth century, registers a joint donation by the sreni-pattagara (pattagara stands for weavers) and concludes that whoever destroys this will be guilty of killing a thousand cows of Varanasi.

25. *E.C.*, vol. iv, G1. 34 in South Kanara district, dated 1372, and *T.T.*, vol. iv, no. 112 of the period of Achyutaraya.

26. *S.I.I.*, vol. iv, no. 391.

27. *The Cholan Purva Pattayam*, ed. C.M. Ramachandra Chettiar, Govt. of Madras, Oriental Series, no. v, (Madras, 1950). While the copper plate inscription claims to belong to the period of Karikala Chola, the reference to the Muslim

invasions shows that it cannot have been written earlier than the thirteenth century and it pertains most probably to the reign of Kulottunga III. Its chronology has been effectively proved by Arokiaswami in his article, 'The Cholan Purva Pattayam: Its Historical Value', *J.I.H.*, vol. xxxii, 1954, pp. 5–10.

28. Ibid., pp. 187–8, 192 to 199 and *passim*.

29. *A.R.E.*, 248 of 1915–16.

30. *A.R.E.*, 108 of 1929–30; 92 of 1933–4, etc.

31. *A.R.E.*, 281 of 1921–2 of a festival.

32. *A.R.E.*, 129 of 1923–4. *Pon* is usually equated with the *kalanju*.

33. The average weight of the *kalanju* in the Chola period was roughly 70 grains of gold. This is more than the weight of the *gadayana* or pagoda of the Vijayanagar period (fifteenth–sixteenth centuries) which steadily averaged around 58 grains of gold.

34. *A.R.E.*, 186 of 1920–1.

35. *A.R.E.*, 514 of 1922.

36. *A.R.E.*, 655 of 1922–3. This coin is also referred to as just *achchu* (*A.R.E.*, 590 of 1922–3 from Coimbatore of the same period) or as *anai-achchu* (*S.I.I.*, vol. v, no. 226 from Perur, also in Coimbatore district, of the period of Vikrama Chola). *Anai-achchu* could have been double the ordinary *achchu*, posssibly like the double pagoda The weight of an ordinary *achchu* averaged around 50 grains.

37. *A.R.E.*, 3 of 1923–4 from Idigarai (Vikrama Chola, twelfth century). The *varaham* is more or less similar to the pagoda or *gadayana*.

38. *A.R.E.*, 6 of 1923–4. One *panam* was equal to a hundred Choliya *kasu* according to a thirteenth century Pandya inscription from Aragalur in Salem district (*A.R.E.*, 439 of 1913–14). It is likely that the reference is to the devalued *kasu* under Kulottunga III rather than the high value *palangasu* of earlier times.

39. *A.R.E.*, 590 of 1922–3.

40. *A.R.E.*, 513 of 1920–1.

41. *T.T.*, vol. i, nos. 70 and 71.

42. *H.A.S.*, vol. xiii, nos. 52, dated 1311, p. 190.

43. *S.I.I.*, vol. x, no. 507 dated 1314.

44. *E.I.*, vol. v, 3A, dated 1161.

45. *A.R.E.*, 108 of 1930–1.

46. *A.R.E.*, 146 of 1912–13.

47. *A.R.E.*, 154 of 1912–13.

48. *A.R.E.*, 267 of 1910–11. An individual merchant from Tiruvorriyur gave 30 *kalanju* of gold, a huge sum, to the Varaha Perumal temple at Tiruvadandai. The reference to donations by the Vellalar are numerous—*S.I.I.*, vol. xiv, no. 202; *S.I.I.*, vol. xix, no. 199, etc.

49. *A.R.E.*, 365 of 1954–5 refers to a donation by a goldsmith of 1 *kalanju* to the temple in Muduturai in Coimbatore.

50. *S.I.I.*, vol. v, no. 670.

51. *A.R.E.*, 172 of 1935–6. *A.R.E.*, 635 of 1916–17 also refers to *udirapatti*, but it is not dated.

52. *S.I.I.*, vol. xix, no. 8 from Kumbakonam belonging to Arinjaya's reign, *S.I.I.*, vol. v, no. 670, tenth century from Kilappalavur in Tirchirapalli, etc.

53. *S.I.I.*, vol. viii, no. 91, an eleventh century inscription from Tiruvannamalai; *A.R.E.*, 208 of 1922–3, twelfth century record from Kanchipuram, etc.

54. George W. Spencer, 'Temple Money-lending and Livestock Redistribution in Early Tanjore', *I.E.S.H.R.*, vol. v, 1968.
55. *S.I.I.*, vol. x, no. 533.
56. *E.C.*, vol. v, Bl, no. 236.
57. *E.C.*, vol. vii, Sr. 112.
58. *E.I.*, vol. xviii, no. 22 E, The suffix 'asura' is extremely interesting and shows that the caste must have worshipped a demon, perhaps to ward off evil effects or that he had been absorbed into the orthodox religious pantheon through a system of assimilation.
59. *H.A.S.*, vol. xiii, no. 10.
60. *A.R.E.*, 248 of 1915–16.
61. *A R.E.*, 452 of 1913–14. A Kaikkola of Kalaiyur (Salem) instituted a car festival and he and his descendants were granted the privilege of a house, a loom, lands and some ritual privileges in the temple.
62. *A.R.E.*, 555 of 1920–1.
63. *A.R.E.*, 467 of 1916–17.
64. *S.I.I.*, xiii, no. 108.
65. *A.R.E.*, 627 of 1909–10. However, these two specific instances cannot be taken into account while assessing the economic status of the weavers because these two donations were obviously made by the Kaikkolar in their capacity as soldiers and not as weavers.
66. 'Nayakar' was the title given to big merchants in the Chola period.
67. *A.R.E.*, 187 of 1927–8.
68. *S.I.I.*, vol. xii, no. 418 of 1909–10.
69. *H.A.S.*, vol. xiii, nos. 10 and 13. See also N.D.I., vol. ii, no. 8, etc.
70. *T.T.*, vol. i, no. 34.
71. *T.T.*, vol. i, no. 108.
72. *A.R.E.*, 281 of 1921–2.
73. *A.R.E.*, 253 of 1907–8 172 of 1927–8, *Inscriptions of the Nellore District* ed. Butterworth and Venugopalachetty (Madras, 1931–8), no. 81, and *A.R.E.*, 400 of 1924–5.
74. *A.R.E.*, 607 of 1922–3.
75. *S.I.I.*, vol. xii, pt. i, nos. 45 and 150.
76. *A.R.E.*, 555 of 1920–1.
77. *A.R.E.*, 126 of 1927–8.
78. *A.R.E.*, 347 of 1923–4, 92 of 1933–4, 6 of 1923–4 and *S.I.I.*, vol. v, no. 417.
79. Burton Stein, ed., *South Indian Temples* (New Delhi, 1978), p. 25ff.
80. *S.I.I.*, vol. vi, no. 258 from Manimangalam in Saidapet, formerly in Chingleput district but now a part of Madras.
81. *Cholan Purva Pattayam*, pp. 188–9, 201, etc.
82. *S.I.I.*, vol. viii, no. 686. In Tiruchirapalli, 20 *ma* made 1 *veli* and 1 *veli* was 6.6 acres.
83. *S.I.I.*, vol. xix, no. 352.
84. *S.I.I.*, vol. xix, no. 365. *Muttuvalperra* refers to a special distinction conferred on this Kaikkola regiment perhaps because of its skill in swordsmanship. The term also occurs in *S.I.I.*, vol. xix, no. 18, etc.
85. *S.I.I.*, vol. v, no. 417.
86. *A.R.E.*, 35 of 1954–5 from Nellore.

87. *S.I.I.*, vol. xix, no. 389; *A.R.E.*, 1 of copper plate 1960–1 etc.
88. *S.I.I.*, vol. x, no. 427 from Peddaganjam in Guntur district, dated 1270, refers to the donation of the entire village with all the taxes to the temple of Visvesvara. Also *S.I.I.*, vol. iv, no. 1373, etc. I am grateful to G.V.S. Lakshmi (Centre for Historical Studies, Jawaharlal Nehru University, Delhi) for providing me with this reference.
89. *A.R.E.*, 172 of 1935–6 from Tiruppattur (Ramanathapuram) of the twelfth century; *A.R.E.*, 92 of 1933–4 of the fourteenth century from Sirudavur (Chingleput), etc.
90. *S.I.I.*, vol. viii, no. 685; *A.R.E.*, 232 of 1924–5. The land was obviously not tax free because in the latter inscription the Kaikkola donees undertake to pay the tax on the land amounting to 120 *panam* in monthly instalments.
91. *S.I.I.*, vol. xi, pt. 1, no. 97. The custom of having a particular number attached to their names was quite common among many communities like the Banajigas, who are referred to as the 'Ainurruvar' or 'five hundred,' and the Teliki 'thousand'. Similarly the Saliya weavers of the Andhra and Karnataka regions are referred to as the 'fifty'. The significance of these numbers is, however, not clear. ·
92. *A.R.E.*, 316 of 1916–17.
93. *A.R.E.*, 596 of 1926–7.
94. *S.I.I.*, vol. x, no. 533.
95. *S.I.I.*, no. vii, no. 425.
96. *S.I.I.*, vol. vii, no. 415.
97. *A.R.E.*, 57 of 1932–3.
98. The term 'Mudali' did not denote any caste in the medieval period, as it does now, but was basically a title indicative of a high status, most often given to military chieftains.
99. *A.R.E.*, 46 of 1921–2, Sengalunirodai in Chingleput.
100. *S.I.I.*, vol. iv, nos. 370 and 371 from Madurai.
101. That this way of acquiring land rights was in fact a general practice in those days is proved by several inscriptions from Tamil Nadu and Karnataka (*E.C.*, vol. v, Bl. 175 dated 1186, etc.). Quite often the reward was in the form of tax concession for the first three years or more. (*E.C.*, vol. iii, Sr. 148 dated tenth century).
102. A. Appadorai, *Economic Conditions of Southern India*, vol. i, pp. 120–1; T.V. Mahalingam, *South Indian Polity*, (Madras, 1967), glossary, p. 427; Noburu Karashima, 'Prevalence of Private Landowning in the Lower Kaveri Valley in the Late Chola Period and its Historical Implication', *Institute for the Study of Languages and Cultures of Asia and Africa* (Tokyo, 1980), pp. 4–5 and *passim*; Burton Stein, *Peasant State and Society*, p. 180.
103. *A.R.E.*, 126 of 1933–4.
104. *A.R.E.*, 347 of 1921–2.
105. *S.I.I.*, vol. iii, no. 64.
106. *A.R.E.*, 362 of 1911.
107. *A.R.E.*, 430 of 1921–2.
108. *A.R.E.*, 66 of 1915–16.
109. *T.T.*, vol. i, no. 34. Pandiyadaraiyan was a staunch Saivite and held the management of the Siva temple of Tiruppaladisvaram udaiya Nayanar in Tiruchchanur.

110. See for instance the name Kaikkola Pallavariyan in *S.I.I.*, vol. xii, pt. 1, nos. 122 and 150 from Tiruvénnainallur. Also *S.I.I.*, vol. v, no. 531 from Tanjavur proper which refers to Kaikkola, Mallavaraiyan, etc.
111. *A.R.E.*, 105 of 1925–6.
112. *S.I.I.*, vol. xiii, no. 108 from Kumbakonam of the period of Rajaraja I, *S.I.I.*, vol. xii, 418 of 1909–10 from South Arcot district. The amount mentioned is 200 *kasu*.
113. M. N. Srinivas, 'A Note on Sanskritization and Westernization' in M. N. Srinivas ed., *Caste in Modern India and other Essays* (Bombay, 1962).
114. Satish C. Misra, 'Indigenization and Islamization in India', *Secular Democracy*, Annual, 1974. Another interesting article on the same theme is, Imtiaz Ahmad, 'The Ashraf and Ajlaf Categories in Indo-Muslim Society', *E.P.W.*, May 1967.
115. M. N. Srinivas, p. 43, has himself given the Lingayats as a leading example of sanskritization and in fact pointed out that the more orthodox Lingayats did not eat food touched or cooked by the Brahmins; he has, however, neither clearly defined nor emphasized this reverse process of sanskritization.
116. *S.I.I.*, vol. iii, pt. iii, no. 128.
117. *S.I.I.*, vol. xii, no. 154.
118. *S.I.I.*, vol. vii, no. 112.
119. *E.C.*, vol. iv, ch. 97.
120. *A.R.E.*, 34 of 1957–8. The reference to Devanga 'thousand' is again parallel to the Saliya 'fifty' or the Teliki 'thousand', i.e. the association of a number with a caste.
121. *A.R.E.*, 47 of 1932–3.
122. *S.I.I.*, vol. viii, no. 195.
123. *Cholan Purva Pattayam*, pp. 206–7.
124. *A.R.E.*, 396 of 1909–10.
125. *S.I.I.*, vol. vi, no. 252; *S.I.I.*, vol. vi, no. 257.
126. *A.R.E.*, 196 of 1912–13.
127. The term Anukkar means one in attendance and also one who is close to the person in authority.
128. 'Padiyilar' literally means 'without husbands' and they were so called because they were not permitted to marry. See K. K. Pillay, 'The Caste system in Tamil Nadu', *Journal of Madras University*, vol. xxix, no. 2, July 1977, p. 30.
129. *Cholan Purva Pattayam*, pp. 200, 206–7 and *passim*.
130. *A.R.E.*, 284 of 1910–11. *T.T.*, vol. i, no. 108 from Tirupati of the period of Yadavarayar (1337) refers to the joint conduct of festivals by the Kaikkolar and the Emperuman Adiyar.
131. C. Balasubramaniam, *Ottakuttar* (in Tamil, n.d.), p. 36.
132. *A.R.E.*, 295 of 1961–2.
133. 'Senguntar Tugil Vidu Tutu' in T. Chandrasekharan ed., *Tutu Tiruttu*, Oriental Manuscripts Series, no. 58 (Madras, 1957), verses 122–5.
134. For instance, the Kammalar (the same as the Pancalar of Karnataka and the Panchanamuvaru of Andhra), trace their origin from Visvakarma, the divine architect. His five sons—Maya, Manu, Tvastri, Silpi and Visvajna—are said to be the progenitors of the five artisans or smiths—carpenter, blacksmith, goldsmith, mason and brazier. (*A.R.E.*, 665 of 1910–11, pt. ii, para 60). The Teliki (oilmen) have a similar legend of their origin which is related in the

Manuvamsa Puranam (Ms. D. 160 of the Catalogue of Telugu Manuscripts in the Mackenzie Collection, Oriental Manuscripts Library, Madras). The Teliki claim to be Kshathriyas from the North and descendants of Manu.

135. *Devanga Puranam*, pp. 1–7.
136. Thurston, vol. ii, p. 156.
137. Ibid., vol. vi, p. 277.
138. *T.T.*, vol. i, nos. 70, 71 and 72.
139. *A.R.E.*, 208 of 1919–20 from Pondicherry.
140. *A.R.E.*, 508 of 1922–3 from Tirukkanapuram in Coimbatore.
141. *A.R.E.*, 208 of 1919–20.
142. *A.R.E.*, 56 of 1912–13; *A.R.E.*, 189 of 1895–6; *A.R.E.*, 120 of 1905–6, etc.
143. *Cholan Purva Pattayam*, pp. 208–9.
144. *A.R.E.*, 248 of 1915–16.
145. *A.R.E.*, 570 of 1922–3.
146. *A.R.E.*, 113 of 1896–7; *S.I.I.*, vol. v, no. 976.
147. *A.R.E.*, 315 of 1954–5.
148. *A.R.E.*, 215 of 1910–11.
149. *E.C.*, vol. x, Ct. 95.
150. *A.R.E.*, 437 of 1921–2.
151. *Sengunta Mannar Kuladipikai*, Thiravavidu Thurai Sivaguru, Saiva Siddanta publication (Madras, 1958), Introduction, pp. 18–19.
152. R. N. Nandi, 'Origins of the Vira Saiva Movement', *I.H.R.*, vol. ii, no. i, July 1975, p. 32. A readable translation of Vira Saiva poetry is to be found in A. K. Ramanujam, ed., *Speaking of Siva* (Penguin Books, 1973).
153. *E.C.*, vol. xxix, no. 19.
154. Abdur Razzaq in R. H. Major ed., *India in the Fifteenth Century*, p. 17. William Methwold, a traveller in the early seventeenth century, refers to the Jangam (i.e. Lingayat)as tailors and says that they were in an impoverished condition. See Methwold's account in W.H. Moreland ed., *Relations of Golconda*, Hakluyt Series (London, 1930), p. 15.
155. Quoted in Burton Stein, 'Social Mobility and Medieval South Indian Hindu Sects', in James Silverburg ed., *Social Mobility in the Caste System of India—A Symposium* (Hague, Netherlands, 1968), p. 83.

Notes to Chapter III

1. *A.R.E.*, 269 of 1913–14 from Chidambaram, South Arcot district.
2. Duarte Barbosa, *The Book of Travels*, Hakluyt Series, tr. by Longworth Dames (London, 1921), vol. ii, p. 59.
3. Abdur Razzaq, 'An Account of his Travels,' in R. H. Major, ed., *India in the Fifteenth Century* (Reprint, New Delhi, 1974), p. 24.
4. *A.R.E.*, 319 of 1911–12.
5. *A.R.E.*, 140 of 1915–16.
6. *A.R.E.*, 263 of 1928–9 from Pennadam, Vriddachalam, South Arcot district, of the period of Devaraya dated 1439. Also *A.R.E.*, 294 of 1910 dated 1418 from Pulipparakoyil, Chingleput district.

7. *Varnaratnakara* of Jyotisvara Thakura, ed. S. K. Chatterji and Babua Misra (Calcutta, 1942), p. 14.

8. Vividavarnaka: 34, cited by Moti Chandra, 'Costumes and Textiles in the Sultanate period,' *J.I.T.H.* no. 6, 1961, p. 27. Not only was cloth known by the caste of the weavers which specialized in weaving them, but sometimes the caste derived its name from its specialization. Thus the Saurashtra weavers of South India (an immigrant community) came to be called *Pattunulkarar* because of their specialization in silk weaving.

9. *Gurjararasavali*: 34.1, 181.5, 35.1, etc. quoted from Moti Chandra, ibid., p. 27.

10. *Varnaratnakara*: 28.

11. George Philips, 'Mahuan's Account of Cochin, Calicut and Aden', *The Journal of the Royal Asiatic Society of Great Britain and Ireland* (1891), p. 345.

12. *S.I.I.*, vol. vii, no. 21.

13. V. Rangacharya (ed.), *Inscriptions of the Madras Presidency*, 3 vols (Madras, 1919), vol. i, no. 446, p. 436.

14. Barbosa, vol. ii, p. 153.

15. The account of Fernao Nuniz translated by Robert Sewell is in *A Forgotten Empire* (New Delhi, 1962), p. 263.

16. The Account of Domingo Paes is in ibid., p. 255.

17. *Varnaratnakara*: 6, and 4.

18. Ibid: 2 and 20. Reference to the fine textiles of Cholapatna is also made in the *Manasollasa*, p. 19.

19. Moti Chandra, p. 32.

20. Tome Pires, *The Suma Oriental*, tr. by Armando Cortesao, Hakluyt Society (London. 1944). vol. i, p. 169, fn.2. Also p. 53 and p. 78.

21. *The Voyage of Frances Pyrard of Laval*, ed. Albert Gray (London, 1887–9), vol. i, pp. 58 and 371.

22. *The Account of J.H.Van Linschoton* (2 vols.) Hakluyt Society (London, 1884), vol. i, p. 91.

23. Barbosa, vol. ii, pp. 77–8, 132, 153, 162 and *passim*.

24. Methwold's *Relations*, in W. H. Moreland, p. 35.

25. Micolo Conti in R. H. Major, pp. 7 and 18.

26. *Rehla* of Ibn Batuta, ed., Mehdi Hussain Gaikwad Oriental Series, no cxxii, p. 192.

27. The List, without any explanatory note, is cited in P. Sree Rama Sarma, *Saluva Dynasty of Vijayanagar* (Hyderabad, 1979), p. 276.

28. *T.T.*, vol. iv, no. 112 of the period of Achyutaraya.

29. *E.C.*, vol. v, Hn. 119, Grama Hobli, Hasan taluq and district Also, *E.C.*, vol. ix Cp. 66, from Virupakshapuram, Hobli, Channapatna taluq, Bangalore district.

30. *E.C.*, vol. v, Ak. no. 40, from Hanibatti in Hasan district.

31. *E.C.*, vol. xi, Mk 1 dated 1557 from Devasamudra Hobli, Chittaldroog district.

32. Abdur Razzaq's account in R. H. Major, p. 17. However, according to Marco Polo, the upper classes among both Hindus and Muslims wore fine muslin on account of the heat, for which variety there was great demand. *Marco Polo*, book ii, p. 361.

33. Fernao Nuniz in Sewell, p. 363.

34. Domingo Paes in ibid., pp. 263, 266, etc. That this kind of costume continued

208   *Textiles and Weavers in South India*

into the seventeenth century is shown by Methwold's description of the people's dresses. Methwold in *Relations*, p. 18, p. 26ff.

35. For figures see Razzaq in Major, Nuniz, in Sewell, pp. 326–7, etc.
36. Paes, p. 254ff.
37. An interesting discussion on the agrarian base of the medieval townships is to be found in R. Tirumalai, *Studies in the History of Ancient Townships of Pudukkottai* (Madras, 1981).
38. See note 109 below.
39. *Further Sources*, vol. iii, p. 52. Also see for instance *A.R.E.*, 284 of 1921–2, para 41, which refers to the rate of taxation on weavers owning land.
40. Tome Pires, vol. i, p. 58.
41. *E.I.*, vol. vi, pp. 230–9. Also *E.C.*, vol. iii, ml. 95, 118; vol. v, Cr. 174.
42. *South Indian Temple Inscriptions*, ed. T. N. Subramanyam, 3 Vols. Oriental Manuscripts Library (Madras, 1953), vol. ii, no. 446.
43. *S.I.I.*, vol. xvi, no. 52, from Srisailam, Nandikotkur taluq, Kurnool district, dated 1515.
44. *Mahuan's account*, p. 342.
45. *The Travels of Pyrard de Laval*, vol. i, p. 247.
46. Barbosa, vol. ii, pp. 172–3ff., 132, 153 etc. The re-export of Chinese silk was an ancient trade. See my Introduction.
47. Caesar Fredrick in *Samuel Purchase: His Pilgrims*, Hakluyt (posthumous), 1563. (Glasgow, 1905), vol. x, p. 127. Hereafter *Pilgrims*. Also see Ralph Fitch, in ibid., p. 191, for the popularity of Pulicat textiles in the Malay Archipelago.
48. Barbosa, vol. ii, pp. 153, 162, 198–9, etc. Scarlet in grain cloth as an import item into Pulicat along with Mecca velvet, vermilion; etc. is mentioned in vol. ii, p. 132, and the same items are mentioned as export commodities to Pegu etc. in p. 153 of the same volume.
49. For a discussion of the situation in the eastern markets cf. Peter Floris, *Voyage to the East Indies* (London, 1934), Hakluyt Series, pp. 27–8 and *passim*. Also introduction by W. H. Moreland, vol. xx.
50. Tome Pires, p. 20, and Barbosa, vol. i, p. 92. The value of a *tanka* is a little more than one-eighth of a rupee.
51. Tome Pires, p. 17 and Barbosa, p. 55.
52. Tome Pires, vol. i, p. 58.
53. Barbosa, vol. i, pp. 65, 178.
54. *Marco Polo*, book i, pp. 349–50. He says that the horses used to die due to mishandling and poor treatment and as a result the king had to buy 2,000 horses every year.
55. Barbosa, vol. i, p. 211.
56. Heras, *Studies in the Aravidu Dynasty of Vijayanagar* (Madras, 1927), pp. 62–3.
57. Barbosa, vol. i, p. 92, and Aden, p. 56ff.
58. Ibid., p. 6.
59. Ibid., vol. ii, pp. 172–3.
60. Ibid., p. 76; also p. 58.
61. Heras, *Studies in the Aravidu Dynasty*, pp. 62–3. Horses had great military significance in the struggles between the native powers.
62. The figures are taken from Appendix B and C of Afzal Ahmad's paper 'Portuguese Trade in the Indian Textiles in the Early Seventeenth Century,'

presented at the 43rd. session of the Indian History Congress held in Kurukshetra.

63. Francois Pyrard of Laval, *Voyage to the Eàst Indies, Maldives and Moluccas*, vol, ii, pt. i, p. 204ff.

64. Refer to the incident of the capture of the Surat ship 'Rahimi' which held a pass and carried a huge cargo in which the queen mother had also invested, in 1613, by the Portuguese. As a consequence, Jahangir and his Deccan allies declared an all out war against them. *The Voyage of Nicholas Dounton*, ed. William Foster, Hakluyt Society (London, 1929), Introduction, p. lxxxii.

65. Pyrard Laval, p. 204. See also W. H. Moreland, *From Akbar to Aurangajeb* (New Delhi, 1972), p. 8.

66. R. Saraswati, 'Political Maxims of Krishnadeva Raya,' *J.I.H.*, vol. iv, pt. 3, p. 77.

67. Abdur Razzaq, 'An account of his Travels,' in R. H. Major ed., *India in the Fifteenth Century*, p. 14.

68. Barbosa, vol. ii, p. 132.

69. Tome Pires, vol. ii, p. 272.

70. The records in the Dutch Koloniel Archief give the price of a yard of cloth in early seventeenth-century Pulicat as 0.05 cruzadoes. Therefore, 240,000 cruzadoes would mean 4.8 million yards of cloth approximately. This price is quoted in Joseph Brennig, 'The Textile Trade of Seventeenth Century Northern Coromandel' (unpublished thesis on micro film, Ann Arbor, Michigan, U.S.A.).

71. Mahuan, p. 345. The reference seems to be the *panam* rather than the *varaha* or pagoda because the value of a pagoda was 7 shillings and 6d and this would make the cost about £4 per piece, which is impossible. Hence the reference must be to the *panam* which was valued at about 6d at this time. Thus the cost of a piece of Chihli cloth must have been around 5 shillings, which is not very cheap. The costly silk by the same standards must have cost over £ 2 per piece, which is quite high.

72. Vasco da gama, *The First Voyage*, p. 132, cited in T.V. Mahalingam *Administration and Social Life Under Vijayanagar*, p. 176.

73. The Account of Nuniz, p. 363.

74. Abdur Razzaq, p. 19.

75. Tome Pires, vol. i, p. 68.

76. Ibid., p. 58 and Barbosa, book i, p. 178. When Vasco da gama came to India, the ruler was Saluva Narasimha. His confused use of the name of the king as being the name of the kingdom has, however, been followed by the subsequent Portuguese travellers who refer to Vijayanagar as Narasinga.

77. Robert Fitch in *Pilgrims*, vol. x, pp. 62–3.

78. Marco Polo in *Foreign Notices*, p. 172.

79. Barbosa, book ii, p. 126.

80. The account of Caesar Fredrick, in *Pilgrims*, vol. x, p. 109.

81. Barbosa, vol. ii, pp. 129–32.

82. Tome Pires, book ii, p. 271.

83. *A.R.E.*, 170 of 1933.

84. *A.R.E.*, 173 of 1933.

85. T. V. Mahalingam, *Administration and Social Life Under Vijayanagar* (Madras, 1976), part ii, p. 165.

86. Tome Pires, book ii, p. 271.

87. *Pilgrims*, vol. x, p. 108.

88. Foster, *English Factory Records* (E.F.I.), 14 volume; (Oxford 1906–27), vol. iv, p. 19. A letter from Achin dated November 1615 by William Nicolls to John Milward refers to the arrival of four ships from Masulipatnam, Nagapatnam and 'Colimat' (Kunimedu).

89. Tome Pires, book ii, p. 271.

90. H.M Elliot, *History of India as told by its own Historians*, ed. J. Dowson, vols. 1–15 (Calcutta, 1952–3), vol. iv, p. 98..

91. The Account of Caesar Fredrick, in *Pilgrims*, vol. x, p. 103.

92. Robert Fitch in ibid., p. 169.

93. *Pilgrims*, vol. x, p. 98 and Barbosa, p. 85.

94. Razzaq, p.7; The Account of Afanasin Nikitin, in R. H. Major, ed., *India in the Fifteenth Century*, p. 19.

95. Tome Pires, vol. i, p. 99.

96. Ibid. vol. ii, p. 270. Pires has used the term 'Shahbandar' to denote its original meaning, a man appointed by the merchants of the different regions as their agent at a port to present them to the state official, to fix up the warehouse and help dispatch their merchandise, etc. (ibid., p. 265.) But later on Shahbandar came to mean the king's official at the port. Refer to Moreland's Introduction in *The Account of Peter Floris* for a description of the evolution of this office.

97. *A.R.E.*, 818 of 1917–18 from Gorantla, Hindapur taluq.

98. *A.R.E.*, 216 of 1963–4 from Vijayamangalam.

99. *S.I.I.*, vol. vii, no. 21 from Omalur.

100. *A.R.E.*, 200 of 1937–8.

101. *T.T.*, vol. iv, no. 112.

102. *S.I.I.*, vol. i, no. 446.

103. Mahuan, p. 342.

104. Ibn Batuta, *Rehla*, Gaikwad Oriental Series, no. cxxii.

105. Tome Pires, vol. ii, pp. 255, 272, etc.

106. K.A. Nilakanta Sastry, *Foreign Notices of South India (From Megasthenes to Mahuan)* (Madras, 1939), p. 307.

107. A corge was a bundle containing twenty pieces of cloth. *The Account of Peter Floris*, p. 70n.

108. Burton Stein 'Coromandal Trade in Medieval India' in John Parker ed., *Merchants and Scholars* (Minneapolis, Minnesota, 1965). This point regarding the decline of merchant guilds, which is mentioned very briefly here, is further elaborated in his article 'Integration of the Agrarian System of South India', in Robert Eric Frykenburg, ed., *Land Control and Social Structure in Indian History* (Madison, Milwaukee, 1969). However, the somewhat simplistic conclusions arrived at by Stein in these earlier articles have been greatly modified by him in *Peasant, State and Society in Medieval South India*. Here his essential arguments are far more sophisticated and he concedes that merchant guilds continued to flourish under the Vijayanagar empire because of the renewed process of urbanization, and that the landed elements forged links with the merchant guilds. See pp. 282, 252 and *passim*.

109. There are innumerable instances of land donation to temples and land ownership by merchants. The areas referred to are the fertile wet lands (*S.I.I.*,

vol. vi, no. 1172; *S.I.I.*, vol. v, no. 812; *S.I.I.*, vol. x, no. 161, etc.) An extremely significant inscription from Peddaganjam (Baptala taluq, Guntur district) of 1270 refers to the donation of an entire village along with the customs duties, taxes, etc. to the temple deity (*S.I.I.*, vol. x, no. 427). That they also had some control over the village castes in some places is shown by the fact that all general contributions of the village communities were made under their leadership (*E.I.*, vol. xviii, no. 22, etc.)

110. *A.R.E.*, no. 322 of 1936–7, *A.R.E.*, 196 of 1927–8, etc.

111. *S.I.I.*, vol. viii, no. 442 from Piranmalai (Ramnad district) etc.

112. Kenneth R. Hall, *Trade and Statecraft in the Age of the Cholas* (New Delhi, 1980).

113. *S.I.I.*, vol. vii, no. 21, *A.R.E.*, 200 of 1937–8, etc., dated 1529 and 1531 respectively. These are just select inscriptions which refer to merchant guilds in connection with the textile trade. But the general inscriptions relating to the functioning of the merchant guilds in the fifteenth—sixteenth centuries are too numerous to be listed here.

114. *A.R.E.*, C.P. 18 of 1917–18 dated 1680.

115. *Amuktamalyada*, iv, verse 35.

116. *A.R.E.*, 170 of 1933.

117. *E.C.*, vol. v, B1.75.

118. *A.R.E.*, 16 of 1935. Also *A.R.E.*, 63 of 1909 of the period of Bhupati Raya.

119. *A.R.E.*, 221 of 1929–30. The term 'Narpattennayira' itself represents a merchant guild.

120. The earliest reference to a weaving site is to be found in an eleventh century inscription from Obalapura, Challakera taluq in Chittaldoorg district, *E.C.*, vol. xi, Cl. 21.

121. *S.I.I.*, vol. ix, pt. 2, no. 516.

122. The *rayarekha* of Alamkonda given in K.A. Nilakanta Sastry and N. Venkataramanayya, ed. *Further Sources of Vijayanagar History*, 3 vols. (Madras, 1946), vol. iii, chap. 29.

123. Mahuan, p. 346.

124. Barbosa, book ii, p. 77.

125. From the account of Ludovico Varthema, pp. 168–9, cited in T.V. Mahalingam, *Administration and Social Life under Vijayanagar*, p. 151.

126. Caesar Fredrick in *Pilgrims*, p. 135.

127. *E.C.*, vol. xi, no. 1.

128. *A.R.E.*, 265 of 1934–5.

129. Refer Table, *A.R.E.*, 247 of 1916 and *A.R.E.*, 209 of 1913.

130. *A.R.E.*, 201 of 1923.

131. Ibid.

132. *A.R.E.*, 201 of 1923.

133. *A.R.E.*, 490 of 1937–8.

134. *A.R.E.*, 622 of 1920; Also *A.R.E.*, 208 of 1934–5 from Nerkunram, Tirukkoyilur, South Arcot district; *A.R.E.*, 228 of 1930–1 from Manamadi in Chingleput district, etc.

135. *A.R.E.*, 247 of 1916; *A.R.E.*, 59 of 1914–15 from Tiruvaigavur (Tanjavur district), refers to the reduction of all taxes by the *idangai* and *valangai* classes due to the same reasons.

136. *A.R.E.*, 1 of 1915–16, appendix D, pt. ii, pp. 152–3. An inscription of the period of the period of Sriranga IV (1756) from Amritaluru (Guntur district) grants

exemption from tax to merchants and weavers on a similar ground for a period of three years. *S.I.I.*, vol. xvi, no. 334.

137. *A.R.E.*, 201 of 1923 from Tiruppulivanam, Kanchipuram taluq, Chingleput district of the period of Virupaksha II. Also, *A.R.E.*, 454 of 1916 dated 1513 from Ambasamudram, Tirunelveli district, and *A.R.E.*, 310 of 1916–17 from the same area.

Notes to Chapter IV

1. Burton Stein's article in John Parker, ed., *Merchants and Scholars*. Also in Frykenburg, ed., *Land Control and Social Structure*. T.V. Mahalingam, though he does not state it in such conclusive terms, seems to hold the same idea for he says, 'The real fact is that, from about the Vijayanagar period in the history of South India, the Government which came to be organized partly on feudal and partly on military basis was not conducive to the active functioning of the village republics'. *South Indian Polity* (Madras, 1967), p. 382.

2. The efforts taken by the Vijayanagar rulers to forge links with the local elements, especially the temples and sectarian leaders, is dealt with in a thought-provoking article by Arjun Appadorai, 'Kings, Sects, and Temples in South India', in Burton Stein, ed., *South Indian Temples* (New Delhi, 1978), pp. 47–75.

3. A record from Nakkarahalu in Hadugallu taluq dated 1562 records that the *adhikari* officers granted *manya* lands to *senabova* (accountant) *tirumallara*, the *gaunda* (headman), *talari* (watchman), *jyotisa* (astrologer) etc. *S.I.I.*, vol. ix, pt. ii, no. 676. *E. C.*, vol. xii, ch. 2 also refers to *manya* being granted to a *jyotisa*.

4. Mark Wilkes, *Historical Sketches of South India*, 3 vols. (London, 1820), vol. i, p. 73.

5. Ibid. A detailed reference to the Ayagar system is also to be found in The *Attavanavyavaharatantram*. This is cited at some length in *Further Sources of Vijayanagar History*, ed W. Venkataramanayya and K. A. Nilakanta Sastry (Madras, 1946), p. 285.

6. *A.R.E.*, 16 C. P. of 1925–6, no. 21 of 1910–11, *E.C.*, vol. xii, Tm. 54, etc.

7. *M.A.R.*, 1928, p. 48.

8. *E.C.*, vol. vii, ch. 62, dated 1565 from Channagiri, Shimoga, for instance, refers to a dispute between two local parties regarding the offices of *senabova, jyotisha* and *purohit*.

9. *M.A.R.*, 1916, para 105.

10. A.V. Venkataratnam, *Local Government in the Vijayanagar Empire* (Prasaranga, University of Mysore, 1972), p. 30.

11. Ibid., p. 37, Saletore's view, that the Vijayanagar kings did not introduce measures by which the powers of the local bodies were curtailed, is quoted with approval by Venkataratnam. To quote Saletore, 'as promoters of the Purvada-Maryade (ancient constitutional usage) it was their endeavour to preserve the old order of things, and to allow the ancient officers to continue under the new government, although . . . they showed their discretion by placing over the local bodies, officers of the Central Government'. B.A. Saletore, *Social and Political Life in the Vijayanagar Empire*, vol. i, p. 342.

12. V. Rangacharya, *Inscriptions of the Madras Presidency*, vol. ii, np. 996 A.
13. *A.R.E.*, 103 of 1906.
14. *T.T*, vol. vi, pt. i, no. 6.
15. *A.R.E.*, 538 of 1916–17.
16. *Amuktamalyada*, canto iv, verse 35.
17. *A.R.E.*, 298 of 1921–2. The inscription gives no clue as to the date nor is it possible to place Vira Sayana Udaiyar, though in the report he is listed as a ruler of Vijayanagar.
18. *S.I.I.*, vol. v, no. 479.
19. *A.R.E.*, 353 of 1911 from Chingleput; *A.R.E.*, 221 of 1929–30, etc.
20. *A.R.E.*, 366 of 1923; *A.R.E.*, 318 of 1916–17, etc.
21. *A.R.E.*, 366 of 1923.
22. *E.C.*, Bn. 66, p. 14.
23. *A.R.E.*, 63 of 1908.
24. *A.R.E.*, 318 of 1916–17.
25. Rangacharya, *Inscriptions of the Madras Presidency*, no. 362.
26. *A.R.E.*, 313 of 1916–17.
27. *A.R.E.*, 353 of 1911.
28. *A.R.E.*, 407 of 1928–9.
29. *A.R.E.*, 221 of 1929–30.
30. *A.R.E.*, 407 of 1928–9.
31. *A.R.E.*, 453 of 1913–14.
32. For a discussion of the shift in the nature of donations from perpetual lamps to *prasadam*, see Arjun Appadorai's article 'Kings, Sects and Temples in South India', pp. 66–7, and ff., also *T.T.*, Introductory Report, p. 129.
33. 1254, the reign of Vijayaganda Gopaladeva, *T.T.*, vol. i, no. 61. Also in the reign of Kulottunga III, virtually the last of the Cholas, *A.R.E.*, 418 of 1909–10.
34. *S.I.I.*, vol. vii, no. 21; *A.R.E.*, 200 of 1937–8, etc..
35. *S.I.I.*, vol. vi, nos. 219 and 220 from Amaravati; also *N.D.I.*, vol. iii, no. 21 from Udayagiri.
36. *S.I.I.*, vol. vi, no. 666.
37. K. S. S Shivanna, 'Kanakadasa's Ramadhanya Charitre—Its Socio-Economic Significance', a paper presented at the 40th session of the Indian History Congress, Waltair, 1979.
38. Cited in T. V. Mahalingam, *Administration and Social Life*, p. 178.
39. *Keyurabhirama* of Manchana, cited in A. Vaidehi Krishnamoorthy, *Social and Economic Conditions in Eastern Deccan* (Secunderabad, 1970), p. 92.
40. *Kreedabhiramamu* of Vallabharaya, ed. Vetturi Prabhakara Sastri (Muktiyala, 1952), verses 54–5.
41. *T.T.*, inscriptions. The majority of the record in this series make some reference to the payment to professionals and menials in the temple. See vol. iii, no. 29 dated 1512, and no. 105 dated 1515, both from the period of Krishnadeva Raya. Also vol. iv, no. 3 dated 1530, no. 39 dated 1535, etc.
42. *A.R.E.*, 407 of 1928–9.
43. *A.R.E.*, 452 of 1913–14.
44. *A.R.E.*, 188 of 1963–4.
45. *A.R.E.*, 189 of 1963–4.
46. *A.R.E.*, 368 of 1923.·

214　　　　　*Textiles and Weavers in South India*

47. *A.R.E.*, 209 of 1934–5.
48. *A.R.E.*, 720 of 1962–3.
49. *S.I.I.*, vol. i, no. 87.
50. *T.T.*, vol. iv, nos. 140 and 258.
51. *A.R.E.*, 346 of 1923.
52. *A.R.E.*, 353 of 1911.
53. *A.R.E.*, 356 of 1911.
54. *A.R.E.*, 8 of 1909, Appendix C.
55. *A.R.E.*, 285 of 1928–9.
56. *A.R.E.*, 99 of 1935–6.
57. *A.R.E.*, 62 of 1908–9.
58. *S.I.I.*, vol. xvii, no. 758.
59. *A.R.E.*, 365 of 1912–13.
60. *A.R.E.*, 356 of 1912–13.
61. *A.R.E.*, 482 of 1909 from Cholapuram, Kovilpatti, Tirunelveli district.
62. *A.R.E.*, 602, 603 and 606 of 1916–17; 320 of 1916–17 and 473 of 1916–17, etc.
63. *A.R.E.*, 486 of 1937–8.
64. *A.R.E.*, 170 of 1933.
65. *S.I.I.*, vol. ix, pt. 2, no. 516.
66. *A.R.E.*, 87 of 1951–2; 318 of 1905–6, 472 and 514 of 1906–7, etc. *E.C.*, vol. vi, Tk. 13, etc.
67. *A.R.E.*, 429 of 1925–6 from South Arcot of the period of Devaraya.
68. *A.R.E.*, 356 of 1923.
69. *A.R.E.*, 473 of 1921–2 of the period of Mallikarjuna, dated 1485.
    A.R.E., 422 of 1925, of the same period.
    A.R.E., 291 of 1928–9.
    A.R.E., 162 of 1918–19.
70. The exact status of Aramvalartta Nayanar is not very clear. It appears that Kachchirayar was the head of the Kanchipuram guild and Aramvalartta Nayanar was the overall head.
71. *A.R.E.*, 291 of 1928–9.
72. *A.R.E.*, 804 of 1917.
73. *S.I.I.*, vol. vi, no. 209.
74. The clash between the weavers and the smiths over privileges is referred to in various inscriptions—*A.R.E.*, 293 of 1928–9 for instance. Several instances are cited by Arjun Appadorai in his monograph *Left-hand Right-hand Castes in South Indian History*.
75. *A.R.E.*, 221 of 1929–30.
76. *A.R.E.*, 229 of 1919–20.
77. The account of Domingo Paes in Sewell, pp. 234, 259.
78. *A.R.E.*, 313 of 1916–17.
79. *A.R.E.*, 602, 603 and 606 of 1916–17. Also *T.T.* inscriptions, *passim*.
80. *A.R.E.*, 196 of 1912–13.
81. *A.R.E.*, 208 of 1912–13.
82. *A.R.E.*, 196, Appendix B, 1912–13.
83. *S.I.I.*, vol. i, p. 22.
84. *T.T.*, vol. i, no. 108.
85. The wages of temple servants are given in several inscriptions pertaining to the Tirumalai-Tirupati temples. *T.T.*, vol. ii, no. 135; *T.T.*, vol. iii, no. 105, no. 29;

T.T., vol. iv, no. 3, etc. There is not much difference in the wages paid to the temple personnel which ranged between 1 to 5 *panams*, but the Sthanathar were paid higher.

86. *T.T.*, vol. ii, no. 85; *T.T.*, vol. iii, no. 7 etc.

87. Abbe Dubois, *Hindu Manners, Customs and Ceremonies of the People of India* (1879; rpt. London, 1978).

88. This opinion is expressed among others by Lewis Rice; *Mysore Gazeteer*, pp. 52–3ff. Also see Hamilton Buchanan's *A Journey from Madras through the countries of Mysore, Canara and Malabar*, 3 vols, (London, 1807). Also refer to Burton Stein *Peasant, State and Society* for his theory of a Brahmin–Vellala alliance against the artisan groups.

89. Arjun Appadorai, 'Left-Hand Right-Hand castes in South India', *I.E.S.H.R.*, vol. xi, nos. 2 and 3, 1974, p. 219.

90. This is what Burton Stein has described as 'opposition which is complementary.' See Stein's article in Richard Fox, ed., *Realm and Region in India* (New Delhi, 1977), pp. 35–6.

91. Only the Kaikkola weavers are specifically mentioned because some weaver castes like the Saliyar of the Tamil country and the Padmasale of the Andhra-Karnatak regions belonged to the *valangai*.

92. *A.R.E.*, 217 of 1916 (Kanchipuram taluq, Chingleput district).

93. *A.R.E.*, 24 of 1944–5.

94. *A.R.E.*, 308 of 1954–5.

95. *A.R.E.*, 315 of 1954–5.

96. *A.R.E.*, 207 of 1929–30.

97. *A.R.E.*, 368 of 1917–18.

98. *A.R.E.*, 293 of 1928–9.

99. Abbe Dubois, p. 26.

100. *S.I.I.*, vol. viii, no. 155.

101. *A.R.E.*, 217 of 1916, For details on the Sanketi Brahmins see Thurston, vol. i. Two other examples of *idangai–valangai* opposition to Brahmins occur in *A.R.E.*, 246 and 254 of 1928–9, though here the issue was not privileges but tax oppression.

102. *A.R.E.*, 422 of 1905.

103. *A.R.E.*, 185 of 1921.

104. *A.R.E.*, 201 of 1936–7.

105. *A.R.E.*, 41 of 1922–3.

106. *A.R.E.*, 103 of 1906–7.

107. *A.R.E.*, 216 of 1917–18.

108. *A.R.E.*, 489 of 1937–8.

109. *A.R.E.*, 92 of 1918–19, para 68.

110. For the growth of urban centres and its links with the Bhakti movement, see R. N. Nandi's article on the 'Origins of the Vira-Saiva movement,' *I.H.R.*, vol. ii, no. i, July 1975. Also see Burton Stein's article on 'Social Mobility and Medieval South Indian Hindu Sects' in Silverburg, ed., *Social Mobility in the Caste System of India* (Hague, 1968), p. 78 and *passim*. Stein's attributing the importance of the Sudras to the existence of large contingents of caste armies in the Vijayanagar period is not correct since most of the caste armies were disbanded after Rajaraja Chola III.

111. *Amuktamalyada*: canto iv, verse 35, p. 230.

112. Stein's article in Silverburg, p. 81.
113. Ibid., p. 90.
114. N. Jagadeesan, *History of Sri Vaishnavism in the Tamil Country (Post-Ramanuja)* (Madurai, 1977), pp. 86, 91–2, 94–5.
115. This aspect is discussed by Stein in Silverburg, pp. 88–9. Also Arjun Appadorai's article in Stein, ed., *South Indian Temples*, p. 59.
116. *T.T.*, vol. ii, nos. 23, 31 and 50, etc.
117. *T.T.*, vol. iii, no. 396, 397.
118. Edgar Thurston, vol. iii, p. 42.
119. H. Buchanan, vol. i, pp. 256–7.
120. Arjun Appadorai in Stein, p. 67.
121. *N.D.I.*, vol. ii, no. 20.
122. Burton Stein 'Temples in the Tamil Country, 1300–1500', in Stein, ed., *South Indian Temples*, pp. 27–8.
123. Thurston, vol. iii, p. 42.
124. The nature of participation of the professional and artisan classes in the Bhakti movement in northern India has been discussed at some length by Irfan Habib in his article 'The Historical background of the monotheistic movements of the 15th–17th Centuries,' Seminar on ideas—Medieval India, Univ. of Delhi, 1965, mimeo.
125. *Hundred Poems of Kabir*, tr. by Rabindranath Tagore, ed. Evelyn Underhill (London, 1970), p. 41.
126. Translated by Sereberiakov in 'The Poetry of Weavers and Tanners', *I.S.P.P.*, vol. viii, 1966–7, p. 194.

Notes to Chapter V

1. Daniel Havert, *Open Ondergang Van Coromandel*, 3 vols. (Amsterdam, 1693), translated as *The Rise and Fall of Coromandel*, Mackenzie Collection (Private), Fol. 88, India Office Library, London, vol. ii, chap. vi.
2. Ibid., chapters i to iv.
3. Streynsham Master, vol. ii, p. 135.
4. *Letters from Fort St. George*, (hereafter *Letters*) 14 March 1696, pp. 16, 22.
5. *A.R.E.*, 244 of 1932–3.
6. *A.R.E.*, 472 of 1925–6.
7. *A.R.E.*, 287 of 1945–4.
8. *A.R.E.*, 356 of 1928–9.
9. *A.R.E.*, 16 of 1935–6; *S.I.T.I.*, vol. ii, no. 506.
10. *A.R.E.*, 411 of 1923–4.
11. *Diary and Consultations*, 28 Sept. 1675, p. 73.
12. *Letters*, 13 Sept. 1688, p. 52; *Diary and Consultations*, 11 June 1694, 21 Nov. 1694, etc.
13. *Dispatches*, 15 Dec. 1676, p. 45.
14. In a petition to the Governor of Fort St. George, the Portuguese inhabitants of Madrasapatam reminded the English that the earliest settlements of weavers

and painters in the region had been made under Portuguese command. *Diary and Consultations*, Jan. 1679, p. 166; *E.F.I.*, vol. v, 12 Sept. 1631, *Dispatches*, 15 Feb. 1688 and 26 Aug. 1698, etc.

15. *E.F.I.*, vol. ii, 6 Nov. 1622, p. 105.
16. *E.F.I.*, vol. iv, 1634, p. 48.
17. *Koloniel Archiefs* (*K.A.*) Letters, lxxix, 28 Nov. 1615.
18. *Diary and Consultations*, 20 Oct. 1674. In their letter dated 29 Sept. 1674, Viranna, Venkata Narain, Pedda Venkatadry, Chinna Venkatadry and other merchants of the Company demanded an upward revision of price on the grounds that they had agreed to take English broad cloth in part payment while the Dutch dealt entirely in liquid capital.
19. *Letters*, 12 Jan. 1665. Also 5 Feb. 1696, p. 9: 'English cloth still not selling, our dependence is wholly on the silver for paying off our debts and carrying on the coast investment.'
20. *Diary and Consultations*, 14 Sept. 1676. Broad cloth given as *Peshkash* to Madanna, Akkanna, Poddala Lingappa, etc.
21. Peter Floris, p. 71.
22. Daniel Havert. vol. i, chap. vi, pp. 110ff.
23. Ibid., p. 172ff.
24. *K.A.*, *Letters*, cccxxvi, 3 Dec. 1628.
25. *K.A.*, *Letters*, D., 16 Nov. 1614.
26. The price of indigo in Surat at various points of time in the seventeenth century is given in Kumari Lily Murgai's unpublished M. Phil dissertation, 'Aspects of the Economy of Ahmedabad during the 17th century,' (Delhi, Jawaharlal Nehru University, 1980).
27. *K.A.*, *Letters*, cccxxvi, 3 Dec. 1628.
28. *K.A.*, *Letters*, xxvii, 1607–8.
29. Cited in J. Irwin, 'Foreign Influences,' in J. Irwin and P.R. Schwartz, ed., *Studies in Indo-European Textile History* (Ahmedabad, 1966).
30. Victoria and Albert Museum. IM 160–1929 and 687–1898 I.S.
31. *Journal of Indian Art*, vol. vii, 1897, plates 92–3.
32. Irfan Habib in his various articles, especially 'Potentialities of change in the Economy of Mughal India', *Socialist Digest*, no. 6, 1972.
33. 'Anonymous Tract' in McCullock, ed., *Early English Tracts on Commerce*, (Cambridge, 1970), pp. 556–9.
34. Palsaert's account, translated by Moreland and Geyl as *Jahangir's India* (Cambridge, 1925), p. 60.
35. *Dispatches*, 2 April 1683, p. 27, 9 June 1686, p. 24, para 33, etc.
36. Irfan Habib 'Notes on the Indian Textile Industry in the 17th Century', *Essays in Honour of S. C. Sarkar* (New Delhi, 1976), pp. 183–4.
37. *T.T.*, vol. iv, no. 112.
38. Irfan Habib, 'Notes on the Indian Textile Industry,' p. 183.
39. *The Diaries of Streynsham Master*, vol. ii, p. 171.
40. See introduction above for Vedic reference to the vertical loom. For a detailed discussion on textile technology, questioning in particular the conclusions of I. Habib, see Vijaya Ramaswamy, 'Notes on the Textile Technology in Medieval India with special reference to the South', *I.E.S.H.R.*, April-June 1980.
41. Export of indigo from Fort St. David and Masulipatnam (besides the Surat

indigo) is referred to in the Company records—*E.F.I.*, 10 Nov. 1656, p. 103; *Dispatches*, 26 Aug. 1698, p. 45, etc. Also of redwood, *Dispatches*, 26 Jan. 1698; *ibid.*, 8 Feb. 1681, p. 73. Red saunders was also known as Calliatore wood. The Company also imported chay (red dye) and attempted to learn its use: *E.F.I.*, 12 Sept. 1631, p. 169.

42. *Dispatches*, 5 Jan. 168.
43. *Diary and Consultations*, 18 Feb. 1675, p. 40 Also Thomas Bowrey, *Countries Round the Bay of Bengal* (London, 1903), pp. 214–15.
44. *Dispatches*, 15 Feb. 1688, p. 167.
45. *Letters*, 18 Aug. 1696, p. 87 and 30 Sept. 1696, p. 90.
46. *Letters*, 30 Nov. 1696, p. 106.
47. *Diary and Consultations* 28 Sept. 1675, p. 73.
48. Ibid., 14 June 1672, p. 6.
49. *Dispatches*, 27 Aug. 1688, p. 148.
50. Methwold's Account in *Relations of Golconda in the Early Seventeenth Century*, ed. W. H. Moreland (London, 1931), pp. 18, 26–7, etc.
51. *Streynsham Master*, vol. i, p. 268 and vol. ii, p. 135.
52. H. Buchanan; *A Journey from Madras through the Countries of Mysore, Canara and Malabar*, Vols. 1–3, (London, 1807), vol. i, p. 40.
53. Ibid., vol. ii, p. 33.
54. *Attavanavyavaharatantram*, Mac. Mss. 15–6–8, in Further Sources, vol. iii, pp. 310–13. Also T. V. Mahalingam, ed., *Mackenzie Manuscripts*, vol. ii, pp. 327–8ff.
55. *The Travels of Peter Mundy*, ed. Richard Carnac Temple (London, 1914), vol. ii, pp. 362, 371.
56. Buchanan, vol. i, pp. 198–200ff.
57. Ibid., p. 221.
58. *O.C.*, 334, 15 Jan 1616.
59. *K.A.*, *Letters*, cclxx.
60. M.N. Pearson, Indigenous Dominance in a Colonial Economy—The Goa Rendas, 1600–1670', *Mare Luso-Indicum*, no. 2 (1972), pp. 61–73, cited in Anthony Disney, *Twilight of the Pepper Empire* (Harvard, 1978), p. 46.
61. *K.A.*, *Letters*, cclxiii, 25 Dec. 1629.
62. *K.A.*, *Letters*, ccclxxxii 12 Dec. 1641.
63. *Travels in India of Tavernier*, ed. V. Ball (London, 1889), pp. 119–20, 143–4, etc. *The Travels of Thevenot and Carreri*, ed. Surendranath Sen (New Delhi, 1949), pp. 119–20, 150, 329, etc.
64. *K.A.*, *Letters*, lxxix, 28 Nov. 1615.
65. K.N. Chaudhuri, *The Trading World of Asia and the English East India Company, 1660–1760* (London, 1978), p. 250.
66. *S.I.I.*, vol. viii, no. 442, from Piranmalai, cited earlier. Also Caesar Fredrick in *Pilgrims*, p. 130, etc.
67. *K.A.*, *Letters*, Dclxiii 20 Sept. 1660.
68. *E.F.I.*, 6 Feb. 1621, p. 119.
69. Peter Floris, pp. 41–2.
70. Pieter Williemsz served the Dutch East India Company from 1603 to 1608 and it was when he was caught indulging in private trade by the Company that he changed his name to Peter Floris and took part in the voyage of the 'Globe' (a ship of the English East India Company) in 1615.

71. Van Leur, *Indonesian Trade and Society, Essays in Asian Social and Economic History* (Hague, 1955), pp. 203–4, 234–5, 242, etc.

72. *K.A.* Letters, lxxxi *A Short Account of the Trade on the Coast of Coromandel Especially Masulipatnam Factory* by Anthony Schorrer, 1615.

73. *K.A.*, dclxiii, 20 Sept. 1660.

74. *K.A.*, dxxxviii.

75. *K.A.*, *Letters*, mxix, 15 Aug. 1633, mxxii, 15 Aug. 1634, etc., cited in Tapan Raychaudhuri, *Jan Company in Coromandel—1605–1690* (Hague, 1962), p. 121.

76. *K.A.*, *Letters*, cclxx, 24 Sept. 1628; cccxxiv, 21 April 1635, dxvii, 8 October 1649, dcxiii, 14 Dec. 1657, etc.

77. *O.C.*, 1201, 1629.

78. *K.A.*, *Letters*, dvi, 5 June 1648; dvii, 19 Sep. 1648; dviii, 22 Nov. 1648, and *passim*.

79. *K.A.*, dxxix, 13 Oct. 1653.

80. Old name for place on the Persian Gulf, now known as *Bandar-Abbas*. *Hobson-Jobson*, p. 384.

81. *E.F.I.*, Thomas Joyce and Nathaniel Wyche at Masulipatnam to the Company, 26 Oct. 1634, p. 48.

82. *E.F.I.*, 31 Jan. 1636, p. 161; *K.A.*, *Letters*, ddxxxvii, 18 Oct. 1644; *K.A.*, xxvii, 1607–8, etc.

83. Flowered, embroidered or brocaded cloth was very popular in Turkey. Since *nim* in Persian means half, the nimguls were half the usual length.

84. *E.F.I.*, 4 March 1647, p. 109.

85. Peter Floris, p. 64, 73–4, etc. Macao is a place on the Pegu river.

86. Ibid., p. 73.

87. *Dispatches*, 11 Sept. 1689, p. 175.

88. Afzal Ahmad, Appendix A to F.

89. Pearson 'Indigenous Dominance, p. 72, cited in Anthony Disney, p. 194, note 68.

90. Anthony Disney, p. 119.

91. Father Antonus Monserrate's Account of Akbar, *Journal and Proceedings of the Asiatic Society of Bengal*, vol. 8, 1912, p. 156; cited in A.I. Chicherov, *India—Economic Development in the 16th–18th Centuries* (Moscow, 1971), p. 115.

92. *E.F.I.*, 6 March 1622, p. 56.

93. India Office Archives, *Court Book VI*, Minutes, dated 6 August 1623, cited in J. Irwin and Schwartz, p. 11.

94. A description of the triangular slave trade can be found in any standard book on the history of the American negroes. See J. H. Franklin, *From Slavery to Freedom* (New York, 1947); Winthrop D. Jordon, *White Over Black, 1550–1812* (Chicago, 1968); Peter Rose, ed., *Americans From Africa* (New York, 1970), etc.

95. *E.F.I.*, 9 Oct. 1647, pp. 163–4.

96. *E.F.I.*, 13 Feb. 1650, p. 297.

97. W. H. Moreland, *From Akbar to Aurangazeb* (London, 1923), pp. 131–2.

98. 'The Textile Trade of Seventeenth Century Northern Cormandel' by J. Brennig (unpublished Ph.D. thesis, Univ. Microfilms, Ann Arbor, Michigan), p. 40; Also K. Glamann, *Dutch Asiatic Trade, 1620–1749* (Hague, 1958).

99. Moreland, *Akbar to Aurangazeb*, p. 129.

100. K. N. Chaudhuri, *The Trading World of Asia*, p. 282. Also refer to the list of orders by the company in the appendix.

101. *E.F.I.*, 10 Nov. 1661, p. 158.

102. *Dispatches*, 12 Dec. 1677, p. 135. A pagoda at that time was reckoned at 8 shillings.

103. *Dispatches*, 22 April 1681, p. 49.

104. *Dispatches*, May 1681, p. 7.

105. *Dispatches*, 26 Jan. 1688.

106. *Dispatches*, 9 Oct. 1682, p. 15.

107. *Dispatch Book*, 16 Nov. 1683, vol. 90, para 18, p. 14; cited in K. N. Chaudhury, p. 287. Also *Dispatches*, 8 June 1676, p. 32, 13 June 1685, pp. 153–5 etc.

108. *E.F.I.*, 1630–3, p. 310.

109. *Dispatches*; 22 July 1681, p. 59; 30 Nov. 1681, p. 69, etc.

110. *Dispatches*, 13 Feb. 1685, p. 153; 9 June 1686, p. 21. Also *Letters*, 12 Dec. 1688, etc.

111. 'The case of several thousand poor of the wool manufacturers ruined by the printing and dyeing of linens in England;' British Museum 816.m 14 (87), cited by Shafaat Ahmad Khan, *The East India Trade in the 17th Century in its Political and Economic Aspects* (London, 1923), p. 286ff. Several other such pamphlets are cited by him on pp. 278–88.

112. 'A Discourse on Trade' (1680) in *Early English Tracts on Commerce*, pp. 307–10ff.

113. Josiah Child, 'The Great Honour and advantage of the East India Trade', pp. 30–1; cited in K. N. Chaudhuri, pp. 278–9.

114. Thomas Mun, 'A discourse of Trade from England upto the East Indies 1621', in *Early English Tracts on Commerce*, p. 9.

115. Thomas Mun, 'England's Treasure by Foreign Trade' (1664) in ibid., p. 135. This idea is expanded in pp. 131, 135–6ff.

116. 'Papers relating to the Linen Drapers' Protest', British Museum, 816, m. 14 (87), quoted extensively by Shafaat Ahmad Khan, pp. 286–8ff. Also Thomas Mun's 'England's Treasure by Foreign Trade' in *Early English Tracts on Commerce*, p. 132: 'In the past 35 years, the winding of raw silk did not employ more than 300. Now it doth set on work above 14,000 souls'.

117. 100 bales of cotton yarn from the Coromandel coast on 14 Dec. 1675 (*Dispatches*, p. 28). In 1676, 50 bales of cotton yarn and 50 bales of Cloretta yarn from the Bay (ibid., 8 June 1676, p. 32). In 1683 and 1684, 150 bales of cotton yarn and 100 bales of linen yarn were exported from the Coromandel coast (ibid., June 1683 and Nov. 1684). The export of cotton yarn from Kolhapur, Masulipatnam, and other regions is frequently referred to in the *Letters* and *Dispatches* of the English East India Company.

118. *E.F.I.*, 13 April 1630, p. 22.

119. *E.F.I.*, 12 Sept. 1631, 1 Oct. 1632, etc; *Dispatches*, 15 Dec. 1676 suggests that, like the Dutch, the Company should also have its own dyers and painters.

120. Daniel Havert, pp. 38 and 84.

121. K. N. Chaudhuri, p. 255.

122. K. Marx, *Capital*, (Moscow, 1974), vol. iii, pt. iv, ch. xx, p. 330.

123. Ibid., p. 334. For a detailed discussion on the master-weavers in the Indian Context, see Vijaya Ramaswamy 'The Genesis and Historical Role of Master Weavers in South Indian Textile Production' *J.E.S.H.O.* (forthcoming).

124. The complete Table is given in J. Brenning, p. 240.

125. *K. A.*, 1294, 8 Jan. 1684, Folio 1519 b, cited in J. Brenning, p. 258. Based on

statistics from Gollapallem, Brenning estimates that 10 per cent of the weaving population owned more than two looms: (ibid., p. 266.

126. *E.F.I.*, 29 Jan. 1653, pp. 152–3, and 4 April 1654, p. 263.
127. *Diary and Consultations*, 19 Nov. 1694, pp. 130–1, and 20 Dec. 1694, p. 143.
128. *Diary and Consultations*, 15 Oct. 1693, pp. 121–2.
129. *Diary and Consultations*, 5 November 1694, p. 123.
130. Buchanan, vol. i, p. 212.
131. Ibid., pp. 212, 216–17, etc.
132. *E.F.I.*, 16 Nov. 1662, p. 175.
133. Methwold in *Relations of Golconda*, p. 16.
134. *A.R.E.*, copper plate 8 of 1952–3.
135. *S.I.I.*, vol. xvi, no. 315.
136. *A.R.E.*, copper plate 18 of 1917–18.
137. *K.A.*, *Letters*, dxli, 6 NN, 1652.
138. *Diary and Consultations*, 25 March 1686, p. 29.
139. *Letters*, 20 March 1687, p. 7.
140. Peter Floris, p. 70.
141. *K.A.*, *Letters*, lxxxvii, 22 Oct. 1615.
142. *K.A.*, *Letters*, cclviii, 27 June 1627.
143. *K.A.*, *Letters*, cclxxxiii, 16 March 1629.
144. *K.A.*, *Letters*, clxxxix, 22 Sept. 1630.
145. *K.A.*, *Letters*, cccxliv, 6 March 1637.
146. *O.C.*, 1451, 1 Oct. 1632.
147. *K.A.*, *Letters*, ddlvii, 19 March 1695, and *passim*.
148. *K.A.*, *Letters*, ddlxxxiv, 6 Dec. 1645, 4 Jan 1646.
149. *K.A.*, *Letters*, ddxcii, 1 May 1646.
150. *K.A.*, *Letters*, div, 3 March 1648.
151. *K.A.*, *Letters*, di, 24 April 1646.
152. *K.A.*, *Letters*, dclxiv, 24 July 1669.
153. *E.F.I.*, 29 Dec. 1640, 27 Jan. 1644, etc., and *K.A.*, *Letters*, 24 April 1646, dxvii, 1 Oct. 1650, etc.
154. *K.A.*, *Letters*, dxxxviii, 14 Dec. 1652 and ibid., di, 24 April 1646.
155. *E.F.I.*, 9 Oct. 1647, p. 166, 27 Aug. 1662, p. 167; *Diary and Consultations*, 14 June 1676, p. 6; 14 Sept. 1676, p. 100, etc. Also *K.A.*, *Letters*, 5 Aug. 1632, Folio 246–7, dl, 19 Jan. 1654, etc. The Dutch, however, borrowed less than the English.
156. *E.F.I.*, 1 March 1654, p. 239.
157. *The Diaries of Streynsham Master*, vol. ii, p. 168.
158. *E.F.I.*, 1 March 1654, p. 238.
159. *Diary and Consultations*, 1693, p. 49. A dollar was reckoned at 4 shillings 6 pence at this time.
160. *K.A.*, *Letters*, ddlxxxiv, 4 Jan. 1646 and dxviii, 23 Nov. 1650, etc.
161. *Letters*, 1 March 1679, p. 12 and *Cuddalore and Porto Novo Consultations*, 26 Feb. 1681, etc.
162. *Diary and Consultations*, 1 March 1694, p. 14, 26 March 1694, p. 27; *Diaries of Streynsham Master*, vol. ii, p. 152, etc.
163. *K.A.*, *Letters*, xxvii, 1607–8.
164. *K.A.*, *Letters*, ccclii, 18 July 1638.

165. *Press List of Ancient Records in the Salem District* 1791 to 1835 (Madras, 1906), vol. 559, 28 April 1800, pp. 301–2; vol. 3173, 21 Oct. 1820, p. 37; vol. 3172, 17 Nov. 1819, pp. 143–4, and 22 May 1819, p. 78, etc.

166. H. Dodwell, 'The Madras Weavers Under the Companyies,' *P.I.H.R.C.*, vol. iv, 1922, p. 44.

167. Peter Floris, p. 14.

168. *Salem District Records*, vol. 559, 16 May 1800, pp. 305–14, vol. 560, 5 Nov. 1800, pp. 69–70, etc.

169. H. Dodwell, p. 44.

170. J. Brenning, p. 267.

Notes to Chapter VI

1. *A.R.E.*, 356 of 1928–9.

2. Cited in C. S. Srinivasachari, 'Right–hand Left–hand Caste Disputes in the early part of the Eighteenth Century, *P.I.H.R.C.*, vol. xii, Gwalior, December 1929, p. 73.

3. *E.C.*, vol. v, Ak. 94.

4. *A.R.E.*, copper plate 18 of 1917–18, dated 1680; *E.C.*, vol. xii, TP 130, and *E.C.*, vol. x, ch. 2, both dated around 1600; and *E.C.*, vol. xii, Ml. 31 dated 1656, etc.

5. *Diary and Consultations*, 19 Nov. 1694, p. 131.

6. H. D. Love, *Vestiges of Madras, 1640–1800*, 3 Vols (London, 1913), vol. i, p. 547.

7. *E.F.I.*, 25 June 1629, p. 342.

8. *E.F.I.*, The Text of Brahmins Declaration, 4 April 1654, p. 256. Also see p. 241.

9. *E.F.I.*, 26 Oct. 1646, p. 52.

10. *E.F.I.*, 4 April 1654, p. 256.

11. Fleet, *Gupta Inscriptions*, no. 18. See also *Indian Antiquary*, vol. 15, no. 162, 1886, p. 194.

12. The peculiar affinity of weavers to the soldiering profession was not unique to the Pattunulkarar. Even the Kaikkolar, for instance, are referred to in the Chola period as 'muttuvalperra Kaikkolar' because of their skill in sword fighting. This point is discussed at some length in chap. ii.

13. One of the most reliable versions of this literary tradition is to be found in Yuchido Norihiko, *Oral Literature of the Saurashtras, India* (1979), pp. 47–52. However, there are different versions of the *Bhovlas* with slight variations perhaps depending on the particular locality in which a group came to settle. Thus the Saurashtras of Kilakkulam mention, apart from Madurai, even Tirunelveli and Papanasam in Tanjavur (ibid., pp. 51–2) Other versions of the *Bhovlas* are to be found in I. R. Dave, *The Saurashtrians in South india* (Rajkot 1976), pp. 32–4, etc. A much earlier version is to be found in *Saurashtra Brahmanar Charitram* (no author) (Madurai, 1914), p. 15. Some of the authorities cited to prove the veracity of these traditions are *The Skandapurana*, the *Bhagvad Gita*, etc!

14. J. H. Nelson, *Manual of the Madurai District* (Madras, 1868), p. 87. Also I.R. Dave, p. 40, etc.

15. *A.R.E.*, 257 of 1927 from Kumbakonam.

16. Yuchido Norihiko, no. 23, p. 144.

17. *Diary and Consultations*, 22 June 1693, p. 100. Simon Halcomb's paper. Also refer William Langhorne's statement, ibid., 28 Sept. 1675, p. 74.

18. *E.F.I.*, 4 April 1654, 'The Brahmins' Declaration', p. 262.

19. Refer to the table on Coromandel textiles in the appendix. For a similar view see Debendra Bijoy Mitra, *Cotton Weavers in Bengal* (Calcutta, 1978), p. 62 and table iv.

20. W. H. Moreland, ed., *Relations of Golconda*, p. 27.

21. *Koloniel Archief*, 1267, 18 April 1652, Fol. 2066, quoted in J. Brennig, p. 263.

22. Tavernier, vol. ii, p. 46.

23. *Streynsham Master*, vol. ii, p. 173, 110 and 371.

24. Thomas Bowry, p. 83.

25. *Factory Records Surat*, 14 Jan. 1738, vol. 23, p. 6; and 22 Feb. 1738, vol. 23, p. 33, cited in K. N. Chaudhuri, p. 268.

26. H. Dodwell, 'The Madras Weavers Under the Company', *P.I.H.R.C.* vol. iv, 1922, p. 43.

27. *Diary and Consultations*, 22 Feb. 1694, p. 12.

28. Buchanan, *A Journey from Madras through the Countries of Kanara and Malabar*, vol. i, p. 216.

29. Elijah Hoole, *A Mission to the South of India* (London, 1829), p. 48.

30. Refer to the table on Coromandel textiles in the appendix.

31. Foster, 27 Dec. 1630, pp. 117–18, Letter from Henry Sill and others at Armagaon to factors at Bantam. The factors themselves comment on the inefficiency of such a method because the merchants compensated themselves by squeezing weavers who ultimately reacted by running away, resulting in serious shortfalls in supply.

32. *Diary and Consultations*, 1 May 1693, p. 74.

33. *Letters from Fort St. George*, 20 June 1696, p. 57.

34. *E.F.I.*, 1659, p. 257. Also *Diary and Consultations*, 18 April 1672, p. 4, p. 6, etc.

35. Cited in K. N. Chaudhuri, p. 265. Also *E.F.I.*, the statement of William Issacs in 1661, p. 58.

36. *Dispatches*, 29 January 1736, p. 31.

37. *Diary and Consultations*, 18 April 1672, pp. 4 and 6. A candy is roughly 400 pounds.

38. *Diary and Consultations*, 23 December 1678, p. 150, and also *Letters to Fort St. George*, 13 March 1628. This and all subsequent reference to paddy prices are to be found in the table attached to this chapter, indicating paddy prices in the seventeenth century at uneven intervals.

39. *Letters to Fort St. George*, 23 March 1693.

40. *Home Miscellaneous Series*, vol. 393, pp. 261–2, cited in K. N. Chaudhuri, p. 265.

41. *E.F.I.*, 31 January 1632, pp. 203–4. Also see 2 Nov. 1630, p. 79, and 27 Dec. 1630, pp. 117–18, etc.

42. Ibid., 4 July 1647, p. 135; 9 Oct. 1647, p. 163; 26 Nov. 1646, p. 55, etc.

43. Ibid., 9 Oct. 1647, p. 163; ibid., 4 January 1647, p. 70, etc.

44. Ibid., 17 Jan. 1659, p. 263, and 11 Jan. 1661, p. 402.

45. *Letters to Fort St. George*, 13 March 1688, p. 25. Also 16th July, 1689, p. 37.

46. *Diary and Consultations*, 20 Sept. 1694, p. 100; ibid., 19 Nov. 1694, p. 130; ibid., 26 Nov. 1694, p. 134, etc.

47. *Original Correspondence*, 16 Jan. 1695, vol. 50, no. 5960; *Dispatches*, 31 Jan. 1695, p. 41.
48. *Letters*, 20 June 1696, p. 57.
49. *Diary and Consultations*, 19 Nov. 1694, p. 130.
50. For a detailed discussion see Richard A. Fresca 'Weavers in Pre-Modern South India', *E.P.W.*, vol. x, no. 30, 26, July 1975.
51. *A.R.E.*, 356 of 1928–9.
52. *A.R.E.*, 411 of 1923–4.
53. *A.R.E.*, C. P. 18 of 1917–18.
54. *A.R.E.*, C. P. 18 of 1917–18.
55. *E.C.*, vol. v, Ak. 94.
56. *E.C.*, vol. xii, M1. 31.
57. *A.R.E.*, 36 of 1945–6.
58. *A.R.E.*, 244 of 1932–3.
59. *A.R.E.*, 472 of 1925–6.
60. *A.R.E.*, 287 of 1943–4.
61. Both the terms *Senkuntam* and *Kaikol* pertain to a peculiar hook-like weapon used by the Chola warriors.
62. The inscription is published in *Sengunta Murasu*, no. 15, November 1975.
63. The incident, known as 'vellanai venradu,' in which the Kaikkola warriors captured a terrible bandit and then spared him in their magnanimity, is narrated here. Another legendary exploit was the self-sacrifice committed by thousands of Kaikkola warriors to provide inspiration to Ottakkutar (a famous poet who flourished in the twelfth century and was himself a Kaikkola) to write the *Itti Eluvatu*.
64. The text of this inscription was provided for me by C. Raju of Erode and Kavignar Kandasami of Rasipuram. The full text is published in *Sengunta Malar*, Silver Jubilee Number (Coimbatore, 1976).
65. *A.R.E.*, 257 of 1927.
66. *E.C.*, vol. xii, Tp. 130.
67. This inscription is said to have been found on the west wall of the shrine of Sri Venkatesa Perumal at Madurai. This is said to be the main piece of evidence presented by the Saurashtras to the Superintendent of Police to bolster their claim to brahmanical status. See *The Caste Questions in the Saurashtra Community*, (Madurai, 1941).
68. John Fryer, *A New Account of the East India and Persia in Eight Letters*, Hak. Soc. (London, 1909–15), vol. i, chap. iii, p. 82.
69. Cited in Srinivasa Iyengar, 'Right-Hand and Left-Hand Caste Disputes in the Early Part of the Eighteenth Century,' *P.I.H.R.C.*, vol. xiii, Gwalior, Dec. 1929, p. 74.
70. *The Diary of William Hodges, 1681–7* Hak. Soc. (London 1886–8), vol. iii, pp. 113–15, 118–19.
71. *E.F.I.*, 1651–4, pp. 135, 245–6 and *passim*.
72. *E.F.I.*, 29 Jan. 1653, pp. 152–3.
73. Moorees were Muslim weavers specializing in the weaving of a particular high grade cloth, while the Kaingaloon weavers specialized in the weaving of cotton cloth for the Malay Archipelago. For both terms, see the glossary of textile terms.
74. Abbe Carre, vol. ii, p. 595.

75. *E.F.I.*, 1 March 1654, p. 240.

76. *E.F.I.*, 1 March 1654, p. 240. The statement shows that the position of the Kammalar had fallen considerably since the days of the Vijayanagar empire, when they vied with the merchants for social honours. Their fall in social status in the seventeenth century is also obvious by the traveller Abbe Carre's comments (1673) that 'the Kavarai weavers are far more esteemed than the Goldsmiths, carpenters and blacksmiths'. Abbe Carre, vol. ii, p. 595.

77. The Palli are basically an agricultural caste and in this particular instance they are clearly in opposition to the 'painters'. But the traveller Abbe Carre (1673) says of them, 'The Pallis are Painters, who do the designing and tracing of the first lines in the manufacture of printed calicoes and stuffs'. Abbe Carre, vol. ii, p. 595.

78. *E.F.I.*, 1 March 1654, pp. 239–41, 243, etc. This incident figures in Greenhill's accusation and also in the brahmins' declaration, ibid., 4 April 1654, p. 256.

79. *E.F.I.*, vol. x, 1655–60, see introduction, pp. 31–2.

80. *Diary and Consultations*, 13 Aug. 1672, p. 131.

81. Ibid., Oct. 1675, p. 76.

82. *Dispatches*, 28 Sept. 1687, p. 90, para 80.

83. *E.F.I.*, 28 Sept. 1687, p. 92, para 97.

84. *Madras Reports*, 1686–92, 3–7, 1, quoted in the travels of Abbe Carre, p. 596.

85. *Diary and Consultations*, 5 Nov. 1694, p. 122.

86. Both these weaver-merchants were originally competing with the East India Company in certain export markets; ibid., 26 Nov. 1693, p. 134.

87. Ibid., 5 Nov. 1694, p. 123.

88. *Letters*, 17 June 1696, pp. 57 and 66.

89. *Diary and Consultations*, 26 June 1707, p. 68.

90. William Hodges, vol. iii, p. 113.

91. *Diary and Consultations*, 26 June 1707, pp. 68–70.

92. Ibid., 15 January 1708, p. 73.

93. William Hodges, vol. iii, pp. 113–15.

Notes to Afterword

1. *Nityananda Kanungo Committee Report*, (New Delhi, 1952).

2. From the unpublished notes of the author's interview with K.S. Parthasarathy at Kanchipuram, 7 October 1985.

3. *Schemes for Handloom Weavers: A New Thrust*, (New Delhi, 1993) p. 8.

4. Memorandum presented to Rajiv Gandhi by Anakaputhur C. Ramalingam, Special Officer Co-optex on behalf of the Tamil Nadu Handloom Weavers' Co-operative Society Ltd in March 1988.

5. *Schemes for Handloom Weavers*, p. 1.

6. *Draft on State Textile Policy*, (Chennai, 1996).

7. Ibid., pp. 104–5.

8. *Textile Policy of Tamil Nadu*, (Chennai, 1998), p. 3.

9. *Report on Textile Policy*, (Chennai, 1998), p. 5.

10. *Textile Policy of Tamil Nadu*, (Chennai, 2000).

11. 'Handloom workers reject panel's suggestions', *Hindu*, 26 February, 2000.

12. The figure is cited in G.J. Sudhakar, 'PrimaryWeavers Co-operatives in the Madras Presidency: 1935–53', *Proceeding of Indian History Congress*, 51st session (Calcutta, 1990).

13. *Report of the Textile Enquiry Committee,* (New Delhi, 1954), vol. I, pp. 16–17.
14. J. Krishnamurty, 'The Distribution of the Indian Working Force,1901–1951' in K.N. Chaudhuri and C.J. Dewey (eds) *Economy and Society: Essays in Indian Economic and Social History,* (Delhi, 1979), p. 273.
15. *Report on the Administration of the Madras Presidency for the year 1934–35,* (Madras, 1936), p. 634.
16. K. Bharathan, 'The Cotton Handloom Industry in Tamil Nadu: Some Characteristics and Aspects of Change from the Post Independence Census Data', (Madras, 1983), working paper no. 34, p. 32.
17. *Santanam Committee Report,* (New Delhi, 1972).
18. K. Keshava Kini, 'The Tamil Nadu State Handloom Weavers Co-operative Society Limited', in *The Kasaragod Weavers' Co-operative Production and Sale Society Ltd. Souvenir,* (Kasargod, 1972), pp. 7–8.
19. *Administrative Report on the Working of Co-operative Societies of Tamil Nadu upto 1975,* (Madras, 1984), pp. 125–6, 132.
20. *Annual Report for 1985 of the Anekal Weavers Co-operative Society,* (Karnataka, 1985).
21. Pakay Sekhsaria, 'Killing the handloom industry', *Hindu,* 14 May 2000. The report is a powerful indictment of APCO's lackadaisical attitude towards Andhra weavers.
22. Asha Krishnakumar, 'Silence of the Looms', *Frontline,* vol.18, issue no. 8, 14–27 April 2001.
23. S. Rangarajan, 'Contemporary Design Development in Handloom', Seminar on Draft: State Textile Policy, Department of Handlooms and Textiles and Tamil Nadu Handloom Weavers Co-operative Society Ltd, held at Chennai in 1996, unpublished report.
24. One of the earliest reports on the traditional strength of the cotton industry in Tamil Nadu, Edgar Thurston, *Cotton Industry in the Madras Presidency,* (Madras, 1906).
25. M. Sonkusley was interviewed by the author on 3 December 1999 at Chennai. Interview is part of the author's fieldwork notes and is unpublished.
26. Author's interview with Nalli Kuppusami Chettiar on 30 January 2000. This interview was later published in *Hindu Business Line,* 20 March 2000.
27. Ibid.
28. Katyayini Chamaraj, 'Empty looms, tenacious existence', *Hindu,* 1 August 1999.
29. 'The Decline of South Indian Arts', *Journal of Indian Art,* no. 29, 1889, pp. 23–4.
30. Author's interview with G. Ramulu on 29 June 1986, master weaver from the Padmasaliya weaving community, Puttapakka, unpublished.
31. Rangarajan, 'Contemporary Design'.
32. Ibid., p. 2.
33. Ibid., p. 6.
34. Author's interview with Nalli Kuppuswami Chettiar at this residence on 30 January 2000, Chennai.
35. Rangarajan, 'Contemporary Design', p. 6 (concluding remarks).
36. Ibid., pp. 104–5.
37. Author's interview with M. Sonkusley, Director, Chennai Weavers Service Centre, 3 December 1999.
38. Rangarajan's 'Contemporary Design', p. 6.
39. Author's interview with S.P. Subramanian at Tiruchchirapalli, 17 June 1986. This is from the author's fieldwork notes. The invention is reported in *Invention Intelligence,* published by the NRDC in their January, 1986 issue.
40. Author's interview with Nalli Kuppusami Chettiar at his residence in Chennai, 3 January 2000.

41. Author's interview with M. Vinay S. Koparde in Bangalore, 2 June 1986. Also conversation with members of the Kuruhina Chetti weaver community (concentrated in Bangalore, Mandya, Chittaldrug, and Hassan districts) at Bangalore on the 2 July 1986. The interview was undertaken as part of the project 'Weavers Folk Traditions in South India' carried out by the author for the Ministry of Commerce between 1985 (The Year of the Handlooms) and 1988 as mentioned earlier. Although the above interview with Koparde is not published in full, a petition given at that time to the author by the Svakulasala and Kuruhina Chettti weavers was provided by the author as an appendix to the project report.

42. Cited in Akurathi Venkateswara Rao ed., *Handbook of Handloom Quotations,* (Hyderabad, 1996).

43. A recent investigative report from Andhra Pradesh focuses on the formation of *The South Indian Handloom Weavers Organsing Committee* (SIHWOC) founded in 1995 to fight for the rights of weavers. There were also other regional and local weavers bodies such as the Tamil Nadu Handloom Weavers' Union or the Chinetha Karmika Samakhya in Prakasam district and Chittoor districts of Andhra Pradesh. Kathyayini Chamaraj, 'Empty Looms, Tenacious Existence', *Hindu,* 1 August 1999. The Satyam Committee report had provoked the SIHWOC to lead a 'Pattini Pattalam' literally 'hunger march' in April 2000 at Chennai.

APPENDIX 1
Currency Equivalents

(The list gives the approximate value of the coins referred to)

Name	Value	Period
1 *Kalanju*	45 to 50 grains of gold (in rare instances 75 grains of gold)	Chola period
2 *Madai* or *Pon*	Value similar to Kalanju	–do–
3 *Panam*	10 Panams = 1 Kalanju	–do–
	15–20 Panams = 1 Pagoda	Vijayanagar period
4 *Pagoda*	52 grains of gold	–do–
5 *Varaha* or	Similar in value to the Pagoda	–do–
Cadavana		–do–
6 *Rupee*	Between 2s 3d and 2s 6d	Seventeenth century
7 *Pagoda*	Between 8s and 9s	–do–
8 *Rial of Eight*	4s 6d	–do–
9 *Cruzado*	10s	–do–
10 *Pardao*	4s	–do–
11 *Rei*	6d	–do–
12 *Copan*	4d	–do–
13 *Fanam (Panam)*	2d	–do–
14 *Larin*	1s 1d	–do–

APPENDIX 2

Volume and Price of Textiles Exported from the Coromandel Coast to England betwen 1675 and 1701, at Uneven Intervals*

Column (A) denotes the volume (number) of piece goods and Column (B) denotes the price per corge (20 pieces) in pagodas

Textile Varieties**	1675		1676		1677		1679		1680		1681		1683		1686	
	A	B	A	B	A	B	A	B	A	B	A	B	A	B	A	B
Longcloth Ordinary	70,000	25–27.5	40,000	25–27.5	60,000	25–27	14,000	23.75	60,000	20–27	70,000	23.75	200,000	–	25,000	–
Longcloth Brown	10,000	47.50–26.25	10,000	47.50–26.25	10,000	47.50–26.25	10,000	26.25–27.5	18,000	17[4]	20,000	26.25–27.5	40,000	–	10,000	–
Longcloth Blue	6,000	30.75	6,000	30.75	–	–	6,000	30.75	–	30.75	10,000	–	20,000	–	–	–
Longcloth Fine	8,000	42.5–47.5	4,000	42.5–47.5	5,000	60–80[2]	–	–	9,000	75–80	10,000	–	28,000	40–80–100	–	–
Longcloth Masulipatnam	–	–	–	–	–	–	6,000	37.5–47.5	(20% cheaper)	–	–	–	–	–	–	–
Salempores Ordinary	80,000	11.5–13.5	40,000	11.5–13.5	50,000 (20% cheaper)	11–13	25,000	11.5–13	65,000	14	84,000	14	200,000	11–16	75,000	–
Salempores Fine	15,000	16–33	8,000	16–33	8,000	25–27	4,000	25–32	10,000	19–28	20,000	19–28	72,000	18–40	10,000	–
Salempores Brown and Blue	–	12–14	–	12–14	–	–	–	–	–	–	–	–	–	–	–	–
Percalles Fine	8,000	13.5–16	4,000	13.5–16	8,000	13–15	10,000	10.25–15	6,000	10.25–15	22,000	13–20	48,000 (cut down by 12,000)	10–20	10,000	–
Moorees Ordinary	6,000	12.50	4,000	12.50	4,000	–	–	12.50	4,000	–	12,000	12.50	–	–	–	–
Moorees Fine	3,000	17–39	2,000	17–39	2,000	–	–	17–25	2,000	17–39		23	26,000	18–50	12,500	–
Moorees Superfine	3,000	–	1,000	–	1,000	–	–	35–39	1,000	–		35.5–39	1,000	–	–	–

Ginghams White	3,000	32.5	3,000	32.5	4,000	–	5,000	–	–	–	–	–	14,000	–	4,000	–
Ginghams Brown	1,000	27–35	1,000	27–35	1,000	–	2,000	22.5–25	2,000	–	3,000	22.5–25	10,000	–	500	–
Ginghams Fine	3,000	–	–	–	–	–	2,000	–	–	–	7,000	–	–	–	–	–
Izarees	1,500	–	2,000	–	2,000	–	–	21.25–26.25	5,000	21.25–26.35	5,000	–	–	–	–	–
Bettilles 20–25 yards	4,000	37–40	3,000	39–42.5	4,000		4,000	–	10,000	37–40[5]	10,000	37–40	40,000	–	30,000	–
Bettilles Warangal	20,000	24	10,000	24	14,000	62[3]	9,000	19.5–25.5	5,000	50	25,000	–	44,000	25–30	–	–
Bettilles Brown	–	39	–	39	–	45	–	–	–	–	–	–	–	–	–	–
Bettilles Coarse	–	–	–	–	–	–	–	–	–	8.5–9.5	–	–	–	–	–	–
Allajaes	6,000	19.5	4,000	19.5	12,000	–	–	17.8–19.5	–	–	12,000	–	24,000	–	8,000	–
Rumals	10,000	–	10,000	–	20,000	–	–	–	–	–			60,000	24–50 rumals per pagoda		
Dimities	–	–	–	–	–	–	–	–	–	–	–	–	–	–	–	–
Diapers	3,000	30	2,000	30	2,000	–	–	–	2000	22.5–24	–	22.5–24	4,000	–	–	–
Neckcloths striped with red }	3,000	20	3,000	–	50,000	–	50,000	35 neck cloth for 1 p.	100,000	35–40 for 1 p. 18–20		35–40 neckcloth for 1p.	–	–	–	–
Neckcloths Fine, 16 or 18 in a piece }							6,000				150,000	18–20				
Sail cloth	20,000	–	10,000	–	10,000	–	10,000	12–13.5	10,000	–	20,000	–	30,000 (40% cheaper)	15,000	–	–
Dungarees	–	–	–	–	12,000	–	–	6.5	4,000	6.25–7	20,000	–	30,000	–	1,000 (50% cheaper)	–
Shifts (Comezes)	–	–	–	–	–	–	–	–	–	–	–	–	– }	–	–	–
Saderunches	–	–	–	–	–	–	–	17.5–19.5	–	–	–	–	20,000 }	–	–	–
Sacerguntes	–	–	–	–	–	–	–	23.5–25	–	–	–	–		–	1,000	–
Callowaypoos	–	–	–	–	–	–	–	23.5–25	–	–	–	–	20,000	–	1,000	–
Cummums	–	–	–	–	–	–	–	–	–	–	–	–	8,000[6]	–	–	–
Salle (Sallalo) of Golconda	–	25.5	–	–	–	–	–	–	–	–	–	–	–	–	–	–

* Figures were not available for the years omitted. Between 1686 and 1690 very few orders were placed. Between 1690 and 1693 no orders were placed.

APPENDIX 2 (*Contd.*)

Volume and Price of Textiles Exported from the Coromandel Coast to England between 1675 and 1701, at Uneven Intervals

Textile Varieties	1688		1690		1693		1695		1696		1698		1700		1701	
	A	B	A	B	A	B	A	B	A	B	A	B	A	B	A	B
Longcloth Ordinary	10,000	20–24	100,000	28–30–40[7] (conimmer cloth)	10,000	25.5–26.5	60,000	25.25–27	8,500	23–26	20,000	27–39	30,000	30.9 middling category = 35–41	10,000	–
Longcloth Brown	5,000	24.18	20,000	28–30[8]	2,000	18–24		–		26	5,000	26	–		middling = 6,000 5,000	–
Longcloth Blue	5,000	27–28	30,000	–	4,000	27–28	1,000	–		29–30	5,000	29–30	3,000		10,000	–
Longcloth Fine	–	–	10,000	–	–	–		70	–	–	5,000	43.75	7,000	65–75	10,000	–
Longcloth Masulipatnam	–	–	–	–	–	–	–	–	–	–	–	–	–	–	–	–
Salempores Ordinary	4,000	10.25–12.5	60,000	–	8,000	10.25–12.05	–	–	2,500	11–12	20,000	–	–	14.18–16.18	25,000 middling = 10,000	–
Salempores Fine	–	–	–	–	–	21–28	3,000	27	–	–	6,000	–	4,000	25–29	7,000	–
Salempores Brown and Blue	5,000	10.25–11.05	6,000	–	–				–	–	5,000	–	–	–	8,000	–
Percalles Fine	–	–	4,000	–	–	–	7,000	10.25–15	–	–	4,000	–	–	–	2,000	–
Moorees Ordinary	–	–	–	–	1,000	–	–	–	–	–	20,000	–	–	–	6,000	–
Moorees Fine	–	–	–	–	–	–	–	–	–	–	5,000	–	–	36 minus 3	6,000	–
Moorees Superfine	–	–	–	–	2,000	39[11] (ginghams striped)	–	–	2,000	39	8,000	35–39	–	–	6,000	–
Ginghams White	–	30–32	20,000	–	–	9–18	–	–	–	–	6,000	–	–	–	–	–
Ginghams Brown	1,000	23–24.18	1,000	–	5,000	30–65 (Madras ginghams = 34)	–	–	2,000	30–39 (4 thread ginghams)	6,000	30–32	–	–	–	–

	C1	C2	C3	C4	C5	C6	C7	C8	C9	C10	C11	C12	C13	C14	C15	C16
Ginghams Fine Izarees	1,500	55–60	10,000	60–65		5,000	21.25–26.25	1,600	60–63	2,000	60–65		65 minus 5	3,000	1,000	
Bettilles 20 to 25 yards	-	-	14,000	11–18						7,000		6,000	38–41	40 corids long = 6,000		
Bettilles Warangal			No demand		3,000	5,000	42.5	3,000	34–37	10,000	34–37	2,000	60–70	10,000		70
Bettilles Brown				18–37		5,000	19.5–25.5					1,500	45–48	50 corids long = 10,000		
Bettilles Coarse			15,000			2,000	25			3,000		5,000		5,000		
Allajaes			50,000			6,000	17.5–19.5			7,000						
Rumals						6,000	23.5–25			2,000						
Dimities										2,000						
Diapers		33 n.c. in 1 p	260,000[9]			2,000	17–35 pieces per pagoda	400	35 n.c. in 1 p.	100,000	50 n.c. for a pagoda					
Neckcloths striped with red			16 in a piece = 5,000	4–5 pieces per pagoda	16 in a piece = 4,000											
Neckcloths Fine, 16 or 18 in a piece	1,500	16–18	18 in a piece = 200,000	17–18 pieces per pagoda	18 in a piece = 1,000		13.5	16 in a piece	17–19	500,000	20 for a pagoda			little or none = 500		
Sail cloth			100,000 (40% cheaper)			2,000										
Dungarees			20,000			10,000	7									
Shifts (Comezes)			20,000[10]							1,000				5,000		
Saderunches			5,000			5,000				4,000				5,000		
Sacerguntes			5,000			6,000								5,000		
Callowaypoos			1,000													
Cummums																
Goa, Concherulas (Chints)						20,000	32.5							5,000		

1. This list sometimes gives the entire range of the prices of longcloth together. In this and in the subsequent figures, 47 pagodas applies only to longcloth fine and not to longcloth brown.
2. The price of longcloth fine is high in comparison to previous years.
3. The price of Warangal bettilles is higher in comparison to previous years.
4. Longcloth brown purchased at Porto Novo is only 17 pagodas per corge.
5. The price of bettilles seems to have been reduced. The 1673 list makes an upward revision from 37–40 pagodas to 39–42.5 pagodas. But in 1680 the Company seems to have gone back to the old price of 37–40 pagodas.
6. After 1683, there is one more order for cummums in 1684 for 20,000 pieces and then no more orders.
7. At Masulipatnam during the time of famine (1690) the price of ordinary longcloth was increased to 40 pagodas per corge. This is one of the few instances where the Company price for cloth went up as a result of famine.
8. Longcloth brown was purchased at Conimeer, where the prices were much cheaper than at Madras or Masulipatnam.
9. The nature of the orders for striped neckcloths provides a clear illustration of the problem faced by the English East India Company with regard to procurement. After huge orders from 1679 to 1681 there are no further orders till 1686, and from 1686 no further orders till 1690. This clearly demonstrates the situation of glut in the market, occasioned by the excessive import of one variety of cloth, and the problem of co-ordination between supply and demand. See Chapter VI.
10 Shifts figure for the first time in the Company lists in 1690.
11. The price eventually paid by the Company was much less, on the ground that the cloth did not match the company musters. The price was reduced from 39 to 35.5 pagodas.

12. The list represents only Masulipatnam musters.
13. The list represents only Fort St George musters.
14. *The Diary and Consultation* of 18 June 1700, p. 42, records the thorough dissatisfaction of the merchants with the fixing of prices according to musters, on the pretext of which all contract prices were greatly reduced. See especially the reduction in the case of fine moorees and fine ginghams.

The Textile Varieties of South India
(Seventeenth Century)

(The list comprises those varieties cited in this work in the context of foreign trade).

Allejaes
Striped cotton, also checks, red and white or blue and white, sometimes embellished with gold and silver thread, 16–17 yards by 1.25 yards wide.

Bafta
Plain cotton cloth, average length 15 cubits; either white or dyed.

Bettilles
From Portuguese *beatilha*: 'veiling'. A muslin much in demand in Europe as neckcloths. Could be dyed red and sometimes striped or flowered with embroidery 14–15 yards long, 1.25 yards wide.

Caingaloons
From Malay *kain*: 'cloth', and *gulong*: 'rolled'. Pertains to cloth patterned in the loom.

Callowaypoos
A kind of flowered chintz, Kaluvayapu, *pu* meaning a flower made at Kalavay village in Atmakur.

Chelas or Chihlies
Could be from Telugu *chila* or sari. A cotton cloth both striped and chequered.

Chindes or Tapechindes
Coarse painted cloth worn in the Malay archipelago as sarongs, requiring no stitching. Also referred to as tape kitchells or tape sarassas.

Cummums
A particular type of Golconda muslin also known as Cummum bettilles.

Dimities
Probably from Persian *Dimyati*, a cotton cloth. Calico woven with raised stripes or fancy figures used for bedroom hanging etc.

Diapers
Plain white 9–10 yards long, 2.5 yards wide, used for babies' napkins. Also with designs for wall hangings etc.

Dragons
Cheap dyed cotton cloth. Usually described as black and red, presumably either striped or chequered.

Dungarees
Plain white, coarse calico, woven mainly in the Goa region.

Ginghams
Pure cotton cloth woven of dyed yarn, i.e. patterned in the loom, either striped or chequered.

Gobar Gaz
Gobar from the Malay word *geber* or coarse cloth. *Gaz* is a measurement. Refers to coarse cloth used as sheeting.

Izarees
According to John Irwin the origin of the word is from the Telugu or Tamil *istree*: 'pressed', possibly because the cloth had a smooth finish. The cloth was mainly used for the making of drawers and trousers and hence a more likely derivation is from the Tamil *nizer*, which means 'drawers'. Usually 8 yards long and 1 yard wide.

Longcloth
The ordinary staple cotton cloth of the Coromandel coast, esteemed for its unusual length—about 37 yards long and 1.25 yards wide. Exported to England for block printing.

Lungees
Cotton plain or painted cloth similar to the *dhoti*, reaching below the knees, very different from *langotee* or loincloth.

Moorees
Superior cotton cloth used as base for chintz making. Generally served as substitute for Holland and French linen. 9–10 yards long and 1 yard 8 inches wide.

Pallampores
Printed calico or chintz produced at Masulipatnam and used mainly as covers and coverlets in England.

Pattas
Cheap dyed cotton cloth, usually striped, worn as waist cloth, varying in style according to the particular local market for which it was intended. For instance there was *patta chara malayu*, i.e. *patta* in Malay style, or *patta macasser*, *patta* in Maccasser style, etc.

Percalles
High grade plain cotton cloth—the type of calico best suited for cloth printing. Dimensions: about 8 yards in length 1 yard in width.

Rambustans
The term is not listed in any of the glossaries but is found in the list of goods from Conimeer (Tanjore Dist.). Rambustan is a Malay word and probably, like all other cloth produced in this region, was an item of barter in the Archipelago.

Rumals
Madras handkerchiefs: 0.75 yard square.

Salempores
Staple cotton cloth produced on the coast ranging from coarse to very fine—either plain white, blue or brown. Usual dimension: 16 yards length, 1 yard width.

Sallalo
Inferior muslin dyed either blue and black or just black, average length 2 vadams 5 spans, width 1 yard.

Sacerguntes
The origin of the word may be from *Sahasra-granthi* (A thousand knots). The material is a sort of spotted muslin, probably patterned in the loom, i.e. tie-dyed before weaving.

Saderunches
Coarse quality patterned cloth.

Shatranji
Coarse striped cotton carpets woven in the Golconda region.

Suffaguzes
Coarse cotton cloth from Persian *saf*: 'plain' or 'clean', and *gaz*: 'coarse cotton'.

General Native Terms

Aanai	Elephant
Abhayaśāsana	Protective charter
Achchu	Print or mould
Aḍaipam	Person who had custody of the betel box
Aḍḍuvu	Measure of grain
Adhikāriyar	Officials
Adikārachoḍi	Customary payments made to a state official at stipulated periods. Same as *Adhikara Peru*
Agrahāram	Brahmin street
Aṇukkar	Personal attendants of king or noble
Anulōma	A man of high caste who married a low-caste woman
Aṟuvai Vīdi	Cloth merchants' street
Aṟuvai Vāṇigar	Cloth merchants
Aṭaivu	Proper place in temple rank
Aṭṭai Sammadam	Annual tax
Avani Aviṭṭam	Annual festival falling in the month of Avani (corresponding to mid-July—mid-August), when Brahmins change their sacred thread
Ayagār	Group of twelve artisans constituting the functionaries of a village
Āyam	Tax
Bānar	Hunting caste
Bannige	Tax on dyers
Biruda	Title
Brahmadēya	Literally 'gifted to Brahmins'. Refers to a village or land gifted to Brahmins
Chīlai	Cloth
Chīlai Cheṭṭi	Cloth merchant
Chīre	Sari

Chetti	Merchant
Dēvadāna	Village or land granted to the temple for its maintenance
Dvijapatra	Flag cloth
Eṇṇaivāṇigar	Oil mongers
Erivīrapaṭṭinam	Place settled by the soldiers attached to merchants. Mercantile town
Gōtra	Term denoting the lineage of a person, family, caste or clan
Haridra	Turmeric
Gouṇḍa	Headman in the Andhra country
Iḍaṅgai	Left-hand; refers to the 'Left-hand castes'
Ilaivāṇigar	Betel-leaf merchants
Irai	Tax
Jāti	Caste
Jāti Ambashṭan	A member of one of the mixed castes
Kaḍamai	Tax
Kiḷavan	Village elder. Also used in the sense of 'landowner'
Kañchi-Kāvaḍi	Bags suspended at both ends of a long pole and slung over the shoulder
Kalasappānai	Sacred vessel used in worship
Kañji	Rice starch
Kāṇi	Heriditary right of possession to land, cultivation, office, etc.
Kāṇikkai	Contribution
Kaṇivilai	Sale of Kani right
Kaṇiyātchi	Possession of Kani right
Karpūra Kāṇikkai	Customary payment for cultivation rights of temple lands and in commutation of the taxes therein
Kaṭṭu	Bundle
Kollan	Blacksmith
Kottali (Gottali)	Tailors
Kuḍikāṇi	Cultivating rights
Kudirai	Horse
Kuli	Measure of land. According to Tanjore measurement, 1 Kuli was equal to 0.0033 acres or 144 sq.ft.

Kūraivānigar	Cloth merchants
Kumbāran	Potter
Kārugar Vīdi	Weavers' street
Kusumba	Red flower used as dye
Laksha	Lac
Ma	Measure of land. Measures tended to differ from one region to another, but according to the Tanjore measurement 20 Ma was equal to 1 Veli, i.e. 1 Ma was equivalent to 0.33 acres or 14,000 sq.ft.
Mahājana	Members of a sabha
Mahāsabhā	Great assembly, usually of Brahmins
Mañjishṭa	Madder
Mānya	Revenue
Manrādi	Shepherds
Mantapam	Meeting place
Mata	Centre, usually religious, but sometimes also used in the sense of the 'centre of a caste organization'
Mēlavaram	The landlord's share of the rent
Mudal	Capital
Nāḍu	Territorial division comprising several villages
Nagaram	Market town attached to a nadu
Nambikkai Paṭṭayam	Charter of protection
Naṟaikkalam	Bugle
Naṭṭār	Members of a nadu assembly
Navarātri	Annual festival of Hindus falling in the month of October or November and lasting nine days
Nāvidar	Barber
Nīli	Indigo
Nīlikkachchai	Cloth dyed with indigo
Nondāviḷakku	Perpetual lamp
Nūlu	Cotton thread
Oḍukku	Probably charge of temple store
Paḍikkāppan	Watchman
Pākkam	Measure of quantity: one-tenth of a Podi

Paṇa	The division of traditional castes, said to be eighteen in number
Paṇḍāram	Sudra priest
Pañju	Cotton
Pañjupeeli	Tax on cotton yarn
Paraiyar	Untouchables employed in the performance of menial services
Parivaṭṭam	Head dress taken from the idol
Parutti	Cotton
Paṭṭāḍai	Silk cloth
Paṭṭagāra	Corporate organization of weavers
Paṭṭi	A measure of land sufficient for a sheep-fold
Paṭṭinam	Port-town
Paṭṭu	Silk
Pavaḍai	Long skirt
Peruvaḷi	Highway
Perumpaḍai	Large army
Pidaran	Headman
Podi	Measure of quantity: one-fifth of a *vandi* or cart-load
Pokkaran	Treasurer
Pradhāni	Chief officer
Prasādam	Food offering made to the deity
Pratilōma	A woman of high caste marrying a low-caste man
Puḍavai	Sari, a six-yard piece worn by women. Also used in the early periods to describe cloth of any kind
Purambaḍi	Outside
Puraṅgāli	Occurs in the context of village functionary but the actual meaning is not clear
Rāgi	Rye
Rājasvam	Confiscation
Rāmānujakūtam	A feeding place for Vaishnavite disciples
Rāsavargam	Merchants
Rātam	Spinning wheel
Ratha	Temple car, the same as *Ter*

Sabha	Assembly of Brahmin landholders of a Brahmin village
Sadisarakkūdam	Square frame fitted on the draw-loom
Samastapraja	Entire population
Samaya	Literally 'religion', but also refers to caste organization
Saṅgu	Conch shell
Santa	Village fair
Sarvamānya	Tax-free land
Senai Angādigal	Armed guards accompanying the merchandise of traders. Alternately a row of shops opened in a military camp
Srēni	Guild or corporation
Srībali	Offering to the deity of flower or fruit
Sthānathār	Temple managers
Sunkam	Customs duty
Tachchan	Carpenter. Also stone mason
Talaichumai	Head-load
Talaikaṭṭu	Head-load
Tanḍu	Palanquin
Taragukāsu	Brokerage fee
Tari	Loom
Tēr	Temple car, the same as *ratha*
Teriñja	Literally 'well-known to one'; its idiomatic meaning is 'trusted' and it refers to the special bodyguards of the king: for example, 'Samarakesari Terinja Kaikkolar'
Terōtsavam	Car festival in the temple
Tēvar aṭimai	Service to the deity
Tēvāram	Hymns composed in Tamil on Lord Shiva
Tirukkavam	Headquarters
Tīrtam	Holy water
Tirumaḍaivilāgam	Area around the temple, called temple-square and sometimes temple-town
Tirunāmattukkāṇi	Land held directly by the temple. Its proceeds were used for carrying on daily worship or for the celebration of festivals

Tirupaḷḷi Eḷuchchi	The ceremony of waking up the deity
Tuṇṇar ⎫	
Tuṇṇakkārar ⎬	All these refer to tailors
Tuṇṇavinajñar ⎭	
Udirapaṭṭi	Money paid to the temple as crime expiation or in memory of a martyr. Alternatively, land given to the descendants of persons who fell fighting
Uḷḷālai	Within, or 'inner apartments'
Upanayanam	Sacred thread ceremony performed for Brahmin boys
Ūr	Village/assembly of a village
Uttirīyam	A piece to cover the upper portion of the body of a male
Vāchanās	Religious sayings. In the present context, sayings of the Virasaivite saints set in metre, like the *dohas* of Kabir
Vaidyan	Physician
Valaṅgai	Right-hand. Refers to the 'Right-hand castes'
Vaṇḍi	Cart
Vāṇigar	Merchants
Vari	Tax
Vāsalvari	House-tax
Veli	Land measure. Roughly $6^1/_4$ acres
Vēsham	Costume
Vēṭṭi	Unstitched cloth worn by men from waist downwards, of roughly two yards in length
Vēṭṭiyan	Low-caste servant of a village. Can also denote one who had to do forced labour—*vishti*, or in modern terms, *corvee*
Vīdi	Street

Select Bibliography

Epigraphy

Annual Report on South Indian Epigraphy (Madras, 1887 onwards).
Annual Reports of the Archaeological Survey of India (1950 onwards).
Andhra Pradesh Government Archaeological Series, ed. P. Sreenivasachar, P.B. Desai, and N. Ramesan (Hyderabad, 1961).
A Collection of Inscriptions on Copper Plates in the Nellore District, ed. Alan Butterworth and V. Venugopal, 3 pts. (Madras, 1931–8).
Corpus Inscriptionum Indicarum, II, Gupta Inscriptions, ed. J.R. Fleet (Calcutta, 1888).
Corpus of Inscriptions in the Nizam's Dominions, Hyderabad Archaeological Series (Calcutta, 1915 to 1956).
'Corpus of Tamil-Brahmi Inscriptions', in N. Nagasamy, ed., *Seminar on Inscriptions* (Madras, 1968).
Epigraphica Carnatica, Mysore Archaeological Series, ed. B. Lewis Rice, 12 vols. (Mysore, 1889–1955).
Epigraphica Indica (Calcutta, 1892 onwards).
Karnatak Inscriptions, ed. R.S. Panchamukhi and B.R. Gopal (Dharwar, 1941).
Mysore and Coorg Inscriptions, ed. Lewis Rice, 3 vols. (London, 1909).
Sewell, R., *Historical Inscriptions of Southern India* (Madras, 1930).
South Indian Inscriptions (1890 onwards).
South Indian Temple Inscriptions, ed. T.N. Subramanyam, 3 vols. (Madras, 1957).
Travancore Archaeological Series, 9 vols. (Travancore, 1910–41).
A Topographical List of the Inscriptions of the Madras Presidency, ed. V. Rangacharya, 3 vols. (Madras, 1919).
Tirumalai - Tirupati Devasthanam Inscriptions, ed. S. Subramanya Sastry and V. Viraraghavacharya, 6 vols. (Madras, 1931–8).

Literature

Agananuru, ed. P.V. Somasundaranar (Madras, 1974).
Amuktamalyada of Krishnadeva Raya, ed. Vedam Venkataraya Sastry (Madras, 1969).

Arthashastra of Kautilya, ed. R.P. Kangle (Bombay, 1963).

Itti Elupatu of Ottakkuttar, ed. with critical commentary by Thiru Murugavel in the *Sengunta Mithiran*, serialized in June-July 1970.

Kreedabhiramamu of Vallabharaya, ed. Vetturi Prabhakara Sastry (Muktiyala, 1952).

Kurunthokai, ed. P.V. Somasundaranar (Madras, 1972).

Madurai Kanchi, in *Pattupattu*, ed. P.V. Somasundaranar (Tirunelveli, 1971).

Manasollasa of Somesvara III, ed. Shrigondekar (Baroda, 1939).

Manimekalai, ed. P.V. Somasundaranar (Madras, 1971).

Mitakshara of Vijsanesvara, ed. J.R. Gharpure (Bombay, 1939).

Narrinai Nanuru, ed. A. Narayanaswami (Madras, 1967).

Periplus of the Erythraean Sea, ed. Wilfred H. Schoff (New York, 1912).

Perumpanarrupadai in *Pattupattu*, ed. P.V. Somasundaranar (Tirunelveli, 1971).

Silappadikaram, ed. P.V. Somasundaranar (Madras, 1969).

Sri Pindanajukti with the Vritti of Malayagiri, Devacand Lalbhai Jaina Pustakodhara (Bombay, 1918).

The Vachanas of Basava, ed. and tr. A.K. Ramanujam under the title *Speaking of Siva* (Penguin, 1973).

General

The Mackenzie Manuscripts, ed. T.V. Mahalingam, 2 vols. (Madras, 1972, 1976).

Oral Tradition—Community Literature

A TRADITIONS RELATING TO THE KAIKKOLAS

Cholar Purva Pattayam, ed. C.M. Ramachandra Chettiar (This is a Kanchipuram Copper Plate which can be dated with fair accuracy to the 13th century. Yet its style and contents are such that it is better classified under 'community literature').

Senguntar Prabhanda Tirattu, ed. Sahapati Mudaliyar (Madras, 1926).

Sengunta Mannar Kuladipikai, ed. Narayanaswami Mudaliyar (Madras, 1908).

Sengunta Kummi of Ramaswamy Kavirayar (Tiruchchengodu, 1925).

B TRADITIONS RELATING TO THE DEVANGAS

Devanga Mulasthambanam of Bommannaiyar (Madras, 1926).
Devanga Puranam of Mambala Kavirayar, early 1900s (exact date not given).
Devanga Puranam, Palanisami Pulavar, based on ancient texts (Coimbatore, 1917).

C THE ORAL TRADITIONS OF THE SAURASHTRAS

The Caste Questions in the Saurashtra Community, Saurashtra Sabha (Madurai, 1941).
A History of the Saurashtrans in Southern India, by the Saurashtra Brahmana Central Board (Madras, 1891).
The Saurashtrans of South India by H.N. Randle (Madurai, 1949).
Saurashtra Brahmana Charitam (in Tamil) (Madurai, 1964).
The Saurashtrians in South India by I.R. Dave (Rajkot, 1976).
Tamilnattil Saurashtrar Mulu Varalaru (in Tamil) by K.R. Sethuraman (Madurai, 1977).
Oral Literature of the Saurashtrans by Yuchido Norihiko (Simant Publications, 1979).
Bhovlas. For a narration of this oral tradition I am grateful to the Saurashtra Sabha, Madurai.

Weaver Community Journals

Sengunta Murasu
Sengunta Malar
Sengunta Mithiran
Saurashtra Mani

Travellers' Accounts

10th–12th   *Arab Geographers Knowledge of Southern India*, ed.
centuries   Muhammad Husayn Nainar (Madras, 1942).
———   *Arab aur Bharat ke Sambandh* by Sulaiman Nadis, translated by Balu Ramachandra Verma (Allahabad, 1930).
c. 1225   'Chau-Ju-Kua's Ethnography' by F.F. Hirth, *Journal of the Royal Asiatic Society of Great Britain and Ireland* (1896).

c. 1300   *The Book of Ser Marco Polo*, ed. Henry Yule and Henri Cordier, 2 vols., Hak. Soc. (reprint, London, 1975).

1333–45   *The Rehla of Iban Batuta,* ed. Mehdi Husain, Gaikwad Oriental Series (Baroda, 1953).

1419–44   *The Travels of Nicolo de Conti*, ed. R.H. Major in *India in the Fifteenth Century*, Hak. Soc. (reprint, New Delhi, 1974).

1442–4   *The Travels of Abdur Razzaq*, ed. R.H. Major, *India in the Fifteenth Century* (reprint, New Delhi, 1974).

c. 1451   'Ma-Huan's Account of Cochin, Calicut and Aden' by George Philips, *Journal of the Royal Asiatic Society of Great Britain and Ireland* (1896).

1468–75   *The Travels of Athanisius Nikitin*, ed. R.H. Major, *India in the Fifteenth Century*, Hak. Soc.

1497–1538   *The Book of Vasco de Gama*, ed. H.E.J. Stanley, Hak. Soc. (London, 1869).

1508–9   *The Book of Duarte Barbosa*, ed. M.L. Dames, Hak. Soc. (London, 1918).

1512–15   *The Suma Oriental of Tome Pires*, ed. A Cortesao, Hak. Soc. (London, 1944).

1520–2   *The Account of Domingo Paes*, ed. Robert Sewell in *A Forgotten Empire* (London, 1900).

1535–7   *The Chronicle of Fernao Nuniz*, ed. Robert Sewell in the *Forgotten Empire* (London, 1900).

1563–81   *The Travels of Caesar de Federici* in *Samuel Purchas, —His Pilgrims*, Hak. Soc., vol. x (Glasgow, 1905).

c. 1579   *The Voyage of Gasparo Balli* in *Samuel Purchas—His Pilgrims*, Hak. Soc., vol. x.

1583–91   *The Voyage of Fobert Fitch* in *Samuel Purchas—His Pilgrims*, Hak. Soc., vol. x (Glasgow, 1905).

1602–10   *The Voyage of F. Pyrard de Laval A. Grey*, ed. Albert Grey, Hak. Soc. (London, 1887–9).

1608–14   *The Account of Anthony Schorer*, ed. W.H. Moreland, *The Relations of Golconda*, Hak. Soc. (London, 1930).

——   *The Account of Anthony Schorer*, ed. C.S. Srinivasachari, *The Indian Historical Quarterly*, vol. 16, no. 4.

1614   *Anonymous Relations*, ed. W.H. Moreland, *The Relations of Golconda*, Hak. Soc. (London, 1930).

1611–15	*The Voyage of Peter Floris* ed. W.H. Moreland, Hak. Soc. (London, 1934).
1618–22	*The Account of William Methwold*, ed. W.H. Moreland, *The Relations of Golconda*, Hak. Soc. (London, 1930).
1640–60	*Travels in India of Tavernier* ed. V. Ball (London, 1889).
1666–7	*The Travels of Thevenot and Carreri*, ed. Surendranath Sen (New Delhi, 1949).
1668–71	*The Travels in India of Abbe Carre*, ed. Charles Fawcet, Hak. Soc. (London, 1948).
1669–79	Thomas Bowry, *A Geographical Account of the Countries Around the Bay of Bengal*, ed. Richard Temple, Hak. Soc. (London, 1903).
1672–81	John Fryer, *A New Account of East India and Persia*, ed. William Crooke, Hak. Soc. (London, 1909–15).
1675–80	*The Diary of Streynsham Master*, ed. Richard Temple, Hac. Soc. (London, 1911).
1681–7	*The Diary of William Hodges*, ed. R. Barlow and Henry Yule, Hac. Soc. (London, 1886–8).
c. 1800	Hamilton Buchanan, *A Journey from Madras through the Countries of Mysore, Canara and Malabar in 1800* (London, 1907).

East India Company Records

GENERAL

The Catalogue of Original Correspondence (72 vols.), 2 vols., London Company's Record Office, 1831. The Original Correspondence of the English East India Company, Nos. 150 to 1494, India Office, London.

The Cuddalore and Porto Novo Consultations, 1681–5, micro film, National Archives, Delhi.

TRANSLATIONS OF DUTCH RECORDS

Letters From India, 1600 to 1694, India Office, London, 1/3/1 to 1/3/86. *Letters From the Seventeen to India*, 1614 to 1620, India Office, London, 1/3/87–94.

Letters From the Governor General to Various Factories, 1617–1699, India Office, London, 1/3/96–100.

PRINTED RECORDS—GENERAL

Danvers, F.C. and W. Foster, ed., *Letters Received by the East India Company from its Servants*, 6 vols. (London, 1896–1902).

Fawcet, Charles, ed., *The English Factories in India*, New Series, 4 vols. (Oxford, 1936–55).

Foster, William, ed., *The English Factories in India*, 1606–27, 1618–69, 13 vols. (Oxford, 1906–27).

McCulloch J.R., ed., *Early English Tracts on Commerce* (Cambridge 1952).

Press List of Ancient Records in the Salem District (Madras, 1906).

Wheeler, Talboys, *Early Records of British India* (reprint, New Delhi, 1972).

RECORDS OF FORT ST GEORGE

The Baramahal Records of the Madras Presidency (Madras, 1907–33).

The Diary and Consultation Books of Fort St George 1672–1766 (Madras, 1910–41).

The Diary and Consultation Book of 1686 (Madras, 1913).

The Diary and Consultation Book of Fort St George, 1684, ed. Pringle (Madras, 1895).

Dispatches from England—1670–1758 (Madras, 1911–32).

Dispatches to England—1694–1746 (Madras, 1916–31).

Letters from Fort St George, 1679–1765 (Madras, 1915–41).

Letters to Fort St George from subordinate factories in 1688 (Madras, 1915).

Census Reports, Gazeteers, Manuals

1871	*Madras Census Report*
1881	—
1881	—
1891	—
1901	—

A Manual of the Chingleput District by C.B. Crole (Madras, 1895).

A Manual of the Coimbatore District by F.A. Nicholson (Madras, 1887).

A Manual of the North Arcot District by H.A. Stuart (Madras, 1895).

A Manual of the Salem District by H.Le Fanu (Madras, 1883).
Anantapur District Gazeteer by W. Francis (Madras, 1906).
Madurai District Gazeteer by W. Francis (Madras, 1904).
Salem District Gazeteer by F.J. Richards (Madras, 1918).
Mysore District Gazeteer by Hayavadana Rao (Mysore, 1911).
Mysore District Gazeteer by Lewis Rice (London, 1897).

Books in English

Anantakrishna Iyer, *Mysore Castes and Tribes*, 4 vols. (Mysore, 1928–35).

Appadorai, A., *Economic Conditions of Southern India* AD *1000–1500* 2 vols., (Madras, 1936).

Appadorai, Arjun, 'Right and Left Castes in South India', (unpublished thesis, Chicago, May 1973).

Arokiaswami, *The Kongu Country* (Madras, 1946).

Baker, G.P., *Calico Printing and Painting in the East* (London 1921).

Balkrishna, *Commercial Relations Between India and England - 1601–1757* (London, 1924).

Basu, D.D., *The Ruin of Indian Trade and Industries* (Calcutta, 1935).

Birdwood, *The Industrial Arts of India* (London, 1980).

Boxer, C.R., *Dutch Seaborne Trade* (London, 1965).

Brennig, Joseph, *The Textile Trade of Seventeenth Century Northern Coromandel* (University Microfilms, Ann Arbor, Michigan, U.S.A.).

Chakraborty, Haripada, *Trade and Commerce of Ancient India–200* B.C. *to 650* A.D. (Calcutta, 1966).

Chicherov, A.I., *Indian Economic Development in the 16th–18th centuries* (Moscow, 1971).

Chaudhuri, K.N., *The Trading World of Asia and the English East India Company, 1660–1760* (London, 1978).

Danvers, Charles, *The Portuguese Empire in India*, 2 vols. (London, 1899).

Dobb, Morris, *Studies in the Development of Capitalism* (London, 1963).

Dubois, Abbe, *Hindu Manners and Customs* (London, 1889).

The Economic Atlas of the Madras State, N.C.E.R.T. (New Delhi, 1962).

Fox, Richard, *Kin, Clan, Raja and Rule* (Oxford, 1971).

——ed., *Realm and Region in Traditional India* (New Delhi, 1977).

Frykenburg, ed., *Land Control and Social Structure in Indian History* (Madison, Milwaukee, 1969).

Furber, Holden, *The John Company at Work* (New York, 1970).
——, *Rival Empires of Trade in the Orient* (Oxford University Press, 1976).
Ganguli, B.N., ed., *Readings in Indian Economic History* (Bombay, 1964).
Glamann, K., *Dutch Asiatic Trade, 1620–1740* (Hague, 1958).
Gramsci, A., *Prison Notebooks* (New York, 1971).
Gupta, Asin Das, *Malabar in Asian Trade* (Cambridge, 1967).
Gururajachar, S., *Economic and Social Life in Medieval Karnataka* (Prasaranga, 1974).
Hadaway, W.S., *Cotton Painting and Printing in the Madras Presidency* (Madras, 1917).
Holder, Edwin, *Monograph on Dyes and Dyeing in the Madras Presidency* (Madras, 1896).
Hamilton, C.G., *Trade Relations Between England and India—1600–1896* (Calcutta, 1919).
Heras, Henry, *Studies in the Aravidu Dynasty of Vijayanagar* (Madras, 1927).
Hoole, Elijah, *Madras, Mysore and the South India* (London, 1844).
Irwin, J. and Schwartz, P.R., *Studies in Indo-European Textile History* (Ahmedabad, 1966).
Jagadeesan N., *History of Sri Vaishnavism in the Tamil Country, (Post-Ramanuja)* (Madurai, 1977).
Kakade G.R., *The Socio-Economic Survey of Weaving Communities in Sholapur* (Poona, 1947).
Khan, Shafaat Ahmad, *The East India Company Trade in the 17th Century in its Economic and Political Aspects* (London, 1923).
Krishnamurthy, Vaidehi, *Social and Economic Conditions in Eastern Deccan* (Madras, 1970).
Kuppuswamy, S.R., *Economic Conditions in Medieval Karnataka* (Dharwar, 1975).
Leur, J.C., *Indonesian Trade and Society* (The Hague, 1955).
Love, H.D., *Vestiges of Old Madras, 1600–1800* (London, 1913).
Mahalingam, T.V., *South Indian Polity* (Madras, 1967); *Administration and Social Life Under Vijayanagar*, Part I (Madras, 1969); *Administration and Social Life Under Vijayanagar* Part II (Madras, 1975).
Majumdar, R.C., *Corporate Life in Ancient India* (Calcutta, 1967).
Meenakshi L., *Administration and Social Life Under the Pallavas* (Madras, 1933).
Mitra, Debendra Bijoy, *The Cotton Weavers of Bengal* (Calcutta, 1978).

Moreland, W.H., *India at the Death of Akbar* (London, 1920).

——, *From Akbar to Aurangzeb* (London 1923).

Moti Chandra, *Trade and Trade Routes in Ancient India* (New Delhi, 1977).

Nanjundayya, *Mysore Castes and Tribes* (Mysore, 1930).

Parker, John, ed., *Merchants and Scholars* (Minneapolis, 1965).

Pillay, K.K., *The Caste System in Tamil Nadu*, Annie Besant Memorial Lectures (Madras, 1977).

Oppert, Gustav, *The Original Inhabitants of India* (reprint, New Delhi, 1972).

Raju, Sharada, *Economic Conditions in the Madras Presidency* (Madras, 1941).

Raman, K.V., *Early History of the Madras Region* (Madras, 1959).

Ramesh, K.V., *History of South Kanara* (Dharwar, 1970).

Rao, Narasimha, *Corporate Life in Medieval Andhra Desa* (Secunderabad, 1967).

Raychaudhuri, Tapan, *Jan Company in Coromandel, 1605–1690* (The Hague, 1962).

Richards, J.F., *Mughal Administration in Golconda* (Oxford, 1975).

Risley, Herbert, *The People of India* (London, 1908).

Saletore, B.A., *Social and Political Life in the Vijayanagar Empire*, 2 vols. (Madras, 1934).

Sastry, K.R.R., *South Indian Guilds* (New Delhi, 1925).

Sastry, K.N., *A History of South India* (Madras, 1976).

Sewell, Robert, *A Forgotten Empire* (London, 1900).

Sherwani, A., *A History of the Qutb Shahi Dynasty* (Delhi, 1974).

Silverburg, J., ed., *Social Mobility in the Caste System of India: A Symposium* (The Hague, 1968).

Singh, R.L., *India—A Regional Geography* (Varanasi, 1971).

Spate, O.H.K., *India and Pakistan - A General and Regional Geography* (London, 1954).

Srinivas, M.N., *Caste in Modern India and other Essays* (Bombay, 1962).

Srinivasachari, C.S., *A History of the City of Madras* (Madras, 1939).

Stein, Burton, *Essays On South India* (New Delhi, 1975).

——, *South Indian Temples* (New Delhi, 1978).

——, *Peasant State and Society in Medieval South India* (New Delhi, Oxford University Press, 1980).

Subramanyam, T.N., *Sangam Polity* (Madras, 1966).

Subbarayalu, Y., *Political Geography of the Chola Country* (Madras, 1973).

Thurston, Edgar, *Castes and Tribes of South India*, 7 vols. (reprint, New Delhi, 1975).

——, *Monograph on the Cotton Industry in the Madras Presidency* (Madras, 1906).

Tirumalai, R., *Studies in the History of Ancient Townships of Pudukkottai*, Institute of Epigraphy (Madras, 1981).

Varadachari and Pundam Baker, *Hand Spinning and Weaving* (Sabarmati, 1926).

Venkataratnam, A.V., *Local Government in the Vijayanagar Empire* (Prasaranga, Mysore, 1972).

Watson, Bruce, *Foundation for Empire—English Private Trade in India, 1659 to 1760* (New Delhi, 1980).

Wilkes, Mark, *Historical Sketches of South India* (London, 1820).

Warmington, *Commerce Between the Roman Empire and India* (London, 1928).

Glossaries - Dictionaries

Barve, V.R., *A Complete Textile Encyclopaedia* (Bombay, 1967).

Clarke, R., *Glossary of South Indian Terms* (Fort St. George, 1817), Mcc.Mss. D. 270.

Hemchandra, A., *Abidana Chintamani*, ed. Nemichandra (Varanasi, 1964).

Hobson-Jobson, A Glossary of Colloquial Anglo-Indian Words and Phrases, ed. William Crooke (London, 1979).

Mahalingam, T.V., Glossary in *South Indian Polity* (Madras, 1967).

Rangachary, V., Glossary in *Inscriptions of the Madras Presidency*, vol. III (Madras, 1919).

Shivaram Apte, V., *Sanskrit–English Dictionary*.

Srinivasachari, P., glossary of Terms, *Hyderabad Archaeological Series*, vol XIII.

Subramanyam, T.N., *Glossary in South Indian Temple Inscriptions*, vol. II

Watt, *Dictionary of Commercial Products*.

Williams, Monier, *Sanskrit–English Dictionary*.

Books in Non-English Languages

Aravanan, ed., *Aivukottu* (Madras, 1973).

Balasubramanyam, *Ottakkuttar* (Madras, n.d.).

Moti Chandra, *Prachin Bharatiya Vesh Bhasha* (Prayag, 1950).

Pandarattar, Sadasiva, *Pirkala Cholargal* (Annamalai, 1974).
Ramachandra Chettiar, *Kongu Nattu Varalaru.*
Rau, Wilhelm, *Weben Und Flechten in Vedischen Indien* (Wiesbaden, 1970).

Articles

Appadorai, Arjun, 'Kings, Sects and Temples in South India 1350–1700', in Stein, ed., *South Indian Temples* (New Delhi, 1978).

Arasaratnam, 'Some Aspects of the Role and Activities of South Indian Merchants, *c.* 1650–1750', Conference, Seminar of Tamil Studies, 1966.

Arasaratnam, 'Indian Merchants and Their Trading Methods', *I.E.S.H.R.*, vol. 3, 1966.

Chakraborty, Haripada, 'Textile Industry in Ancient India 300B.C. to 300 A.D.', *J.I.H.*, Golden Jubilee Volume, Kerala, 1973.

Chaudhury, K.N., 'The Structure of Indian Textile Industry in the Seventeenth and Eighteenth Centuries', *I.E.S.H.R.*, II, 1974.

Dirks, Nicholas S., 'Political Authority and Structural Change in Early South Indian History', *I.E.S.H.R.*, vol. XIII, 1969.

Dixit, G.S. 'Economic Conditions in the Reign of Krishna Devaraya', *Vijayanagar Six Centenary Volume*, ed. C. Shivaramamurthy (Dharwar, 1931).

Dodwell, W.H., 'The Madras Weavers under the Company', *P.I.H.R.C.*, vol. IV, 1922.

Fletcher, 'The Improvement of Cotton in the Bombay Presidency', *The Agricultural Journal of India*, vol. I, no. IV, 1906.

Fresca, R.A., 'Weavers in pre-Modern South India', *E.P.W.*, vol. X no. 30, July 1975.

Grammie, G.A., 'The Cultivation of Cotton in India', *The Agricultural Journal of India*, vol. III, no. 2, 1908.

Gupta, H.L. 'The Economic Impact of the West on Indian Industries', *J.I.H.*, vol. 38, pt. 1, 1960.

Habib, Irfan, 'The Historical Background of the Monotheistic Movements of the 15th–17th Centuries', Seminar on Ideas, Medieval India, University of Delhi, 1965, Mimeo.

Habib Irfan, 'Notes on the Indian Textile Industry in the Seventeenth Century', *S.C. Sarkar Felicitation Volume* (New Delhi, 1976).

Habib Irfan, 'Technological Changes and Society, 13th and 14th Centuries', 31st session of the Indian History Congress, 1969.
——, 'The Technology and Economy of Mughal India', *I.E.S.H.R.*, vol. XVI, 1980.
Hall, Kenneth, R., 'International Trade and Foreign Diplomacy in Early Medieval South India', *J.E.S.H.O.*, vol. XXI, pt. 1, 1978.
Imtiaz Ahmad, 'The Aahraf-Ajlaf Categories in Indo-Muslim Society', *E.P.W.*, May 1967.
Indrapala, K., 'Some Medieval Mercantile Communities of South India and Ceylon', *Journal of Tamil Studies*, vol. II, no. 2, Oct. 1970.
Irwin, John, 'Indian Textile Trade in the Seventeenth Century - Coromandel Coast', *J.I.T.H.*, pt. 2, 1956.
——, 'European Influence on Indian Textile History', *J.I.T.H.*, 1959.
——, 'Golconda Cotton Paintings of the Early Seventeenth Century', Lalit Kala (New Delhi, 1958).
——, Social Relations in the Textile Trade of the Seventeenth Century', *I.S.P.P.*, vol. I, no. 2, 1960.
Kulkarni, A.R., 'Villages Life in the Deccan in the Seventeenth Century', *I.E.S.H.R.*, vol. XI, 1967.
Mishra, Satish S., 'Indigenisation and Islamisation in India', *Secular Democracy*, Annual, 1974.
Moreland, W.H., 'From Gujarat to Golconda in the Reign of Jahangir', *J.I.H.*, vol. 17, 1938.
Moti Chandra, 'Costumes and Textiles in the Sultanate Period', *J.I.T.H.*, no. 6, 1961.
Nandi, R.N., 'Origins of the Vira Saiva Movement', *The Indian Historical Review*, vol. II, no. 1, 1975.
Panchamukhi, R.S., 'The Coinage of the Vijayanagar Dynasties', in C. Shivaramamurthy ed., *Vijayanagar Sixth Centenary Volume* (Dharwar, 1931).
Pillay, K.K., 'Social Conditions as reflected in the Jivakachintamani', *J.I.H.*, *Golden Jubilee Volume* (Kerala, 1973).
Poonen, T.I., 'Early History of the Dutch Factors of Masulipatnam and Petapoli', *J.I.H.*, vol. 27, 1949.
Qaisar, J., 'The Brokers in Medieval India' in *The Indian Historical Review*, vol. I, no. 2, 1974.
Ray, Jogesh Chandra, 'Textile Industry in Ancient India', *Journal of Bihar and Orissa Research Society*, vol. III.
Saletore, B.A., 'Some Aspects of the Overseas Trade of Vijayanagar

From the Accounts of European Travellers', *B.C. Law Commemoration Volume*, Calcutta, 1945.

Sanders, A.J., 'The Saurashtrans in Madurai, South India', *Journal of the Madras University*, vol. I, no. 1, 1928.

Saraswati, 'Political Maxims of Krishnadeva Raya', *J.I.H.*, vol. IV, pt. III.

Schlingloff, D., 'Cotton Manufacture in Ancient India', *J.E.S.H.O.*, vol. 17, 1974.

Sen, S.P., 'Indian Textiles in South East Asian Trade in the Seventeenth Century', *Journal of South East Asian History*, Singapore, vol. 3, 1962.

Serebriakov, I.D., 'Poetry of Weavers and Tanners', *I.S.P.P.*, vol. 8, 1966–7.

Srinivasa Iyengar, 'The Origins of the Left Hand–Right Hand Castes', *Journal of the Andhra Historical Research Society*, vol. IV pts. I and II, July and October 1929.

Srinivasa Iyengar, 'Right Hand and Left Hand Caste Disputes in the Early Part of the Eighteenth Century', *P.I.H.R.C.*, vol. XII (Gwalior, 1929).

Stein, Burton, 'Coromandel Trade in Medieval India', in John Parker ed., *Merchants and Scholars* (Minneapolis, 1965).

——, '*Social* Mobility and Medieval South Indian Hindu Sects', in J. Silverburg, ed., *Social Mobility in the Caste System of India*.

——, 'The State and Agrarian Order in Medieval South India', in Burton Stein, ed., *Essays on South India* (New Delhi, 1975).

——, 'The Segmentary State in South Indian History', in Richard Fox, ed., *Realm and Region in Traditional India* (New Delhi, 1977).

——, 'Integration of the Agrarian System of South India', in R.E. Frykenburg, ed., *Land Control and Social Structure in Indian History* (Madison, 1969).

——, 'Temples in Tamil Country (1300–1750)', in Burton Stein, ed., *South Indian Temples* (New Delhi, 1978).

Venkatarama Iyer, K.R., 'Medieval Trade, Craft and Merchant Guilds in South India', *J.I.H.*, vol. 25, 1974.

Index of Names